Taking
SIDES

Clashing Views on Controversial Issues in World Civilizations
Volume I
From Ancient Times to the Rise of National States

Edited, Selected, and with Introductions by

Joseph R. Mitchell
Howard Community College

Helen Buss Mitchell
Howard Community College

William K. Klingaman
University of Maryland, Baltimore County

and

R. K. McCaslin

Dushkin/McGraw-Hill
A Division of the McGraw-Hill Companies

To our families

Cover Art Acknowledgment

Charles Vitelli

Library of Congress Cataloging-in-Publication Data

Main entry under title:
   Taking sides: clashing views on controversial issues in world civilizations, volume i from ancient times to the rise of national states/edited, selected, and with introductions by Joseph R. Mitchell and Helen Buss Mitchell.—1st ed.
   Includes bibliographical references and index.
   1. Civilization. I. Mitchell, Joseph R., *comp*. II. Mitchell, Helen Buss, *comp*. III. Klingaman, William K., *comp*. IV. McCaslin, R. K., *comp*.

901

0-697-42299-2   ISSN: 1094-7582

 Printed on Recycled Paper

PREFACE

In *Taking Sides: Clashing Views on Controversial Issues in World Civilizations*, we identify the issues that need to be covered in the teaching of world civilizations and the scholarly and readable sources that argue these issues. We have taken care to choose issues that will make these volumes multicultural, gender-friendly, and current with historical scholarship, and we frame these issues in a manner that makes them user-friendly for both teachers and students. Students who use these volumes should come away with a greater understanding and appreciation of the value of studying history.

One of the valuable aspects of this book is its flexibility. Its primary intended use is for world civilization courses, world history courses, and other courses that pursue a global/historical perspective. However, since more than half the issues in this volume focus on Western civilizations, teachers of Western civilization will be able to use these issues within the framework of their teaching and then assign the non-Western civilization issues as comparative studies or supplements for placing the Western materials in a wider context.

Plan of the book   This book is made up of 17 issues that argue pertinent topics in the study of world civilizations. Each issue has an issue *introduction*, which sets the stage for the debate as it is argued in the pro and con selections. Each issue concludes with a *postscript* that makes some final observations and points the way to other questions related to the issue. In reading the issue and forming your own opinions, you should not feel confined to adopt one or the other of the positions presented. There are positions in between the given views or totally outside them, and the *suggestions for further reading* that appear in each issue postscript should help you to find resources to continue your study of the subject. We have also provided Internet site addresses (URLs) in the *On the Internet* page that accompanies each part opener. At the back of the book is a listing of all the *contributors to this volume*, which will give you information on the historians and commentators whose views are debated here.

A word to the instructor   An *Instructor's Manual With Test Questions* (multiple-choice and essay) is available through the publisher. A general guidebook, *Using Taking Sides in the Classroom*, which discusses methods and techniques for integrating the pro-con approach into any classroom setting, is also available. An online version of *Using Taking Sides in the Classroom* and a correspondence service for Taking Sides adopters can be found at www.cybsol.com/usingtakingsides/. For students, we offer a field guide to analyzing argumentative essays, *Analyzing Controversy: An Introduc-*

tory Guide, with exercises and techniques to help them to decipher genuine controversies.

Taking Sides: Clashing Views on Controversial Issues in World Civilizations, Volume 1, is only one title in the Taking Sides series. If you are interested in seeing the table of contents for any of the other titles, please visit the Taking Sides Web site at http://www.dushkin.com/takingsides/.

Acknowledgments   We would like to thank Larry Madaras of Howard Community College, fellow teacher, good friend, and coeditor of *Taking Sides: Clashing Views on Controversial Issues in American History,* for suggesting we pursue a Taking Sides volume in world civilizations and for introducing us to the editorial team at Dushkin/McGraw-Hill. We are also grateful for the assistance of Jean Soto, Susan Myers, James Johnson, Keith Cohick, and the entire staff of the Howard Community College Library for their assistance with this volume.

Special thanks go to David Dean, list manager for the Taking Sides series; David Brackley, developmental editor; and Tammy Ward, administrative assistant, for their assistance in this project. Without their professionalism, encouragement, and cooperation, this volume would not have been the manageable pleasure that it has been.

We hope you enjoy using this book. Please send us any comments you have on its contents, especially suggestions for additions and deletions, to Taking Sides, Dushkin/McGraw-Hill, Sluice Dock, Guilford, CT 06437 or to tsides@mcgraw-hill.com.

Joseph R. Mitchell
Howard Community College

Helen Buss Mitchell
Howard Community College

CONTENTS IN BRIEF

PART 1   THE WORLD OF THE ANCIENTS   1

Issue 1.   Did *Homo Sapiens* Originate in Africa?   2

Issue 2.   Did Egyptian Civilization Originate in Africa?   22

Issue 3.   Did Greek Civilization Have Semitic and African
　　　　　　Origins?   42

Issue 4.   Did the Benefits of the First Emperor of China's Rule
　　　　　　Outweigh the Human Costs?   62

Issue 5.   Did Christianity Liberate Women?   80

Issue 6.   Did the Roman Empire Collapse Under Its Own
　　　　　　Weight?   100

Issue 7.   Does the Ninth Century Mark the End of the Dark
　　　　　　Ages?   118

PART 2   THE WORLD IN TRANSITION   141

Issue 8.   Does the Modern University Have Its Roots in the Islamic
　　　　　　World?   142

Issue 9.   Were Environmental Factors Responsible for the Collapse
　　　　　　of the Mayan Civilization?   160

Issue 10. Were the Crusades an Early Example of Western
　　　　　　Imperialism?   178

Issue 11. Did Women and Men Benefit Equally from the
　　　　　　Renaissance?   200

Issue 12. Should Christopher Columbus Be Considered a
　　　　　　Hero?   218

Issue 13. Did Calvinism Lay the Foundation for Democracy in
　　　　　　Europe?   236

Issue 14. Did Tokugawa Policies Strengthen Japan?   248

Issue 15. Did Oliver Cromwell Advance Political Freedom in
　　　　　　Seventeenth-Century England?   270

Issue 16. Did Indian Emperor Aurangzeb's Rule Mark the Beginning
　　　　　　of Mughal Decline?   296

Issue 17. Did Peter the Great Exert a Positive Influence on the
　　　　　　Development of Russia?   318

CONTENTS

Preface   1

Introduction: World Civilizations and the Study of History   x

PART 1   THE WORLD OF THE ANCIENTS   1

ISSUE 1.   Did *Homo Sapiens* Originate in Africa?   2
YES: Allan C. Wilson and Rebecca L. Cann, from "The Recent
African Genesis of Humans," *Scientific American*   4
NO: Alan G. Thorne and Milford H. Wolpoff, from "The
Multiregional Evolution of Humans," *Scientific American*   12

The late Allan C. Wilson and Rebecca L. Cann, both molecular biologists,
state that modern humans are descended from a single woman who lived
in Africa around 200,000 years ago. Anthropologists Alan G. Thorne and
Milford H. Wolpoff maintain that modern humans developed simultaneously
in different parts of the world.

ISSUE 2.   Did Egyptian Civilization Originate in Africa?   22
YES: Clinton Crawford, from *Recasting Ancient Egypt in the African
Context: Toward a Model Curriculum Using Art and Language*   24
NO: Kathryn A. Bard, from "Ancient Egyptians and the Issue of
Race," in Mary R. Lefkowitz and Guy MacLean Rogers, eds., *Black
Athena Revisited*   33

Clinton Crawford, an assistant professor who specializes in African arts and
languages as communications systems, asserts that evidence from the fields
of anthropology, history, linguistics, and archaeology prove that the ancient
Egyptians and the culture they produced were of black African origin. Assistant professor of archaeology Kathryn A. Bard argues that although black
African sources contributed to the history and culture of ancient Egypt, the
country's people and culture were basically multicultural in origin.

ISSUE 3.   Did Greek Civilization Have Semitic and African
            Origins?   42
YES: Martin Bernal, from "Black Athena: The African and
Levantine Roots of Greece," in Ivan Van Sertima, ed., *African Presence
in Early Europe*   44

NO: John E. Coleman, from "Did Egypt Shape the Glory That Was Greece? The Case Against Martin Bernal's *Black Athena,*" *Archaeology*   **52**

Professor of government Martin Bernal argues that racism and anti-Semitism among past classical scholars caused them to ignore the African and Near Eastern roots of Greek culture and civilization. Professor of classics John E. Coleman argues that although racism and anti-Semitism did exist among classical scholars, it did not influence their work. He maintains that the idea that Greek culture and civilization have African and Near Eastern roots cannot be proved.

ISSUE 4.   Did the Benefits of the First Emperor of China's Rule Outweigh the Human Costs?   **62**

YES: Arthur Cotterell, from *The First Emperor of China: The Greatest Archeological Find of Our Time*   **64**

NO: T'ang Hsiao-wen, from "A Refutation of Some Confucian Fallacies Concerning the Causes of the Downfall of the Ch'in Dynasty," in Li Yu-ning, ed., *The First Emperor of China*   **72**

English historian Arthur Cotterell argues that the ruthless policies of emperor Qin Shihuangdi caused thousands of deaths among the Chinese peasantry and impoverished much of the surviving population. Chinese scholar T'ang Hsiao-wen, adopting a Marxist approach, praises Qin Shihuangdi for centralizing the Chinese state and for his willingness to attack the aristocratic slave owners.

ISSUE 5.   Did Christianity Liberate Women?   **80**

YES: Monique Alexandre, from "Early Christian Women," in Pauline Schmitt Pantel, ed., *A History of Women in the West, vol. 1: From Ancient Goddesses to Christian Saints*   **82**

NO: Karen Armstrong, from *The Gospel According to Woman: Christianity's Creation of the Sex War in the West*   **90**

Professor of religious history Monique Alexandre argues that there were a variety of roles for women—including prophetess, widow, deaconess, donor, and founder—that indicated a more liberated status for women in the early centuries of Christianity. Professor of religious studies Karen Armstrong finds examples of hostility toward women and fear of their sexual power in the early Christian Church, which she contends led to the exclusion of women from full participation in a male-dominated church.

ISSUE 6.   Did the Roman Empire Collapse Under Its Own Weight?   100

YES: Solomon Katz, from *The Decline of Rome and the Rise of Mediaeval Europe*   102

NO: Arther Ferrill, from *The Fall of the Roman Empire: The Military Explanation*   109

History professor Solomon Katz summarizes the internal causes that led to the decline of the Roman Empire and argues that the growth of the empire carried with it the seeds of its own destruction. History professor Arther Ferrill maintains that the primary cause of the fall of the Roman Empire was external and that attacks by the barbarian tribes along the periphery of the empire ultimately caused the collapse of the state.

ISSUE 7.   Does the Ninth Century Mark the End of the Dark Ages?   118

YES: Kevin Reilly, from *The West and the World: A Topical History of Civilization*   120

NO: Joseph Dahmus, from *The Middle Ages: A Popular History*   129

Kevin Reilly, a world historian and textbook author, paints a portrait of the postclassical period as dark and bloody and argues that it established a tradition of violence in Western civilization. Joseph Dahmus, a professor of medieval history, portrays the period as a not-so-dark age filled with cultural, political, and religious advancement.

PART 2   *THE WORLD IN TRANSITION*   141

ISSUE 8.   Does the Modern University Have Its Roots in the Islamic World?   142

YES: Mehdi Nakosteen, from *History of Islamic Origins of Western Education* A.D. *800–1350*   144

NO: Charles Homer Haskins, from *The Rise of Universities*   152

Professor of history and philosophy of education Mehdi Nakosteen traces the roots of the modern university to the golden age of Islamic culture (750–1150 C.E.). He argues that Muslim scholars assimilated the best of classical scholarship and developed the experimental method and the university system, which they passed on to the West before declining. The late historian Charles Homer Haskins (1870–1937) traces the university of the twentieth century to its predecessors in Paris and Bologna, where, he argues, during the twelfth and thirteenth centuries the first universities in the world sprang up.

ISSUE 9. Were Environmental Factors Responsible for the
Collapse of the Mayan Civilization?   160

YES: Richard E. W. Adams, from *Prehistoric Mesoamerica*, rev. ed.   162

NO: George L. Cowgill, from "Teotihuacan, Internal Militaristic
Competition, and the Fall of the Classic Maya," in Norman
Hammond and Gordon R. Willey, eds., *Maya Archaeology and
Ethnohistory*   169

Professor of anthropology Richard E. W. Adams argues that although military
factors played a role in the Mayan demise, a combination of internal factors
was more responsible for that result. Professor of anthropology George L.
Cowgill contends that although there is no single explanation for the Mayan
collapse, military expansion played a more important role than scholars originally thought.

ISSUE 10. Were the Crusades an Early Example of Western
Imperialism?   178

YES: Hugh Trevor-Roper, from *The Rise of Christian Europe*   180

NO: Marcus Bull, from "The Pilgrimage Origins of the First
Crusade," *History Today*   192

Historian Hugh Trevor-Roper looks to the secular motivation of the knights
of the Crusades and argues that they represented another example of Western
imperialism. Marcus Bull, a lecturer in medieval history, stresses the continuity that the First Crusade had with the pilgrimage tradition in medieval
Europe.

ISSUE 11. Did Women and Men Benefit Equally from the
Renaissance?   200

YES: Mary R. Beard, from *Woman as Force in History: A Study in
Traditions and Realities*   202

NO: Joan Kelly-Gadol, from "Did Women Have a Renaissance?" in
Renate Bridenthal, Claudia Koonz, and Susan Stuard, eds., *Becoming
Visible: Women in European History*, 2d ed.   209

Historian Mary R. Beard contends that during the Renaissance, Italian women
of the higher classes turned to the study of Greek and Roman literature and
committed themselves alongside men to developing well-rounded personalities. Historian Joan Kelly-Gadol argues that women enjoyed greater advantages during the Middle Ages and experienced a relative loss of position and
power during the Renaissance.

ISSUE 12. Should Christopher Columbus Be Considered a Hero? 218

YES: Paolo Emilio Taviani, from *Columbus: The Great Adventure, His Life, His Times, and His Voyages,* trans. Luciano F. Farina and Marc A. Beckwith 220

NO: Basil Davidson, from *The Search for Africa: History, Culture, Politics* 229

Italian television writer and biographer Paolo Emilio Taviani defends the traditional view of Christopher Columbus as a hero of the West. British journalist Basil Davidson, a longtime popularizer of African history, lays the blame for slavery and racism on Columbus.

ISSUE 13. Did Calvinism Lay the Foundation for Democracy in Europe? 236

YES: Kenneth Scott Latourette, from *A History of Christianity, vol. 2: A.D. 1500–A.D. 1975,* rev. ed. 238

NO: Owen Chadwick, from *The Reformation* 243

Kenneth Scott Latourette, a professor of missions and Oriental history, asserts that Protestantism—Calvinism, in particular—contributed to the development of individualism and democracy in Western culture and politics. Owen Chadwick, a professor of ecclesiastical history, states that there was little democracy in Calvin's political ideal.

ISSUE 14. Did Tokugawa Policies Strengthen Japan? 248

YES: Marius B. Jansen, from "Tokugawa and Modern Japan," *Japan Quarterly* 250

NO: Milton W. Meyer, from *Japan: A Concise History,* 3rd ed. 262

Historian Marius B. Jansen asserts that the Tokugawa emperors' policies, which were designed to restore order and stability to Japan, paved the way for Japan's remarkable rise to world power in the twentieth century. Historian Milton W. Meyer contends that the imperial Tokugawa conservatism preserved outmoded political and social institutions, closed off attractive trade opportunities, and turned Japan into an authoritarian nation.

ISSUE 15. Did Oliver Cromwell Advance Political Freedom in Seventeenth-Century England? 270

YES: Peter Gaunt, from *Oliver Cromwell* 272

NO: John Morrill, from "Introduction," in John Morrill, ed., *Oliver Cromwell and the English Revolution*   **283**

Peter Gaunt, a lecturer in history and president of the Cromwell Association, argues that Oliver Cromwell's religious convictions led him to promote policies of "liberty of conscience." John Morrill, a lecturer in history and a former president of the Cromwell Association, maintains that Cromwell can best be described as a religiously devoted libertarian but a political authoritarian.

ISSUE 16.   Did Indian Emperor Aurangzeb's Rule Mark the Beginning of Mughal Decline?   **296**

YES: Jadunath Sarkar, from *A Short History of Aurangzib, 1618–1707,* 3rd ed.   **298**

NO: S. M. Ikram, from *Muslim Civilization in India*   **309**

Historian Jadunath Sarkar argues that the Indian emperor Aurangzeb's reign aggravated already-contentious divisions between Muslims and Hindus. Historian S. M. Ikram defends the reign of Aurangzeb as the last effective defense of Muslim rule on the subcontinent.

ISSUE 17.   Did Peter the Great Exert a Positive Influence on the Development of Russia?   **318**

YES: Vasili Klyuchevsky, from *Peter the Great,* trans. Liliana Archibald   **320**

NO: Peter Brock Putnam, from *Peter: The Revolutionary Tsar*   **330**

Historian Vasili Klyuchevsky, dismissing the cruelty of Peter the Great's methods, argues that the myriad Petrine reforms helped Russia compete with western European nations. Historian Peter Brock Putnam argues that the human and financial costs of Peter's reforms outweighed their benefits, particularly for the Russian peasantry.

Contributors   **338**

Index   **342**

INTRODUCTION

World Civilizations and the Study of History

Helen Buss Mitchell

WHAT IS A CIVILIZATION?

What do we mean by the term *civilization?* Usually it designates a large group of people, spread out over a vast geographical area. In the modern world, we typically think in terms of nations or states, but these are a relatively recent development, traceable to sixteenth-century Europe. Before the rise of national states, the land that we call Europe belonged to a civilization known as Christendom—the unity of people ruled by the spiritual and temporal power of the Christian Church. At that time, other great civilizations of the world included China, Africa, India, Mesoamerica, and the Islamic Empire.

Civilization began about 5,000 years ago, when humans reached high levels of organization and achievement. When we look at world civilizations, we are considering the ancient and the contemporary versions of human alliances. Even in this age of national states, perhaps it makes sense to think of the West (Europe and North America) as a civilization. And the movement for European unity, which includes attempts to create a common currency, suggests that Europe may be thought of as a civilization despite its division into many separate nations. Postcolonial Africa is a continent of separate countries, and yet, in some ways, it remains a unified civilization. China, once a vast and far-flung group of kingdoms, has united as a civilization under communism. And Islam, which united the warring tribes of the Arabian Peninsula in the seventh century, is again defining itself as a civilization. What would be gained and what would be lost by shifting our focus from the national state to the much larger entity civilization?

Civilizations are systems for structuring human lives, and they generally include the following components: (1) an economic system by which people produce, distribute, and exchange goods; (2) a social system that defines relationships between and among individuals and groups; (3) a political system that determines who governs, who makes the laws, and who provides services for the common good; (4) a religious and/or intellectual orientation by which people make sense of the ordinary and extraordinary events of life and history—this may appear as a formal religious system, such as Judaism, Christianity, Islam, Buddhism, or Hinduism, or as an intellectual/values system, such as communism, Confucianism, or democracy; and (5) a cultural system, which includes the arts, and symbol systems, which give expression and meaning to human experience. Some of these components stand out more clearly than others in the selections in this volume, but all of them are present to one degree or another in every civilization.

WHAT IS HISTORY?

History is a dialogue between the past and the present. As we respond to events in our own world, we bring the concerns of the present to our study of the past. What seems important to us, where we turn our attention, how we approach a study of the past—all these are rooted in the present. It has been said that where you stand determines what you see. This is especially true with history. If we stand within the Western tradition exclusively, we may be tempted to see its story as the only story, or at least the only one worth telling. And whose perspective we take is also critical. From the point of view of the rich and powerful, the events of history take one shape; through the lens of the poor and powerless, the same events can appear quite different. If we take women as our starting point, the story of the past may present us with a series of new surprises.

Presentism

Standing in the present, we must be wary of what historians call *presentism*, that is, reading the values of the present back into the past. For example, if we live in a culture that values individualism and prizes competition, we may be tempted to see these values as good even in a culture that preferred communalism and cooperation. And we may miss a key component of an ancient civilization because it does not match what we currently consider to be worthwhile. We cannot and should not avoid our own questions and struggles; they will inform our study of the past. Yet they must not warp our vision. Ideally, historians engage in a continual dialogue in which the concerns but not the values of the present are explored through a study of the past.

Revisionism

History is not a once-and-for-all enterprise. Each generation will have its own questions and will bring new tools to the study of the past, resulting in a process called *revisionism*. Much of what you will read in this book is a product of revisionism in that the featured historians have reinterpreted the past in the light of the present. You will find that whereas one generation might value revolutions, the next might focus on their terrible costs. Likewise, one generation might assume that great men shape the events of history, while the next might look to the lives of ordinary people to illuminate the past. There is no final answer, but where we stand will determine which interpretation seems more compelling to us.

As new tools of analysis become available, our ability to understand the past improves. Bringing events into clearer focus can change the meanings that we assign to them. Many of the selections in this book reflect new attitudes and new insights made possible by the tools that historians have recently borrowed from the social sciences.

The New Social History
Proponents of the new social history reject what they call "history from the top down." This refers to the previous generation of historians who had sometimes acted as if only the influential—often referred to as the "great man"—had a role in shaping history. Social historians assume that all people are capable of acting as historical agents rather than being passive victims to whom history happens. With this shift in attitude, the lives of slaves, workers, all women, and children become worthy of historical investigation. Social historians call this technique of examining ordinary people's lives "history from the bottom up."

Tools of the New Social History
Because the poor and powerless seldom leave written records, other sources of information must be analyzed to understand their lives. Applying the methods of social scientists to their own discipline, historians have broadened and deepened their field of study. Archaeological evidence, DNA analysis, the tools of paleoanthropology, and computer analysis of demographic data have allowed the voiceless to speak across centuries. Analyzing "material culture" (the objects that the people discarded as well as the monuments and other material objects they intended to leave as markers of their civilizations), for example, reveals to historians the everyday lives of people. At certain points in human history, to own a plow made the difference between merely surviving and having some surplus food to barter or sell. What people left to their heirs can tell us how much or how little they had while they lived. Fossil evidence and the analysis of mitochondrial DNA—the structures within cells that we inherit only from our mothers—may each be employed, sometimes with strikingly different results, to trace the migrations of preliterate peoples. As we continue to dig, for instance, we find our assumptions confirmed or denied by the fossils of once-living organisms. Evidence of sea life on the top of a mountain lets us know that vast geologic changes have taken place. And, in another example, our genetic material—our DNA—has information scientists are just now learning to decode and interpret that may settle important questions of origin and migration.

The high-speed comparative functions of computers have allowed historians to analyze vast quantities of data and to look at demographic trends. Consider this question: At what age do people marry for the first time or have a child? Looking at the time between marriage and the birth of a first child can help us to calculate the percentage of pregnant brides and to gain some insight into how acceptable or unacceptable premarital sex may have been to a certain population at a certain time in the context of an expected future marriage. If we study weather patterns and learn that certain years were marked by periods of drought or that a glacier receded during a particular time period, we will know a little more about whether the lives of the people who lived during these times were relatively easier or more difficult than those of their historical neighbors in earlier or later periods.

Broadening the Perspective
Stepping outside the Western tradition has allowed historians to take a more global view of world events. Accusing their predecessors of Eurocentrism, some historians have adopted a view of world history that emphasizes Africa's seminal role in cultural evolution. Also, within the Western tradition, women have challenged the male-dominated perspective that studied war but ignored the family. Including additional perspectives complicates our interpretations of past events but permits a fuller picture to emerge. We must be wary of universalism—for example, the assumption that patriarchy has always existed or that being a woman was the same for every woman no matter what her historical circumstances. If patriarchy or the nuclear family has a historical beginning, then there must have been a time when some other pattern existed. If cultures other than the West have been dominant or influential in the past, what was the world like under those circumstances?

Race, Class, and Gender
The experience of being a historical subject is never monolithic. That is, each of us has a gender, a race, a social class, an ethnic identity, a religion (even if it is atheism or agnosticism), an age, and a variety of other markers that color our experiences. At times, the most important factor may be one's gender, and what happens may be more or less the same for all members of a particular gender. Under other circumstances, however, race may be predominant. Being a member of a racial minority or of a powerful racial majority may lead to very different experiences of the same event. At other times social class may determine how an event is experienced; the rich may have one story to tell, the poor another. And other factors, such as religion, ethnic identity, or even age, can become the most significant pieces of a person's identity, especially if prejudice or favoritism is involved. Historians generally try to take into account how race, class, and gender (as well as a host of other factors) intersect in the life of a historical subject.

Ethnocentrism
All cultures are vulnerable to the narrow-mindedness created by *ethnocentrism*—the belief that one culture is superior to all others. From inside a particular culture, certain practices may seem normative—that is, we may assume that all humans or all rational humans must behave the way that we do or hold the attitudes that we hold. When we meet a culture that sees the world differently than we do, we may be tempted to write it off as inferior or primitive. An alternative to ethnocentrism is to enter the worldview of another and see what we can learn from expanding our perspective. The issues in this book will offer you many opportunities to try this thought experiment.

Issues of Interpretation

Often historians will agree on what happened but disagree about why or how something occurred. Sometimes the question is whether internal or external factors were more responsible for a happening. Both may have contributed to an event but one or the other may have played the more significant role. Looking at differing evidence may lead historians to varying interpretations. A related question considers whether it was the circumstances that changed or the attitudes of those who experienced them. For example, if we find that protest against a situation has been reduced, can we conclude that things have gotten better or that people have found a way to accommodate themselves to a situation that is beyond their control?

Public or Private?

Another consideration for historians is whether we can draw firm lines between public and private worlds. For instance, if a person is highly respected in private but discriminated against in public, which is the more significant experience? Is it even possible to separate the two? In the postindustrial world, women were able to exercise some degree of autonomy within the sphere of home and family. This might have compensated for their exclusion from events in the wider world. On the other hand, can success in the public sphere make up for an emotionally impoverished or even painful personal life? Every person has both a public and a private life; historians are interested in the balance between the two.

Nature or Nurture?

It seems plausible that our experiences within the private sphere, especially those we have as children, may affect how we behave when we move outside the home into a more public world. However, some of what we are in both worlds may be present at birth—that is, programmed into our genes. When historians look at the past, they sometimes encounter one of the puzzles of psychology and sociology: Are we seeing evidence of nature or nurture? That is, does biology or culture offer the more credible explanation for people's behavior through history? Do women and men behave in particular ways because their genetic makeup predisposes them to certain ways of acting? Or is behavior the result of an elaborate system of socialization that permits or rewards some actions while forbidding or punishing others? If people in the past behaved differently than those in the present do, what conclusions may we draw about the relative influence of nature and nurture?

Periodization

The student of the past must wonder whether or not the turning points that shape the chapters in history books are the same for all historical subjects. The process of marking turning points is known as *periodization*. This is the more or less artificial creation of periods that chunk history into manageable segments by identifying forks in the road that took people and events in new directions. Using an expanded perspective, we may find that the traditional turning points hold for men but not for women or reflect the experiences of one ethnic group but not another. And when periodization schemes conflict, which one should we use?

It is also important to keep in mind that people living at a particular moment in history are not aware of the labels that later historians will attach to their experiences. People who lived during the Middle Ages, for example, were surely not aware of living in the middle of something. Only long after the fact were we able to call a later age the Renaissance. To those who lived during what we call the Middle Ages or the Renaissance, marriage, childbirth, work, weather, sickness, and death were the primary concerns, just as they are for us today. Our own age will be characterized by future historians in ways that might surprise and even shock us. As we study the past, it is helpful to keep in mind that some of our assumptions are rooted in a traditional periodization that is now being challenged.

Continuity or Discontinuity?

A related question concerns the connection or lack of connection between one event or set of events and another. When we look at the historical past, we must ask ourselves whether we are seeing continuity or discontinuity. In other words, is the event we are studying part of a normal process of evolution, or does it represent a break from a traditional pattern? Did the Industrial Revolution take the lives of workers in wholly new directions, or did traditional behaviors continue, albeit in a radically different context? Questions of continuity versus discontinuity are the fundamental ones on which the larger issue of periodization rests.

Sometimes events appear continuous from the point of view of one group and discontinuous from the point of view of another. Suppose that factory owners found their world and worldview shifting dramatically, whereas the lives and perspectives of workers went on more or less as they had before. When this is the case, whose experience should we privilege? Is one group's experience more historically significant than another's? How should we decide?

The Power of Ideas

Can ideas change the course of history? People have sometimes been willing to die for what they believe in, and revolutions have certainly been fought, at least in part, over ideas. Some historians believe that studying the clash of ideas or the predominance of one idea or set of ideas offers the key to understanding the past. What do you think? Would devotion to a political or religious cause lead you to challenge the status quo? Or would poor economic conditions be more likely to send you into the streets? Historians differ in ranking the importance of various factors in influencing the past. Do people challenge the power structure because they feel politically powerless, or because they are hungry, or because of the power of ideas?

A related question might be, What makes a person feel free? Is it more significant to have legal and political rights, or is the everyday experience of personal autonomy more important? If laws restrict your options but you are able to live basically as you choose, are you freer than someone who has guaranteed rights but feels personally restricted? And, again, does the public sphere or the private sphere exert the greater influence? Suppose that you belong to a favored class but experience gender discrimination. Which aspect of your experience has a greater impact? On the other hand, suppose you are told that you have full political and economic rights and you are treated with great respect but are prevented from doing what you like. Will you feel freer or less free than the person who is denied formal status but acts freely? In the quest to understand the past, these questions are interconnected, and they are becoming increasingly difficult to answer.

THE TIMELINESS OF HISTORICAL ISSUES

If you read the newspaper or listen to the news, you will find that there are a confusing number of present-day political, economic, religious, and military clashes that can be understood only by looking at their historical contexts. The role of the United States in world events, the perennial conflicts in the Middle East, China's emerging role as an economic superpower, the threat posed by religious fundamentalism, Africa's political future, the question of whether revolutions are ever worth their costs—these concerns of the global village all have roots in the past. Understanding the origins of conflicts increases the possibility of envisioning their solutions. The issues in this book will help you to think through the problems that are facing our world and give you the tools to make an informed decision about what you think might be the best courses of action.

In a democracy, an informed citizenry is the bedrock on which a government stands. If we do not understand the past, the present will be a puzzle to us and the future may seem to be out of our control. Seeing how and why historians disagree can help us to determine what the critical issues are and where informed interpreters part company. This, at least, is the basis for forming our own judgments and acting upon them. Looking critically at clashing views also hones our analytic skills and makes us thoughtful readers of textbooks as well as magazines and newspapers.

WHY STUDY WORLD CIVILIZATIONS?

At times it seems that the West's power and dominance in the world make its story the only one worth studying. History, we are sometimes told, is written by the winners. For the Chinese, the Greeks, the Ottoman Turks, and many other victors of the past, the stories of other civilizations seemed irrelevant, unimportant, and not nearly as valuable as their own triumphal sagas. The Chinese considered their Middle Kingdom the center of the world; the Greeks labeled all others barbarians; and the Ottoman Turks never expected to lose their position of dominance. From our perspective in the present, these stories form a tapestry. No one thread or pattern tells the tale, and all stories seem equally necessary for a complete picture of the past to emerge.

Any single story—even that of a military and economic superpower—is insufficient to explain the scope of human history at a given moment in time. Your story is especially interesting to you. However, as we are learning, any one story achieves its fullest meaning only when it is told in concert with those of other civilizations, all of which share an increasingly interconnected planet. As communications systems shrink the Earth into a global village, we may be ignoring the rest of the world at our own peril. At the very least, the study of civilizations other than our own can alert us to events that may have worldwide implications. And, as we are beginning to learn, no story happens in isolation. The history of the West, for example, can be accurately told only within a global context that takes into account the actions and reactions of other civilizations as they share the world stage with the West. As you read the issues that concern civilizations other than those of your heritage, stay alert for what you can learn about your own civilization.

On the Internet . . .

Duke Papyrus Archive
The Duke Papyrus Archive provides electronic access to texts about and images of 1,373 papyri from ancient Egypt.
http://scriptorium.lib.duke.edu/papyrus/

Fossil Evidence for Human Evolution in China
This site introduces the fossil evidence for human evolution in China. It includes a catalog of Chinese human fossil remains; links to other sites dealing with paleontology, human evolution, and Chinese prehistory; and other resources that may be useful for gaining a better understanding of China's role in the emergence of humankind.
http://www.cruzio.com/~cscp/index.htm

HyperHistory Online
HyperHistory presents 3,000 years of world history via a combination of colorful graphics, life lines, time lines, and maps. Its main purpose is to convey a perspective of world historical events and to enable the reader to hold simultaneously in mind what was happening in widely separated parts of the world.
http://www.hyperhistory.com/online_n2/History_n2/a.html

PART 1

The World of the Ancients

Beginning with the question of the origins of humankind, this section covers the development of the world's earliest civilizations; the religious, educational, economic, social, political, environmental, cultural, and intellectual challenges they faced; how they responded to them; and what resulted from that process. It is during this period that the first history originated, and with that began a never-ending process of analysis and reevaluation of historical information.

■ Did *Homo Sapiens* Originate in Africa?

■ Did Egyptian Civilization Originate in Africa?

■ Did Greek Civilization Have Semitic and African Origins?

■ Did the Benefits of the First Emperor of China's Rule Outweigh the Human Costs?

■ Did Christianity Liberate Women?

■ Did the Roman Empire Collapse Under Its Own Weight?

■ Does the Ninth Century Mark the End of the Dark Ages?

ISSUE 1

Did *Homo Sapiens* Originate in Africa?

YES: Allan C. Wilson and Rebecca L. Cann, from "The Recent African Genesis of Humans," *Scientific American* (April 1992)

NO: Alan G. Thorne and Milford H. Wolpoff, from "The Multiregional Evolution of Humans," *Scientific American* (April 1992)

ISSUE SUMMARY

YES: The late Allan C. Wilson and Rebecca L. Cann, both molecular biologists, state that modern humans are descended from a single woman who lived in Africa around 200,000 years ago.

NO: Anthropologists Alan G. Thorne and Milford H. Wolpoff maintain that modern humans developed simultaneously in different parts of the world.

Where did we come from? This question strikes at the heart of human existence. For each individual, its answer provides an identity that no one else can share. When it is applied universally to all humankind, it can provide answers that go back to the origin of the species: How did we get here? From whom are we descended? How old are we? To what extent are we all related?

In the twentieth century, the origin of our ancestors was determined by the most recent fossilized discovery. With each time period, the location shifted from one part of the world to another, until the last generation's pioneering work placed the origins of our ancestors firmly in East Africa. But this answers only the origins part of the human puzzle. When did these "ancestors" evolve into *Homo sapiens*, and where did this occur?

Answers to these questions have come within the domain of scientists known as *paleoanthropologists.* Relying on fossil discoveries and the latest tools and methodologies used to analyze and evaluate them, these scientists have done much to provide information regarding the origins of humankind. But, recently, they have been joined in the quest by another group of scientists —molecular biologists (or molecular geneticists)—who have used advances in the study of DNA in their search for answers to the same questions.

In 1987 the latter group published their findings, thus firing the opening shots in what would be an interdisciplinary conflict within the scientific community. By examining the mitochondrial DNA, taken from the placentas of women representing every identifiable racial and ethnic group possible, they concluded that approximately 200,000 years ago, our earliest traceable human ancestor existed in Africa. This species migrated throughout the world, thus making Africa the birthplace of *Homo sapiens*. This is known as the "out-of-Africa" theory.

The popular media has picked up on the debate: articles in *Time*, *Newsweek*, the *New York Times*, and many other publications have publicized the new findings, naming our common ancestor "Eve" and proclaiming her to be "the mother of us all."

For a time, the DNA proponents seemed to dominate the world's attention with "Eve." But it did not take long for some paleoanthropologists to fire back. Claiming the reasoning of the DNA disciples to be flawed, they offered evidence to support a multiregional approach to the evolution of humankind, in which prehistoric creatures originated in Africa, migrated to other parts of the world, and then separately evolved into *Homo sapiens*. This has been referred to as the "multiregional" theory in regard to the origins of humankind.

Although the media has made this seem more like a battle between the old school paleoanthropologists and the new school molecular biologists than it really is, there are fundamental differences in the arguments developed by both sides that require further research and evaluation. In the April 1992 issue of *Scientific American*, the two sides squared off for a page-by-page debate on the subject. In the following reproductions of those articles, the late Allan C. Wilson and Rebecca L. Cann, both molecular biologists, restate their original 1987 findings, for which DNA-related evidence was used to prove the "out-of-Africa" theory. Paleoanthropologists Alan G. Thorne and Milford H. Wolpoff refute this theory, arguing that the reasoning of its proponents is flawed. They offer support for their own "multiregional" approach to *Homo sapiens*'s evolution.

It is hoped that the publicity generated by this debate will lead to further studies into the origins of humankind. Perhaps we will then be closer to definitive answers to the questions stated in the first paragraph of this introduction.

YES

Allan C. Wilson and
Rebecca L. Cann

THE RECENT AFRICAN
GENESIS OF HUMANS

In the quest for the facts about human evolution, we molecular geneticists have engaged in two major debates with the paleontologists. Arguing from their fossils, most paleontologists had claimed the evolutionary split between humans and the great apes occurred as long as 25 million years ago. We maintained human and ape genes were too similar for the schism to be more than a few million years old. After 15 years of disagreement, we won that argument, when the paleontologists admitted we had been right and they had been wrong.

Once again we are engaged in a debate, this time over the latest phase of human evolution. The paleontologists say modern humans evolved from their archaic forebears around the world over the past million years. Conversely, our genetic comparisons convince us that all humans today can be traced along maternal lines of descent to a woman who lived about 200,000 years ago, probably in Africa. Modern humans arose in one place and spread elsewhere.

Neither the genetic information of living subjects nor the fossilized remains of dead ones can explain in isolation how, when and where populations originated. But the former evidence has a crucial advantage in determining the structure of family trees: living genes must have ancestors, whereas dead fossils may not have descendants. Molecular biologists know the genes they are examining must have been passed through lineages that survived to the present; paleontologists cannot be sure that the fossils they examine do not lead down an evolutionary blind alley.

The molecular approach is free from several other limitations of paleontology. It does not require well-dated fossils or tools from each part of the family tree it hopes to describe. It is not violated by doubts about whether tools found near fossil remains were in fact made and used by the population those remains represent. Finally, it concerns itself with a set of characteristics that is complete and objective.

A genome, or full set of genes, is complete because it holds all the inherited biological information of an individual. Moreover, all the variants on it that appear within a population—a group of individuals who breed only with one another—can be studied as well, so specific peculiarities need not distort the interpretation of the data. Genomes are objective sources of data because they present evidence that has not been defined, at the outset, by any particular evolutionary model. Gene sequences are empirically verifiable and not shaped by theoretical prejudices.

The fossil record, on the other hand, is infamously spotty because a handful of surviving bones may not represent the majority of organisms that left no trace of themselves. Fossils cannot, in principle, be interpreted objectively: the physical characteristics by which they are classified necessarily reflect the models the paleontologists wish to test. If one classifies, say, a pelvis as human because it supported an upright posture, then one is presupposing that bipedalism distinguished early hominids from apes. Such reasoning tends to circularity. The paleontologist's perspective therefore contains a built-in bias that limits its power of observation.

As such, biologists trained in modern evolutionary theory must reject the notion that the fossils provide the most direct evidence of how human evolution actually proceeded. Fossils help to fill in the knowledge of how biological processes worked in the past, but they should not blind us to new lines of evidence or new interpretations of poorly understood and provisionally dated archaeological materials.

* * *

All the advantages of our field stood revealed in 1967, when Vincent M. Sarich, working in Wilson's laboratory at the University of California at Berkeley, challenged a fossil primate called *Ramapithecus*. Paleontologists had dated its fossils to about 25 million years ago. On the basis of the enamel thickness of the molars and other skeletal characteristics, they believed that *Ramapithecus* appeared after the divergence of the human and ape lineages and that it was directly ancestral to humans.

Sarich measured the evolutionary distance between humans and chimpanzees by studying their blood proteins, knowing the differences reflected mutations that have accumulated since the species diverged. (At the time, it was much easier to compare proteins for subtle differences than to compare the genetic sequences that encode the proteins.) To check that mutations had occurred equally fast in both lineages, he compared humans and chimpanzees against a reference species and found that all the genetic distances tallied.

Sarich now had a molecular clock; the next step was to calibrate it. He did so by calculating the mutation rate in other species whose divergences could be reliably dated from fossils. Finally, he applied the clock to the chimpanzee-human split, dating it to between five and seven million years ago—far later than anyone had imagined.

At first, most paleontologists clung to the much earlier date. But new fossil finds undermined the human status of *Ramapithecus*: it is now clear *Ramapithecus* is actually *Sivapithecus*, a creature ancestral to orangutans and not to any of the African apes at all. Moreover, the age of some sivapithecine fossils was downgraded to only about six million years. By the early 1980s almost all paleontologists came to accept Sarich's more recent date for the separation of the human and ape lines. Those who continue to reject his methods have been reduced to arguing that Sarich arrived at the right answer purely by chance.

Two novel concepts emerged from the early comparisons of proteins from different species. One was the concept of inconsequential, or neutral, mutations. Molecular evolution appears to be dominated by such mutations, and they accumulate at surprisingly steady rates in surviving lineages. In other words, evolution at the gene level results mainly from the relentless accumulation of mutations that seem to be neither harmful nor beneficial. The second concept, molecular clocks, stemmed from the observation that rates of genetic change from point mutations (changes in individual DNA base pairs) were so steady over long periods that one could use them to time divergences from a common stock.

* * *

We could begin to apply these methods to the reconstruction of later stages in human evolution only after 1980, when DNA restriction analysis made it possible to explore genetic differences with high resolution. Workers at Berkeley, including Wes Brown, Mark Stoneking and us, applied the technique to trace the maternal lineages of people sampled from around the world.

The DNA we studied resides in the mitochondria, cellular organelles that convert food into a form of energy the rest of the cell can use. Unlike the DNA of the nucleus, which forms bundles of long fibers, each consisting of a protein-coated double helix, the mitochondrial DNA comes in small, two-strand rings. Whereas nuclear DNA encodes an estimated 100,000 genes—most of the information needed to make a human being—mitochondrial DNA encodes only 37. In this handful of genes, every one is essential; a single adverse mutation in any of them is known to cause some severe neurological diseases.

For the purpose of scientists studying when lineages diverged, mitochondrial DNA has two advantages over nuclear DNA. First, the sequences in mitochondrial DNA that interest us accumulate mutations rapidly and steadily, according to empirical observations. Because many mutations do not alter the mitochondrion's function, they are effectively neutral, and natural selection does not eliminate them.

This mitochondrial DNA therefore behaves like a fast-ticking clock, which is essential for identifying recent genetic changes. Any two humans chosen randomly from anywhere on the planet are so alike in most of their DNA sequences that we can measure evolution in our species only by concentrating on the genes that mutate fastest. Genes controlling skeletal characters do not fall within this group.

Second, unlike nuclear DNA, mitochondrial DNA is inherited from the mother alone, unchanged except for chance mutations. The father's contribution ends up on the cutting-room floor, as it were. The nuclear genes, to which the father does contribute, descend in what we may call ordinary lineages, which are of course important to the transmission of physical characteristics. For our studies of modern human origins, however, we focus on the mitochondrial, maternal lineages.

Maternal lineages are closest among siblings because their mitochondrial DNA has had only one generation in which to accumulate mutations. The degree of relatedness declines step by step as one moves along the pedigree, from first cousins descended from the maternal grandmother, to second cousins descended from a common maternal great-grandmother and so on. The farther back the genealogy goes, the larger the circle of maternal relatives becomes, until at last it embraces everyone alive.

Logically, then, all human mitochondrial DNA must have had an ultimate common female ancestor. But it is easy to show she did not necessarily live in a small population or constitute the only woman of her generation. Imagine a static population that always contains 15 mothers. Every new generation must contain 15 daughters, but some mothers will fail to produce a daughter, whereas others will produce two or more. Because maternal lineages die out whenever there is no daughter to carry on, it is only a matter of time before all but one lineage disappears. In a stable population the time for this fixation of the maternal lineage to occur is the length of a generation multiplied by twice the population size.

* * *

One might refer to the lucky woman whose lineage survives as Eve. Bear in mind, however, that other women were living in Eve's generation and that Eve did not occupy a specially favored place in the breeding pattern. She is purely the beneficiary of chance. Moreover, if we were to reconstruct the ordinary lineages for the population, they would trace back to many of the men and women who lived at the same time as Eve. Population geneticists Daniel L.

Hartl of Washington University School of Medicine and Andrew G. Clark of Pennsylvania State University estimate that as many as 10,000 people could have lived then. The name "Eve" can therefore be misleading—she is not the ultimate source of all the ordinary lineages, as the biblical Eve was.

From mitochondrial DNA data, it is possible to define the maternal lineages of living individuals all the way back to a common ancestor. In theory, a great number of different genealogical trees could give rise to any set of genetic data. To recognize the one that is most probably correct, one must apply the parsimony principle, which requires that subjects be connected in the simplest possible way. The most efficient hypothetical tree must be tested by comparison with other data to see whether it is consistent with them. If the tree holds up, it is analyzed for evidence of the geographic history inherent in elements.

In 1988 Thomas D. Kocher of Berkeley (now at the University of New Hampshire) applied just such a parsimonious interpretation to the interrelatedness of the mitochondrial DNA of 14 humans from around the world. He determined 13 branching points were the fewest that could account for the differences he found. Taking the geographic considerations into account, he then concluded that Africa was the ultimate human homeland: the global distribution of mitochondrial DNA types he saw could then be explained most easily as the result of no more than three migration events to other continents.

A crucial assumption in this analysis is that all the mitochondrial lineages evolve at the same rate. For that reason, when Kocher conducted his comparison of the human mitochondrial DNAs, he also included analogous sequences from four chimpanzees. If the human lineages had differed in the rate at which they accumulated mutations, then some of the 14 human sequences would be significantly closer or farther away from the chimpanzee sequences than others. In fact, all 14 human sequences are nearly equidistant from the chimpanzee sequences, which implies the rates of change among humans are fairly uniform.

The chimpanzee data also illustrated how remarkably homogeneous humans are at the genetic level: chimpanzees commonly show as much as 10 times the genetic variation as humans. That fact alone suggests that all of modern humanity sprang from a relatively small stock of common ancestors.

Working at Berkeley with Stoneking, we expanded on Kocher's work by examining a larger genealogical tree made up from 182 distinct types of mitochondrial DNA from 241 individuals. The multiple occurrences of mitochondrial DNA types were always found among people from the same continent and usually in persons who lived within 100 miles of one another. Because the tree we constructed had two main branches, both of which led back to Africa, it, too, supported the hypothesis that Africa was the place of origin for modern humans.

One point that jumps out of our study is that although geographic barriers do influence a population's mitochondrial DNA, people from a given continent do not generally all belong to the same maternal lineage. The New Guineans are typical in this respect. Their genetic diversity had been suspected from linguistic analyses of the remarkable variety of language families—generally classified as Papuan—spoken on this one island [see "The Austronesian Dispersal and the Origin of Languages," by Peter Bellwood; SCIENTIFIC AMERICAN, July 1991]. On our genealogical tree, New Guineans showed up on several different branches, which proved that the common female ancestor of all New Guineans was not someone in New Guinea. The population of New Guinea must have been founded by many mothers whose maternal lineages were most closely related to those in Asia.

That finding is what one would expect if the African origin hypothesis were true: as people walked east out of Africa, they would have passed through Asia. Travel was probably slow, and during the time it took to reach New Guinea, mutations accumulated both in the lineages that stayed in Asia and in those that moved on.

Thus, people who are apparently related by membership in a common geographic race need not be very closely related in their mitochondrial DNA. Mitochondrially speaking, races are not like biological species. We propose that the anatomic characteristics uniting New Guineans were not inherited from the first settlers. They evolved after people colonized the island, chiefly as the result of mutations in nuclear genes spread by sex and recombination throughout New Guinea. Similarly, the light skin color of many whites is probably a late development that occurred in Europe after that continent was colonized by Africans.

During the early 1980s, when we were constructing our genealogical tree, we had to rely on black Americans as substitutes for Africans, whose mitochondrial DNA was difficult to obtain in the required quantities. Fortunately, the recent development of a technique called the polymerase chain reaction has eliminated that constraint. The reaction makes it possible to duplicate DNA sequences easily, and infinitum; a small starting sample of DNA can expand into an endless supply [see "The Unusual Origin of the Polymerase Chain Reaction," by Kary B. Mullis; SCIENTIFIC AMERICAN, April 1990].

The polymerase chain reaction enabled Linda Vigilant, now at Pennsylvania State University, to redo our study using mitochondrial DNA data from 120 Africans, representing six diverse parts of the sub-Saharan region. Vigilant traced a genealogical tree whose 14 deepest branches lead exclusively to Africans and whose 15th branch leads to both Africans and non-Africans. The non-Africans lie on shallow secondary branches stemming from the 15th branch. Considering the number of African and non-African mitochondrial DNAs surveyed, the probability that the 14 deepest branches would be exclusively African is one in 10,000 for a tree with this branching order.

Satoshi Horai and Kenji Hayasaka of the National Institute of Genetics in Japan analogously surveyed population samples that included many more Asians and individuals from fewer parts of Africa; they, too, found that the mitochondrial lineages led back to Africa. We estimate the odds of their arriving at that conclusion accidentally were only four in 100. Although these statistical evaluations are not strong or rigorous tests, they do make it seem likely that the theory of an African origin for human mitochondrial DNA is now fairly secure.

*   *   *

Because our comparisons with the chimpanzee data showed the human mitochondrial DNA clock has ticked steadily for millions of years, we knew it should

be possible to calculate when the common mother of humanity lived. We assumed the human and chimpanzee lineages diverged five million years ago, as Sarich's work had shown. We then calculated how much humans had diverged from one another relative to how much they had diverged from chimpanzees—that is, we found the ratio of mitochondrial DNA divergence among humans to that between humans and chimpanzees.

Using two different sets of data, we determined the ratio was less than 1:25. Human maternal lineages therefore grew apart in a period less than $1/25$th as long as five million years, or less than 200,000 years. With a third set of data on changes in a section of the mitochondrial DNA called the control region, we arrived at a more ancient date for the common mother. That date is less certain, however, because questions remain about how to correct for multiple mutations that occur within the control region.

One might object that a molecular clock known to be accurate over five million years could still be unreliable for shorter periods. It is conceivable, for example, that intervals of genetic stagnation might be interrupted by short bursts of change when, say, a new mutagen enters the environment, or a virus infects the germlike cells, or intense natural selection affects all segments of the DNA. To rule out the possibility that the clock might run by fits and starts, we ran a test to measure how much mitochondrial DNA has evolved in populations founded at a known time.

The aboriginal populations of New Guinea and Australia are estimated to have been founded less than 50,000 to 60,000 years ago. The amount of evolution that has since occurred in each of those places seems about one third of that shown by the whole human species. Accordingly, we can infer that Eve lived three times 50,000 to 60,000 years ago, or roughly 150,000 to 180,000 years ago. All our estimates thus agree the split happened not far from 200,000 years ago.

Those estimates fit with at least one line of fossil evidence. The remains of anatomically modern people appear first in Africa, then in the Middle East and later in Europe and east Asia. Anthropologists have speculated that in east Africa the transition from anatomically archaic to modern people took place as recently as 130,000 years ago [see "The Emergence of Modern Humans," by Christopher B. Stringer; SCIENTIFIC AMERICAN, December 1990].

On the other hand, a second line of evidence appears to conflict with this view. The fossil record shows clearly that the southern parts of Eurasia were occupied by archaic people who had migrated from Africa to Asia nearly a million years ago. Such famous fossils as Java Man and Beijing Man are of this type. This finding and the hypothesis that the archaic Eurasian population underwent anatomic changes that made them resemble more modern people led to the multiregional evolution model: similar evolutionary changes in separate geographic regions converted the inhabitants from archaic small-brained to modern big-brained types.

Huge levels of gene flow between continents, however, would be necessary to maintain human populations as one biological species. The multiregional evolution model also predicts that at least some genes in the modern east Asian population would be linked more closely to those of their archaic Asian predecessors than to those of modern Africans. We would expect to find deep lineages in Eurasia, especially in the Far East. Yet surveys in our laboratories and in others, involving more than 1,000 people from Eurasia and its mitochondrial DNA satellites (Australia, Oceania and the Americas), have given no hint of that result.

It therefore seems very unlikely that any truly ancient lineages survive undetected in Eurasia. We simply do not see the result predicted by the regional model. Moreover, geneticists such as Masatoshi Nei of Pennsylvania State University, Kenneth K. Kidd of Yale University, James Wainscoat of the University of Oxford and Luigi L. Cavalli-Sforza of Stanford University have found support for an African origin model in their studies of nuclear genes.

*   *   *

Proponents of the multiregional evolution model emphasize they have documented a continuity of anatomic morphologies between the archaic and modern residents of different regions; they insist these morphologies would be unlikely to evolve independently in any invading people. For that argument to hold true, it must also be shown that the cranial features in question are truly independent of one another—that is, that natural selection would not tend to favor certain constellations of functionally related features. Yet we know powerful jaw muscles may impose changes on the mandible, the browridge and other points on the skull; circumstances that promoted the evolution of these features in one population might do so again in a related population.

Other paleontologists also dispute the evidence of continuity. They argue modern populations are not linked to past ones by morphological characteristics that evolved uniquely in the fossil record. Instead fossils and modern populations are united by their shared retention of still older ancestral characteristics. The continuity seen by believers in multiregional evolution may be an illusion.

The idea that modern humans could cohabit a region with archaic ones and replace them completely without any mixture may sound unlikely. Nevertheless, some fossil finds do support the idea. Discoveries in the caves at Qafzeh in Israel suggest Neanderthals and modern humans lived side by side for 40,000 years, yet they left little evidence of interbreeding.

How one human population might have replaced archaic humans without any detectable genetic mixing is still a mystery. One of us (Cann) suspects infectious diseases could have contributed to the process by helping to eliminate one group. Cavalli-Sforza has speculated the ancestors of modern humans may have developed some modern trait, such as advanced language skills, that effectively cut them off from breeding with other hominids. This and related questions may yield as molecular biologists learn how to link specific genetic sequences to the physical and behavioral traits those sequences influence.

Even before then, further studies of both nuclear and mitochondrial DNA will render more informative genetic trees. Particularly enticing are the sequences on the Y chromosome that determine maleness and that are therefore inherited from the father alone. Gerad Lucotte's laboratory at Collège de France has indirectly compared such sequences in an effort to trace paternal lineages to a single progenitor—"Adam," if you will. Those preliminary results also point to an African homeland, and with further refinements this work on paternal lineages may be able to provide an invaluable check on our results for maternal lineages. Unfortunately, base changes accumulate slowly on useful regions of the Y chromosome, making it technically difficult to conduct a detailed genealogical analysis.

Still more progress can be expected in the immediate future, as molecular biologists learn to apply their techniques to materials uncovered by our friendly rivals, the paleontologists. Preliminary molecular studies have already been conducted on DNA from mummified tissues found in a Florida bog and dated to 7,500 years ago. Improved methods of extracting DNA from still older fossilized bone now appear close at hand. With them, we may begin building the family tree from a root that was alive when the human family was young.

NO

Alan G. Thorne and Milford H. Wolpoff

THE MULTIREGIONAL EVOLUTION OF HUMANS

Two decades ago paleoanthropologists were locked in a debate about the origin of the earliest humans. The disagreement centered on whether the fossil *Ramapithecus* was an early human ancestor or ancestral to both human and ape lineages. Molecular biologists entered that discussion and supported the minority position held by one of us (Wolpoff) and his students that *Ramapithecus* was not a fossil human, as was then commonly believed. Their evidence, however, depended on a date for the chimpanzee-human divergence that was based on a flawed "molecular clock." We therefore had to reject their support.

Today the paleoanthropological community is again engaged in a debate, this time about how, when and where modern humans originated. On one side stand some researchers, such as ourselves, who maintain there is no single home for modern humanity—humans originated in Africa and then slowly developed their modern forms in every area of the Old World. On the other side are workers who claim that Africa alone gave birth to modern humans within the past 200,000 years. Once again the molecular geneticists have entered the fray, attempting to resolve it in favor of the African hypothesis with a molecular clock. Once again their help must be rejected because their reasoning is flawed.

Genetic research has undeniably provided one of the great insights of 20th-century biology: that all living people are extremely closely related. Our DNA similarities are far greater than the disparate anatomic variations of humanity might suggest. Studies of the DNA carried by the cell organelles called mitochondria, which are inherited exclusively from one's mother and are markers for maternal lineages, now play a role in the development of theories about the origin of modern human races.

Nevertheless, mitochondrial DNA is not the only source of information we have on the subject. Fossil remains and artifacts also represent a monumental body of evidence—and, we maintain, a much more reliable one. The singular importance of the mitochondrial DNA studies is that they show one of the origin theories discussed by paleontologists must be incorrect.

With Wu Xinzhi of the Institute of Vertebrate Paleontology and Paleoanthropology in Beijing, we developed an explanation for the pattern of human evolution that we described as multiregional evolution. We learned that some of the features that distinguish major human groups, such as Asians, Australian Aborigines and Europeans, evolved over a long period, roughly where these peoples are found today.

Multiregional evolution traces all modern populations back to when humans first left Africa at least a million years ago, through an interconnected web of ancient lineages in which the genetic contributions to all living peoples varied regionally and temporally. Today distinctive populations maintain their physical differences despite interbreeding and population movements; this situation has existed ever since humans first colonized Europe and Asia. Modern humanity originated within these widespread populations, and the modernization of our ancestors was an ongoing process.

An alternative theory, developed by the paleontologist William W. Howells of Harvard University as the "Noah's ark" model, posited that modern people arose recently in a single place and that they subsequently spread around the world, replacing other human groups. That replacement, recent proponents of the theory believe, must have been complete. From their genetic analyses, the late Allan C. Wilson and his colleagues at the University of California at Berkeley concluded that the evolutionary record of mitochondrial DNA could be traced back to a single female, dubbed "Eve"

in one of his first publications on the issue, who lived in Africa approximately 200,000 years ago. Only mitochondrial DNA that can be traced to Eve, these theorists claim, is found among living people.

* * *

How could this be? If Eve's descendants mixed with other peoples as their population expanded, we would expect to find other mitochondrial DNA lines present today, especially outside Africa, where Eve's descendants were invaders. The most credible explanation for the current absence of other mitochondrial DNA lineages is that none of the local women mixed with the invading modern men from Africa—which means that Eve founded a new species. Wilson's reconstruction of the past demands that over a period of no more than 150,000 years there was a complete replacement of all the preexisting hunter-gatherers in Africa and the rest of the then inhabited world; later, the original African features of the invading human species presumably gave way to the modern racial features we see in other regions.

An analogy can highlight the difference between our multiregional evolution theory and Wilson's Eve theory. According to multiregional evolution, the pattern of modern human origins is like several individuals paddling in separate corners of a pool; although they maintain their individuality over time, they influence one another with the spreading ripples they raise (which are the equivalent of genes flowing between populations). In contrast, the total replacement requirement of the Eve theory dictates that a new swimmer must jump into the pool with such a splash that it drowns all the other swimmers. One of these two views of our origin must be incorrect.

Mitochondrial DNA is useful for guiding the development of theories, but only fossils provide the basis for refuting one idea or the other. At best, the genetic information explains how modern humans might have originated if the assumptions used in interpreting the genes are correct, but one theory cannot be used to test another. The fossil record is the real evidence for human evolution, and it is rich in both human remains and archaeological sites stretching back for a million years. Unlike the genetic data, fossils can be matched to the predictions of theories about the past without relying on a long list of assumptions.

The power of a theory is measured by how much it can explain; the scientific method requires that we try to incorporate all sources of data in an explanatory theory. Our goal is to describe a theory that synthesizes everything known about modern human fossils, archaeology and genes. The Eve theory cannot do so.

The Eve theory makes five predictions that the fossil evidence should corroborate. The first and major premise is that modern humans from Africa must have completely replaced all other human groups. Second, implicit within this idea is that the earliest modern humans appeared in Africa. Third, it also follows that the earliest modern humans in other areas should have African features. Fourth, modern humans and the people they replaced should never have mixed or interbred. Fifth, an anatomic discontinuity should be evident between the human fossils before and after the replacement.

* * *

We are troubled by the allegations that beginning about 200,000 years ago one group of hunter-gatherers totally replaced all others worldwide. Although it is not uncommon for one animal species to replace another locally in a fairly short time, the claim that a replacement could occur rapidly in every climate and environment is unprecedented.

We would expect native populations to have an adaptive and demographic advantage over newcomers. Yet according to the Eve theory, it was the newcomers who had the upper hand. How much of an advantage is necessary for replacement can be measured by the survival of many hunter-gatherer groups in Australia and the Americas; they have persisted despite invasions by Europeans, who during the past 500 years arrived in large numbers with vastly more complex and destructive technologies.

If a worldwide invasion and complete replacement of all native peoples by Eve's descendants actually took place, we would expect to find at least some archaeological traces of the behaviors that made them successful. Yet examining the archaeology of Asia, we can find none. For instance, whereas the hand ax was a very common artifact in Africa, the technologies of eastern Asia did not include that tool either before or after the Eve period. There is no evidence for the introduction of a novel technology.

Geoffrey G. Pope of the University of Illinois has pointed out that six decades of research on the Asian Paleolithic record have failed to unearth any indication of intrusive cultures or technologies. Types of artifacts found in the earliest Asian Paleolithic assemblages continue to appear into the very late Pleistocene. If invading

Africans replaced the local Asian populations, they must have adopted the cultures and technologies of the people they replaced and allowed their own to vanish without a trace.

Archaeological evidence for an invasion is also lacking in western Asia, where Christopher B. Stringer of the Natural History Museum in London and a few other researchers believe the earliest modern humans outside of Africa can be found at the Skhūl and Qafzeh sites in Israel. The superb record at Qafzeh shows, however, that these "modern" people had a culture identical to that of their local Neanderthal contemporaries: they made the same types of stone tools with the same technologies and at the same frequencies; they had the same stylized burial customs, hunted the same game and even used the same butchering procedures. Moreover, no evidence from the time when Eve's descendants are supposed to have left Africa suggests that any new African technology emerged or spread to other continents. All in all, as we understand them, the Asian data refute the archaeological predictions implied by the Eve theory.

Perhaps that refutation explains why Wilson turned to a different advantage, asserting that the invasion was successful because Eve's descendants carried a mitochondrial gene that conferred language ability. This proposal is yet to be widely accepted. Not only does it conflict with paleoneurology about the language abilities of archaic humans, but if it were true, it would violate the assumption of Wilson's clock that mitochondrial mutations are neutral.

The remaining predictions of the Eve theory relate to abrupt anatomic changes and whether the earliest recognizably modern humans resembled earlier regional populations or Africans. With the fossil evidence known at this time, these questions can be unambiguously resolved in at least two and possibly three regions of the world. The most convincing data are from southern and northern Asia.

The hominid fossils from Australasia (Indonesia, New Guinea and Australia) show a continuous anatomic sequence during the Pleistocene that is uninterrupted by African migrants at any time. The distinguishing features of the earliest of these Javan remains, dated to about one million years ago, show they had developed when the region was first inhabited.

Compared with human fossils from other areas, the Javan people have thick skull bones, with strong continuous browridges forming an almost straight bar of bone across their eye sockets and a second well-developed shelf of bone at the back of the skull for the neck muscles. Above and behind the brows, the forehead is flat and retreating. These early Indonesians also have large projecting faces with massive rounded cheekbones. Their teeth are the largest known in archaic humans from that time.

A series of small but important features can be found on the most complete face and on other facial fragments that are preserved. These include such things as a rolled ridge on the lower edge of the eye sockets, a distinctive ridge on the cheekbone and a nasal floor that blends smoothly into the face.

This unique morphology was stable for at least 700,000 years while other modern characteristics continued to evolve in the Javan people. For example, the large fossil series from Ngandong, which recent evidence suggests may be about 100,000 years old, offers striking proof that the Javans of that time had brain sizes in the modern range but were otherwise remarkably similar to much earlier individuals in the region.

* * *

The first inhabitants of Australia arrived more than 60,000 years ago, and their behavior and anatomy were clearly those of modern human beings. Their skeletons show the Javan complex of features, along with further braincase expansions and other modernizations. Several dozen well-preserved fossils from the late Pleistocene and early Holocene demonstrate that the same combination of features that distinguished those Indonesian people from their contemporaries distinguishes modern Australian Aborigines from other living peoples.

If the earliest Australians were descendants of Africans, as the Eve theory requires, the continuity of fossil features would have to be no more than apparent. All the features of the early Javans would need to have evolved a second time in the population of invaders. The repeated evolution of an individual feature would be conceivable but rare; the duplication of an entire set of unrelated features would be unprecedentedly improbable.

Northern Asia also harbors evidence linking its modern and ancient inhabitants. Moreover, because the similarities involve features different from those significant in Australasia, they compound the improbability of the Eve theory by requiring that a second complete set of features was duplicated in a different population.

The very earliest Chinese fossils, about one million years old, differ from their Javan counterparts in many ways that parallel the differences between north Asians and Australians today. Our research with Wu Xinzhi and independent research by Pope demonstrated that the Chinese fossils are less robust, have smaller and more delicately built flat faces, smaller teeth and rounder foreheads separated from their arched browridges. Their noses are less prominent and more flattened at the top. Perhaps the most telling indication of morphological continuity concerns a peculiarity of tooth shapes. Prominently "shoveled" maxillary incisors, which curl inward along their internal edges, are found with unusually high frequency in living east Asians and in all the earlier human remains from that area. Studies by Tracey L. Crummett of the University of Michigan show that the form of prehistoric and living Asian incisors is unique.

This combination of traits is also exhibited at the Zhoukoudian cave area in northern China, where fully a third of all known human remains from the Middle Pleistocene have been found. As Wu Rukang of the Chinese Academy of Sciences has pointed out, even within the 150,000 or more years spanned by the Zhoukoudian individuals, evolutionary changes in the modern direction, including increases in brain size, can be seen. Our examinations of the Chinese specimens found no anatomic evidence that typically African features ever replaced those of the ancient Chinese in these regions. Instead there is a smooth transformation of the ancient populations into the living peoples of east Asia.

Paleontologists have long thought Europe would be the best source of evidence for the replacement of one group, Neanderthals, by more modern humans. Even there, however, the fossil record shows that any influx of new people was neither complete nor without mixture. In fact, the most recent known Neanderthal, from Saint-Césaire in France, apparently had the behavioral characteristics of the people who succeeded the Neanderthals in Europe. The earliest post-Neanderthal Europeans did not have a pattern of either modern or archaic African features. Clearly, the European Neanderthals were not completely replaced by Africans or by people from any other region.

Instead the evidence suggests that Neanderthals either evolved into later humans or interbred with them, or both. David W. Prayer of the University of Kansas and Fred H. Smith of Northern Illinois University have discovered that many allegedly unique Neanderthal features are found in the Europeans who followed the Neanderthals—the Upper Paleolithic, Mesolithic and later peoples. In fact, only a few Neanderthal features completely disappear from the later European skeletal record.

Features that persist range from highly visible structures, such as the prominent shape and size of the nose of Neanderthals and later Europeans, to much more minute traits, such as the form of the back of the skull and the details of its surface. A good example is the shape of the opening in the mandibular nerve canal, a spot on the inside of the lower jaw where dentists often give a pain-blocking injection. The upper part of the opening is covered by a broad bony bridge in many Neanderthals, but in others the bridge is absent. In European fossils, 53 percent of the known Neanderthals have the bridged form; 44 percent of their earliest Upper Paleolithic successors do, too, but in later Upper Paleolithic, Mesolithic and recent groups, the incidence drops to less than 6 percent.

In contrast, the bridged form is seen only rarely in fossil or modern people from Asia and Australia. In Africa the few jaws that date from the suggested Eve period do not have it. This mandibular trait and a number of others like it on the skull and the rest of the skeleton must have evolved twice in Europe for the Eve theory to be correct.

In sum, the evolutionary patterns of three different regions—Australasia, China and Europe—show that their earliest modern inhabitants do not have the complex of features that characterize Africans. There is no evidence that Africans completely replaced local groups. Contrary to the Eve theory predictions, the evidence points indisputably toward the continuity of various skeletal features between the earliest human populations and living peoples in different regions.

* * *

If Africa really were the "Garden of Eden" from which all living people emerged, one would expect to find evidence for the transition from archaic to modern forms there—and only there. Following the lead of the German workers Reiner Protsch of Goethe University in Frankfurt, some paleontologists did argue that modern *Homo sapiens* originated in Africa because they believed the earliest modern-looking humans were found there and that modern African racial features can be seen in these fossils. But the African evidence is sparse, fragmentary and for the most part poorly dated; it includes materials that do not seem to fit the Eve theory.

Early human remains from Africa, such as the Kabwe skull from Zambia, are extremely rare and are presumed to be at least 150,000 years old. Later transitional fossils from Morocco, Ethiopia, Kenya and South Africa confirm the expectation that local modernization occurred in Africa, as it did everywhere else. No pattern in the fossils, however, indicates the previous emergence of skeletal features that uniquely characterize modern humans generally or even modern Africans in particular.

The evidence for a great antiquity of modern-looking people is based primarily on the interpretation of bones from three sites: The Omo site in Ethiopia and the Klasies River and Border Cave sites in South Africa. Some of the Omo and Border Cave individuals resemble modern humans, but all the remains are fragmentary. Most of the Omo remains were found on the surface, not in datable strata. The estimate of their age, which is based on inappropriate dating techniques, is widely considered to be unreliable. Some of the Border Cave bones, including the most complete cranium, were dug out by local workmen looking for fertilizer and are of unknown antiquity. Other human bones found at a 90,000-year-old level are chemically different from animal bones found there. They may actually be more recent burials dug into the cave.

The best excavated remains are from the Klasies River Mouth Cave and are securely dated to between 80,000 and 100,000 years ago. Some of the skull fragments are small and delicate and are said to "prove" that modern humans were present. Yet a comparative analysis of the entire sample by Rachel Caspari of Albion College showed that others are not modern looking at all. Two of the four lower jaws do not have chins, so thorough proof of a modern jaw is lacking. The single cheekbone from the site is not only larger than those of living Africans but also larger and more robust than those of both the earlier transitional humans and the archaic humans found in Africa. The claim that this sample contains modern Africans is highly dubious and does not justify the proposal that the earliest modern humans arose in Africa.

* * *

With the disproof of the unique African ancestry theory for the living people of most areas and the lack of evidence showing that modern people first appeared in Africa, we conclude that the predictions of the Eve theory cannot be substantiated. We must wonder why the analysis of mitochondrial DNA suggested a theory so contrary to the facts. Perhaps the mitochondrial DNA has been misinterpreted.

The basic difficulty with using mitochondrial DNA to interpret recent evolutionary history stems from the very source of its other advantages: in reproduction, the mitochondrial DNA clones itself instead of recombining. Because mitochondrial DNA is transmitted only through the maternal line, the potential for genetic drift—the accidental loss of lines—is great: some mitochondrial DNA disappears every time a generation fails to have daughters.

The problem is analogous to the way in which family surnames are lost whenever there is a generation without sons. Imagine an immigrant neighborhood in a large city where all the families share a surname. An observer might assume that all these families were descended from a single successful immigrant family that completely replaced its neighbors (just as Eve's descendants are supposed to have replaced all other humans). An alternative explanation is that many families immigrated to the neighborhood and intermarried; over time, all the surnames but one were randomly eliminated through the occasional appearance of families that had no sons to carry on their names. The surviving family name would have come from a single immigrant, but all the immigrants would have contributed to the genes of the modern population. In the same way, generations without daughters could have extinguished some lines of mitochondrial DNA from Eve's descendants and her contemporaries.

Any interpretation of the surviving mitochondrial DNA mutations in populations consequently depends on a knowledge of how the size of the populations has changed over time and how many maternal lines may have vanished. Random losses from genetic drift after a reconstruction of the tree of human mitochondrial DNA branching by pruning off signs of past divergences. Each uncounted branch is a mutation never taken into account when determining how long ago Eve lived.

Changes in population sizes have been dramatic. In parts of the Northern Hemisphere, some human populations shrank because of climate fluctuations during the Ice Ages. Archaeological evidence from both Africa and Australia suggests that similar population reductions may have taken place there as well. These reductions could have exacerbated genetic drift and the loss of mitochondrial DNA types.

At the end of the Ice Ages, along with the first domestication of animals and plants, some populations expanded explosively throughout a wide band of territory from the Mediterranean to the Pacific coast of Asia. Although the number of people expanded, the number of surviving mitochondrial DNA lines could not—those lost were gone forever.

Human populations with dissimilar demographic histories can therefore be expected to preserve different numbers of mutations since their last common mitochondrial DNA ancestor. They cannot be used together in a model that as- sumes the lengths of mitochondrial lineages reflect the age of their divergence. One cannot assume, as Wilson does, that all the variation in a population's mitochondrial DNA stems solely from mutations: the history of the population is also important.

* * *

A major problem with the Eve theory, therefore, is that it depends on an accurate molecular clock. Its accuracy must be based on mutation rates at many different loci, or gene positions. Yet genes in the mitochondrial DNA cannot recombine as genes in the nucleus do. All the mitochondrial DNA genes are the equivalent of a single locus. The molecular clock based on mitochondrial DNA is consequently unreliable.

Mitochondrial DNA may not be neutral enough to serve as the basis for a molecular clock, because some data suggest that it plays a role in several diseases. Because of random loss and natural selection some vertebrate groups—cichlid fish in Lake Victoria in Africa, American eels, hardhead catfish and redwing blackbirds, for example—have rates of mitochondrial DNA evolution that are dramatically slower than Wilson and his colleagues have claimed for humans. A number of molecular geneticists disagree with Wilson's interpretation of the mitochondrial genetic data.

The molecular clock of Wilson and his colleagues has, we believe, major problems: its rate of ticking has probably been overestimated in some cases and underestimated in others. Rebecca L. Cann of the University of Hawaii at Manoa and Mark Stoneking of Pennsylvania State University, two of Wilson's students, admitted recently that their clock was able to date Eve only to between 50,000 and

500,000 years ago. Because of the uncertainty, we believe that for the past half a million years or more of human evolution, for all intents and purposes, there is no molecular clock.

Putting aside the idea of a clock, one can interpret the genetic data in a much more reasonable way: Eve, the ultimate mitochondrial ancestor of all living humans, lived before the first human migrations from Africa at least one million years ago. The spread of mitochondria would then mark the migration of some early human ancestors into Eurasia when it contained no other hominids. Such an interpretation can fully reconcile the fossil record with genetic data. We propose that future research might more productively focus on attempts to disprove this hypothesis than on attempts to recalibrate a clock that clearly does not work.

The dramatic genetic similarities across the entire human race do not reflect a recent common ancestry for all living people. They show the consequences of linkages between people that extend to when our ancestors first populated the Old World, more than a million years ago. They are the results of an ancient history of population connections and mate exchanges that has characterized the human race since its inception. Human evolution happened everywhere because every area was always part of the whole.

Neither anatomic nor genetic analyses provide a basis for the Eve theory. Instead the fossil record and the interpretation of mitochondrial DNA variation can be synthesized to form a view of human origins that does fit all the currently known data. This synthetic view combines the best sources of evidence about human evolution by making sense of the archaeological and fossil record and the information locked up in the genetic variation of living people all over the world. The richness of human diversity, which contrasts with the closeness of human genetic relationships, is a direct consequence of evolution. We are literally most alike where it matters, under the skin.

POSTSCRIPT

Did *Homo Sapiens* Originate in Africa?

The recent debate over human origins has been clouded by the emergence of race and political correctness as factors to be included in the equation. Those with Afrocentric viewpoints resist any attempt to deny Africa its status as humankind's place of origin, and they see racism as being behind any scheme to do so. See Milford Wolpoff and Rachel Caspari, *Race and Human Evolution* (Simon & Schuster, 1996), pp. 43–47, for an analysis of this current controversy. It is hoped that this diversion will not in any way obfuscate the search for answers to the questions inherent in this debate—questions that are important to an understanding of the origins of human existence.

This issue is a classic example of the influence that technology can have on an academic discipline and its work. New tools now make it possible for scholars to produce results that were only dreamed about a generation ago. But is it possible that too much importance can be placed on the tools and that the search for humankind's origins could end up a "tail wagging the dog" situation?

For further research, the Wolpoff and Caspari book listed above is a good starting point. Written by proponents of the multiregional theory, it obviously leans toward that side of the argument. Stephen Jay Gould, in *Dinosaur in a Haystack: Reflections in Natural History* (Harmony Books, 1995), pp. 101–107, offers an interesting update and commentary on the multiregional/out-of-Africa debate while leaning toward support for a common ancestry (probably African). Fossil hunter Richard Leakey and Roger Lewin, in *Origins Reconsidered: In Search of What Makes Us Human* (Doubleday, 1992), provide a balanced view of the debate and what might ultimately come from it in a chapter entitled "Mitochondrial Eve and Human Violence." Michael D. Lemonick, in "How Man Began," *Time* (March 14, 1994), presents a balanced view of the debate, which could be useful as a summary of the issue.

Finally, Jean M. Auel's *Clan of the Cave Bear* (Crown, 1980) presents a fictional account of the "dawn of humankind" through the eyes of a woman. A film version of this work is also available.

ISSUE 2

Did Egyptian Civilization Originate in Africa?

YES: Clinton Crawford, from *Recasting Ancient Egypt in the African Context: Toward a Model Curriculum Using Art and Language* (Africa World Press, 1996)

NO: Kathryn A. Bard, from "Ancient Egyptians and the Issue of Race," in Mary R. Lefkowitz and Guy MacLean Rogers, eds., *Black Athena Revisited* (University of North Carolina Press, 1996)

ISSUE SUMMARY

YES: Clinton Crawford, an assistant professor who specializes in African arts and languages as communications systems, asserts that evidence from the fields of anthropology, history, linguistics, and archaeology prove that the ancient Egyptians and the culture they produced were of black African origin.

NO: Assistant professor of archaeology Kathryn A. Bard argues that although black African sources contributed to the history and culture of ancient Egypt, the country's people and culture were basically multicultural in origin.

For a place that is considered by many to be the birthplace of humankind, Africa has not been treated kindly by its neighbors. Exploitation of every kind —culminating with the heinous Atlantic slave trade and resultant imperialism—has marked Africa's experiences with the outside world. Westerners, in particular, developed theories to prove African inferiority in order to justify their barbaric actions. No field of academic endeavor escaped this prejudicial treatment, and by the nineteenth century Africa had been totally denied its history, and its culture had been denigrated as savage and primitive.

It is not surprising, therefore, that when most of Africa gained independence after World War II, the continent's intellectuals sought to reaffirm their continent's rich and glorious past and to eradicate the onus placed upon them by Western historians and scientists. With assistance from African American scholars such as W. E. B. Du Bois, African historians—led by the Senegalese scientist and historian Cheikh Anta Diop—sought to write history from an African perspective in order to provide the continent with a positive account of its past. The Afrocentric view of history came of age during this time.

With archaeological discoveries suggesting that humankind originated in East Africa, it was natural for Africa's historians to explore the connections between black Africa and ancient Egyptian civilization. Their findings seemed to confirm the interrelatedness of the two. Hence, these historians concluded that one of the oldest and most respected ancient civilizations was African in origin.

But is this claim totally accurate? Many scholars today maintain that ancient Egypt possessed a cosmopolitan, multicultured society, one that was influenced by all of its neighbors. While acknowledging African influences on Egyptian society, these scholars hold that the claims of the Afrocentrists are too broad and historically inaccurate. In their opinion, to deny Egypt its multicultural past does a great disservice to all concerned parties.

In recent years, history has been used by some to promote racial or ethnic pride and solidarity. Although every group has a right to seek the glories of its past, exaggerations and false claims benefit no one. Those who have seen their past distorted beyond recognition, such as Africans and African Americans, maintain that they are merely rewriting their history to give credibility to what has been denied for centuries.

In the following selections, Clinton Crawford, using evidence from a variety of academic disciplines—history, linguistics, archaeology, anthropology, and art—argues that ancient Egypt was indeed African in origin. Those who believe so, he states, "share a common ideological concern, namely that the social and political histories of the Egyptians must be told truthfully." Kathryn A. Bard analyzes the same information and comes to a different conclusion —that ancient Egyptians were "North African peoples, distinct from Sub-Saharan blacks" and that anyone who claims that Egypt was a black or white civilization is promoting "a misconception with racist undertones that appeals to those who would like to increase rather than decrease the racial tensions that exist in modern society."

Clearly, the battle lines have been drawn in a scholarly debate that is likely to last well into the twenty-first century.

YES

ORIGIN AND DEVELOPMENT OF
THE ANCIENT EGYPTIANS

This [selection] discusses the origin, development, and interrelationship of the people and the culture of ancient Egypt. When people and their culture are viewed as reciprocal, we can understand more fully the evolution of a culture.

Slowly but surely, American academia is beginning to admit the centrality of Egyptian civilization and its sub-Saharan antecedents to the history of the arts and sciences. It is impossible to reprise this debate in any detail here, but let us at least develop the outlines of the discourse. It is also imperative that ancient Egypt be understood as a Black civilization if it is to be a source of self-esteem for African-Americans.

Consider the following oft-cited remarks from Count C. F. Volney's *Ruins of Empire:*

> There [at Thebes, ancient metropolis of Upper Egypt], a people, now forgotten, discovered, while others were yet barbarians, the elements of the arts and science. A race of men now rejected for their *sable skin and frizzled hair,* founded on the study of the laws of nature, those civil and religious systems which still govern the universe. (Volney 1991: 16–17)

This eighteenth-century scholar was puzzled by characterizations of the "Negro" slaves of the western hemisphere because they looked very similar to the indigenous Africans he met in Egypt. Volney attempted to prove that the indigenous Africans in Egypt were similar to the American "Negro" slaves on the basis of his description of the Sphinx of Gizeh. He described the monument's facial characteristics—a common determinant of racial origin—as identical with all people of the Black races.

Similarly, a contemporary of Volney, Baron Denon (1798), also sought the identity of the ancient Egyptians through an examination of the Sphinx. He described the portraits he examined as having the indigenous African characteristics—broad noses, thick lips, and wooly hair. Denon argues that his drawings document an accurate appearance of the Sphinx's head before

From Clinton Crawford, *Recasting Ancient Egypt in the African Context: Toward a Model Curriculum Using Art and Language* (Africa World Press, 1996). Copyright © 1996 by Africa World Press. Reprinted by permission. References omitted.

Napoleon's troops destroyed some of the evidence of its "Negroid looks" (ben-Jochannan, 1989, p. 14).

The list of historians and artists who affirm Volney's and Dennon's work is long. Among them are the German scholar and explorer Frobenius (1910), and Egyptian art historian Cyril Aldred (1956, 1961; 1962). On numerous occasions both scholars have made reference to the racial characteristics of the ancient Egyptians. Hopefully, Reba Ashton-Crawford's faithful rendering of the head of King Aha, or Narmer-Memes, together with the photograph of the Boston Museum of Fine Arts bust of Khafre, may help convert those who have been misled by the modern falsification that the makers of ancient Egypt were not Negroid and African.

Among other scholars on the long list, Cheikh Anta Diop, who is well known in the disciplines of history, egyptology, and anthropology, has advanced well-researched arguments in support of the position that the ancient Egyptians were Africoid and undoubtedly "black" in racial origin. Supporting Diop is Yosef ben-Jochannan, a renowned scholar of ancient and contemporary history and egyptology. Other supporters are Basil Davidson, Ivan Van Sertima, John Henrik Clarke, Chancellor Williams, Leonard Jefferies, Frank Snowden, and James Brunson.

Foremost, ben-Jochannan (1989) places the controversy in its historical context. Ben-Jochannan and Chancellor Williams (1976) argue that the ancient Egyptians were always referred to by the Greeks and Romans as people whose descendants came from the interior of Africa. He cites many examples from ancient texts which validate the point.

For example, Manetho (early and third century B.C.), a high priest of mixed Egyptian and Greek parentage, who wrote the first chronology of the Egyptian dynasties, testifies to the undisputed Negroid origin of the ancient Egyptians. Ben-Jochannan, as if unsatisfied with Manetho's accounts, recalls the many works of Herodotus which referred to the Egyptian as black. Herodotus observed that the probability of encountering men with black skin, woolly hair, without any other ethnic feature common of Negroes, is scientifically nil. To term such individuals as "whites" with black skin because of their fine features is no less absurd than the appellation "blacks" with white skin. If the absurdity of the latter is applied to three-fourths of the Europeans who lack Nordic features, then what can one conclude? Looking at these two appellations and their contradictions, one can conclude that a pseudo-scientific approach has given way to inaccurate generalization (History of Herodotus, p. 115). This decree by Herodotus is but one of many such testimonies by the Greek "father of history," who made many pilgrimages to Egypt in the fifth century B.C.

Over the span of several centuries, from the fall of ancient Egypt to sometime in the 1800s, classical authors of antiquity [cited by Anta Diop (1974) and ben-Jochannan (1989)] had no difficulty classifying the physical characteristics of the ancient Egyptians. Diop commends Aristotle (389–332 B.C.), Lucan the Greek (125–190 A.D.), Aeschylus (525–456 B.C.), Strabo (58–25 A.D.), and Diodorus of Sicily (63–14 B.C.), among many others, for bearing out this evidence about the ancient Egyptians. Each of the ancient historians usually included a graphic description of the ancient Egyptians. For example, Diodorus of Sicily described the Egyptians as follows:

> The Ethiopians say that Egyptians are one of their colonies which was brought into Egypt by Osiris.... It is from them that the Egyptians have learned to honor kings and gods and bury them with such pomp; sculpture and writing were invented by the Ethiopians. (Anta Diop, 1974, pp. 1–2)

Diodorus' account supports Herodotus' statement. Diop employs Diodorus' account to illuminate at least two plausible implications: (1) that Ethiopia is an older civilization than Egypt; (2) that the Egyptians were a different race than the Ethiopians. Diodorus seriously discussed the possibility of considering the ancient Egyptians to be either close neighbors (separated by a physical barrier—a cataract) or actual descendants of Black Africans (Ethiopians). Herodotus, in Histories II (457–450 B.C.) had stated that the Colchians, Ethiopians, and Egyptians bore all of the Negroid racial characteristics of thick lips, broad nose, woolly hair, and dark complexion—a statement that parallels Diodorus' observations, documented many years later.

Despite the testimonies of the ancients, ben-Jochannan and Diop also sought new data to support their position. Ben-Jochannan uses many strategies to advance his claims. Conspicuously, some of the strategies included examining the names and terminologies which the African Egyptians used to describe themselves and their country. He also reviews the works of some of the modern-day scholars who have advanced the claim of an Indo-European/Caucasian genesis for the ancient Egyptians. Furthermore, to counter what he regards as a deliberate attempt to discredit the contributions of

a great Black civilization, ben-Jochannan cites the findings from Ellio Smith's examination of mummies from the tombs of Egyptian Royalty (1912).

Ben-Jochannan argues that before the Greeks imposed the name *Egyptos* on the people of *Alke-bu-lan* (modern day Africa), the linguistic and papyrological evidence show that the Egyptians called their land *Kimit, Kham, Ham, Mizrain,* and *Ta-Merry.* It cannot be coincidental, according to ben-Jochannan, that the same words chosen to describe the empire of the ancient "Egyptians" also refer to the land and its people as "children of the sun." The fact remains, these people were of dark pigmentation. And it is no mistake that even the Greek word *Egyptos* means "land of the dark people."

In addition to his linguistic and papyrologic evidence, ben-Jochannan cites that the Nile Valley and (African) Great Lakes High Cultures, peopled by Blacks of Egypt and its close neighbor Nubia, had an organized system of education called the Mysteries System.... At the height of ancient Egyptian culture, the Grand Lodge of Alexandria was known as the world center of learning. Those foreign to ancient Egypt who did not attend the main educational center received training at the "established subordinate Lodges of the Osirica—which was centered in the Grand Lodge at Luxor, Nubia" (ben-Jochannan, 1989, p. xxv). This puts into a new perspective the well-known fact that the Greek philosophers Socrates, Aristotle, and Pythagoras all testified to the education they received from the Egyptians.

Having established the ancient Egyptian preference for how they wanted to be called and the consistent testimonies of other ancients, ben-Jochannan focuses primarily on several examples of the racist hypotheses which are still used in academic circles as authentic scholarship on Africa, especially as it relates to Egypt.

To expose some of the racist hypotheses, ben-Jochannan examines several attempts to undermine the Negroid origin of the ancient Egyptians. The most striking appeared in the January 9th, 1972 issue of the *New York Times* in a report by Donald Janson of his interview with archaeologist Ray Winfield Smith, of the Museum of the University of Pennsylvania. The article concerned a computer reconstruction of a bas-relief sculpture in which Queen Nefertiti is shown with the same pear-shaped, elongated torso used to characterize her husband, pharaoh Akhenaten, and all other persons during their reign. Their stylized portrayal represented the aesthetic choice of King Akhenaten and Queen Nefertiti's reign—a shift away from the conventional royal portrayal to a more naturalistic style. In apparent ignorance of the aesthetic shift of the eighteenth dynasty, Smith interpreted Akhenaten's "long, narrow face, hatchet chin, thick lips, thick thighs and spindly legs" as the manifestation of apparent glandular trouble associated with the syndrome of "a physical monstrosity" (p. 12), namely, "an extreme case of destructive peridontal disease—badly abscessed teeth which results in long narrow face, thick lips, and hatchet chin." Moreover, he insisted that the outstanding and intelligent achievements of Akhenaten's reign, particularly monotheism, cannot be attributed to him. Instead, Smith credited Nefertiti (who is generally perceived to be of European extraction) with the idea of monotheism, and with the change of aesthetic canons in art. Janson goes on to quote Smith's speculation that the abnormalities of Akhenaten are usually accompanied by sterility, so that Nefertiti's four daughters could not have been his. In his conclusion on Akhenaten, Smith compounded the pharaoh's plight by suggesting that Queen Nefertiti generally stood in her husband's shadow, an indication she had no need to embarrass him about his ineptness.

Winfield Smith's analysis of the Akhenaten bas-relief may not necessarily be racist, but rather one isolated incident plagued with errors. Ben-Jochannan, however, uses this article to illustrate the vicious, deliberate errors and the racism still leveled at people from Africa. He invites his readers to compare the facial characteristics of Akhenaten with those of all people indigenous to Africa and their descendants living in North America, the Caribbean, Brazil, and other parts of South America, and with the descriptions of the Egyptians by ancient Greek and Roman historians. Are we to understand that all those people who seem to fit Smith's description of Akhenaten were/are actually physically deformed?

In his quest to present further convincing evidence about the origin of the ancient Egyptians, ben-Jochannan uses some of the mummies presently on display at the Egyptian Museum in Cairo. These mummies represent many of the various facial types present in Egypt before and after the Dynastic periods. Referring to Smith's illustration, ben-Jochannan observes that most "reconstructions" of the ancient Egyptians we generally see are of the "C" type, which bears the facial characteristics of Europeans. Most people, however, if shown the majority of mummies and surviving sculpture in the round, would not have great difficulty deciding the racial origin of the ancient Egyptian. If ben-Jochannan has presented forceful and cogent evidence of the negroid origin of the ancient Egyptians, the findings presented in Anta Diop's great work, *African Origin of Civilization: Myth or Reality* (1974), are utterly convincing.

Like his contemporary ben-Jochannan, Diop presents evidence from the accounts of ancient Greeks and Romans. Beyond the ancients' testimonies, Diop employs several other approaches—linguistic, totemic, physical anthropology, microscopic analysis, osteological measurements, blood-group typing, cultural data, and the papyrus documents which illustrate how the Egyptians saw themselves. From the wealth of data Diop presents, I will focus on his scientific evidence, which has received the greatest attention from people in archaeology, anthropology, egyptology, history, and linguistics.

Diop (cited, Van Sertima, 1989) prefaces his argument by citing the theory of paleontologist Louis Leakey (cited, Diop, 1974), which has received general acceptance. Central to Leakey's theory is mankind's monogenetic and African origin. His evidence shows that man of 150,000 years ago was "morphologically identical with the man of today" and was "living in the regions of the Great Lakes of Africa, at the sources of the Nile and no where else" (p. 9). Justifying the morphological identity claim, Leakey advances two important points. First, it was out of pure necessity that the earliest men were "ethnically homogeneous and negroid" (p. 9). In defense of this assumption, Leakey uses Gloger's law, which posits that living organisms most likely adapt to their environment by developing characteristics peculiar to the given circumstances. In the case of human beings, Leakey insists, "warm blooded an-

imals evolving in a warm humid climate will secrete black pigment (eumelanin)" (p. 9). Leaky implies that if mankind originated in the areas of the tropics, around the latitude of the Great Lakes of Africa, then logic would lead us to conclude that early man of this region had a dark pigmentation. Consequently, those who moved to other climatic regions must have adapted appropriately. Accordingly then, he argues that the "original stock" was split into different races, and this is one possible conclusion. To ensure that his hypothesis is taken seriously, Leakey points to the geographical constraints of early man, identifying the only two routes available to early man for migration to other continents—the Sahara and the Nile Valley.

To support his position about the African origin of the ancient Egyptians, Diop (1974) uses the historical background of the Nile Valley route and the peopling of that Valley by Negroid races. In substance, although the evidence provided by the physical anthropologists can be used to build "reliable and definitive truths, and sound scientific conclusions," the criteria used to supposedly finalize a solution of this problem are arbitrary, thus giving way to "scientific hair-splitting" (p. 129). He cites many studies which exemplify the hair splitting of the varying percentage of negroid presence in the Valley from the distant prehistoric ages to predynastic times. Diop examines one of the conclusions in Emile Massoulard's *Histoire et protohistoire d' Egypt* (1949). Massoulard states that the Negadah skulls are said to belong to a homogeneous group and therefore can provide sufficient data for a general conclusion about the racial origin. He cites that the dimensions of the skulls' total height, length, breadth of face, nasal capacity and so forth, approximate that of the present-day negro. However, he insists that "the nasal breadth, height of orbit, length of palate and nasal index," seem similar to Germanic peoples. Generally, those who argue for the caucasian origin of the early Egyptians bypass the evidence which suggests negroid characteristics of predynastic Negadian people. Instead they focus almost exclusively on the few racial characteristics akin to the white races.

The other studies Diop cites include Thomson and Randall MacIver's 1949 study of skulls from El Amrah and Abydos, and Keith Falkenburger's recent study of 1,800 male skulls from the Egyptian populations ranging from predynastic to present day. Falkenburger's conclusions report 36 percent Negroid, 33 percent Mediterranean, 11 percent Cro-Magnoid, and 20 percent are estimated to be either Cro-Magnoid or Negroid. Falkenburger's percentage of Negroid skulls during the predynastic period of Egypt is higher than Thomas and Randall MacIver's findings of 25 percent men and 28 percent women.

Consequentially, Diop's analysis considers the discrepancies among the percentages of Negroid, Mediterranean, Cromagnoids, and cross-bred individuals. He draws our attention to what is, perhaps, the most salient of all the arguments put forth. Common to all these arguments is that all bodies of evidence converge at a point which shows that the Egyptian population in the predynastic epoch was Negroid. In view of the common and convincing evidence about the Negro origin of predynastic Egypt, those who insist on arguments that the Negro presence came later remain suspect (Diop, 1974, pp. 129–131).

To further reverse the present-day hypothesis of "White African/Egyptians," Diop employs the science of microscopic analysis of skin to accurately define ethnic affiliation. Since melanin (eumelanin), which determines color of pigmentation, is known to be virtually indestructible, and the scientific community widely agrees that the melanin in animal skin and fossils has survived for millions of years, Diop reasons that the skin of the Egyptian mummies (unparalleled specimens of embalming technique) are prime subjects for melanocyte analysis. Although melanin is mainly found in epidermis, it also penetrates the epidermis and lodges in the dermis. For example, the sample of mummies examined from the Marietta excavation in Egypt shows a higher level of melanin than in any "white skinned races" (p. 125). He assures us that if a similar analysis is done on the best preserved mummies in the Cairo Museum, the result will parallel his findings, proving that the ancient Egyptian belongs to the black races.

Osteological measurements were also a part of Diop's scientific analysis. In physical anthropology, the measurement of bones is a more accepted criterion than craniometry for accurately determining the distinctions of race. In other words, by means of osteological measurement one can differentiate the racial characteristics of a white and a black. Citing the study of the distinguished nineteenth-century German scientist Lepsius, Diop reconfirms that the ancient Egyptians belong to the black races, for, even though physical anthropology has progressed in its methodology, Lepsius' findings have not been invalidated by the new approaches. For example, his notation of some specific characteristics unique to the Egyptian skeleton still stands unchallenged. Lepsius contends that the bodily proportions, especially the short arms, are consistent with the negroid or negrito physical type.

Further, in his quest to provide more substantive evidence for the identity of the ancient Egyptians, Diop examines the etymology of the pharaonic language to see what they called themselves. Connected to the idea of self-description, Diop finds only one term that was designated for this purpose. That word was *kmt*, which literally translated means "the negroes." It is, according to Diop, the strongest term existing in pharaonic language to indicate blackness. Likewise, the character used to symbolize the word *kmt* in hieroglyph is "a length of wood charred at both ends" and not "crocodile scale" (as is commonly misinterpreted). Actually, the word *kmt* is etymologically related to the well-known word *Kamit*, which is common in modern anthropological literature. Diop cautions, however, against the manipulation of modern anthropological literature, which seeks to distort the meaning of the word *kmt* to have it imply "white." To guard against misinformation, he redirects our attention to the authenticity of the pharaonic mother tongue where the word *kmt* meant "coal black." (For an extensive discussion of the grammar of the pharaonic language see his *The African Origin of Civilization* [1974])....

In divine epithets, according to Diop, "black" or "negro" was invariably used to identify the chief beneficent gods of Egypt. Thus, for example, *kmwr* means the "great Negro" (for Osiris). More importantly, *km* always precedes the names of the revered gods of Egypt: for example, Apis, Min Thot, Isis, Hathor, and Horus.

Many other scholars besides ben-Jochannan and Anta Diop who have succeeded in re-establishing the true origin of the ancient Egyptians also point out the African influence on the development of Greco-Roman civilization. Whereas it is not possible within the scope of this work to review many of those who have argued for the Negroid origin of the ancient Egyptians, I must not neglect to mention the challenging and thought-provoking work of Martin Bernal in *Black Athena* Volumes I and II (1987 and 1991, respectively). *Black Athena Volume I* is particularly important for establishing the racial origin of the ancient Egyptians and their contributions to a great civilization. Convinced by the archaeological findings for at least 7,000 years, he asserts that the Egyptian population comprised African, South-West Asian, and Mediterranean types. Furthermore, historically speaking, the farther south one moves along the Nile Valley, where the upper Egyptian Kingdoms had influence, "the darker and more negroid the population becomes" (p. 242). In fact, the darker and more negroid population is still dominant in these regions today.

Bernal's overall view of the ancient Egyptians is summarized in his introduction. He asserts that the Egyptian population was fundamentally African/Black and that the African dominance was remarkable in the Old and Middle Kingdoms before the approximately 150 years of Hyksos reign, which notably was restricted to Lower Egypt. Supporting the claim of African dominance, Bernal joins Basil Davidson and James Brunson (cited, Van Sertima, 1989) in affirming that the most important and powerful dynasties were I–IV, VI, XI–XIII, XVII–XVIII, and XXV, and that the pharaohs of these dynasties were black (Bernal, 1987, p. 242).

Notwithstanding that Bernal devotes little time to the racial origin of the ancient Egyptians, he echoes the views of Diop, ben-Jochannan, and others with respect to what the ancients thought of the Egyptians. He professes that the ancient Greeks unanimously agreed upon the cultural supremacy of the Pharoanic civilization. Judging from how eloquently and respectfully the ancients wrote about the Egyptians, Bernal believes, if it were possible for the Greeks to review some of the modern arguments that deny the Black African origin of ancient Egypt, they would rebuke the absurdity of early nineteenth-century scholarship. Bernal enforces his position by recalling the fact that the Greeks of the Classical Age went to Egypt to learn philosophy, mathematics, history, and many more arts and sciences. In short, Egypt was the center of learning.

Closely associated with the modern distortion of the ancient Egyptian racial origin, Bernal argues, modern racism and slavery figured prominently in the modern debasement of the negroid presence in early Egyptian civilization. Bernal suggests that those people who imposed the most brutal form of human degradation upon African people through the slave trade employed a strategy which included "proving" that Blacks were biologically incapable of creating a civilization as magnificent as Egypt. By thus establishing the so-called "biological truth," the perpetrators of racism and "continental chauvinism" were able to discount the genius of Black Egyptians and replace it with an Indo-Asiatic, white model of civilization. The mission, then, of many nineteenth- and twentieth-century historians was to maintain this status quo as "truth" despite many contradictions (Bernal, 1987, pp. 240–247).

The arguments presented here are a mere sampling of the voluminous body of findings that addresses the question of the racial origin of the ancient Egyptians. Ben-Jochannan, Anta Diop, Van Sertima, Bernal, and Williams are only a few of the modern scholars who have given credence to the testimonies of the ancients about the racial composition of the ancient Egyptians. The Greeks, in particular, maintained a reverence for the genius of the African civilization, Egypt, which was responsible for so many of their own cultural advancements.

By presenting convincing scientific evidence about the racial characteristics of the ancient Egyptians, Diop in particular helps write an important chapter in human history for the benefit of all people, especially downtrodden African peoples. The findings are overwhelmingly in favor of classifying the ancient Egyptians as belonging to the negro race.

Finally, in my arguments, I have used the work of contemporary observers— Volney, Denon, Aldred, ben-Jochannan, Chandler, Anta Diop, and museums with Egyptian art collections—who have presented written and photographic documentation about the physical characteristics of the ancient Egyptians. In every case that I have cited favoring the African/Negroid origin of the Egyptians, none of the sources sought to discount or discredit the importance of European civilization. In fact, the proponents of the African origin of Egyptian civilization share a common ideological concern, namely that the social and political histories of the Egyptians must be told truthfully. Those who are interested in having this truth told understand the need to recast Egypt into its rightful historical position. Diop and ben-Jochannan warn that the re-establishing of African history should not be used as a tool of divisiveness, but rather as a unifying force on behalf of all mankind.

This [selection] has addressed the reconsideration and accurate representation of the origin of the ancient Egyptians. In the discussion I have cited the findings of Yosef ben-Jochannan, Chiekh Anta Diop, and Martin Bernal. Generally speaking, the evidence of ancient Greek and Roman accounts affirms the African influence on ancient Egypt. In addition, scientific data from osteological measurement, eumelanin analysis, and cranium measurements independently support the argument that the ancient Egyptians were Black. As further evidence, the etymology of pharaonic language was examined to find out how the ancient Egyptians referred to themselves. Finally, photographic evidence of ancient Egyptian sculpture supplies mute yet eloquent testimony about the origin of the ancient Egyptians.

NO

Kathryn A. Bard

ANCIENT EGYPTIANS AND
THE ISSUE OF RACE

Egypt straddles two major geographical regions: the continent of Africa and the Middle East. Because it was located on the African continent, ancient Egypt was an African civilization, though perhaps its African identity has been subtly minimized within the discipline of Near Eastern studies, which has its roots in European Orientalism of the nineteenth century. Many earlier European scholars working in Egypt, particularly during the days of the British empire, assumed that ancient history began with Egypt and Mesopotamia—in other words, that the earliest civilizations were Near Eastern ones, and ancient Egypt could be understood as such (and not as an African civilization). Some scholars, such as Sir Flinders Petrie (1899, 10) and Walter Emery (Emery 1967, 39), assumed that civilization was introduced into Egypt by an invading dynastic race from southwestern Asia, who replaced the prehistoric hunters and gatherers and early farmers living along the Nile —peoples much too primitive to "invent" civilization.

It is now known that as the land bridge between Asia and Africa, Egypt was the recipient of earlier technological developments in southwestern Asia, especially agriculture. The major cereal cultigens, emmer wheat and barley, as well as the domestic sheep/goat, are species not known in their wild form in Africa; they were domesticated much earlier, in southwestern Asia, and only later introduced into Egypt (Wetterstrom 1993, 200). There is no archaeological evidence, however, to suggest that a large-scale migration of peoples from southwestern Asia brought farming into Egypt, and the mechanisms by which domesticated cereals and perhaps the technology of farming were introduced into Egypt remain unclear. But recent research on the Predynastic period in Egypt (ca. 4000–3000 B.C.E.), including my excavations near Nag Hammadi in Upper Egypt, has shown that the cultural roots of Egyptian civilization are indeed indigenous (Hoffman, 1988, 47).

Less clear, however, has been the issue of race in ancient Egypt. The modern concept of race was unknown to the ancient Egyptians. Non-Egyptians were identified by their ethnic/tribal affiliations or by the region/country from which they came. Most physical anthropologists in the second half of this century do not believe that pure races ever existed, and they view the concept of "race" as a misleading one for their studies (Trigger 1978, 27). But a number of Afrocentrists have claimed that black civilization began with ancient Egypt. The very title of Martin Bernal's *Black Athena* alludes to the putative roots of Greek—and therefore Western civilization—as a black African civilization in Egypt.

Ancient Egyptians were Mediterranean peoples, neither Sub-Saharan blacks nor Caucasian whites but peoples whose skin was adapted for life in a subtropical desert environment. Ancient Egypt was a melting pot; peoples of different ethnic identities migrated into the Nile Valley at different times in its prehistory and history. The question of whether ancient Egyptians were black or white obscures their own identity as agricultural peoples of *Kmt*, as opposed to *dšrt*, the barren "Red Land" of the desert. *Kmt* means "Black Land," the fertile floodplain of the lower Nile Valley, where cereal crops grew in such abundance. It does not mean "Land of Blacks."

Egyptians were Egyptians, the people of *Kmt*. The name points to the importance of the Nile in their lives. Unlike that of other early riverine civilizations, the Egyptian floodplain required no fallow time, nor was salinization of soils a problem with irrigation agriculture (Butzer 1976, 90). The economic base of pharaonic civilization was provided by the incredibly rich potential of cereal agriculture in the Egyptian Nile Valley. Egyptians were the indigenous farmers of the lower Nile Valley, neither black nor white as races are conceived of today.

Just who the ancient Egyptians were can be addressed by several types of evidence: language, historical records, the material culture, and physical remains (usually skeletons from burials). Evidence may be used to study cultural and biological relationships between different groups as well as within groups. For the most part, analyses of the different types of evidence have to be pursued independently, using different data because of the very different variables of such data; only after that can relationships between the different data be studied—within a specific cultural context.

Looking first at the linguistic evidence, there is nothing that links Egypt to other areas in Africa except very generally Egyptian, the language spoken by the ancient Egyptians and written on monuments in hieroglyphs, evolved over more than four thousand years, to be finally replaced by Arabic following the Arab invasion in the seventh century C.E. Egyptian is classified by linguists as one of the five main groups of what is called the Afro-Asiatic language family. The other languages in this family include the Semitic languages spoken in southwestern Asia (including modern Arabic and Hebrew); Berber, spoken by Berbers in North Africa to the west of the Nile; the Chadic languages, spoken in northern Central Africa in the vicinity of Lake Chad; and the Cushitic languages spoken in the Horn of Africa, such as Galla in eastern Ethiopia (and probably covering Omotic; cf. Greenberg 1955, 43). Egyptian is so distinctly different from these languages in its structure and vocabulary as to be classified by itself. But it is more closely related to other languages in the Afro-Asiatic family than to any Indo-European languages or to the Bantu languages spoken today in Sub-Saharan Africa. In the New Kingdom (ca. 1558–1085 B.C.E.), when Egypt had an empire in southwest Asia, more Semitic words appeared in what is called Late Egyptian, but this can be explained by increased interaction with Semitic-speaking peoples, and not with other Africans (although that too certainly occurred). The linguistic evidence, then, points to the relative isolation of speakers of Egyptian in relation to other languages spoken in Africa.

Another important type of evidence for the study of ancient populations is from the physical remains that have been preserved in Egyptian burials. D. E. Derry, who studied the physical remains of Old Kingdom elites buried at Giza (excavated in the first decade of this century by George Reisner of Harvard University), took skull measurements and concluded, like Petrie and Emery, that the pyramid builders were a dynastic race of invaders, probably from the East, "who were far removed from any negroid element" (1956, 81).

As practiced by Derry, however, craniometry is no longer considered a valid statistical means for evaluating genetic relationships of ancient populations. A more recent analysis of nonmetrical variations in skulls (Berry and Berry 1973) suggests that the Egyptian samples show genetic continuity from Predynastic times through the Old and Middle Kingdoms—over two thousand years—with a shift in the New Kingdom, when there were considerable infiltrations of new peoples into the Nile Valley. In this same study the Egyptian skulls were then analyzed with samples from the northern Sudan (the Neolithic site of Jebel Moya), West Africa (Ashanti), Palestine (the site of Lachish), and Turkey (Byzantine period). Not surprisingly, the Egyptian skulls were not very distinct from the Jebel Moya skulls but were much more distinct from all others, including those from West Africa. Such a study suggests closer genetic affinity between peoples in Egypt and the northern Sudan, which were close geographically and are known to have had considerable cultural contact throughout prehistory and pharaonic history. But the Egyptian and the Jebel Moya samples also seemed no more related to the samples from southwestern Asia in Palestine and Turkey than to modern (black) populations of West Africa (Berry and Berry 1973, 206).

Clearly more analyses of the physical remains of ancient Egyptians need to be done using current techniques, such as those Nancy Lovell at the University of Alberta is using in her work (see A. L. Johnson and N. Lovell 1994). Two problems, however, hinder such studies. First, graves in Egypt have been robbed since prehistoric times. Intact tombs, such as Tutankhamen's, are the great exception, and even his tomb had been penetrated twice in antiquity by robbers. Second, many skeletons excavated by earlier archaeologists working in Egypt were either not kept, or have been stored so poorly that today they are in very bad condition. The prehistoric burials that I excavated in 1978 at Naqada in Upper Egypt were sent off to storage in the basement of the Cairo Museum, never to be seen again. Even for the same age/sex group within a burial sample representing one small village community (in which there probably was some or even considerable intermarriage), there can be significant skeletal variability, and large samples need to be analyzed so that statistical findings will be valid. But nonskeletal features, which are the ones most frequently used to distinguish race today, have long since disappeared in the physical remains of burial—even when they have been mummified as in pharaonic Egypt (Trigger 1968, 11).

It is disturbing to me as an archaeologist that archaeological evidence—the artifacts, art and architecture of ancient Egypt—has been identified with race and racial issues. Racial issues, which in all fairness have arisen because of racial inequalities in the United States and elsewhere, have been imposed on the material remains of a culture even though these remains do not in themselves denote race. I am reminded of the excavation report of the Wellcome expedition at the site of Jebel Moya (Addison 1949). The English archaeologists who worked there in 1911–12 were certain that the advanced stone tools they excavated had to have been made by a prehistoric people who were white. This seems like a ridiculous conclusion today: stone tools thousands of years old cannot tell us the race of their makers any more than they can tell us what language their makers spoke.

The conventions of Egyptian art, as established by the beginning of the First Dynasty (ca. 3050 B.C.E.) do not represent humans as seen in perspective by the eye, but represent them in an analytic manner that transforms reality. The head, arms, and legs are drawn in profile; the torso is depicted frontally. Art may sometimes be grossly mannered and exaggerated, as it was during the reign of Akhenaten (ca. 1363–1347 B.C.E.) because of religious and cultural reforms conceptualized by that pharaoh. The conventions of Egyptian art were those of the crown and elites associated with the crown, and what is characteristic of Egyptian style in art for the most part represents a very small segment of the population.

Who and what were depicted on the walls of temples and tombs depended on Egyptian beliefs and ideology. Art was functional, and much of what is seen today in museums was created for the mortuary cult. Ancient Egypt was a class-stratified society, and age and sex in art were differentiated by scale of figures, style of dress, and symbols of status or office, as well as by skin tone. Statues and reliefs of women were painted in lighter tones of yellow ochre-based paint; men were painted in darker tones of red ochre-based paint. This is not to suggest that all Egyptian men were darker than all Egyptian women, but rather that established artistic conventions served to convey such ideas as sex differentiation. Such conventions, however, were not hard and fast rules, and there are many known exceptions. For example, in the tomb of Queen Nefertari, Rameses II's chief wife, the queen's skin is painted a brown (red ochre) color in a scene where she is playing a board game, as a contrast to the solid background of yellow ochre paint.

Non-Egyptian Africans, as well as Asiatics, were usually depicted in representational art as distinctly different from Egyptians, especially in their clothing and hairstyles. In the well-known scenes from the Eighteenth Dynasty tomb of Rekmire, Asiatics, Cretans, and Nubians are painted in registers bringing tribute to the court of Tuthmoses III. The Nubians, from the Nile Valley south of the First Cataract at Aswan, are painted in darker skin tones than the Asiatics, and are depicted with more prognathous jaws than the Egyptians. Bringing exotic goods and pets that originated in regions south of Nubia, the Nubians also carry gold ingots shaped into large rings. Nubia had little agricultural potential compared to Egypt, but rich gold mines were located there in *wadis* to the east of the Nile. That in part explains why Egypt occupied Nubia and built forts and temple towns there in the Middle and New Kingdoms.

Nubians bearing gold ingots and exotic tribute in paintings from the tomb of Huy (Thebes, no. 40), dating to the time of Tutankhamen, wear long, pleated Egyptian robes, but their hairstyles and large earrings are distinctly non-Egyptian. They have neck markings that may represent scarification, a practice unknown in ancient Egypt, and their facial features may possibly be interpreted as prognathous. In one scene an elite Nubian woman is depicted standing in a cart drawn by oxen, something in which Egyptian women would never have ridden. The Nubian tribute-bearers are painted in two skin tones, black and dark brown. These tones do not necessarily represent actual skin tones in real life but may serve to distinguish each tribute-bearer from the next in a row in which the figures overlap. Alternatively, the brown-skinned people may be of Nubian origin, and the black-skinned ones may be from farther south (Trigger 1978, 33). The shading of skin tones in Egyptian tomb paintings, which varies considerably, may not be a certain criterion for distinguishing race. Specific symbols of ethnic identity can also vary.

Nor are black Africans depicted by standardized conventions. The scenes of Queen Hatshepsut's expedition to the land of Punt, from her Eighteenth Dynasty mortuary temple at Deir el-Bahri, show a land very different from Egypt. Punt is thought to have been located along and to the west of the Sudanese/Eritrean coast (Kitchen 1993). The houses of the Punt peoples were hemispherical and built on elevated posts, unlike the rectangular mudbrick houses of Egyptians. Punt was the source of incense, ivory, and ebony, and tribute-bearers are seen carrying these goods to the seafaring Egyptians. A grossly obese "queen" of Punt is very unlike the lithe Egyptian upper-class women shown in tombs of this period. The "king" of Punt, whom she follows, is depicted in an Egyptian loincloth, but with a long and very un-Egyptian beard.

Though some Egyptian details appear, the ethnographic details in the Punt expedition scenes portray a culture that is distinctly non-Egyptian. But what race the Punt peoples were cannot really be determined from these scenes. Egyptian artists or scribes who accompanied this expedition recorded very distinctive ethnographic details, but the Puntites' facial features look more Egyptian than "black." Identifying race in Egyptian representational art, again, is difficult to do —probably because race (as opposed to ethnic affiliation, that is, Egyptians versus all non-Egyptians) was not a criterion for differentiation used by the ancient Egyptians.

As enemies of Egypt—peoples who threatened the boundaries of Egypt's kingdom—Nubians and Asiatics were depicted generically on the walls of Egyptian temples in the New Kingdom. The enemies of Egypt were shown as bound captives, being vanquished by pharaoh. On Egyptian temples in Nubia, reliefs showing such scenes must have had as one of their purposes the intimidation of local people. It was the duty of the king to destroy Egypt's enemies, and this is what is symbolized on the handle of a cane and on a footstool from Tutankhamen's tomb, both carved with generic Asiatic and Nubian captives. The Nubians carved on these two artifacts have very different facial features from those of the bearded Asiatics, but the facial features of both types of foreigners differ from the sculpture of Tutankhamen in the tomb.

Given that conventions for differentiating ethnic identity varied, as did artistic conventions for skin tones, anomalies in Egyptian art cannot be used with any certainty for drawing inferences about the race of ancient Egyptians. A limestone female head found in Giza tomb 4440, dating to the Fourth Dynasty (ca. 2613–2494 B.C.E.), is described in the catalogue of the Museum of Fine Arts in Boston as "of negroid type with thick lips, wide nostrils, and full cheeks" (W. S. Smith 1960, 35). A limestone head representing the woman's husband, also from tomb 4440, is distinctly different in its facial features: "the aquiline type of face so characteristic of some of the members of the Cheops family" (Smith, 35). Neither of these heads is painted, so their skin tones are unknown. The genre (called "reserve heads"), known only from the Fourth Dynasty, suggests more individualistic portraits than are usual in Egyptian art, and this female head "of negroid type" is different from other known reserve heads. As the identity of the person represented is unknown, her place in Egyptian society cannot be ascertained—though she certainly was a woman of high position.

A sandstone statue of Mentuhotep II, the king who unified Egypt and founded the Middle Kingdom in the twenty-first century B.C.E., was found in a pit to the east of the king's mortuary complex at Deir el-Bahri. The king is shown wearing a white robe and the red crown of Lower Egypt—and his skin is painted black. But as with analogous cases noted above, paint applied to a statue offers no real indication of his actual skin color. Black-painted skin could be symbolic of something of which we are unaware four thousand years later.

Perhaps better known than the painted statue of Mentuhotep II are the two New Kingdom figures of Tutankhamen that Howard Carter found guarding the entrance to that king's burial chamber. The black, resin-covered skin on these two wooden figures is contrasted by their gold skirts, sandals, headdresses, and jewelry (Reeves 1990, 128). These two black renditions of the king contrast the lighter-toned paintings of him on the walls of the burial chamber, and with the colored inlay on the back of the famous golden throne. Other art in this tomb likewise depicts a young man with brown skin, in keeping with Egyptian artistic conventions. Far from suggesting that the king had black skin, the two guardian figures of Tutankhamen may appear black simply because resin was applied to the skin areas. It is possible, too, that the resin was originally lighter and became dark over time. Resin, a costly and exotic import in ancient Egypt, was a material befitting a king who was to go to the afterlife displaying all forms of worldly wealth.

The people who lived south of Egypt are also known from archaeological evidence excavated in Nubia. From the fourth millennium B.C.E., when complex society evolved in Egypt, there is evidence in Lower Nubia of what archaeologists call the A-Group culture: people who traded with the Egyptians for Egyptian craft goods found in their burials. But with the founding of the First Dynasty in Egypt, ca. 3050 B.C.E., the newly unified Egyptian state penetrated into Lower Nubia, probably by military campaigns, and the A-Group disappeared there. Who the A-Group were in terms of race cannot be ascertained from the artifacts in their graves, but their locally made grave goods demonstrate a different material culture from that of the Predynastic Egyptians (Trigger 1976, 33).

From the Old Kingdom (ca. 2686–2181 B.C.E.) there is some archaeological evidence of small-scale Egyptian settlements in Lower Nubia, but by the late Old Kingdom a group of indigenous peoples, known to archaeologists as the C-Group, moved into Nubia as Egyptian occupation ended. After Egypt was reunified during the Middle Kingdom (ca. 2040–1786 B.C.E.), large mudbrick forts were built along the Nile in the region of the Second Cataract (near the modern-day border of Egypt and the Sudan). But evidence of the C-Group in Lower Nubia is also known to date to the Middle Kingdom, and the C-Group culture actually survived the Egyptian withdrawal from Nubia at the collapse of the Middle Kingdom.

During the Middle Kingdom a powerful African polity arose whose capital was at Kerma near the Third Cataract in the Nile, in the northern Sudan. In Egyptian texts this culture is called "Kush." The eastern cemetery at Kerma was excavated by George Reisner, and artifacts from eight very large round tumuli are now in the Museum of Fine Arts in Boston (Reisner 1923a). These tumuli are of a different architecture than Egyptian tombs. Some of them, moreover, contained human sacrifices, not found in Egyptian burials (with the possible exception of the First Dynasty royal tombs at Abydos). A Swiss archaeologist currently excavating the town and cemetery at Kerma estimates that there are 30,000 to 40,000 burials (Bonnet 1992, 613). The sway of Kerma extended into Lower Nubia until the reunification of Egypt at the beginning of the New Kingdom.

With Egyptian control in the New Kingdom extending as far south as Gebel Barkal near the Fourth Cataract, where a temple to the god Amen was built, the Kerma kingdom came to an end. Egyptians restored the Middle Kingdom forts in Lower Nubia and built temple towns farther south. But after the collapse of the New Kingdom, ca. 1085 B.C.E., a new Kushite power eventually arose at Gebel Barkal, where the cult of Amen continued to be practiced. The earliest burials in the royal cemetery at el-Kurru near Gebel Barkal (see Dunham 1950), also excavated by George Reisner, date to around 850 B.C.E. A hundred years later the first Kushite garrisons were established in southern Egypt during the reign of the Kushite king Piye, who later established his rule over all of Egypt (Trigger 1976, 140, 145). The Twenty-fifth Dynasty (ca. 760–656 B.C.E.), whose kings were all Kushites, ruled in Egypt for about sixty years. The later kings of this dynasty were frequently at battle with the Assyrian army, which finally succeeded in ending Kushite control in Egypt. Piye built the first pyramid tomb at el-Kurru, whereas in Egypt pyramids as royal burial monuments had not been built for a thousand years. Later Kushite kings were mummified, according to Egyptian custom, and spread the cult of Amen throughout Nubia.

The archaeological evidence of African kingdoms south of Egypt, at Kerma and Gebel Barkal, suggests distinctly different cultures that came into contact with Egypt. During the Twenty-fifth Dynasty the polity centered at Gebel Barkal actually controlled Egypt for a period. Cultural connections, if any, between the earlier Kerma kingdom and the later kingdom centered farther up the Nile at Gebel Barkal are uncertain, but the well-preserved burials recently excavated at Kerma by Bonnet (1992) provide a new source of information about Nubian populations.

Presumably the Kushites buried at Kerma and later at el-Kurru were related to the Nubians depicted in New Kingdom tomb paintings, as opposed to blacks living farther south in Africa, but once again the evidence seems ambiguous. Skin color, which is considered a criterion for race, cannot be determined from skeletal remains, and the evidence of representational art is problematic. The archaeological evidence at Kerma and el-Kurru points to African cultures that were different from Egyptian culture but that were responsible nonetheless for major cultural achievements. The Kushite peoples were considered non-Egyptians by Egyptians—in other words, ethnically different—but how physically different they were has yet to be determined by physical anthropologists. In any event, they are certainly better candidates for "black" African kingdoms than is ancient Egypt.

Culturally and linguistically the ancient Egyptians were different from other peoples living outside the Nile Valley, as well as those farther south and east. From textual and representational evidence it may be shown that ancient Egyptians had a sense of ethnic identity—of being Egyptian, as opposed to non-Egyptian. Today in Africa there are many different ethnic groups speaking many different languages. With the exception of South Africa, identity in Africa today is not by race or, for the most part, by nation, but by ethnic or tribal affiliation, which often has a close association with a spoken language or dialect. Ancient Egypt was definitely the earliest African civilization and as such certainly had an influence not only on the other cultures that arose in the Near East, but also on the states that arose farther south in Africa —at Kerma, Gebel Barkal, and later at Meroë. The evidence cited here strongly suggests that the ancient Egyptians were North African peoples, distinct from Sub-Saharan blacks. But to state categorically that ancient Egypt was either a black—or a white—civilization is to promote a misconception with racist undertones that appeals to those who would like to increase rather than decrease the racial tensions that exist in modern society.

POSTSCRIPT

Did Egyptian Civilization Originate in Africa?

It is sad that so much of the current debate regarding the origin of Egyptian civilization is influenced by today's volatile racial climate.

Afrocentrists consider the view that ancient Egypt had multicultural origins to be another attempt by Eurocentrist scholars to "whitewash" African history. Those who oppose the Afrocentric view of the origins of Egyptian civilization claim that they are merely supporting the facts as they have been uncovered. These scholars assert that they fail to see how anyone can benefit from a distorted historical record, regardless of reason.

Martin Bernal's *Black Athena* (Rutgers University Press, 1987) brought renewed interest to the Egyptian/African debate, even though it was not his intention to do so. But his provocative title, which indicates African roots for the Greek goddess of wisdom, certainly caught the attention of Afrocentrists, who have embraced the book as supportive of their own views on the nature and origins of ancient Egypt. In a September 23, 1991, *Newsweek* article, Bernal suggested that "African Athena" might have been a more accurate title for his work. *Black Athena* is a difficult read, but a quick perusal of the work is a most enlightening experience, especially Bernal's exposure of the pro-Aryan bias of past scholars, which is the root of the problem here.

Support for the Afrocentric view of Egyptian civilization can be found in several books by Cheikh Anta Diop: *The African Origins of Civilization: Myth or Reality?* (Lawrence Hill Books, 1974); *Civilization or Barbarism: An Authentic Anthropology* (Lawrence Hill Books, 1981); and the chapter entitled "Origin of the Ancient Egyptians" in G. Mokhtar, ed., *Ancient Civilizations of Africa*, volume 2 of UNESCO's *General History of Africa* (University of California Press, 1981).

The multicultural side of this debate can be found in a number of articles in *Black Athena Revisited* edited by Mary R. Lefkowitz and Guy MacLean Rogers (University of North Carolina Press, 1996). Lefkowitz, in *Not Out of Africa: How Afrocentrism Became an Excuse to Teach Myth as History* (Basic Books, 1996), deals mainly with the question of the Egyptian influence on Greek civilization, but she also devotes space to the issue of Egypt's early roots.

Two excellent videotape series that cover every aspect of the African experience and touch on the issue analyzed here are Ali A. Mazrui, *The Africans: A Triple Heritage* (Program 2, "Anatomy of a Continent"), and *Africa: A Voyage of Discovery With Basil Davidson* (Program 1, "Different But Equal").

ISSUE 3

Did Greek Civilization Have Semitic and African Origins?

YES: Martin Bernal, from "Black Athena: The African and Levantine Roots of Greece," in Ivan Van Sertima, ed., *African Presence in Early Europe* (Transaction Books, 1985)

NO: John E. Coleman, from "Did Egypt Shape the Glory That Was Greece? The Case Against Martin Bernal's *Black Athena*," *Archaeology* (September/ October 1992)

ISSUE SUMMARY

YES: Professor of government Martin Bernal argues that racism and anti-Semitism among past classical scholars caused them to ignore the African and Near Eastern roots of Greek culture and civilization.

NO: Professor of classics John E. Coleman argues that although racism and anti-Semitism did exist among classical scholars, it did not influence their work. He maintains that the idea that Greek culture and civilization have African and Near Eastern roots cannot be proved.

Greece has been considered by many to be the birthplace of Western civilization. Scholars have agreed that everything that is considered important in the West—philosophy, mathematics, science, democratic government, art and architecture, drama, poetry, epics, mythology to enrich our imagination, language, and so on—was rooted in a place called "Hellas," the land of the ancient Greeks. The message was simple: to understand Western civilization one had to understand the Greeks. Or so it was thought!

In 1987 Martin Bernal published the first of his projected four-volume *Black Athena* series, and the ancient world and its present-day scholars have never been the same. The subtitle said it all: *The Afroasiatic Roots of Classical Civilization*. Volume 2, published in 1991, added more fuel to the fire.

In both volumes Bernal developed the following theses: (1) The scholarly community from the eighteenth century through most of the twentieth century was blatantly racist and anti-Semitic and, thus, incapable of considering the fact that some of Greek civilization could have come from African or Semitic sources; and (2) there is substantial evidence to support the idea that people from both the Near East (Semites) and Africa (Egyptians) played an important role in transmitting their culture to Greece, where it became part of the intellectual and cultural backbone of Western civilization.

Once the classicists caught their breath, they began to reply to Bernal's charges in increasing numbers. In both scholarly journals and popular magazines, the words "Martin Bernal replies" were frequently used, as Bernal was forced to answer his many critics. This avalanche of criticism reached its apex in 1996 with the publication of *Black Athena Revisited* edited by Mary R. Lefkowitz and Guy MacLean Rogers (University of North Carolina Press), in which 20 scholars contributed articles criticizing various aspects of Bernal's work.

Bernal was not without allies. Basil Davidson, one of the twentieth century's leading historians on Africa, has come to Bernal's defense, as have a number of scholars who see in his work a justification for their Afrocentric view of history. With race consciousness and political correctness entering the fray, it seems likely that this debate will not end in the near future. And what will happen when volume 3 is published?

In the following selection, Bernal states his theses and develops arguments to support them. The first is that classicists in past eras were racists and anti-Semites and that these biases adversely influenced their work. The second thesis is that ancient Greek civilization had Afroasiatic roots. Bernal uses all of the sources available to him, and he relies heavily on linguistics (his original field of endeavor) to prove his points.

In the second selection, John E. Coleman answers Bernal's challenges, mounting a counterattack against his theses and the evidence used to support them. He states that although racism was evident in classical studies during the past two centuries, it did not play a major role in the scholarship developed by those working in the field. He then questions the conclusions drawn by Bernal, examining the very same sources that Bernal uses. A slightly enlarged version of the article reprinted here is contained in *Black Athena Revisited*.

Despite the acrimony that this debate may have engendered, Bernal has done classical studies a great service. Coleman himself admits that *Black Athena* is an "inspiring broad scholarly and popular reexamination of the relationship between the Greeks and the Near Eastern world." Such is the nature of historical revisionism and what develops from it.

YES

Martin Bernal

BLACK ATHENA: THE AFRICAN AND LEVANTINE ROOTS OF GREECE

In [another] publication I discuss the economic, political, social and intellectual environments in which the new discipline of *Altertumswissenschaft* or "Classics" was established. To do this I have found it useful to distinguish between two models for the origins of Ancient Greece which I called the "Ancient" and the "Aryan." Most of us have been educated within the latter. According to this, Greek culture was the result of one or more invasions of Greece by Indo-European speakers from the north. They conquered the native population who were supposed to have been soft but civilized. Apart from having been "white" or "Caucasian" and definitely not "Semitic" or African, very little is known about these "pre-Hellenes" except from the many linguistic traces of a non-Indo-European culture left in Greece. In this way the painful impossibility of maintaining that Greece was purely Indo-European has been to some extent alleviated by the type of mixture envisaged. It is seen as an Aryan conquest of non-Aryans but unlike the Aryan conquest of India, the original inhabitants of Greece were Caucasian. Thus no fundamental racial impurity was involved.

... [T]he only evidence that can be adduced to support a northern invasion there is the fact that Greek is fundamentally an Indo-European language and as there is a strong likelihood that the original proto Indo-European was spoken in the region now known as the Ukraine there must have been a cultural flow from the north. However, how and when this language came to be spoken in Greece is unknown. So too are the origins of the many non-Indo-European elements in the Greek language, toponyms and divine and mythological names.

There is furthermore no tradition of a northern invasion of Greece. This in fact has been a problem for 19th and 20th century scholars who have been convinced of the invasion's central role in the formation of Greek culture. As J. B. Bury put it, in his standard history of ancient Greece:

> "The true home of the Greeks before they won dominion in Greece had passed clean out of their remembrance, and they looked to the east not to the north, as the quarter from which some of their ancestors had migrated."

What Bury saw as their faulty memory, I describe as the Ancient Model. This historical scheme is referred to by most Greek writers concerned with understanding their distant past, omitted by one or two, and denied only by Plutarch in what is generally seen to be an outburst of spleen against Herodotus. According to it, Greece had originally been inhabited by primitive tribes, Pelasgians and others, and had then been settled by Egyptians and Phoenicians who had built cities and introduced irrigation. The latter had brought the alphabet and the former had taught the natives the names of the gods and how to worship them. The earliest royal dynasties were supposed to have had both divine and Egyptian or Phoenician descent.

This Ancient Model was discredited in the last quarter of the 18th century, through a process that cannot be linked to any new evidence or source of information. It must therefore be associated with other intellectual shifts. I maintain that these were the new predominance of romanticism, racism and the concept of progress. Romanticism was important because in its attack on the universality of the Enlightenment, it emphasized peculiarity and the importance of place and kinship in the information of cultures. This was accompanied by the belief that demanding or stimulating environments, particularly the cold ones of mountains or the north, produced the most virtuous peoples. Thus such a virtuous race as the Greeks could not have derived their culture from the south and east.

Closely associated with romanticism was the rise of systematic racism, the belief that there was an integral connection between virtue or manliness and skin color. Both trends were clearly influenced by the Northern European need to denigrate the peoples they were exterminating, enslaving and exploiting in other continents. European expansion and the arrogance and optimism that flowed from it were also important in the new predominance of the paradigm of progress. Thus, where in previous centuries the greater antiquity of the Egyptians and the Phoenicians gave them cultural superiority, the idea that "later is better" clearly benefited the Greeks. Closely related to this was the growing cult of youth and dynamism. Until the 18th century the perceived antiquity and stability of Egypt and China made them foci of admiration. In the new intellectual climate these became marks of failure.

This interwoven cluster of beliefs found the Ancient Model intolerable. Greece, the pure childhood and epitome of youthful and dynamic Europe, could not have gained its civilization from the static and senile cultures of the southern and racially inferior Egyptians....

At this point, however, I must introduce a complication to my scheme, by distinguishing between two branches of the Aryan Model, the Broad and the Extreme. The Broad Aryan Model, established in the first half of the 19th century, denied the tradition of Egyptian influence on Greece but for the most part accepted that of the Phoenicians. The Extreme Aryan Model, which arose towards the end of the century, rejected the idea of Semitic influence as well. Since the late 18th century, there had been little doubt that the superior race was the "Caucasian" one, to use a term coined in the period. The "Caucasians" included not only Europeans but "Semites" to use another new term. With the establishment of the Indo-European language family a new concept emerged, that of two master-races, the Aryans and the Semites. These were seen in perpetual dialectic. The Semites had given the world religion and poetry and the Aryans manliness, democracy, philosophy, science, etc.

In classical scholarship this allowed the legendary Phoenician role in Greece to be accepted. Indeed to some extent their reputation rose to take up the slack left by the absence of the Egyptians. This was particularly true in Victorian England where, for obvious reasons, the image of stern seamen who spread civilization while making a tidy profit from selling cloth and a little bit of slave trading, was quite appealing. In Germany, however, this idea was never so widely accepted and German scholars were central to the formation of what I call the Extreme Aryan Model in which neither Egyptians nor Phoenicians were supposed to have had any significant influence on the formation of Greek civilization....

In the case with which we are concerned it could well be that the Aryan Model made better sense of Greek history than the Ancient one externally, in its relations with the *Weltenschauung* of the historians concerned. It does not necessarily mean that it provided any better "internal" explanation of the origins of Greece. Given that most scholars today do not share the views of romantic ethnicity and racial hierarchy which provided a large part of the basis for the dismissal of the Ancient Model and the creation of the Aryan one, it would seem appropriate to test the internal heuristic values of the two....

The headings under which the comparison will be undertaken are the following: intrinsic, documents, archaeology, [and] language....

INTRINSIC

The proponents of the Ancient Model living between 500 B.C. and 500 A.D. were nearer to the period concerned than advocates of the Aryan one after 1800 A.D. Though the former lived over a millennium after the alleged invasion they had at their disposal abundant materials in both Egypt and Phoenicia. On the other hand access to them was largely through Egyptians and Phoenicians who may well have wanted to glorify their own traditions especially in relation to those of Greece. In Greece itself there was, *pace* conventional wisdom, no period of complete illiteracy between the Bronze and the Iron Ages. Thus some native written records supplemented by those from Egypt and Phoenicia, oral traditions, archaeological and even architectural remains gave Greek historians after the 5th century considerable information about their past.

They appear to have been torn in their attitudes to the idea of derivation of their higher culture from Egyptians and Phoenicians. Some writers appear to have been pleased to find deep historical roots for their culture through these older civilizations. On the other hand many clearly did not like the cultural inferiority in which such a historical pattern put them, especially as the Egyptians and Phoenicians were still very much around. This unhappiness may provide an explanation why Thucydides failed to mention what was in his time a very widespread view of history.

In most respects 19th and 20th century classicists and Ancient Historians have less information. It is true that Egyptologists can read Egyptian better than most of the Greeks who went to Egypt. They cannot of course read it as well as the Egyptian informants of the Greeks. Moreover, unlike the ancient Greeks, modern historians cannot experience Ancient Egyptian Society or question Ancient Egyptians. Surviving written records from the Levant [the countries bordering on the eastern Mediterranean] are negligible in comparison to those we know to have existed 2,000 years ago. It is true that archaeology has enabled us to know more about the material culture of Egypt and Greece—though not Phoenicia—than any one in the past 1,500 years. This, however, does not put us beyond the ancients themselves who lived at the end of a period of extraordinary cultural continuity of 3,000 years.

Proponents of the Aryan Model have not however based their claim for superiority on quantity of information. For them what matters is not the amount of information but the use made of it. In their eyes they and they alone have treated it "scientifically" hence the term *Altertumswissenschaft* "Science of Antiquity." For them, just as the railways, steamships and telegraphs transcended all previous means of transport and communication, their scientific and skeptical historical approach or "method" has put them on a categorically higher plane than all their predecessors, especially the "credulous" Greeks.

For them the Ancient Model was a delusion. Just as 'scientific' historians had to discount all the Greek references to centaurs, sirens and other mythical creatures who offended against the laws of natural history, the Ancients' view of Greece as civilized by Africans and Near Easterners, had to be removed, because it went counter to "racial science." It was in this "scientific" spirit that the medical term "Egyptomania" was coined. This was seen as a delusion that affected otherwise rational Greeks with the belief that Egypt was central to their culture.

The claim to be "scientific" simply because they were living in a period of technological breakthrough is inherently suspect. Nevertheless, the classicists were undoubtedly right when they maintained that the Greek historians held many views incompatible with our own scientific paradigms. These, however, are not especially significant to the question of whether or not Greece was civilized by Egyptians and Phoenicians. On the other hand the racial views of the founders of classics are central to the question of the historicity of the settlements. While, as stated above, the Greeks were torn on their desirability, Ancient Historians of the 19th and 20th centuries have had no such ambivalence. They have wanted or even needed to keep Greece purely European and certainly not have it colonized by Africans and Asians.

To conclude this section, the division is not between skepticism and credulousness, it is one over which group is to be believed; the Ancients with more information and more confused attitudes towards Greek relations with Phoenicians and Egyptians or the Classicists with their "scientific method" and their clear cut paradigmatically based preferences.

DOCUMENTS

Although the Aegean in the 2nd millennium is often thought to be prehistoric, this is not, in fact, the case. First of all, we know that much, if not all, of it was literate during this period. Secondly the nearby Levant and Egypt, both of which were fully literate, had contact with the region.

The only surviving and comprehensible documents from the Aegean are the tablets in Linear B found on both Crete and the Mainland from the 14th and 13 centuries B.C. They are written in a Greek which contains many acknowledged Semitic Loanwords and many Egyptian ones too. The tablets are administrative records of palatial economies with striking resemblances to those of the Levant and Mesopotamia. These parallels extend to the system of weights and calques of bureaucratic phraseology. There are also a number of personal names such as Aikupitijo and Misarijo (Egyptian) and Turijo (Tyrian), showing the presence of people from these places in the Bronze Age Aegean. Unfortunately, there are no historical texts in Linear B. So, although the tablets prove that there was considerable Eastern influence in Greece in the Late Bronze Age there is no specific evidence to settlements or an invasion.

The same is true of texts from the Levant. Tablets from the great Syrian port of Ugarit from the 14th and 13th centuries show not only that its officials knew about Crete but also that they were trading with it. A 14th century letter from a king of Tyre to the Egyptian pharaoh mentions a king of Danuna who may well have lived in Greece.

Egyptian sources are more plentiful. Crete is referred to in a document that may date back to the First Intermediate Period in the 22nd century B.C. References to the Aegean became more frequent in the Hyksos period ±1720–1570 B.C. The Hyksos were a group of largely Semitic-speaking northerners who conquered and ruled Lower Egypt for most of this period. As far back as the 3rd century B.C., historians have linked this period to the biblical tradition of a sojourn in Egypt. They have also related the Hyksos expulsion by native Egyptians to the Exodus. This period also makes traditions among the Greeks themselves of settlements of Danaans and the movement from Egypt to Greece of the Phoenician Cadmus.

Interestingly however rulers of H3w Nbw, a country that has plausibly been identified with the Aegean, seem to have been allied with the Egyptians against the Hyksos. In any event there was close contact between the two regions at the end of the Hyksos period and the beginning of the 18th Dynasty, c1650–1550. It is from this time that we have a list of names from Kftiw (Crete). This contains some Semitic, some Hurrian, many Egyptians names and others of unknown origin. Apart from the ethnic mix this portrays, it shows Egyptian interest in and claim to know about the island. This emphasis is all the more remarkable in view of the extremely poor documentation on any subject in this period.

The years for which there is most evidence of close relations between Egypt and the Aegean are those from 1450 to 1320 during which the New Kingdom had an empire in the Levant.

In this period there are records of missions from the islands to Egypt and there is no doubt that at least the Egyptians saw the relationship as one of suzereinty. From this period there is also a list of Cretan and Mainland place-names showing that Egyptian knowledge of the region was relatively detailed.

Before leaving the Egyptian documents we should mention the... publication of a major inscription from Mit Rahina in Memphis dating from the middle of the 12th Dynasty, the early 19th century B.C. This details the activities of Egyptian pharaohs by both land and sea in the Levant and beyond. Archaeological evidence from a royal religious foundation of the period indicates that at least indirect contact with the Aegean was made at this period. This raises the real possibility of Egyptian expeditions to this region which could conceivably be related to the Egyptian claim, reported by Diodorus, that Kekrops the founder of Athens had come from Egypt. One of the pharaohs mentioned on the inscription (Senwosret I) is called by his *prenomen* Kheper kare' or should it be kakheperre'?

Beyond this, the inscription has much wider ramifications. Firstly it shatters once and for all the aryanist myth that Egyptians never went to sea. It also alters the balance between the relative worth of ancient writings and modern Egyptology. The former had given details of the massive conquests of Sesostris and Memnōn who can be identified with the pharaohs mentioned. These descriptions have been as absurd by 19th and 20th century ancient historians because no corroborative evidence for them had been found by Egyptology. This shows how much "science" can miss and how dangerous the "argument from silence" can be even in such a relatively well dug country as Egypt.

Apart from this, however, there is no Egyptian evidence of any possible conquests or settlements in the Aegean. Thus, as with the Linear B texts, all that can be seen from the documents is that there was considerable contact between Greece and the East Mediterranean in the 2nd millennium B.C.

ARCHAEOLOGY

Plutarch writing in the 2nd century A.D. gave a detailed description of a discovery made 500 years previously of Egyptian objects with an inscription in Boitia

in Central Greece. Here, however, we will restrict ourselves to modern archaeology. This has found no commemorative Stela or other inscription recording Egyptian or Semitic settlements. On the other hand near the middle of the 2nd millennium, the time specified by the Ancient Model as that of the main Afroasiatic settlements, there appears to have been a sharp break in the material culture of Greece. The Middle Helladic Period ±2000–1600 B.C. seems to have been a poor one. Towards its end, however, there appears to have been a drastic social change. This is shown by the extraordinarily rich finds from Shaft and Tholos graves of the period. The graves' pottery is of the same style found before, indicating some continuity. The rich metal work, however, has no Greek precedent. Although distinctive in style the pieces have affinities with contemporary or slightly earlier work from Syria, Egypt and Crete. The graves' wealth would seem to indicate great social stratification. If, as would seem plausible, grave-goods show the real or ideal occupations of their occupants, the new society was very warlike. The graves are full of spears, knives *and* swords, a new weapon recently developed in south west Asia.

This evidence is interpreted by Aryanists in one of two ways. One, that local chieftains became rich and imported and imitated oriental goods; two, that Greeks went to Egypt to fight as mercenaries and returned with new weapons, techniques and artistic styles. The evidence can equally well be interpreted as showing that the tombs were those of the Egypto-Phoenician of Hyksos warrior ruling class. This, in fact, is the position taken in the canonical *Cambridge Ancient History*. However, the author of this section remains within the Aryan Model by insisting that the Hyksos chieftains had no lasting effect on Greek culture. Further support for a link between Mycenae and West Semites comes from the fact that both at the former and Byblos the royal cemetery consisted of a partial circle of shaft graves. If anything therefore the archaeological evidence supports the Ancient Model. Archaeology is however too blunt a tool to provide any certainty on this.

LANGUAGE

It must be emphasized at this point that there is absolutely no doubt that Greek is fundamentally an Indo-European language. This is shown by its morphology; case and personal endings, and by its core vocabulary, pronouns, prepositions, numbers and verbs and nouns of every-day agricultural life. On the other hand over 50% of its lexicon, especially in the semantic areas of luxuries, political—not family—relationships, law, religion and abstraction are non-Indo-European. The commonest pattern for languages resulting from conquest and settlement is that seen in English, Swahili and Vietnamese in which the natives preserve the core but the conquerors introduce the vocabulary of urban culture. Using this analogy Greek could not have been the result of an Aryan conquest of Pre-Hellenes but could well have been one from Egyptian and Phoenician colonization. There is, however, another pattern in that found in Turkish and Hungarian in which the conquerors absorbed the cultivated language of their victims. In these cases, however, the outsiders retain their own vocabulary for military terms. In Greek nearly all words for weapons and military organizations are non-Indo-European. Thus to maintain the Aryan Model one has to postulate a typologically unique resulting language.

I believe that many, if not most, of the non-Indo-European elements in Greek can be explained in terms of Egyptian or West Semitic. There is thus no need to postulate a pre-Hellenic substratum.

In the 17th, 18th, and 19th centuries, large numbers of Semitic etymologies for Greek words were proposed. Since 19880, however, most of these have been discarded. Egyptian was not read until after the establishment of the Aryan Model. Therefore, apart from an interesting attempt by Barthélemy in the 18th century to derive Greek words from roots found in Coptic, no attempt has been made to find fundamental loans from Egyptian into Greek.

In both cases, however, loans have been accepted in areas that do not disturb the Aryan Model. Thus, no-one objects to deriving "ebony" from the Egyptian *hbny* or 'sesame' from the West Semitic SS. In fact a number of more 'central luxuries' whose etymologies from West Semitic were accepted when though to be late have now been attested in Linear B. These include *khitōn* "clothes" and *khrysos* "gold." By contrast other etymologies, such as *bōmos* "altar, high-place" from *bāmah* with the same meaning, are dismissed without discussion, even though non-Indo-European etymology for it has proposed. The simplest explanation for these different standards is that the Extreme Aryan Model can not tolerate the presence of Semitic loan-words in central semantic fields such as religion. There are, however, several other plausible etymologies in the same area. Some of these like *nektar* from *niqtar* "smoked or distilled wine," have been proposed before. Others have not: like *kudos*

YES Martin Bernal / 51

"divine glory or vileness" from KDS with the same meaning; *naiō* "dwell" and *naos* "divine dwelling" from NWH with the same general and specific connotations and *Sphag-* from SPK "sacrifice by cutting the throat." In the absence of competitors they seem very plausible.

The Egyptian origin of the Greek *makarios* 'blessed' from *m3'hrw* "true of voice," the title given to the dead who have passed the test of judgment is increasingly accepted. Other Egyptian legal terms would seem equally plausible; see for instance *martyros* from *mtrw* "witness" and *timā* "honour" in both warfare and law from an Egyptian form attested in Demotic as *tym3'* "cause to become just." Similarly *orthos* "straight upright" would seem to come from *w3t* plumbline or cord used in architectural planning (the vulture aleph' represented by "3" had a value close to *r* in Early and Middle Egyptian)....

To turn now to weapons; the derivation of the Greek *xiphos* "sword" from the Egyptian *sft* with the same meaning has been generally accepted. That of its synonym *phasganos* from the Semitic PSG "cleave" would seem equally plausible. These two words are of particular importance as they denote one of the new weapons of the Shaft Grave Period. The sword also played a central role in mythology, as the magical weapon of the conquering heroes like Perseus and Theseus whose enemies seldom, if ever, possessed them. The other military breakthrough of the period was the chariot. Harma the Greek word for this

would seem to come from "tackle" as there is a large number of related words in the semantic field: "net, rope, string together." The whole cluster can be plausibly derived from an Afroasiatic root HRM with the same meaning, found in both Semitic and Egyptian.

These are only a few of the many hundred more or less plausible Egyptian and Semitic etymologies for Greek words, most of which have no Indo-European competitors. Cumulatively they would seem to form a sufficient proportion of the Non-Indo-European elements in Greek to allow one to dismiss the hypothetical Pre-Hellenic substratum. This would be replaced by an Egyptian and Phoenician superstrate, needed if one is to sustain the Ancient Model....

It could be asked whether this apparently abstruse historiographical problem has any relevance today. Why should one disturb Classics with its harmless mysteries. My answer to this is on two levels. Firstly I believe it is methodologically important to attack Romantic scholarship the combination of romanticism and positivism. According to it what is not proven is beyond the reach of reason. This is doubly misleading because it gives exaggerated and sometimes mistaken respect to the "certain" and it can be used to inhibit fruitful estimation on the basis of plausibility. Secondly, Romantic scholarship has used this double technique to maintain a myth of European isolation from and superiority over the rest of the world which is as historically misleading as it is politically pernicious.

NO
John E. Coleman

DID EGYPT SHAPE THE GLORY THAT WAS GREECE?

Two of the four projected volumes of *Black Athena*, Martin Bernal's sweeping study of Greek civilization and prehistory, have appeared, and it is not too early for an assessment. The work is receiving wide media attention for its message that "Afro-Asiatic roots" were basic in the formation of Classical Greek culture and that these roots have been ignored because of a prevailing racist vision of an ancient Greece unblemished by African and Semitic cultural debts. But is Bernal's picture of Greek history accurate and are his accusations of racism in scholarship true?

His argument rests on claims that Greece was invaded or colonized by the Hyksos, a Semitic-speaking Canaanite people from southern Syro-Palestine, in the eighteenth and seventeenth centuries B.C.; that it underwent massive cultural changes as a result of these invasions and subsequent contact; and that the classical Greeks of the first millennium B.C. knew of these invasions and resultant changes. This is what Bernal calls the "Ancient Model" of the development of Greek civilization.

Scholars agree that the Hyksos infiltrated and later came to rule Egypt during the Second Intermediate period (generally dated ca. 1660–1550 B.C.). They were eventually expelled from Egypt by Ahmose, the first Pharaoh of the 18th Dynasty (1550–1525), and he and his immediate successors subsequently campaigned in southern Syro-Palestine and established their hegemony over it. Bernal claims that the Hyksos also invaded Greece, although historical sources do not support this.

Invasions of Greece are mentioned neither in the third-century B.C. history of Egypt written by Manetho, an important source for the Hyksos, nor by any Bronze Age source. Egyptian and Canaanite second-millennium documents rarely mention the Aegean, and when they do they suggest that the peoples of Egypt and Canaan (i.e., Syro-Palestine) were familiar with Aegean peoples only as traders and, occasionally, as raiders. Mycenanean Linear B documents from the second half of the second millennium B.C. provide no evidence for Hyksos invasions; on the contrary, the rarity of foreign names suggests that

From John E. Coleman, "Did Egypt Shape the Glory That Was Greece? The Case Against Martin Bernal's *Black Athena*," *Archaeology*, vol. 45, no. 2 (September/October 1992). Copyright © 1992 by The Archaeological Institute of America. Reprinted by permission.

an Egyptian or eastern Mediterranean presence in the Bronze Age Aegean was very slight.

There is also a serious chronological problem with Bernal's proposed date for a Hyksos invasion at the beginning of the Aegean Late Bronze Age. The recent redating of the volcanic eruption of Thera to 1628 B.C. indicates that the Late Bronze Age began no later than 1700 B.C. The possibility of Hyksos activity in the Aegean at this early date is very unlikely, for it would predate the Hyksos rise to power in Egypt. Bernal's thesis that the Hyksos were responsible for Egyptian influences on Greece presupposes that they adopted Egyptian culture before invading Greece.

Furthermore, Egyptian or Canaanite objects, although more frequent later, are rarely found in Greece at the time of the supposed invasions. Although Bernal claims that the shaft graves at the Late Bronze Age citadel of Mycenae in southern Greece contained Egyptian objects and that the burials they contained were therefore those of Hyksos princes, he fails to mention that the Egyptian attributions are doubtful. Emily Vermeule, Harvard University's Bronze Age authority, concludes in *The Art of the Shaft Graves at Mycenae* (Cincinnati, 1975) that "there is nothing truly Egyptian in the shaft graves."

Before Bernal's work, only one other scholar, Frank Stubbings, a University of Cambridge classicist, had maintained that the shaft graves contained Hyksos princes. Others argued that they contained the first Indo-European speakers to arrive in Greece, whether from the Balkans to the north or from eastern Anatolia and the Caucasus. Still others, in what I think is the correct view, have emphasized the continuity between the shaft graves and the preceding Middle Bronze Age culture in Greece. As this wide divergence of opinion demonstrates, the evidence of the shaft graves is at best inconclusive and cannot in itself support the claim for Hyksos invaders.

In fact, all scholars agree that the strongest outside influence on the shaft graves of Mycenae comes not from the East but from Minoan Crete. Since at that time the Minoans were culturing more advanced than the Greek mainland and had closer interconnections with the eastern Mediterranean, possible reflections of Egyptian or eastern Mediterranean customs in the shaft graves are best explained as having come indirectly through Minoan Crete.

Bernal is on safe ground when he emphasizes extensive interconnections between the Aegean and the eastern Mediterranean from the sixteenth century B.C. on. The Aegean is generally recognized as being part of a well-developed network of trade and perhaps even diplomacy in the eastern Mediterranean. As the Late Bronze Age shipwrecks at Cape Gelidonya and Kaş attest, copper and tin were brought to the Aegean from the eastern Mediterranean or father east. However, although such contacts may have influenced cultural developments in the Aegean, the evidence does not support Bernal's claims of massive borrowings. For example, it is central to his thesis that there was decisive influence from Egypt and Canaan on Greek religion. Yet Egyptian divinities are significantly different from Greek ones in their ubiquitous associations with animals and birds, and not a single recognizable Egyptian or Canaanite god is mentioned in Mycenaean Greek Linear B documents. Instead, the names are those known from later times, such as Zeus, Poseidon, and

Hera. That these divine names themselves are derived from Egyptian and Canaanite ones is also highly doubtful. Hesiod's *Theogony*, a description of the origin of the world and the gods, composed around 700 B.C., names more than 120 divinities and characters, almost all explicitly connected with Greek lands. Zeus and the other Olympian gods, for instance, live on Mount Olympus. I challenge Bernal, or other champions of massive eastern influence, to identify in Near Eastern or Egyptian sources more than one or two of the names mentioned in *Theogony*. None of the most characteristic Egyptian or Near Eastern divinities occur, such as Amun-Ra, Osiris, Baal, Seth, and Astarte.

Bernal cites no unequivocal instance of cultural borrowing significant enough to be considered basic to Aegean civilization in the Late Bronze Age. Minoan society, for instance, had many unique features and, although some artistic techniques and subjects come from the eastern Mediterranean, many are distinctively Aegean (e.g., bare-breasted females with flounced skirts and bull-leaping). Some alleged borrowings may actually have been Aegean exports to Egypt and Syro-Palestine rather than the reverse. For instance, the "flying gallop," a pose in which animals are depicted with front legs stretched forward and rear legs backward, occurs earlier in the Aegean and probably spread from there to Egypt and the Eastern Mediterranean. And there is no prototype in Egypt and Syro-Palestine for the palatial *megaron* (hall), the focus of Mycenaean society. The frescoes with Minoan subjects from Avaris, Egypt, and Tel Kabri, Palestine, are far more plausibly explained as due to Cretan traders sailing eastward than to Hyksos invaders going westward.

A further argument against Hyksos invasions is that Aegean peoples continued to use their local syllabic scripts, Linear A and Linear B, whereas they never used Egyptian hieroglyphics or Near Eastern cuneiform. Except for dubious arguments about letter forms, there is also no evidence for Bernal's claim that the Semitic alphabet was introduced to Greece in the fifteenth or fourteenth century B.C. On the contrary, since the alphabet is first attested in Greece no earlier than about 750 B.C., it is improbable that it was used there for 600 years or more and left no indication in the archaeological record. Furthermore, neither Linear A nor Linear B show signs that another writing system was in simultaneous use.

Bernal also supports his thesis of massive cultural borrowings by citing Egyptian and Semitic loan words in classical Greek. Some of these, particularly those designating foreign commodities, such as papyrus, ebony, natron, and sesame, are best explained as resulting from trade contacts. Others he cites are dubious, especially the personal and place names. After all, proper nouns often lack demonstrable etymologies and, inasmuch as those Bernal cites are truly foreign to Greek and the Indo-European family of languages to which Greek belongs, other source languages as plausible as Egyptian may be suggested. We know, for instance, that the Greeks borrowed place names from the pre-Greek inhabitants of the Aegean, and other loans from that source may go unrecognized. Words also surely came into Greek from the language of the Minoans. Although Minoan Linear A is undeciphered, good evidence exists that it was not an Indo-European language. When items of trade and doubtful names are removed from Bernal's lists, few words remain to support his views of foreign conquest and influence.

In short, there are good reasons for denying such strong cultural influences on the Aegean in the second millennium B.C., as Bernal postulates. Mycenaean civilization, as revealed by archaeological and documentary evidence, differs significantly from that of Egypt and Syro-Palestine. There is no evidence that Egyptian or Canaanite scripts or languages were used in the Aegean in the Bronze Age or that Egyptian or Canaanite gods were worshiped there. The available Bronze Age evidence, rather than supporting Bernal's thesis, is strongly opposed to it.

What about the ancient Greek belief in invasions from Egypt or Syro-Palestine? The picture here is far from straightforward. The Homeric and Hesiodic poems, the earliest sources on Greek beliefs about their past, do not support the view that there was a general Greek belief in such invasions (Bernal's "Ancient Model"), since they make no mention of invasions or immigration from Egypt or Syro-Palestine and generally show only a limited awareness of the eastern Mediterranean....

The Greek historian Herodotus (mid-fifth century B.C.), despite his belief in the coming of Danaos and Kadmos to Greece, provides equivocal evidence at best for Bernal's position. Herodotus' knowledge of the Bronze Age is sketchy and inaccurate. For instance, the Hyksos were apparently unknown to him, since they are not even mentioned for their role in Egyptian history let alone as invaders of Greece. Inaccuracies include his insertion of the Greek mythological character Proteus into the sequence of Pharaohs and his dating of the Great Pyramid builders near the end rather than the beginning of Egyptian history. Thucydides, who knew of Herodotus' histories, makes no mention of invasions or influence from Egypt or Syro-Palestine. Furthermore, Plutarch explicitly disagrees with many of Herodotus' claims of Egyptian influence and accuses him of "using worthless Egyptian stories to overthrow the most solemn and sacred truths of Greek religion" (*On the Malice of Herodotus*, 14)....

The vagueness of classical Greeks like Herodotus about the Bronze Age is understandable, given their very limited sources of information. The Bronze Age had ended some 700 years earlier and the "Dark Ages," a period of at least 300 years during which writing was lacking and cultural memories were orally transmitted, had intervened between the Bronze Age and the time of Homer and Hesiod. The Homeric poems, the principal source on the "heroic age" for later Greeks, present a distorted and anachronistic picture of the Mycenaean period, showing, for instance, that the former existence of Linear B writing had been completely forgotten. Furthermore, although some classical Greeks were familiar with Egypt, there is no evidence that they ever had access to accurate historical records. By the time of Herodotus, Egypt had long since ceased to be a leading center of civilization—in his day it was a part of the Persian Empire—and priests, a primary source of historical information for the Greeks, were not likely to have been well-informed. The ancient "tour guides," who escorted Greeks and others around Egyptian monuments, were likely illiterate and even less informed than the priests. Furthermore, classical Greeks were totally unaware that their own language belonged to a family (Indo-European) different from that to which the Egyptian and Semitic languages belonged. Hence, even if they had unanimously believed in invasions from the east, we would have reason to be skeptical in the absence of independent evidence. Egyptian civilization seemed to Greeks demonstrably older, as indeed it was, and the temptation to ascribe the origins of civilized customs to the older civilization was irresistible in view of the scarcity of precedents in what the Greeks knew of their own past. That the Greeks embroidered their accounts of Egypt and the eastern Mediterranean with mythical characters of their own invention, such as Proteus, Danaos and Kadmos, demonstrates how ignorant they were of Bronze Age events.

* * *

Has classical scholarship been racist, as Bernal contends? Instances of racism are undeniable and are to be deplored and condemned. Bernal has done a great service in charting the course of racism in the nineteenth and earlier twentieth century and in drawing attention to contemporary racist attitudes. However, one is not entitled to conclude without further evidence that racism was the predominant reason for widely accepted scholarly views. Surely all scholarship should be judged primarily on the basis of the evidence and arguments it presents. As Bernal acknowledges, even racist scholars may reach correct conclusions.

Racism, for instance, was not necessarily decisive in the increasing skepticism in the eighteenth and nineteenth centuries about the influence of Egypt and the eastern Mediterranean on Greece. Other, more plausible reasons can be given for the change in attitudes. The higher standards of rational analysis during the eighteenth-century Enlightenment was surely a factor. Another is that Greece itself, which had suffered a long decline during the later Byzantine Empire and the Turkish occupation, began again to be visited and its ancient remains studied by educated Europeans. James Stuart and Nicholas Revett, for instance, were in Athens in the 1750s and their four-volume *Antiquities of Athens* (published between 1762 and 1816), had a tremendous public impact; the detailed drawings of the Parthenon and other classical monuments inspired many an example of Greek Revival architecture in Europe and America. Classical Greek civilization could now be seen as manifestly different from that of Egypt, which was also becoming better known as a result of Napoleon's expedition of 1798.

Enormous increases in knowledge occurred simultaneously with the worst of racist preconceptions. Two nineteenth-century advances not sufficiently emphasized by Bernal were central to the changes in attitude toward Greece and Egypt: the discovery that Greek was a member of an Indo-European family of languages and the decipherment of Egyptian hieroglyphics, which made it possible to study Egyptian testimony directly. Comparison of Egyptian and Greek texts soon showed that Egypt, for all its impressive achievements, had never reached the level of the Greeks in philosophy, history and science. Cuneiform was also deciphered in the mid-nineteenth century and the reading of ever increasing numbers of texts in the Semitic languages of the Near East revolutionized our knowledge of the Bronze Age.

The Bronze Age in the Aegean was hardly known before 1870, when Heinrich Schliemann began digging at Troy. The rediscovery of Minoan Crete began only with the excavations of Sir Arthur Evans at Knossos in 1900. Linear B was deciphered only in 1952. Such developments provided us with far more information about the Bronze Age than was available either to ancient Greeks or to earlier scholars. The availability of so much new evidence, coupled with scholarly analysis, has surely been the major driving force in the changes in our historical interpretations.

One of the most striking features of Bernal's work is his characterization of sources, both ancient and modern, as following one of three "models," which he calls the "Ancient Model," the "Aryan Model," and the "Revised Ancient Model." My doubts about the "Ancient Model" and about the predominant role of racism in modern scholarship, which Bernal labels the "Aryan Model," have already been expressed. A further question remains, however: What purpose is served by lumping almost all nineteenth- and twentieth-century scholarship together and describing it as "Aryanist," as Bernal does? There have in fact been a multiplicity of approaches that can be categorized by less emotionally laden terms, such as positivism, diffusionism, functionalism, etc. So far as I can tell, the only common feature in the views of scholars categorized by Bernal as "Aryanist" is their belief that Greek is an Indo-European language introduced by people coming from somewhere to the north or east of Greece. This view, however, is almost universally accepted. Bernal himself accepts it.

Scholars today would not call themselves Aryanists, given the connection of the term with the horrors of Nazi Germany. Although "Indo-Aryan" was formerly used as a general term for the family of Indo-European languages, it was already giving way to "Indo-European" before the rise of the Nazis and the terms "Aryan" or "Indo-Aryan" are now restricted in scholarly use to a group of languages spoken in India. Greek was in any case never considered a member of this Indo-Aryan group of languages. The use of terms such as "Indo-European model" and "Indo-Europeanist" would therefore have been far more appropriate (even if, in my view, an unjustifiable oversimplification) and far less inflammatory. It is difficult to escape the conclusion that Bernal uses "Aryan Model," "Aryanist," "extreme Aryanist," etc. in an unfair attempt to stigmatize scholarly opponents. Contemporary classical scholarship cannot be shoe-horned into any single framework or model, let alone an "Aryan" one. Bernal's statements about scholarly conservatism continue to carry the insulting connotation that anyone who disagrees with him has accepted a racist position, whether consciously or not. Not only is Bernal's attitude contrary to the principles of open inquiry but it is especially unfair to those of African or Jewish descent who not infrequently express doubts about his claims.

Bernal also often implies that his work, like that of archaeologists Cyrus Gordon and Michael Astour, and other scholars with similar views, has been ignored or rejected primarily because of racism (including anti-Semitism), or because of a scholarly conservatism that masks racist attitudes....

While Bernal's claims of prejudice may be true, or partly true in a few instances, there are other plausible reasons for the negative reactions, including the doubts I mention below about his scholarly methods. Furthermore, his claims of victimization act as a preemptive strike against potential criticism, since people are reluctant to risk possible charges of racism for speaking out. In any case, *Black Athena* has been more widely discussed in both scholarly and general forums than most books and can hardly be said to have been ignored.

Bernal is not the first modern scholar to try to make a case for massive eastern Mediterranean influences on Greek civilization. Cyrus Gordon's *The Common Background of Greek and Hebrew Civilizations*, for instance, came out in 1962 and Michael Astour's *Hellenosemitica* in 1967. What is new about Bernal's work, besides his emphasis on Egypt rather than the eastern Mediterranean as a source of Greek roots, is his structuring of the argument in terms of competing paradigms. What, then, about the plausibility of Bernal's paradigm, his "Revised Ancient Model" (which holds that Classical Greek civilization was the product of African and Asian invasions of, and influences on a Bronze Age Aegean previously peopled in part by speakers of Greek) as a general proposition?

First, given the variety of current scholarly views that his "Aryan Model" represents, his claim that his "Revised Ancient Model" should be considered an alternative and competing explanation creates, to my mind, a false dichotomy. Existing views and theories simply do not form the monolithic whole that he postulates. Second, Bernal's general position rests on the plausibility of the specific claims he makes, whether in the areas of political and military history, archaeology, cultural and religious history, linguistics, mythology, and the like. A case that is implausible but that cannot be ruled out as impossible, as so often happens with archaeology, is not a strong one, and implausible cases in several areas of study do not strengthen the overall proposition.

Hence, it seems to me a sign of the general weakness of Bernal's position that, as he says in the preface to *Black Athena* II, "I abandoned the attempt to apply disciplinary rigour to the material in favour of 'thick description' involving many different types of information simultaneously."

In fact, the absence of rigorous argument is everywhere apparent in *Black Athena*. Examples include Bernal's fundamental reliance on the historical accuracy of myths and on farfetched etymologies, his failure to discuss adequately evidence that tends to contradict his views, and his frequent reasoning that because it is not impossible for such-and-such a thing to have happened, therefore it probably did happen. His terms are often defined in such a vague and all-encompassing way that falsification of his argument is impossible. Consider, for instance, the following passage on the Hyksos: "The hypothesis proposed here is that the royalty buried in the Shaft Graves and the other early Mycenaean tombs were Hyksos invaders from Syria, who probably spoke Hurrian and possibly even Indo-Iranian. However, the majority of the ruling class were Levantine Semitic-speakers together with significant numbers of Egyptians and Cretans, most of whom probably spoke a Semitic language themselves." Bernal's Hyksos, it seems, were such a mixed group that almost any non-Mycenaean trait may be claimed for them.

Bernal's general aim to provide an alternative to the view that what we call "Western civilization" was predominantly a European creation, has been embraced by some supporters of multiculturalism. Although I support multiculturalism, particularly the expansion and mainstreaming of teaching about African civilizations, I doubt that *Black*

NO John E. Coleman / 59

Athena will ultimately have a positive influence on current debates. The cultures of Africa and western Asia are worthy of study for their own merits. Exaggerated claims for Afro-Asiatic influence on ancient Greece may provoke a reaction against studying such non-European cultures on the grounds that they did not make such contributions as are claimed.

There is a positive side to Bernal's work, despite his failure to convince. The traditional disciplines are sometimes narrow, and racism has undoubtedly contributed toward ancient Greece.

Bernal offers healthy challenges to conventional wisdom. Through its extraordinary breadth and wealth of detail, his work forces would-be critics to expand their horizons far beyond their areas of expertise. The heated reception he often receives shows that his challenges are being heard at a basic level. *Black Athena*'s greatest contribution, in my view, is that it is inspiring broad scholarly and popular reexamination of the relationship between the Greeks and the ancient Near Eastern world.

POSTSCRIPT

Did Greek Civilization Have Semitic and African Origins?

The emergence of race as an issue has brought Bernal's work to a higher plane of controversy. Afrocentrists see in his work an affirmation of their desire to reinterpret history in a light that is more favorable to Africans. That many of the past scholars of the ancient world were racists comes as no surprise to them; that is precisely why they believe that the human record has to be rewritten. And attempts to criticize their work are often marked by insinuations that perhaps the racism of the past is not yet dead.

Bernal has certainly espoused the cause of Afrocentrism; some of his scholarship is directly related to it. However, he has expressed some reservation about some uses (and misuses) of his work. In fact, he has said that "African Athena" would have been a more accurate title for his work.

Any analysis of the sources related to this issue must begin with Bernal. A summary of his major arguments might be better than attempting to read the difficult *Black Athena*. Bernal also replies to Coleman's criticism in "The Case for Massive Egyptian Influence in the Aegean," *Archaeology* (September/October 1992), the same issue in which Coleman's article was published. Another article that provides a useful summary is "Out of Egypt, Greece," *Newsweek* (September 23, 1991). Support for Bernal is also evident in Basil Davidson's *The Search for Africa: History, Culture, Politics* (Random House, 1994) in a chapter entitled "The Ancient World and Africa: Whose Roots?"

As far as Bernal's critics are concerned, *Black Athena Revisited* edited by Mary R. Lefkowitz and Guy MacLean Rogers (University of North Carolina Press, 1996) may be all that is necessary. The editors and contributors are to be congratulated for placing so much criticism in one volume and making it so accessible to the average reader. Its organization and scholarship, whether one agrees with it or not, makes it an indispensable source as far as this issue is concerned.

Bernal's work in this field is only half complete. We await the next two volumes for a continuation of the debate.

ISSUE 4

Did the Benefits of the First Emperor of China's Rule Outweigh the Human Costs?

YES: Arthur Cotterell, from *The First Emperor of China: The Greatest Archeological Find of Our Time* (Holt, Rinehart & Winston, 1981)

NO: T'ang Hsiao-wen, from "A Refutation of Some Confucian Fallacies Concerning the Causes of the Downfall of the Ch'in Dynasty," in Li Yu-ning, ed., *The First Emperor of China* (International Arts and Sciences Press, 1975)

ISSUE SUMMARY

YES: English historian Arthur Cotterell argues that the ruthless policies of emperor Qin Shihuangdi caused thousands of deaths among the Chinese peasantry and impoverished much of the surviving population.

NO: Chinese scholar T'ang Hsiao-wen, adopting a Marxist approach, praises Qin Shihuangdi for centralizing the Chinese state and for his willingness to attack the aristocratic slave owners.

Between 403 and 221 B.C. China endured nearly two centuries of civil strife known as the "warring states" period. During this time, political authority in China was fragmented among eight major states—Chu, Han, Wei, Song, Qi, Yan, Zhao, and Qin—that were engaged in almost ceaseless warfare among themselves. In 259 B.C. Prince Zheng ascended to the throne of Qin at the age of 13. Using the Qin army, which had been hardened by fighting against constant barbarian pressure, Prince Zheng began attacking the neighboring Chinese states. In a series of encounters, he gradually subdued them until, in the year 221 B.C., he emerged as the sole ruler of a united Chinese state.

Over the following decade, Zheng—who adopted the name of Qin Shihuangdi, "First Emperor of the Qin Dynasty"—ruthlessly transformed China into a unified state. He destroyed the existing feudal political structure and established a system of 36 commanderies that were ruled by imperial officials responsible only to the emperor. Aristocratic families were disarmed and forced to live in the capital city, where Qin could keep an eye on them. Fortifications and walls between states were destroyed, and communication throughout the empire was enhanced by an ambitious program of building roads and canals. Qin also promoted the use of a single written Chinese language and standardized weights, measures, and wagon wheel gauges to facilitate trade and transportation. To enforce his authority, Qin and his advisers implemented a ferocious code of laws, with harsh and specific punishments for even the most minor offenses. His most ambitious project was the construction of the Great Wall, actually an attempt to link a series of existing walls in northern China that were designed to keep out the barbarian raiders known as the Xiongnu (ancestors of the ancient Huns).

Traditional Chinese historians have reluctantly acknowledged the accomplishments of Qin Shihuangdi but have decried his ruthless methods. The Great Wall and the system of roads and canals were constructed primarily through conscripted labor, and the brutal treatment of the workers led to hundreds of thousands of deaths. Moreover, Qin suppressed Confucian learning, going so far as to bury several hundred Confucian scholars alive. Given the fact that most Chinese scholars over the following two centuries adhered to Confucian ideology, it is not surprising that Qin Shihuangdi's historical reputation remained poor until the twentieth century.

In the following selections, Arthur Cotterell puts forth a modern version of the traditional interpretation of Qin Shihuangdi. (Since Cotterell employs the Wade-Giles system of translating Chinese names, the emperor is identified in his text as Ch'in Shih-huang-ti.) Cotterell admits that Qin's policies increased trade and established the imperial political system that governed China for more than 20 centuries, but he insists that Qin's regime was far too overbearing partly because of Qin's own uncontrollable fits of temper and his indifference to the misery of his subjects.

Writing during the late twentieth century, under the influence of the communist ideology of the People's Republic of China, T'ang Hsiao-wen describes the rule of Qin Shihuangdi in terms of an ongoing class struggle. According to this Marxist interpretation, the first emperor deserves praise for suppressing the aristocratic, feudal rulers who preceded him, identified here as the "restoration forces of the slave owners." Qin's short-lived dynasty thus becomes a necessary stage in the historical process, a victory for the rising landowning class over the slave owners who had dominated Chinese society during the warring states period. T'ang Hsiao-wen also supports Qin's attacks upon the Confucian scholars and defends Qin for instituting a powerful central government with near-absolute authority over its subjects.

YES   Arthur Cotterell

THE FIRST EMPEROR OF CHINA

The demise of Ch'u after Wang Chien's victory assured the triumph of Ch'in and the unification of China. The campaigns of 222 and 221 BC were the last in the series of attacks on feudal states initiated by King Cheng. By adopting the title of Ch'in Shih-huang-ti, Cheng staked his claim to be the first ruler of all the Chinese people. He was conscious of the uniqueness of his position, a lone monarch whose territories were bordered by no other civilized nation. The isolation of China from the other centres of civilization persuaded the ancient Chinese that they lived in the centre of the world. Major physical barriers such as the Gobi desert, the Yunnan and Tibetan plateaus, and the Himalayan mountain range ensured that contact between China and West and South Asia was minimal. The Great Wall, the major piece of civil engineering commissioned by the First Emperor in 214 BC, completed the landward encirclement. This 'ten thousand *li* city-wall' was more than a defence against the fierce nomadic peoples of the northern steppes. It symbolized the orderliness of China. Beyond its crenellations lay the uncivilized wastes of the outer world; inside its winding course the regulated lives of the First Emperor's subjects maintained the fabric of civilization. If Ch'in Shih-huang-ti did nothing else, he demonstrated to the Chinese the value of unity. Since 221 BC the country has been united for a longer period than it has been disunited, thus making China an exception to the rule that in the pre-modern era large states did not endure. As the first Sung Emperor was later to ask a rival who begged for independence in AD 960: 'What wrong have your people committed to be excluded from the Empire?' It had become inconceivable that any province should seek to isolate itself: the empire was the Greece and Rome of East Asia. China was the civilized world.

In accepting the arguments of Li Ssu against the reintroduction of feudal holdings, the First Emperor evidently recognized that his reign was a turning-point in history. In 221 BC Ch'in Shih-huang-ti commented:

> 'If the whole world has suffered from unceasing warfare, this is the fault of feudal lords and kings. Thanks to my ancestors, the Empire has been pacified for the first time. If I restored feudal holdings, war would return. Then peace could never be found!'

From Arthur Cotterell, *The First Emperor of China: The Greatest Archeological Find of Our Time* (Holt, Rinehart & Winston, 1981). Copyright © 1981 by Holt, Rinehart & Winston. Reprinted by permission.

The ruthless determination that had directed the 'Tiger of Ch'in' in his defeat of the feudal states was soon apparent in the organization of the Ch'in empire. In order to unify China he was obliged to become one of the great destroyers of history. Lacking any degree of economic integration, the Ch'in empire was insecure in two main directions—the east and the north. The deposed feudal aristocracy posed an internal threat, especially in the lower valley of the Yellow river, while in the north there was danger from the Hsiung Nu nomads, probably the Huns who invaded the Roman Empire in the fifth century AD. Military control seemed the quickest and most efficient way of bringing about stability. Therefore an edict abolished feudal holdings and extended the Ch'in pattern of freehold farmers to all China. The *nung*, the peasant farmers, were simply made liable for taxes, unpaid labour on state projects, and military service. Between 221 and 213 BC wealthy or formerly noble families were moved from their homes throughout the empire to residences in Hsienyang where, isolated from their supporters, they remained without influence. In the resettlement programme of 221 BC alone some 120,000 families were reportedly moved. The empire itself was divided into new administrative areas: thirty-six commanderies *(chun)*, which in turn were subdivided into districts or prefectures *(hsien)*. Each commandery was under the authority of a civil administrator *(chun-shou)* and a military governor *(chun-wei)*. Appointed by and responsible to the central Ch'in government, these two officials worked under the watchful eye of an overseer *(chien-yu-shih)*. The overseer appears to have been added to the provincial system as a means of keeping Hsienyang up to date on local developments and of checking on the implementation of central policies. The *hsien* were governed by prefects *(ling)*. This centralized bureaucratic government left no room for feudalism and in a modified form it was to be the basis of the imperial system in China down to this century.

In the *Shih Chi* we read that the First Emperor had all the weapons of the empire brought to Hsienyang, 'where they were melted into bells and bell supports, and made into twelve metal human figures, each weighing thousands of pounds, these being set up within the imperial palace'. Apart from disarming the population, he also unified 'the laws and rules and weights and measures'. It was decreed that 'carts were all to be made of equal gauge and that the characters used in writing were to be made uniform'. This standardization flowed naturally from the centralization of the empire. The regionalism of the Chan Kuo period, albeit less pronounced than that of earlier times, had been accompanied by considerable diversification. Variable axle lengths, for example, caused the transfer and reweighing of goods at borders, because of the differing distance between cartwheel ruts from one state to another. An equal hindrance to trade was the variety of coinage. Bronze coins known by their distinctive shapes —the 'knife money' originally minted by Ch'i, the different 'spade monies' of Han, Chao, Wei, Sung and Yen, the 'checker pieces' of Ch'u, and not least the 'round money' of Ch'in—were not readily exchangeable. Although the First Emperor was more concerned about taxation than trade, the edict which established Ch'in coinage as the imperial standard greatly aided commercial activity. The freer interchange of people and commodities fostered a wider national consciousness but it did not excessively enrich the merchant class.

From the *Ch'ien-Han Shu (The History of the Former Han Dynasty)*, a work dating from the beginning of the Christian era, it would appear that the Ch'in empire levied heavy taxes both in money and kind. According to this history, the First Emperor took half of the agricultural production in tax-grain, increased thirty times the tax on profits derived from the sale of salt and iron, and levied a poll-tax. Equally demanding was his use of compulsory service. In 212 BC 'he mobilized the men from families living on the left side of village gateways to guard the frontiers'. As a result, the remaining peasant farmers were unable to cultivate all the land and 'there was a shortage of food'. Requisitions of cloth also added to the misery of rural poor, whose fundamental welfare paradoxically even the most extreme Legalists recognized as the foundation of the state. During the last troubled years of the Ch'in dynasty, Li Ssu was forced to admit that the government was too overbearing. Imprisoned by Erh Shih-huang-ti, the Second Emperor, the Grand Councillor lamented in 208 BC that 'the empire was taxed heavily, without regard for the cost'.

However, the location of the imperial capital in the Wei river valley was militarily sound. From Hsienyang, protected on three sides by mountain or wasteland, Ch'in Shih-huang-ti could sweep down the valley of the Yellow river into the lowlands or retire into an almost impregnable stronghold whenever the forces of the eastern provinces were organized. A network of tree-lined roads radiating from the capital was begun so that imperial orders and troops could be rapidly conveyed to the furthest out-posts. The five major trunk roads focused on Hsienyang each measured about fifteen metres (forty-nine feet) across and totalled some 7,500 kilometres (4,661 miles) in length. Lesser roads fanned out from this strategic grid, penetrating such remote areas as the upper reaches of the Yang-tze valley. One amazing route led south-west towards Yunnan, then outside the imperial frontier, and for many kilometres it ran in 'hanging galleries' suspended along the precipitous walls of gorges. Hanging galleries were wooden balconies jutting out from the cliff-face: they carried a road about five metres (sixteen feet) wide. The imperial trunk roads were policed and provided with post-stations. At the latter there were stables and couriers in readiness for the relay service, living quarters for officials and authorized travellers, and cells for prisoners moving under guard. In the method of road construction used, the Chinese had already anticipated the technique of John McAdam. Whereas the Roman road might be described as a wall laid on its side, the Ch'in road was essentially a thin, convex, watertight shell made of rammed earth, resting on ordinary subsoil. The light and elastic road surface partly accounts for the speed with which the First Emperor's engineers built a system more extensive than the Roman one. The sheer determination of the ruler must be counted as the other factor.

The resentment felt over the geographical location of the capital, tucked away in the north-western corner of the empire, was connected with the regret expressed by many *shih* over the abolition of feudalism. In 213 BC Li Ssu took advantage of the First Emperor's wilfulness to strike at this opposition and recommend the Burning of the Books. 'These scholars', he said, 'learn only from the old, not from the new, and employ their learning to oppose our rule and confuse the black-headed people... Let all historical records but those of Ch'in be destroyed.' Except for the volumes contained in the imperial library, it was therefore decreed that all works other than official Ch'in annals and utilitarian treatises on divination, the practice of agriculture and medicine, should be collected for burning. Furthermore, those who dared to quote the old songs or records were to be publicly executed. What the Grand Councillor feared was an alliance between the old feudal aristocracy and Confucian scholars.

He need not have worried. In 212 BC the superstitious anger of Ch'in Shih-huang-ti himself brought about a court purge. Being told by his Taoist advisers that his efforts towards immortality were being frustrated by a malignant influence at court, he decided to protect his own divinity by keeping his movements secret. Although 'he gave orders for the two hundred and seventy palaces and pavilions within two hundred *li* of Hsienyang to be connected by causeways and covered walks... and made disclosure of his whereabouts punishable by death', the First Emperor remained dissatisfied with the daily arrangements, especially after the Taoists quit the capital without notice. The *Shih Chi* relates,

> When the emperor heard of their flight he was beside himself with rage. 'I collected all the writings of the empire and burned those which were of no use,' he fumed. 'I assembled a host of scholars and alchemists to start a reign of peace, hoping the latter would find marvellous herbs... (Instead they have) wasted millions without obtaining any elixir... (while) the other scholars are libelling me, saying that I lack virtue. I have had inquiries made about the scholars in the capital and I find that some of them are spreading vicious rumours to confuse the people.'

Four hundred and sixty scholars were found guilty. They were buried alive in Hsienyang as a warning against further defiance of his wishes. Even more were banished to frontier areas, including the crown prince, Fu-su, who protested against these policies. Prince Fu-su had dared to suggest that such severity against Confucian scholars would unsettle the population. The First Emperor's answer was the continued destruction of all city and other local walls that could have helped local separatist movements.

It was the measure introduced to deal with the Hsiung Nu nomads, namely the building of the Great Wall, that spread dissension among the peasant farmers. This project was an immense task. Meng T'ien, the prominent Ch'in general, was ordered to set up a line of fortresses in 214 BC, but surprisingly few details were recorded of the complex logistics that must have been involved. He had already cleared the nomads from the Ordos desert and driven the imperial highway northwards from Hsienyang to Chiu-yuan in the upper Yellow river valley. In his biography of the general, Ssu-ma Ch'ien tells us that Meng T'ien built 'a Great Wall, constructing its defiles and passes in accordance with the configuration of the terrain'. The vastness of the scheme appears to have aroused superstitious fears as well as widespread discontent. Of his enforced suicide in 209 BC, Meng T'ien said:

> 'Indeed I have a crime for which to die. Beginning at Lin-t'ao, and extending to Liao-tung, I have made ramparts and ditches over more than ten thousand *li*, and in that distance it is impossible that

I have not cut through the veins of the earth. This is my crime.'

Ssu-ma Ch'ien, however, comments that the general's death had less to do with geomancy than his 'little regard for the strength of the people'. In fact, Meng T'ien and Prince Fu-su were commanded to commit suicide in an edict forged by Li Ssu and the eunuch Chao Kao, after the death of the First Emperor. Yet Ssu-ma Ch'ien is correct about the harsh enforcement of Ch'in law. Literally armies of men, conscripts and convicts, toiled on the construction of the Great Wall, working and dying in the mountains and wastes of the northern frontier. Through the mobilization of labour on such an unprecedented scale, Ch'in Shih-huang-ti hoped to solve the problem of the Hsiung Nu as well as provide employment for the great reservoir of labour made idle by the end of war and the abolition of serfdom. The almost continuous use of the corveé in public works certainly did much to accelerate social change. Surnames appear for the first time. There was room in the administrative hierarchy for a new man literally to make a name for himself. But there is no denying that the apparently endless demands of the Ch'in dynasty on the ordinary people led directly to the popular uprisings that occurred after the death of the First Emperor and dethroned his feeble successors. The terrible lot of the labourers who worked under Meng T'ien is recalled in the famous legend of Meng Chiang-nu, whose conscripted scholar-husband succumbed to the hard conditions and was buried in the Great Wall. Having recovered his bones through divine aid, Meng Chiang-nu had the misfortune to be admired there by the First Emperor during a tour of inspection. Anxious above all to ensure a proper burial for her husband, the faithful widow overcame her revulsion for the emperor and agreed to enter the imperial harem once her husband's remains had been given a state funeral on the shores of the Eastern Sea. The ceremony over, Meng Chiang-nu leapt into the waves so as to join her husband in death.

Another policy of the First Emperor was encouragement of the southward movement of the Chinese people. He was anxious to halt any drift to the north in case the farmers of the northern outposts might abandon agriculture and take up stock-rearing, so strengthening the nomad economy. The Great Wall was intended to keep the First Emperor's subjects in as well as to keep his barbarian enemies out. Imperial armies first moved south against the Yueh people, who had reestablished a state beyond the old Ch'u border. Next he sent a waterborne expedition up the Hsiang river, a tributary of the Yangt-ze that rises on the boundary of the present-day province of Kwantung. By 210 BC the campaign had extended the First Emperor's authority into the West river basin, reaching the coast in the vicinity of modern Hong Kong. While the peoples of Nan-hai ('Sea South') were by no means assimilated or firmly controlled, they were irrevocably tied to the empire. The cutting of the Magic Canal near Ling-ling joined the Yang-tze and West river systems and facilitated the flow of men and materials southwards.

Ch'in Shih-huang-ti was efficient and hard working; he handled 'one hundred pounds of reports' daily, and he undertook frequent tours of the empire. In Legalist terms he must rank as a successful ruler. On the other hand, there was little in his reign to mitigate against the insensitivity of Legalism. His own personal drive was the engine within the Ch'in juggernaut, as his outbursts of fury on encountering obstacles only too clearly show. When in 219–218 BC, for instance, he found crossing the Yang-tze river difficult because of a gale, the First Emperor placed the blame on the river-goddess whose temple stood on a mountain close by. In retaliation he ordered 3,000 convicts to fell all the trees on its slopes, leaving the mountain bare.

The three attempted assassinations undoubtedly increased the Emperor's anxiety about dying, a weakness exploited by the scholar-magicians Hsu Fu and Lu, but the unique position of the ruler, as overlord of all within the Four Seas, also contributed to his dilemma. The concentration of wealth and prestige about a single man gave rise to expectations hitherto unknown in China. Was Cheng not the greatest king who had ever lived? Was it not fitting that his earthly reign should end in the attainment of immortality? The First Emperor's capital, palace and tomb were as lavishly planned as the Great Wall itself; and they were not regarded as extraordinary by the ruler himself. His absolute power made comparison odious. As the fugitive Taoist adept Lu noted in 212 BC, 'No fewer than three hundred astrologers are watching the stars, but these good men, for fear of giving offence, merely flatter the emperor and dare not speak of his faults. It is he who decides all affairs of state, great and small.' Yet it would seem that after the execution of the scholars that year in Hsienyang the First Emperor did leave the government more in the hands of his closest advisers, Li Ssu and Chao Kao. The discovery of a meteorite in 211 BC worried him enormously. When it was reported that someone had inscribed on the stone, 'After Ch'in Shih-huang-ti's death the land will be divided', he had the people living in the neighbourhood exterminated and the stone pulverized. 'Then the emperor', according to the *Shih Chi*, 'unable to find happiness, ordered the court scholars to write poems about immortals and pure beings, and wherever he went he made musicians set these to music and sing them.'

The First Emperor died in 210 BC while on a tour of the eastern provinces. Having progressed down the Yang-tze river and along the coast of the Yellow sea, he had a dream one night about a contest with a sea-god which had assumed a human form. In consequence he was advised to hunt a monstrous fish with a repeater crossbow, so that by slaying it he would remove the evil spirit which was keeping him from making contact with the immortals. After disposing of what was most likely a whale at Ch'ifu, the First Emperor sickened and died within a month or so. Because they feared for their lives, Li Ssu and Chao Kao suppressed the news of the emperor's death, forged an edict ordering both the heir apparent Prince Fu-su and General Meng T'ien to commit suicide, and then forged a will entrusting the empire to the late emperor's second son, Hu-hai. As if the First Emperor were still alive, the imperial party travelled back to the capital. 'The coffin was borne in a litter escorted by the emperor's favourite eunuchs, who presented food and official reports as usual and issued imperial commands from the covered litter. . . . But it was summer and the litter began to smell. To disguise the stench the escort was told to load a cart with salted fish.' Thus it was that the body of Ch'in Shih-huang-ti, the would-be immortal ruler, returned to Hsienyang, following a cartload of mouldering fish; the very terror inspired by his own title meant that such a final indignity could happen without anyone daring to inquire. In the capital, the *Shih Chi* tells us, 'the crown prince Hu-hai succeeded to the throne as the Second Sovereign Emperor, and in the ninth month the First Emperor was buried at Mount Li.' ...

The burden of taxation and compulsory labour pressed hard enough on the population during the reign of the First Emperor, but it was after his death in 210 BC that the load became intolerable. Utterly indifferent to the sufferings of his subjects, the Second Emperor pressed on with grandiose schemes, rigorously enforced the laws, and overcame shortages in the capital by wholesale requisitions. Ssu-ma Ch'ien comments tersely: 'All members of the imperial house were intimidated while ministers who protested were accused of slander. So high officials drew their salaries but did nothing, and the common people were afraid.' Ssu-ma Ch'ien would have us believe, that in his death cell Li Ssu himself realized the mistake of supporting the Second Emperor. The tremendous taxations alienated the empire, and though at the time of this reflection in 208 BC the first rebellions had been suppressed, those unmistakable signs of breakdown and disorder that were to indicate in later Chinese history an impending dynastic change were apparent. The situation was summed up by a noted Han scholar, Tung Chung-shu, who wrote:

> The exactions of frontier military service and of public labour each year were thirty times more than in antiquity. The land taxes, poll-taxes, and taxes on profits from sales of salt and iron were twenty times greater. There were some people cultivating the lands of the rich, who suffered a tax of five tenths of their produce. Therefore the poor often wore the clothing of oxen acid horses and ate the food of dogs and swine. They were burdened by avaricious and oppressive officials, and executions increased in an arbitrary manner. The people were aggrieved but had no one to rely on. They fled into the mountains and forest and became brigands. Those clothed in red filled half the road, and the number of those yearly condemned to imprisonment amounted to thousands and even to as many as ten thousand.

Allowing for anti-Legalist sentiment and literary exaggeration by the archproponent of Confucianism under the Han emperors, the picture given of Ch'in repression is startling....

* * *

The administrative system which the Han emperors took over from the Ch'in proved to be one of the most stable frameworks for social order ever developed. Despite the initial association with totalitarianism, the Chinese succeeded in evolving from it a bureaucratic government staffed by educated men. The model official after 202 BC was to be the Confucian scholar. He was a man firm in principle and benevolent in outlook: he served the throne and protected the ordinary people. It is not a little ironic that the single-minded autocracy of Ch'in Shih-huang-ti gave place to the Celestial Empire so admired by the European Enlightenment. 'A remarkable fact and quite worthy as marking a difference from the West' Matteo Ricci wrote seventeen hundred years later, 'is that the entire kingdom is administered by the Order of the Learned, the Philosophers. The responsibility for orderly management of the entire realm is wholly and completely committed to their charge and care.' How vexed Li Ssu would have been to learn that the labours of a lifetime had inadvertently established a unified and enlightened empire in which the creative genius of Chinese civilization could flower. In his death cell he foresaw the collapse of the Ch'in dynasty: 'Outlaws will come to Hsienyang, and deer wander through the palace courtyard.' But he had no inkling of the second empire to be founded by the socially insignificant Liu Pang. Nor would he have expected to see a new imperial capital arise in 200 BC at Ch'ang-an, across the Wei river from Hsienyang. The last word on Ch'in belongs perhaps to the Han scholar and statesman Chia I, who offered, fifty years after the event, this telling reason for its overthrow by the first peasant rebellion in Chinese history. Chia I said Ch'in fell because it failed 'to realize that the power to conquer and the power to hold what has been won are not the same'.

NO

T'ang Hsiao-wen

A REFUTATION OF SOME CONFUCIAN FALLACIES CONCERNING THE CAUSES OF THE DOWNFALL OF THE CH'IN DYNASTY

The Spring and Autumn and Warring States periods were an age of great up-heaval in Chinese society, marked by stormy slave uprisings and the surging struggle of the newly rising landlord class to seize power, which gradually brought about the replacement of the slavery system by the feudal system. In 221 B.C., the statesman of the newly rising landlord class, Ch'in Shih-huang, "arose to carry on the glorious achievements of six generations. Cracking his long whip, he drove the universe before him" (Chia l, "The Faults of Ch'in") and completed the great task of unifying the six states and founding China's first autocratic centralized feudal state. After the unification of the whole country, Ch'in Shih-huang resolutely and thoroughly implemented the Le-galist line, emphasizing the present while slighting the past, and vigorously carried out a series of reforms in the economic base and in the superstruc-ture, achieving conspicuous results. The founding of the Ch'in dynasty was of great and far-reaching significance in Chinese historical development. How-ever, this first feudal dynasty in Chinese history lasted only fifteen years; in 206 B.C. it was overthrown by the great peasant uprising led by Ch'en Sheng and Wu Kuang.

Why did the Ch'in dynasty fall so fast? This has always been an important question of fierce controversy between the Confucian and Legalist schools. The reactionary rulers and the reactionary Confucian scholars through all ages, right up to the renegade and traitor Lin Piao and company, all made a big fuss over this question. They concocted many fallacies and slandered and attacked Ch'in Shih-huang and his Legalist political line with great aban-don. A thorough criticism of the fallacies spread by reactionary Confucian scholars on this question is of great significance toward arriving at a correct appraisal of Ch'in Shih-huang, summing up more properly the historical ex-perience of the struggle between Confucianism and Legalism, and deepening the criticism of Lin Piao and Confucius.

* * *

On the question of the causes of the downfall of the Ch'in dynasty, the first fallacy fabricated by the reactionary Confucian scholars was the "theory that the Legalist line destroyed Ch'in." They Preposterously asserted that because Ch'in Shih-huang "followed the laws of Shen [Pu-hai] and Shang [Yang] and implemented the theories of Han Fei" ("Biography of Tung Chung-shu" in *History of the Han*), he "seized the country by force and maintained power through the laws, thus failing in both beginning and end, and therefore Ch'in fell" ("Compulsory Labor Service" in *Debates on Salt and Iron*). They blamed the Legalist line for the downfall of the Ch'in dynasty in a vain attempt to deny the progressive role played by the Legalist line in history. This was a complete waste of effort.

Actually the opposite was true. Originally, Ch'in was a small feudal state in the western part of China. Until the early years of the Warring States period, it was still rather backward, and was looked upon by the various eastern states as a "barbarian" country. Later, Ch'in carried out Shang Yang's political reforms, implemented the Legalist line and, as a consequence, rapidly became strong and prosperous. Ch'in Shih-huang was an outstanding statesman of the Legalist school. Within a short period of time he unified the six states and established the first centralized feudal state. This was precisely the result of the victory of the progressive Legalist line over the reactionary Confucian line and of Ch'in's long adherence to implementing the Legalist line. In the book *Lieh Tzu* there is a graphic fable: A Confucian scholar named Meng from the state of Lu went to

Ch'in to peddle his Confucian learning, in order to get an official position and strike it rich. The king of Ch'in sharply pointed out that "in the current struggle among the feudal lords, only troops and food are of importance. To use benevolence and righteousness to rule my state would be the way to ruin." After duly punishing this reactionary scholar, the king of Ch'in expelled him from the land ("Shuo Fu" in *Lieh Tzu*). This literary fable is a reflection of the actual struggle. The power-holders of the newly rising landlord class in the state of Ch'in realized through their political experience that the doctrines of Confucius and Mencius were "the way to ruin" and that the Confucian line would lead to national destruction. The historical fact that Ch'in developed from a weak state to a strong state and finally unified the whole empire proved that only the Legalist line could make a state wealthy and powerful. The so-called "theory that the Legalist line destroyed Ch'in" is a fallacy which confused black and white. As Chang T'ai-yen stated, "that Ch'in ultimately fell was not the fault of the laws" ("On Ch'in Government" [Ch'in cheng chi]).

To be sure, as the political power of the newly rising landlord class, the Ch'in dynasty, beside performing the revolutionary function of assailing the restoration forces of the slave owners, also oppressed and exploited the peasants, and there was from the very beginning an irreconcilable class contradiction between it and the peasantry. However, this kind of contradiction developed by stages, and it had not yet reached an intense degree during the reign of Ch'in Shih-huang. At the time, the contradiction between the newly rising landlord class and the restoration forces of the slave owners was more violent, and there was a real danger that the restoration forces of the slave owners might overthrow and usurp the political power of the landlord class. Owing to the landlord class' own class limitations, and because this class had only recently seized national power, those in power were not sufficiently aware of this danger and also lacked experience in ruling. Hence, the subsequent usurpation of power by Chao Kao was by no means fortuitous. After Chao Kao came to power, he vigorously carried out restoration activities, completely abolished the Legalist line, and further intensified the class contradiction between the peasants and the landlords. Under such circumstances, large-scale peasant uprisings eventually erupted. It is apparent that the rapid downfall of the Ch'in dynasty was the evil result produced by the abolition of the Legalist line and that the usurpation of power by Chao Kao was a turning point. . . .

* * *

Without exception, reactionary Confucian scholars through the ages have cursed Ch'in Shih-huang through gritted teeth for adopting the revolutionary measure of "burning the books and burying Confucian scholars alive." The "theory that the burning of the books and burying Confucian scholars alive caused the downfall of Ch'in" was another fallacy used by them to attack Ch'in Shih-huang. They said that Ch'in Shih-huang "severely banned literature and forbade the possession of books"; "hence the dynasty was destroyed after he had ruled as Son of Heaven for [only] fourteen years" ("Biography of Tung Chung-shu" in *History of the Han*). "Were the Confucian scholars buried by Ch'in or was Ch'in buried by the Confucian scholars?" (*Ch'üan T'ang wen*). "The imperial

achievement withered before the smoke from the bamboo slips and silks had dispersed" (from a poem by Chang Chai of the T'ang dynasty). And so on and so forth, over and over again, went the explanation that Ch'in Shih-huang's "burning of the books and burying Confucian scholars alive" led to the downfall of Ch'in dynasty.

Was the downfall of the Ch'in dynasty caused by Ch'in Shih-huang's "burning of the books and burying Confucian scholars alive"? It was not. "Burning the books and burying Confucian scholars alive" was Ch'in Shih-huang's revolutionary policy for the purpose of assailing the restoration forces of the slave owners and consolidating the dictatorship of the newly rising landlord class.

"Any given culture (as an ideological form) is a reflection of the politics and economics of a given society, and in turn it has a tremendous influence and effect upon that society's politics and economics." After Ch'in Shih-huang unified the whole country, in order to consolidate the political system and economic base of the newly rising landlord class, there was an urgent need to establish a culture adapted to it so as to secure the predominant position within the superstructure of the Legalist ideology of the newly rising landlord class. At the time, the struggle within the cultural sphere between the newly rising landlord class and the declining slave-owner class was extremely violent. The reactionary Confucian scholars who were the spokesmen of the declining slave-owner class utilized the positions they occupied in the cultural sphere in various ways to create public opinion in favor of restoration and to carry out restoration activities, thereby seriously affecting the implementation of the various policies and laws of the Ch'in government and threatening the consolidation of the political power of the newly rising landlord class. In light of the frenzied attacks launched by the slave-owner class, Ch'in Shih-huang adopted the decisive measure of "burning the books and burying Confucian scholars alive" to deal heavy blows to the restoration forces of the slave owners. The "burning of the books and burying Confucian scholars alive" did not weaken Ch'in Shih-huang's imperial achievement, but strengthened it. It effectively realized the dictatorship of the landlord class over the slave-owner class in the ideological and cultural sphere.

However, Ch'in Shih-huang had one great flaw: he did not strike at the restoration forces hard enough, or suppress them thoroughly. After the establishment of the Ch'in dynasty, he forcibly moved 120,000 influential and wealthy families from all parts of the country to Hsien-yang, thus forcing them to move far away from their old dens. This was a blow to the restoration forces. But the Ch'in government did not adopt effective measures for exercising dictatorship over these reactionary slave owners. On the contrary, this in fact further concentrated the restoration forces in the Hsien-yang area. It was no coincidence that the restoration activities of the reactionary Confucian scholars were especially blatant in the Hsien-yang area. On the other hand, the remnant forces of the slave owners represented by the old aristocracy of the six states and the reactionary Confucian scholars were still ubiquitous, waiting for an opportunity to act and constantly dreaming of restoration. Some of them brazenly committed armed robbery, and still more surreptitiously carried out covert activities. A descendant of the old aristocracy of the state of Ch'u, Hsiang

Yü, secretly studied the art of war at home and prepared himself "to fight ten thousand men" in a rash attempt to seize political power from Ch'in Shih-huang and "take his place" ("Basic Annals of Hsiang Yü" in *Historical Records*). K'ung Fu, the eighth generation descendant of Confucius, secretly hid the Confucian classics "to await someone to come searching for them" (*Tzu-chih t'ung-chien*). What was especially dangerous was that some representatives of the restoration forces had wormed their way into the Ch'in government. For example, Ch'en Yü and Chang Erh, the descendants of the old aristocracy of the state of Wei, changed their names and became "village gatekeepers" in Ch'in, thus slipping into the basic-level government of Ch'in ("Biographies of Chang Erh and Ch'en Yü" in *Historical Records*). Chao Kao wormed his way into the central government organs of Ch'in. These restoration forces were a grave threat to Ch'in's political power.

The Legalist Han Fei had said, "By carefully examining the laws and executing those who arrogate authority, there will be no criminals in the country" ("The Principal Way" in *Han Fei Tzu*). He advocated taking firm steps to suppress the restoration forces of the slave owners. However, Ch'in Shih-huang merely buried alive the 460 Confucian scholars in Hsien-yang, but adopted virtually no measures at all to suppress and eradicate the dangerous enemies who had wormed their way deep into the government and who were carrying out restoration activities behind his back. In the case of such a representative figure of the restoration forces as Chao Kao, although Ch'in Shih-huang discovered that he had committed a "serious crime," he still pardoned him, retained him, and "restored his official titles" ("Biography of Meng T'ien" in

Historical Records). Li Ssu knew that Chao Kao was plotting a coup d'etat, and since he was chancellor at the time, he could have eliminated Chao Kao and company. But he did not do this, and at the crucial moment, showed himself intolerably weak and compromising.

The revolution of the newly rising landlord class was a revolution that replaced the slavery system with the feudal system. "The result was that one kind of system of exploitation was replaced by another. It was neither necessary nor possible for them to thoroughly suppress counterrevolution." Owing to his class limitations, Ch'in Shih-huang naturally could not thoroughly suppress counterrevolution. The ineffectiveness of Ch'in Shih-huang's blows against the restoration forces of the slave owners was a major cause of "the downfall after [only] two generations" of his government.

The reactionary Confucian scholars insisted on lumping together "the burning of the books and burying Confucian scholars alive" and the fall of the Ch'in dynasty. They melodramatically asked, "Were the Confucian scholars buried by Ch'in or was Ch'in buried by the Confucian scholars?" This demonstrated that they were extremely afraid of and hostile to the revolutionary act of "burning the books and burying Confucian scholars alive" and that they stubbornly and steadfastly maintained the position of regression and restoration. Lin Piao and company also maliciously attacked Ch'in Shih-huang for "burning the books and burying Confucian scholars alive." After the failure of the counterrevolutionary coup d'etat at the Second Plenum of the Ninth CCP Central Committee, they buzzed like flies that had flown into a wall and moaned that "the imperial achievement withered before the smoke from the bamboo slips and silk had dispersed" to give vent to their implacable hatred for the proletarian dictatorship, in a vain attempt to restore capitalism through a counterrevolutionary coup d'etat. But this was only a pipe dream, for their counterrevolutionary conspiracy could never have succeeded.

* * *

The "theory that resistance to the Hsiung-nu led to the downfall of Ch'in" is another fallacy fabricated by reactionary Confucian scholars. They preposterously asserted that Ch'in Shih-huang's sending of Meng T'ien to fight the Hsiung-nu led to "the fall of the Ch'in dynasty" ("Denouncing Shang Yang" in *Debates on Salt and Iron*). It is an unmitigated capitulationist fallacy to claim that resistance to the raids of the military regime of the Hsiung-nu slave owners would lead to the fall of the state.

During the Warring States period, in the initial stage of the slavery system, the Hsiung-nu were a powerful nomadic people to the north of China with a backward economy and culture. The slave-owning Hsiung-nu aristocrats were savage and ruthless and accustomed to looting and plundering. They constantly encroached upon other fraternal peoples and made raids into Chinese territory. Each autumn, when their horses were well-fed and strong, they banded together, and relying upon the superior military power of their cavalry, entered Chinese territory to capture prisoners, valuables, and livestock. They constituted an extremely serious threat to the consolidation of Ch'in political power and to the security of the lives and property of the people of all nationalities in the north.

During the period of Ch'in Shih-huang's unification of the six states, the slave-owning regime of the Hsiung-nu tried to profit from others' misfortunes by making constant incursions to the south. The head of the slave owners of the state of Yen also attempted "to befriend the shan-yu in the north" so as to block unification by Ch'in. Therefore, in 215 B.C., after Ch'in Shih-huang unified China, he sent the famous general Meng T'ien at the head of an army of 300,000 to attack the Hsiung-nu in the north. Large stretches of land, including the Ordos area, which had been occupied by the Hsiung-nu slave owners, were recovered. Subsequently, Ch'in established 44 prefectures in the north, reclaimed land, and built the Great Wall. These measures were of great significance in consolidating the Ch'in central government, safeguarding the life and property of the people of all nationalities in the north, and expediting economic and cultural development.

Those reactionary Confucian scholars pretended to show sympathy for the people and attacked Ch'in Shih-huang's war of resistance against the Hsiung-nu as "having no regard for the lives of the people." They preposterously asserted that the war of resistance against the Hsiung-nu led to "physical exhaustion" and "financial depletion" and caused the people "to nurse grievances" leading to peasant uprisings which brought about the downfall of the Ch'in dynasty. This is malicious slander of the broad masses of the people and soldiers, who had opposed national oppression and actively participated in the war of resistance against the Hsiung-nu; it is also a serious distortion of history.

Chairman Mao has said, "National struggle is, in the final analysis, a ques-tion of class struggle." The struggle between the Ch'in dynasty and the Hsiung-nu was actually a struggle of the newly rising landlord class and the broad masses of laboring people against the slave-owning aristocrats. The Ch'in dynasty's war of resistance against the raids of the Hsiung-nu slave-owning aristocracy was a just war, which was in accordance with the interests and demands of the masses of the people. The reactionary Confucian scholars had an ulterior motive in keeping silent and saying nothing about the just and progressive nature of the anti-Hsiung-nu war while deliberately highlighting the sufferings from the war and distorting the historical facts. Chao Kao and company murdered Meng T'ien, the famous general who had resisted the Hsiung-nu, thus seriously sabotaging Ch'in Shih-huang's undertaking to resist the Hsiung-nu. By concocting the fallacy that "resistance to the Hsiung-nu led to the downfall of Ch'in," the reactionary Confucian scholars actually adopted a capitulationist attitude toward the raids and plundering of the Hsiung-nu slave owners in a vain attempt to make use of the butchers' knives of the Hsiung-nu slave owners to attain their objective of throttling the revolution and stemming progress. The renegade Lin Piao inherited the mantle of the reactionary Confucian scholars and maliciously attacked Ch'in Shih-huang's policy of resisting the Hsiung-nu. In May 1960 he went on a pilgrimage to pay homage to the so-called Temple of Meng Chiang-nü[1] This completely exposed Lin Piao's repulsive counterrevolutionary face.

* * *

On the question of the causes of the downfall of the Ch'in dynasty, the reactionary rulers through the ages distorted history and fabricated fallacies in a vain attempt to obliterate the historical achievements of Ch'in Shih-huang and the progressive role of the Legalist school and to create a foundation upon which they could honor Confucianism, oppose Legalism, and engage in restoration and regression. Lenin said, "Historical development follows a tortuous path, full of twists and turns" (*Selected Works of Lenin*, Vol. 3, p. 492). The downfall of the Ch'in dynasty was one of the twists and turns in the course of the development of the newly emerging feudal system. However, the tide of historical development cannot be stemmed. Chao Kao and his ilk tried their utmost to switch the direction of historical development and vainly attempted to restore the outdated slavery system. They were nothing more than a praying mantis trying to halt a cart with its forelegs. All subsequent dynasties used the laws and institutions of Ch'in. The various institutions enacted by Ch'in Shih-huang were in accordance with the requirements of historical development and they played their role in Chinese feudal society for a long time. Chairman Mao has said, "Regression eventually produces the reverse of its promoters' original intentions. There never has been an exception to this rule, at present or in the past, in China or elsewhere." More than 2,000 years ago, Chao Kao went against the tide of history to engage in restoration and regression. As a result, he was killed and his clan exterminated; he left a bad name for thousands of years, and became a pile of dogshit spurned by mankind. Today, Lin Piao followed the example of Confucius in "self-restraint and returning to the rites." He vainly attempted to overthrow the dictatorship of the proletariat, restore capitalism, and turn back the wheel of history. Eventually, he came to an ignominious end, smashed to pieces, leaving a foul name for thousands of years to come. There is nothing at all strange about this.

NOTES

1. Famous in legend because she traveled in search of her husband, who had been conscripted by the Ch'in government to work on the construction of the Great Wall. By the time she reached the Wall, her husband was dead and buried, and her wailing at his grave caused part of the wall to collapse. Cf. "What Is the Origin of 'The Wailing of Mend Chiang-nü at the Great Wall'?" pp. 65–67.

POSTSCRIPT

Did the Benefits of the First Emperor of China's Rule Outweigh the Human Costs?

In the second half of the twentieth centry, the debate over the merits of Qin Shihuangdi's rule has continued to play a significant role in Chinese political life. Chinese rulers have traditionally appealed to the past to legitimize their own regimes and stigmatize their opponents; accordingly, during the cultural revolution of 1966–1976, supporters of Mao Zedong branded their enemies— particularly Lin Piao, the Communist Party leader who favored the introduction of a modified form of capitalism into China—as counterrevolutionaries who followed the same line as Qin's enemies. So long as the People's Republic of China is governed by the iron hand of an absolutist regime, Qin is likely to remain a hero in that country's official histories.

Western views of Qin's dynasty are more ambivalent. General histories that place Qin Shihuangdi in the context of Chinese history are John King Fairbank's *China: A New History* (Harvard University Press, 1992); *The Chinese: Their History and Culture* by Kenneth Scott Latourette (Macmillan, 1971); Hilda Hookham's *A Short History of China* (St. Martin's Press, 1970); and William K. Klingaman's *The First Century* (HarperCollins, 1990).

ISSUE 5

Did Christianity Liberate Women?

YES: Monique Alexandre, from "Early Christian Women," in Pauline Schmitt Pantel, ed., *A History of Women in the West, vol. 1: From Ancient Goddesses to Christian Saints* (Belknap Press, 1992)

NO: Karen Armstrong, from *The Gospel According to Woman: Christianity's Creation of the Sex War in the West* (Anchor Press, 1987)

ISSUE SUMMARY

YES: Professor of religious history Monique Alexandre argues that there were a variety of roles for women—including prophetess, widow, deaconess, donor, and founder—that indicated a more liberated status for women in the early centuries of Christianity.

NO: Professor of religious studies Karen Armstrong finds examples of hostility toward women and fear of their sexual power in the early Christian Church, which she contends led to the exclusion of women from full participation in a male-dominated church.

When we look at the past, we can either focus on external events and actions or concentrate on the somewhat elusive attitudes of long-dead historical subjects. In the readings that follow, we have a choice of which approach to accept.

In determining whether or not Christianity liberated women, it is necessary to decide what liberation means. If a relatively powerless group is held in high regard by those in power, for example, will they feel liberated regardless of whether or not they play public roles? Or is it the public roles that create a feeling of liberation, even if the group in question feels hostility from the power structure? Granting that both acceptance and prominence combine to produce genuine liberation, which (if either) can be absent and still permit us to use the word *liberation*?

With this issue—as with others—we must beware of bringing our own value systems into the past. The real challenge is to try to imagine how early Christian women regarded their own status in the new religion. Were they accepted by some leaders and rejected by others? Did freedom of action make them oblivious to the attitudes of those who feared and hated them? From what we are able to learn by reading existing documents, did the women of the early Christian Church feel liberated from the more patriarchal world of first-century Palestinian Judaism? And, regardless of how they felt, does our assessment of their status merit the conclusion that Christianity liberated them?

Before the Christian Church became institutionalized and before a theology was clearly defined, early converts acted out of personal conviction, and they put their religious fervor to work in making the world a better place. Remember that in the early centuries Christians were persecuted by the Roman occupying forces because they refused to worship the emperor. In Palestine, Christianity was an underground religion until the early fourth century, when the Holy Roman Emperor Constantine made it the state religion. Outside the Palestinian world, missionaries rapidly made Greek converts so that Gentile, or non-Jewish, Christians would outnumber Jewish ones by the third century. Many of the women you will read about in the following selections lived in the Greek-speaking world, which was the first to accept Christianity in large numbers.

Only recently have women been admitted to the clergy in Protestant Christianity, and they are still excluded from the Roman Catholic priesthood. Can we find the seeds of this exclusion in the attitudes of the past as well as the historic precedents of women filling significant roles?

In the selections that follow, Monique Alexandre notes that the Christian Church maintains that it has been a consistent defender of the dignity and worth of women, especially their religious calling or vocation. Although others have charged the Christian Church with contributing significantly to the oppression of women, Alexandre warns us not to read the present controversies concerning women's roles in religious and secular life back into the early history of the Christian Church. That must be judged, she maintains, on its own terms. Karen Armstrong finds that modern culture is uncomfortable with sex, and she traces the roots of hostility between men and women to the early days of Western Christianity. The Eastern Church —what is today the Russian and Greek Orthodox branch of Christianity— which split with the Western Church in an act of mutual excommunication in 1054, is judged by Armstrong as less misogynistic, or less inclined toward the hatred of women.

YES

Monique Alexandre

EARLY CHRISTIAN WOMEN

JEWISH WOMEN IN THE CHRISTIAN ERA

In Palestine during the time of Jesus women, excluded from public life, were expected to conform, as wives, mothers, and housekeepers, to the model of the "virtuous woman." When they left home, they wore veils. Men maintained a prudent silence, as Josi ben Johanan admonished them: "Do not speak much with a woman." This precept was glossed as follows: "Do not speak much with thy own wife, say the sages, much less with thy neighbor's wife." Whence this maxim: "He who speaks too much with women invites evil, neglects the study of the Law and will end in Gehenna." Only princesses and common women, particularly in the countryside, were exempt from this ideal reclusiveness. In Alexandria, Greek custom reinforced Jewish moral teaching: "While outdoor life is suitable for men in time of peace as well as war," for females "domestic life and diligence in the home are best. Maidens, cloistered within the home, must not venture further than the door of the gynaeceum. Grown women may not venture further than the door of the house."

At age twelve or even sooner girls passed from their father's authority to their husband's. If Jewish women could be divorced not only for "something shameful" but, according to Hillel's interpretation, for nothing more than immodesty or a disagreeable appearance, they also enjoyed exceptional rights when it came to divorce. The *ketouba,* or marriage contract, carefully specified the amount of the dowry due the husband, but this same amount had to be repaid to the woman in case of divorce. The wife retained ownership of certain property of her own, of which the husband became the usufructuary. The token to be paid in case of separation or death of a spouse was also specified. A woman's testimony was not admissible evidence in court, according to Flavius Josephus, "owing to the frivolity and temerity of the sex." The Talmudic treatise *Nidda* specified how long women were to remain excluded from society because of contagious impurity following menstruation, other loss of blood, and childbirth (forty days after the birth of a boy, twice as long after a girl).

Because of this destructive potential the participation of women in religion was also restricted. Women were exempt from pilgrimages to Jerusalem at Passover, Simchas Torah, and Succoth and excluded from the morning and evening Sh'ma (the prayer "Hear, O Israel! the Lord our God, the Lord is one"). These positive religious precepts thus did not apply to women, but many negative precepts did. Thrice daily the pious Jew repeated this prayer: "Blessed be God for not making me a Gentile... for not making me a peasant... for not making me a woman, because women are not required to observe the commandments."

At home women were responsible for dietary and sexual purity but played little religious role in the strict sense. True, they enjoyed the privilege of lighting the sabbath candles and baking the sabbath bread, and it was their task to wash and dress the bodies of the dead and to mourn their passing. But blessings and prayers were reserved for men.

Polytheism had its goddesses and priestesses, but monotheism boasted hereditary priesthood, from which women were excluded more stringently than ever during the time of the Second Temple. Flavius Josephus described "the unbreachable barriers that protect purity... four concentric porticoes, each with its own particular guard according to the law... Anyone could enter the outer portico, even strangers. Only menstruating women were barred. The second portico was open to Jewish men and their wives, so long as they were free of all taint. The third was open to male Jews, spotless and purified. And the fourth was open to priests wearing their sacerdotal robes. As for the Holy of Holies, only the chief rabbis in their special robes could enter."

Gone were the days when women tended "the door of the tabernacle."

Women were not required to attend synagogue for sabbath readings and sermons, which were already common at the dawn of the Christian era. Even if present, they did not count toward the *minyan*, the minimum number of men necessary for public prayer. "Out of respect for the congregation," they could not be called upon to read. They probably sat in a separate section of the synagogue, although the archaeological evidence is not very clear. Perhaps they were separated from the male congregation by a low wall, such as that described by Philo in his accounts of sabbath meetings of the Therapeutae in Alexandria.

But there may be another side to the story. Bernadette Brooten has examined nineteen Greek and Latin inscriptions dating from the first century B.C. to the sixth century A.D. and from various sites in Asia Minor, Italy, Egypt, and Palestine. In them women are designated as heads of synagogues (*archisynagogos/archisynagogissa*), leaders (*archegissa/arche*), elders (*presbytera/presbyterissa*), mothers of the synagogue (one Latin inscription reads *pateressa!*), and even priestesses (*hiereia/hierissa*). These honorific titles are similar to those applied to men, and there is evidence as well of donations made by women. Clearly women were generous givers, and wealthy, prominent women did have influence, particularly in Asia Minor and Italy. But did they have religious duties in the synagogue?

Women were exempt, or excluded, from the study and teaching of the Torah, which, following the destruction of the Temple, became more than ever the central focus of Judaism. In the first century A.D. Rabbi Eliezar, who was married to the learned Ima Shalom, nevertheless said that "to teach Torah to one's daughter is to teach her obscenities." To be sure, the statement was controversial. But legendary traditions pertaining to Ima Shalom and Beruriah, the daughter of Rabbi Hanania ben Teradyon, martyred under Hadrian, and wife of Rabbi Meir, and who was said to be "capable of reading three hundred traditions of three hundred masters in a winter's night," were apparently exceptions that confirm the rule. And was not the fate of Beruriah an object lesson? For all her defiance of the rabbis' low opinion of women's intelligence, she was almost seduced by one of her husband's students and committed suicide out of shame.

To be sure, Jews honored the memory of the "Mothers" of *Genesis:* Sarah, Rachel, and Rebeccah. They honored the seven prophetesses of old, especially Miriam, Deborah, judge of the people, and Huldah under King Josiah. They exalted the women who had freed the people of Israel: Esther, the widow Judith, chaste wives like Susannah who triumphed over calumny, and martyrs like the mother of the Maccabees. Yet not even the brilliance of these figures can blind us to so sweeping a condemnation as Flavius Josephus': "Woman, the Law says, is inferior to man in all things. Hence she must obey not force but authority, because God has given power to man."

WOMEN OF THE GOSPEL

With the gospel texts a marked change occurred. The genealogy of Joseph, "the husband of Mary," in Matthew is unusual for a biblical text in that it names four atypical women: Thamar, the foreign woman who, with face veiled and by means of prostitution, deceived her father-in-law in order to perpetuate the lineage; Rachab, the Jericho prostitute, who ensured Israel's survival upon entering the Promised Land; Ruth the Moabite; and the woman "that had been the wife of Urias," the beloved of David, Bathsheba, whose sin was pardoned by the birth of Solomon.

The gospels of Matthew and Luke emphasize the virginity of Mary, who is made pregnant by the Holy Spirit as foretold by Isaiah 7:14: "Behold, a virgin shall conceive, and bear a son, and shall call his name Immanuel." Joseph's dream, the adoration of the magi, the flight to Egypt in Matthew and even more prominently in Luke, the annunciation, the visitation, the nativity, the announcement to the shepherds, the presentation in the Temple, Jesus lost and found among the Doctors—all these are narrative fragments that were ripe for further development, which they received in the second-century Apocrypha, especially the Protoevangelium of James. All the new episodes—Anne's encounter with Joachim, the childhood of Mary and her presentation at the Temple, her wedding with Joseph, the virgin birth and the incredulity of Salome, the midwife whose desiccated hand is healed —encourage Marial piety and the ideal of virginity. They also furnished future Christian iconography with a rich supply of images. In Luke the figures of Elizabeth, the sterile woman who becomes the mother of John the Baptist, and Anne, the prophetic widow who heralds the deliverance of Israel, accompany the central figure of Mary, with her "fiat" of submission and "magnificat" of exultation in weakness. Subsequent allusions to Mary are rare, as religious bonds took precedence over ties of blood, but such episodes as the marriage at Cana and Mary standing at the foot of the cross with the beloved disciple of Jesus left an indelible mark on Christian memory, as did Mary's presence among the apostles praying for Jesus after the Ascension. The earliest allusion to Mary is in Paul: "God sent forth his Son, made of a woman." The importance of this feminine role in the theology of the Incarnation is clear.

Jesus' relations with women seem to have been remarkably free, given the reserve that Jewish custom in his day required. He is received by Martha and Mary, neither of whom is married, and demonstrates his friendship by resurrecting their brother Lazarus. When his disciples find him talking to a Samaritan at Jacob's well in Sichem, they "marvelled that he talked with the woman. Yet no man said, What seekest thou? or, Why talkest thou with her?" Barriers were broken down in the most surprising ways. Jesus preached to foreign women like the "schismatic" Samaritan and healed even the daughter of a Canaanite. The traditional hierarchy was overturned in favor of the despised: "The publicans and the harlots go into the kingdom of God before you," Jesus tells the high priests and elders of the Temple. In a well-known passage he forgives the many sins of a woman who "loved much" because she, to the horror of the Pharisees, is willing to anoint his feet with ointment. The pardon granted to the adulterous woman and the disarray of her male accusers can be seen in the same light. So can the message to the Samaritan woman who has been married five times and is now living as a concubine. Even female impurity is transcended: a bleeding woman touches the hem of Jesus' cloak and is cured. He also takes pity on the poorest of women, the widows protected by the Law: he resurrects the only son of the widow of Nain, as Elijah before him had resurrected the son of the widow of Sarepta. The poor widow who casts in "two mites" is praised more than the rich men making their gifts to the temple treasury.

The identity of the "saved" women who followed Jesus out of Galilee varies with the source. In Luke, after the passage about the anointment, we read: "And the twelve were with him. And certain women, which had been healed of evil spirits and infirmities, Mary called Magdalene, out of whom went seven devils, and Joanna the wife of Chuza, Herod's steward, and Susanna, and many others, which ministered unto him of their substance." It is a diverse group of women that sets out with Jesus on the road in defiance of custom. In all the lists Mary Magdalene comes first. Unlike the Twelve, these women have not received an explicit call, nor are they dispatched on clear missions. Yet in contrast to the abandonment of Jesus by the disciples, the presence of the women is emphasized—at a distance according to the Synoptics but near the cross according to John. As was customary in Judaism, the women are present when Jesus is wrapped in his shroud, and it is they who prepare perfumes and fragrances for anointing the body. Matthew names Mary Magdalene and the other Mary; Mark, Mary Magdalene, Mary, mother of James, and Salome; Luke, Mary Magdalene, Joanna, and Mary, mother of James; and John, only Mary Magdalene.

All four versions break with Jewish custom by making women, and particularly Mary Magdalene, witnesses to the resurrection and responsible for informing the disciples. To be sure, masculine incredulity is apparent in Mark and Luke. But the special place of women, who are the first to see the resurrected Christ, is therefore all the more significant, especially in the celebrated *Noli me tangere* scene in John. Memory of that special role would be preserved in prayer and imagery....

The Charisma of Prophetesses

Although the institutional place of women was strictly limited and women, in keeping with Jewish custom, were excluded from positions of authority, they played a more important charismatic role. In Luke three women—Mary, Elizabeth, and Anne—are reminiscent of the prophetesses of the Old Testament. The early Christian community experienced the outpouring of the Holy Spirit at Pentecost: "And it shall come to pass in the last days, saith God, I will pour out of my Spirit upon all flesh: and your sons *and your daughters* shall prophesy." A passage in the Acts alludes to Paul's visit to the home of Philip the Evangelist, one of the Seven, who "had four daughters, virgins, which did prophesy." In the congregation of Corinth men and women both prayed and prophesied. But while men were enjoined to bare their heads, women were required to keep theirs covered as a sign of power (*exousia*), dignity, and decency, and out of respect "for the angels" present as mediators of human prayer. Thus the order of creation was respected, with man enjoying priority over woman and interdependence in the Lord. This complex passage is still a matter of debate among exegetes.

Already true prophetesses were distinguished from false. In Revelations there is a denunciation of Jezebel, a woman of Thyatira "who claims to be a prophetess" and teacher. The gift of revelation would continue to flourish for a long time to come. In the second century Justin spoke of "Christian men and women who receive gifts from the Spirit of God." In 203 in Carthage the martyr Perpetua experienced visions. But these gifts were difficult to control, and heretical sects could lay claim to them as readily as the orthodox. When the Montanists made such claims in the second century, the Church began to play down the importance of prophecy, particularly among women....

WIDOWS AND DEACONESSES IN THE CHURCH

In the Church hierarchy the bishop was the dispenser of the sacred word and sacraments. He was assisted by priests and deacons. As the distinction between clergy and laity grew increasingly rigid, women were allowed a place in the ecclesiastical institution, but a limited one. In both east and west widows took on a spiritual and charitable role that gradually became confounded with the growing women's monastic movement in the last thirty years of the fourth century. At certain times and in certain places, mainly in the east, deaconesses who fulfilled a variety of functions were invested with ministries until roughly the tenth century. Here too feminine monasticism eventually subsumed these roles.

Widows. Along with orphans, the poor, the sick, prisoners, and strangers, widows had been portrayed as people in need of assistance in Christian text from I Timothy 5:16 onward. A portion of the Sunday collection was set aside for them. In Rome in 251 Bishop Cornelius counted 1,500 widows and paupers receiving aid from the Church. In return, the recipients of such aid were covered by certain special precepts in "apostolic" texts. Thus

Polycarp wrote to the Philippians: "May they be wise [*sophronousas*] in the faith they owe the Lord, intercede constantly for all, avoid calumny, slander, false witness, love of money, and all evil, in the knowledge that they are the alter of God."

But, as already in I Timothy 5:5, one group of widows stood out: those who pledged themselves to remain continent, to join an order (*tagma ton cheron, cherikon; ordo viduarum, viduatus*). This ideal of chaste renunciation at first seemed to make these widows a model for virgins, with whom they were sometimes associated. Ignatius referred to "virgins called widows." Other reports mention a similar confusion. Soon, however, the luster of virginity would outshine that of widows, not only in merit but also in competition for precedence within the Church.

Did widows have a place among the ecclesiastical orders? Tertullian in passing says that they did. But Hippolytus of Rome, in his third-century *Apostolic Tradition*, noted that widows of long standing could, after a period of probation, "be instituted by speech [and] joined to others but not ordained." No hand was to be placed on such a widow, because she was not making an oblation and had no liturgical services to perform. The widow was not ordained but instituted (*kathistatai*) for prayer, which was for everyone. Most of the texts state that a widow, in order to be instituted, had to have been married only once (Greek: *monandros*; Latin: *univira*). Her profession and vow of continence had to be irrevocable. For Basil of Caesarea breaking this vow meant excommunication. The age of admission was set at fifty or sixty, though it was not always respected.

Foremost among the obligations of the widow was prayer; I Timothy 5:5 had established this principle, and Hippoly-

tus had followed it in *Apostolic Tradition*. We find it too in the *Didascalia Apostolorum*, a compilation that probably originated in Syria in the third century. When ordered to do so by a bishop, widows were supposed to pray at the bedside of the sick, lay on hands, and fast. The asceticism of the widow's commitment was further emphasized in *Apostolic constitutions*, a late-fourth-century compilation from Syria or Constantinople. Prayer was to be coupled with fasting and vigils on the model of Judith.

In both the *Didascalia* and the *Constitutions*, however, the limits of widows' activities were carefully circumscribed. They were subject to the authority of bishops and deacons. Without express orders, no widow was permitted to visit any person's home for the purpose of eating, drinking, fasting, receiving gifts, laying on hands, or praying. The inner life came first: widows were the "altar of God" and must prove themselves to be just as solid as an altar. They were *cherai* (widows), not *perai* (sacks used by mendicants). They were to pray at home and go out to help others. They were at first advised, then ordered, not to perform baptisms. They were denied the right to teach, especially about Christ's passion and redemption. At most they were permitted to repeat elementary answers to basic questions: Christians must not worship idols, there is only one God. Such warnings suggest that women, instead of devoting themselves to prayer, may have been encroaching on territory that male clerics considered their own private preserve.

Deaconesses. Second-century texts offer no clear evidence concerning women's service to the Church. In Hermas' *The Shepherd* the woman representing the Church proposes that one copy of her book be sent to Clement, who will circulate it to other cities, and another to Grapta, who will alert widows and orphans. In a letter to Trajan, Pliny speaks of *ancillae... ministrae* whom he has subjected to torture in Bithynia. The Latin word may correspond to the Greek *diakonos*, but we are told nothing about what services these women might have performed. Pliny is contemptuous, seeing in their religion nothing more than "an absurd, extravagant superstition." His contempt may have been heightened by the humble status of these female slaves, who had been invested with official responsibilities by a community consisting of "many people of all ages and walks of life and of both sexes... in the cities, towns, and countrysides infected by this contagious superstition." Like Blandina in Lyons in 177 and Felicity in Carthage in 203, who were also slaves but without official religious functions, these victims of torture were notable for their courage. Note too the confidence of this *ekklesia* of mixed composition.

In the third century the *Didascalia Apostolorum* defined the status of the female deaconess (*he diakonos, gyne diakonos*) in the east. In the ecclesial typology the bishop was said to be in the image of God; the deacon, of Christ; the deaconess, of the Holy Spirit; and the priests, of the Apostles. The bishop named deacons to perform certain necessary tasks and deaconesses to serve women. The number of deacons and deaconesses depended on the size of the congregation. The deacon's duties were extensive and included assisting the bishop, especially during the celebration of the Eucharist, and maintaining decorum in church. By contrast, the deaconess' duties were limited to the service of other women: "Let a deaconess anoint the women" during baptism. "And when the woman being baptized emerges from the water, let the deaconess welcome her and teach her how the seal of baptism is to be preserved intact in purity and sanctity." Furthermore, "a deaconess is necessary to visit pagan homes in which there are female believers, and to visit women who are sick, and to wash those who are recovering from an illness." The *Didascalia* stressed the importance of this apparently new ministry by pointing out that Christ was served by deaconesses: Mary Magdalene, Mary, daughter of James and mother of Josiah; the mother of the sons of Zebadiah; and others....

Women enjoyed power as donors and founders. They played a role in the transition from ancient euergetism to Christian charity, church assistance of the poor, and monasteries. Some were obscure, like those who donated inscriptions in honor of their husbands. Others stood alone: "In virtue of her vow, Peristeria has made the mosaic in the nave" of the Stobi basilica; Matrona too was mentioned as the donor of a mosaic.... Aristocratic donors in the east and west were celebrated by their ecclesiastical biographers. After doing penance for a divorce followed by remarriage, Fabiola (died 399) founded the first hospital (*nosokomion*) in Rome, where she took care of the sick and the aged. She was generous to clerics, monks, and virgins throughout Italy. Upon her return from Jerusalem with Pammachius, who became a monk after the death of his wife Pauline, Fabiola founded a hostelry for travelers (*xenodochium*) at Porto Romano.

The generosity of widows had long been an important source of wealth for the Church. Porphyry accused Christians of "persuading women [to distribute] their fortunes and their property among the poor," reducing them to beggary. When Melania the Elder left Rome for a pilgrimage to Egypt, she brought with her a casket containing 300 pieces of silver and gave it to Pambo, a hermit. She supported orthodox deportees in Jerusalem and later founded there a monastery, where, according to Palladius, she and Rufinus received "all who come to pray: bishops, monks, and virgins, edifying them and aiding them from their resources... They gave gifts and food to the clergy of the city."...

Most important of all, women's power from the inception to the final victory of Christianity lay in the communicative character of their faith. It was easier for women than for men to free themselves from the social and political constraints of the ancient city, and often women seem to have been in advance of men from the same family. Their influence at home encouraged others to convert, so that women played a crucial role in the transmission of the faith. In 2 Timothy I:5 we read: "I call to remembrance the unfeigned faith that is in thee, which dwelt first in thy grandmother Lois, and thy mother Eunice."...

Women also led the way to still greater religious commitment. After obtaining a cure for Evagrius and restoring him to his anchoritic life, Melania the Elder returned to Italy from Jerusalem. There "she met the blessed Apronianus, a most worthy man, who was a pagan. She taught him the catechism and made him a Christian. And she persuaded him to remain continent with his wife, his niece Avita. While her counsel she fortified the resolve of her granddaughter Melania and her husband Pinianus and taught the catechism to her daughter-in-law Albina, the wife of her son. Then, having persuaded them all to sell what they possessed, she took them back to Rome and showed them how to live a noble and serene life."

NO

Karen Armstrong

THE RESULT: EVE

From almost the earliest days of Western Christianity, men started to see women as sexually dangerous and threatening, and in the grip of this fear they started a process which would eventually push women away from the male world into a separate world of their own. This might at first seem an odd development: neither Jesus nor Paul had pushed women away, but had worked closely with them and granted them full equality with men. However, later books of the New Testament, particularly the First Epistle to Timothy, which was probably written at the beginning of the 2nd century some sixty years after Paul's death, have a very different message. By this time Christianity is coping with the Gentile world of the late Empire and its terrors of sexual excess. A fear of sexuality had changed official Church policy toward women:

> I direct that women are to wear suitable clothes and to be dressed quietly and modestly without braided hair or gold and jewellery or expensive clothes; their adornment is to do the sort of good works that are proper for women who profess to be religious. During instruction, a woman should be quiet and respectful. I am not giving permission for a woman to teach or to tell a man what to do. A woman ought not to speak, because Adam was formed first and Eve afterwards, and it was not Adam who was led astray but the woman who was led astray and fell into sin. Nevertheless, she will be saved by childbearing, provided she lives a modest life and is constant in faith and love and holiness.
>
> —(1 Timothy 2:9–15)

When Paul had told the women in Corinth to keep quiet in Church, there was no hint of sexual disgust, nor was there any idea that women were potentially wicked (they just have to remember their place!) In 1 Timothy we have something different and sinister. Woman is not just inferior, she is wicked also, because of Eve. Eve fell into sin first and led Adam into sin. This is a theme which will recur again and again in the writings of the Early Fathers, and is also a deeply sexual idea.

From Karen Armstrong, *The Gospel According to Woman: Christianity's Creation of the Sex War in the West* (Anchor Press, 1987). Copyright © 1987 by Karen Armstrong. Reprinted by permission of Doubleday, a division of Bantam Doubleday Dell Publishing Group, Inc.

The author of 1 Timothy begins his remarks about women with directions about the sort of clothes they should wear. Glancing through the works of the Fathers, it is extraordinary how much time they devoted to writing about women's dress—a concern that should have been beneath them. Diatribes about the way women load themselves with jewelry, cake their faces with makeup and douse themselves with perfume crop us with extreme frequency. One of the first was written by Tertullian in the 3rd century. In a treatise written to his "best beloved sisters" in the faith, Tertullian glides from affection and respect to an astonishing attack:

> If there dwelt upon earth a faith as great as we expect to enjoy in heaven, there wouldn't be a single one of you, best beloved sisters, who, from the time when she had first "known the Lord" and learned the truth about her own condition, would have desired too festive (not to say ostentatious) a style of dress. Rather she would have preferred to go about in humble garb, and go out of her way to affect a meanness of appearance, walking about as Eve, mourning and repentant, so that by her penitential clothes she might fully expiate what she has inherited from Eve: the shame, I mean, of the first sin, and the odium of human perdition. *In pains and anxieties dost thou bear children, woman; and toward thine husband is thy inclination and he lords it over thee.*[1] And do you not know that you are each an Eve? The sentence of God on this sex of yours lives in this age: the guilt must of necessity live too. *You* are the devil's gateway: *you* are the unsealer of that forbidden tree: *you* are the first deserter of the divine law: *you* are she who persuaded him whom the devil was not valiant enough to attack. *You* destroyed so easily God's image, man. On account of *your* desert—

that is death—even the Son of God had to die. And do you think about adorning yourself over and above your tunics of skins.

> —(*On Female Dress*, I:i)

It is exactly the same complex of ideas that we find, less clearly articulated, in 1 Timothy: female appearance, Eve, childbirth. It seems at first sight strange that this enormous attack—each woman is completely responsible for destroying men and crucifying Christ—should start and finish with something as apparently unimportant as women's clothes. What prompts Tertullian's virulent attack is pure irrational fear. As the treatise goes on, we see that it is wholly about sex. Woman is as much of a temptation to man as Eve was to Adam, not because she is offering him an apple but because she is offering the forbidden fruit of sex. She can cause a man to lust after her just by walking around looking beautiful. "You must know," Tertullian insists, "that in the eye of perfect Christian modesty, having people lusting after you with carnal desire is not a desirable state of affairs but is something execrable" (II, ii). He is thinking of Jesus' words when he said that a man who looks at a woman lustfully has already committed adultery in his heart. Jesus was not making a particular issue of lust here, but was illustrating his admirable religious insight that mere external conformity to a set of rules is not enough for the truly religious man. It is the attitude in his heart that counts, not a meticulous performance of burdensome commandments. Tertullian twists this potentially liberating idea into a truly frightening view of the moral world. "For as soon as a man has lusted after your beauty, he has in his mind already committed the sin which his lust was imagining and he perished because of this, and you [women] have been made the sword that destroys him" (II, ii). A man's lustful glance may be entirely involuntary, but he still perishes. The woman is guilty of destroying him just as Eve was guilty of destroying Adam. She may have had absolutely no intention of tempting him—she may not even realize that she has caused any lustful thoughts at all, but she is still guilty. Both the man and the woman have sinned even though what happened was quite beyond their control.

Tertullian is quite clear that women are to blame: "even though you may be free of the actual crime, you are not free of the odium attaching to it" (II, ii). This means that, far from dressing up and making herself look pretty and desirable, a woman has a duty to look as unattractive as she possibly can:

> ... it is time for you to know that you must not merely reject the pageantry of fictitious and elaborate beauty, but even the grace and beauty you enjoy naturally must be obliterated by concealment and negligence, because this is just as dangerous to the people who glance at you. For even though comeliness is not to be censured exactly, because it is certainly a physical felicity and a kind of goodly garment of the soul, but it is to be feared, because of the injury and violence it inflicts on the men who admire you.
>
> —(II, ii)

This is an oft-repeated theme for Tertullian. In his treatise *On the Veiling of Virgins*, it surfaces in a particularly disturbed form. St. Paul had said that women had to wear veils in Church "because of the angels." Here he was referring to the legend of the "Sons of God," the "angels" who

lusted after earthly women and came down from heaven to mate with them.

> For if it is "because of the angels"—those beings of whom we read as having fallen from God and from heaven because of lusting after women—who can presume that it was bodies already defiled and relics of human lust which the angels yearned after, but that rather that they were inflamed for virgins, whose bloom pleads an excuse for human lust? ... So perilous a face, then, ought to be kept shaded, when it has cast stumbling stones even so far as heaven. This face, when it stands in the presence of God, at whose bar it already stands accused of driving the angels from their heavenly home, may blush before the other angels who didn't fall as well.
>
> —(*On the Veiling of Virgins*, VII)

There is something extremely unpleasant here. It is not simply the view that sex always defiles a woman, so that afterward she is merely a "relic of human lust," a memory of a shameful act. There is also a horrible leering prurience about unsullied virgins being especially lustworthy, and there is a real terror in the idea that a woman's beauty is so dangerous and powerful that it can even cause angels to abandon heaven and fall irretrievably into sin. If even angels are not safe from a woman's beauty, then what hope is there for mere men? A woman must keep her "perilous" face hidden. She must disguise her beauty, or she will destroy men just as surely as Eve destroyed Adam. Already, years before Augustine would finally formulate for the West the doctrine of Original Sin, the emotional trinity which exists at the heart of that doctrine has been formed in the Christian neurosis of Tertullian: woman, sex and sin are fused together in his mind indissolubly. The only hope for man is that women hide themselves away—veil their faces from man's lustful eyes, hide their beauty by disfiguring themselves and make themselves ugly and sexless in the penitential garb that befits each woman as an Eve.

Christian men were told to inhabit a separate world from women. When Jerome wants to defend his friendship with the noble Roman lady St. Paula, who became one of his staunchest disciples, he stresses the fact that he was scrupulous about keeping away from women:

> Before I became acquainted with the household of the saintly Paula all Rome was enthusiastic about me. Almost everyone concurred in judging me worthy of the highest office in the Church. My words were always on the lips of Damasus of blessed memory. Men called me saintly: men called me humble and eloquent. Did I ever enter a house of any woman who was included to wantonness? Was I ever attracted by silk dresses, flashing jewels, painted faces, display of gold? No other matron in Rome could dominate my mind but one who mourned and fasted, who was squalid with dirt, almost blind with weeping. All night long she would beg the Lord for mercy, and often the sun found her still praying. The psalms were her music, the Gospels her conversation: continence was her luxury, her life a fast. No other could give me pleasure, but one whom I never saw munching food.

> —(Letter xiv: To Asella)

For Jerome the only good woman is a sexually repulsive one. Paula has made herself "repellent." When Jerome went to visit her, he felt disgusted by her and his virtue was quite safe. He was in no sexual danger. Paula herself would have been delighted by this appalling description; she was only one of the new breed of Roman ladies who were taking up the ascetic life and mutilating themselves physically and spiritually in this way. This pattern of mutilation is one that recurs in all sorts of psychological and physical ways among the women of Western Christianity. By telling a woman that she should not be physically attractive if she wanted to consort with men and still be virtuous, Jerome and his like were deeply damaging the women who obeyed them.

If a woman is not repulsive then she must be isolated and ostracized. In his letter to Nepotian, a young priest, Jerome tells him that he must be careful to keep himself away from women, even the most innocent and virtuous women, unless they are sexually repellent:

> A woman's foot should seldom or never cross the threshold of your humble lodging. To all maidens and to all Christ's virgins show the same disregard or the same affection. Do not remain under the same roof with them; do not trust your chastity. You cannot be a man more saintly than David, or more wise than Solomon. Remember always that a woman drove the tiller of Paradise from the garden that had been given him. If you are ill let one of the brethren attend you, or else your sister or your mother or some woman of universally approved faith. If there are no persons marked out by ties of kinship or reputation for chastity, the Church maintains many elderly women who by their services can both help you and benefit themselves, so that even your sickness may bear fruit in almsgiving.... There is a danger for you in the ministrations of one whose face you are continually watching. If in the course of your clerical duties you have to visit a widow or a virgin, never enter the house alone.... Never sit alone without witnesses with a woman in a quiet place.

If there is anything intimate she wants to say, she has a nurse or some elderly virgin at home, some widow or married woman. She cannot be so cut off from human society as to have no one but yourself to whom she can trust her secret.

—(Letter lii)

Merely sitting with a woman or letting her nurse you is to put yourself in grave danger. Women, therefore, have to be shunned, even if they are in trouble and need help. A woman is to be avoided and left alone in a world which is quite apart from men.

It becomes part of the advice that is given to your aspirants of both sexes who want to lead virtuous Christian lives. Men are to shun women, and women are urged to withdraw from the world and take themselves off into a separate and totally female existence. Inevitably that will be maiming, even without the fasting and the deliberate physical mutilation that the woman is urged to undertake in the name of physical penance. Simply by being deprived of the realities of the male world, by being deprived of education and normal activity, women were only being able to function in half the world. However, the most destructive thing of all was the sexual disgust which drove women into their separate worlds. There is a continual process of repulsion which we have already seen in Tertullian, a process which is neurotic and probably not even conscious. You begin speaking lovingly to your "best beloved sisters" and you end up castigating "Eve." Jerome has exactly the same reaction. Here he is writing to a young girl who has written asking for his advice about the Christian life. Jerome urges her to lock herself away from the world. Simply by walking around she will inspire male

lust, however virtuous she is. In fact, virtue itself can turn a man on:

What will you do, a healthy young girl, dainty, plump, rosy, all afire amid the fleshpots, amid the wines and baths, side by side with married women and with young men. Even if you refuse to give what they ask for, you may think that the asking is evidence of your beauty. A libertine is all the more ardent when he is pursuing virtue and thinks that the unlawful is especially delightful. Your very robe, coarse and sombre though it be, betrays your unexpressed desires if it be without crease, if it be trailed upon the ground to make you seem taller, if your vest be slit on purpose to let something be seen within, hiding that which is unsightly and disclosing that which is fair. As you walk along your shiny black shoes by their creaking give an invitation to young men. Your breasts are confined in strips of linen, and your chest in imprisoned by a tight girdle. Your hair comes down over your forehead or over your ears. Your shawl sometimes drops, so as to leave your white shoulders bare, and then, as though unwilling to be seen, it hastily hides what it unintentionally revealed. And when in public it hides the face in a pretence of modesty, with a harlot's skill it shows only those features which give men when shown more pleasure.

—(Letter cxvii)

It is not surprising that Jerome doesn't let himself near women, because this letter shows him to be sexually obsessed and one of the great voyeurs of all time. He has obviously studied women minutely, and is pruriently eager to pick up each and every movement, every mannerism. He is even excited by the creaking of a woman's shoe. Watching a woman walk down the street, he immediately imagines her underwear; his eyes are skinned to catch a glimpse of her white shoulders. It is taken for granted that she is teeming with lust. Every movement, intentional or unintentional, is a sign of her "unexpressed" sexual desire. What Jerome is doing is over-sexualizing women because of his own sexual repression. *He* is rampantly frustrated so he tells women that *they* are sexually insatiable. He has forgotten here that he is writing to a good little girl, who has asked him for advice. He is so lost in his fantasy that by the end of the paragraph he is comparing her to a harlot. In just the same way Tertullian begins by calling his readers "best beloved" and ends by calling them "Eve." Christian love for women easily modulates into sexual hatred.

Woman then is man's deepest enemy. She is the harlot who will lure a man to his doom because she is Eve, the eternal temptress. Just as Original Sin comes to be linked with sex, so woman is Eve because she is sexual. Jerome's pathological disgust with sex is shown in his letter to Furia, who had written to seek his advice about getting married again:

> The trials of marriage you have learned in the married state: you have been surfeited to nausea as though with the flesh of quails. Your mouth has tasted the bitterest of gall, you have voided the sour unwholesome food, you have relieved a heaving stomach. Why would you put into it again something which has already proved harmful to you. *The dog is turned to his own vomit again and the sow that was washed to her wallowing in the mire.*
>
> —(2 Peter 2:22)

What must Furia have felt like when she received this letter? Again she seems to have been a virtuous woman, a genuine and enthusiastic Christian, but because of her sexuality she would have been made to feel foul and sinful. Jerome is clear that she is sexually obsessed and voracious. As a widow she must be inflamed by the "pleasures of the past." The widow "knows the delights that she has lost and she must quench the fire of the devil's shafts with the cold streams of fast and vigil." Jerome sees a woman as having such strong sexual cravings that if she dresses attractively she is crying out for sex, her "whole body reveals incontinence." Again he sees her as luring poor unsuspecting men into sex and sin. Woman is Antichrist:

> What have rouge and white lead to do on a Christian woman's face? The one simulates the natural red of cheeks and lips, the other the whiteness of the face and neck. They are fires to inflame young men, stimulants of lustful desire, plain evidence of an unchaste mind. How can a woman weep for her sins when tears lay her skin bare and make furrows on her face? Such adorning is not of the Lord, it is the mask of Antichrist.
>
> —(Letter liv)

Reading this one might assume that Jerome is writing about prostitutes whose garish makeup advertises their availability. In fact here, as elsewhere, he was writing about ordinary Roman matrons who used frequently to wear cosmetics at this time.

This hostility and fear of women's sexual powers we see again and again. Augustine sees danger even in the virtuous women of the Old Testament, sometimes with ludicrous results. Trying to come to terms with the sex lives of the Patriarchs, he presents Abraham and Isaac copulating with their wives dutifully but with enormous distaste, in order to obey God's command to found the Chosen Race. They would far rather have abstained. Abraham, Augustine says, had to go on copulating with his wife Sarah for years before he managed with God's help to conceive his son Isaac. Abraham, who seems to have been a highly sexed man, would have read all this with considerable bewilderment. Isaac, Augustine continues, was more fortunate. The Bible only mentions his having sex once, and he was lucky enough to produce the twins, Esau and Jacob, straight off so he never had to do it again. When he came to Jacob, however, who had twelve sons, Augustine is in a bit of a quandary. This looks like zeal in excess of duty. However, he decides that Jacob would gladly have followed the example of Isaac and only had sex once in his life, but his two wives, Leah and Rachel, kept pestering him because of their excessive lust and sexual greed, forcing the holy Patriarch to abandon his high ideals. Yet Rachel and Leah are good women. For Augustine, as for his predecessors Jerome and Tertullian, all women, however virtuous, are men's enemies. "What is the difference," he wrote to a friend, "whether it is in a wife or a mother, it is still Eve the temptress that we must beware of in any woman" (Letter 243, 10).

There is no room for this enemy in the male world. Indeed, there is no room for her at all in God's plan. Augustine seems puzzled about why God made women at all. It is not possible that she was a friend and helpmate to man. After all, "if it was good company and conversation that Adam needed, it would have been much better arranged to have two men together, as friends, not a man and a woman" (De Genesis ad Litteram IX, v, 9).

The only reason he made women was for the purposes of childbearing. Luther shared this view. The only vocation he could see for a woman was to have as many children as possible, so that all the more people could be led to the Gospel. It didn't matter what effect this might have on women: "If they become tired or even die, that does not matter. Let them die in childbirth—that is why they are there." There was no other way that a woman could help man. Her place was "in the home" (the famous phrase was actually coined by Luther). There was no place for her in the male world of affairs. Similarly Calvin, who is virtually the first Christian theologian to speak favorably of women, might insist that woman *was* created to be a companion to man and that marriage was instituted by God precisely for that companionship, but his Geneva was entirely male dominated, and women's role as a companion was confined to the domestic female world of the home. Protestantism shared fully the misogyny that the Fathers had bequeathed to the Catholic Church. When Lutherans at Wittenberg discussed the question whether women were really human beings at all, they were not discussing anything new. Theologians had always been perplexed about women's place in God's plan. Thomas Aquinas was as puzzled as Augustine had been about why God had made her at all and decided that woman was a freak in nature:

As regards the individual nature, woman is defective and misbegotten, for the active force in the male seed tends to the production of a perfect likeness in the masculine sex; while the production of woman comes from a defect in the active force or from some material indisposition, or even from some external influence.

—(*Summa Theologica*, IV, Part I. Quaest. XCII, art 1, 2)

It does not help that Aquinas decides that womankind in *general* is human. The "individual nature" of women is a defect, an idea he picked up from Aristotle's biology. The norm is the male. Every woman is a failed man.

* * *

Women are therefore emotionally excluded from the male world, for all that Paul had originally insisted upon sexual equality. Even now that we are breaking into the male preserves we still tend to feel ill at ease in it. Recent surveys show that college women are even more afraid of success today than they were when Betty Friedan did her original survey in the early 1960s. Dons at Oxford and Cambridge have complained about the quality of women who are gaining admission to the colleges that used to be all-male. They have asked schools to stop sending them girls who are polite, efficient and well-behaved, and instead send them students who will argue with them as aggressively as the boys do. Breaking into the male world is not simply a matter of opportunity. It is a question of attitude on the part of both men and women. Women are still ambiguous and fearful in these new male worlds that have recently been opened to them. They are still maintaining their guilty apologetic stance. For centuries they have been excluded not simply because they were supposed to be inferior but because they inspired sexual fear and disgust in men. Marilyn French's novel *The Women's Room* puts this humorously when she imagines the male world of Harvard terrified to admit women in case they drip menstrual blood all over this pure male preserve. Where Moslems have traditionally locked their women into harems inside their homes because they owned and valued them, men in the Christian West have locked their women outside their lives because they hate them, exiling women to a lonely, separate world.

NOTES

1. Genesis 3:16. Tertullian quotes God's words to Eve after the Fall.

POSTSCRIPT

Did Christianity Liberate Women?

Eusebius (263–339 C.E.) was a Greek Christian and an intimate friend of the emperor Constantine who wrote the only surviving account of the first 300 years of Christian Church history. Sometimes called the Christian Herodotus, he certainly earned the title Father of Ecclesiastical (church) History. A translation of his work by G. A. Williamson, *The History of the Church* (Dorset Press, 1984), is easy to obtain.

In the early years of Christianity, different schools of what would later become theology existed side by side. One of these was Gnosticism, a mystical worldview that predominated in Greece and Rome. Remarkable for its androgynous view of God as father and mother, Gnosticism was condemned as the first heresy primarily because of its insistence that God only appeared to suffer and die in the person of Jesus. Four Gnostic gospels, part of what scholars call the Nag Hammadi library, found in Egypt in the 1940s, are available in Marvin W. Meyer's translation in *The Secret Teachings of Jesus* (Vintage Books, 1986). Elaine Pagels has also written about Gnosticism in *The Gnostic Gospels* (Vintage Books, 1989) and about the origin of evil in *Adam and Eve and the Serpent* (Vintage Books, 1989).

A documentary sampling of women in history from the ancient Greeks to the modern Victorians may be found in *Not in God's Image* edited by Julia O'Faolain and Lauro Martines (Harper & Row, 1973). Including both religious and nonreligious writings, this book places Western attitudes toward women in a broader context. The image of God is a critical element in understanding Christian attitudes toward women. If women are included in the image of God, then they are eligible for full membership within Christianity; if, however, the image of God is strictly a male one, then women must necessarily be excluded or marginal. Two books shed considerable light on this question: *God, a Biography* by Jack Miles (Alfred A. Knopf, 1995), which considers God the protagonist of the Hebrew scriptures (what Christians call the Old Testament), and Karen Armstrong's *A History of God: The 4,000-Year Quest of Judaism, Christianity and Islam* (Alfred A. Knopf, 1993), which traces the image of God through all three religions of the book.

Feminist theory points to an Eve/Mary split within Christianity. According to this thesis, women are offered only two roles—Eve, the temptress whose disobedience brought about the loss of Eden, or Mary, the mother of Jesus whose obedience to the will of God made possible human salvation. The two extremes represented by these roles seem to exclude all living women. If Mary is held up as an ideal—as she clearly has been during certain periods of Christian history—then women, if they remain pure and demure, may share in the honor accorded Mary. However, to slip even slightly from the perfection embodied by Mary is to fall all the way to the disdain accorded Eve. There is no middle ground. Film historians call this the virgin/whore split and cite numerous examples of film heroines who play out one of these two roles. Students may be interested in reading Molly Haskell's *From Reverence to Rape: The Treatment of Women in the Movies* (Penguin Books, 1974) and Marjorie Rosen's *Popcorn Venus* (Avon Books, 1973), which explore this theme.

ISSUE 6

Did the Roman Empire Collapse Under Its Own Weight?

YES: Solomon Katz, from *The Decline of Rome and the Rise of Mediaeval Europe* (Cornell University Press, 1955)

NO: Arther Ferrill, from *The Fall of the Roman Empire: The Military Explanation* (Thames & Hudson, 1986)

ISSUE SUMMARY

YES: History professor Solomon Katz summarizes the internal causes that led to the decline of the Roman Empire and argues that the growth of the empire carried with it the seeds of its own destruction.

NO: History professor Arther Ferrill maintains that the primary cause of the fall of the Roman Empire was external and that attacks by the barbarian tribes along the periphery of the empire ultimately caused the collapse of the state.

Few historians would challenge the assertion that the decline and fall of the Western Roman Empire was one of the most momentous developments in history. The causes of that decline, however, have occasioned heated debate, particularly as each generation seeks to determine whether or not the fall of Rome carries lessons—or warnings—for its own political leaders. It is not a question with simplistic answers, for the transformation of the Roman Empire into its various successor states was an extraordinarily complex phenomenon that involved numerous causes, both internal and external.

The Roman Empire was founded in the first century B.C. by Augustus Caesar, who fashioned political institutions that suited his own particular style of leadership. Succeeding emperors found it difficult to maintain the balance that Augustus had achieved; nevertheless, by the first decade of the first century A.D., the boundaries of the empire stretched from Britain in the west to North Africa in the south, and to the edge of the Persian Gulf in the east. The empire reached its zenith during the reign of Trajan, and it remained relatively prosperous for another century and a half. In the third century, however, a long process of decline commenced, which accelerated following the reign of Valentinian I (364–375), who split the empire into separate western and eastern sectors. Over the next 100 years, the empire continued to disintegrate; the final Roman emperor was overthrown in 476.

Historians have advanced scores of theories to explain the fall of the Roman Empire. In his classic, six-volume work *History of the Decline and Fall of the*

Roman Empire (1776–1788), English historian Edward Gibbon noted several dozen such theories, but he refrained from endorsing any single explanation himself. Since that time, some historians have focused upon the disintegration of the imperial economy as the crucial factor. Others have suggested that the unwieldy and excessively conservative political institutions of the doddering empire doomed it to eventual extinction. Still other historians have argued that specific policies of ambitious or dim-witted emperors were primarily responsible for the collapse of the Roman state.

Solomon Katz rejects any single-causation theories for the fall of Rome. Specifically, he rejects the argument that the empire was slain by barbarian invasions. After all, Rome had resisted equally formidable attacks by barbarians before the disastrous assaults of the late fifth century; therefore, the key must lie in internal factors that sapped the strength and will of the empire to resist. In the selection that follows, Katz argues that the decline actually began when territorial expansion ceased in the early second century. From that point on, he says, the central government in Rome had to govern and protect a vast empire using only the resources that existed within the empire. The results included autocratic administrative controls, a bloated bureaucracy that relied upon repressive regulations to survive, and excessive taxation on a dwindling middle class to support an army to defend the empire's far-flung frontiers. By the start of the fifth century, Katz asserts, Rome suffered from a disintegration of central authority, an expanding gap between rich and poor, and a breakdown of morale that left the Western Roman Empire an easy prey for invaders.

Arther Ferrill displays less interest in long-term, internal causes of Roman decline. In the second selection, he concentrates instead on the struggle of the Roman armies to defend the borders of the empire. He argues that the Roman Empire still showed signs of remarkable vigor in the late fourth century. It was the military losses of 407–410, including the sack of Rome and the loss of Britain, that Ferrill believes started Rome on its downhill spiral. From that point on, the strategic position of the Western Roman Empire began to deteriorate, as the imperial frontiers began to shrink. For Ferrill, therefore, the key to the fall of Rome lay in the destruction of Roman military power in the fifth century, a development that was exacerbated by the empire's reliance on non-Roman troops and the general loss of morale among the empire's fighting men. Consequently, the Roman Empire in the West succumbed to the barbarian attacks, while the Eastern Roman Empire, based in Constantinople and untouched by similar military disasters, was able to survive.

YES

Solomon Katz

DECLINE AND FALL

From St. Augustine (354–430), in whose lifetime Italy and Rome were overrun by barbarian invaders, to the present, historians, philosophers, and theologians have sought an answer to one of the central problems of history: what caused the decline of the Roman Empire? What were the forces of dissolution? What were the weaknesses in the Roman Empire? What, in the words of the great eighteenth-century historian Edward Gibbon, were "the most important circumstances of its decline and fall: a revolution which will ever be remembered, and is still felt by the nations of the Earth?"

For each generation the question has had a topical as well as a historical interest. Consciously or not, men have sensed in that decline a foreshadowing of the fate of their own civilization and have tried, by seeking the causes of Rome's decline, to escape the same misfortune. Their own basic assumptions about the meaning of history, their own philosophy of history, have inevitably dictated the answers which men have given to the question....

PROBLEMS IN EVALUATING THE DECLINE

The decline of the Roman Empire was neither sudden nor cataclysmic, but was a gradual process extending over several centuries. We have already examined many of the disquieting symptoms of decay and disintegration which appeared during the third and even the second century A.D., and we have seen how successive emperors applied force and compulsion in order to maintain the integrity of the Empire. Important as their achievement was, Diocletian and Constantine succeeded only in postponing the collapse of the Roman Empire, not in preventing it. After the death of Constantine in 337, the signs of decay increased, and the world of the fifth and sixth centuries, while it preserved many elements of ancient civilization, was already recognizably mediaeval. On the soil of the western half of the Roman Empire, Germanic kingdoms were established; while in the East, Byzantine emperors ruled as heirs to the Romans. Trade continued, but on a diminishing scale, and agriculture was increasingly on the basis of large, self-sufficient estates worked by serfs who were bound to the soil. The pagan cults yielded to Christian-

From Solomon Katz, *The Decline of Rome and the Rise of Mediaeval Europe* (Cornell University Press, 1955). Copyright © 1955 by Cornell University. Reprinted by permission. Notes omitted.

ity, the Christian church built a strongly centralized administrative system, and classical learning was adapted to Christian needs or was superseded by Christian theology.

Roman armies had been defeated by Germanic invaders before, but the catastrophic defeat of the Romans in 378 at the battle of Adrianople... was a dramatic proof that the imperial government was unable to offer effective resistance to invasion. This was underscored in 410, when the barbarians occupied and sacked Rome. Finally in 476 Romulus Augustulus, the last Roman emperor in the West, lost his throne and soon the invaders gained full control of the western half of the Roman Empire. The Empire had experienced other crises in the past and had surmounted them; now it was unable to rally. A government which for centuries had untied almost the whole civilized world into one empire was disintegrating. Meanwhile the acceptance of Christianity by the emperors and the vast majority of their subjects was both cause and effect of a profound transformation in the civilization of the ancient world. To this theme Gibbon gave a title which has become traditional: *The Decline and Fall of the Roman Empire*. Closer study has revealed that Gibbon exaggerated the extent of decline: there were elements of vitality as well as signs of decay in the centuries after the Antonine Age. Some historians, indeed, have insisted that there was no real decline, but merely a transformation of civilization. Nevertheless, if from whatever point of view— political, economic, or cultural—we compare the Roman world of the third and fourth centuries with the Empire during the first two centuries, we find indisputable evidences of decline.

Whether we designate what occurred as change or decline, we are concerned with a very complex phenomenon. Many of the explanations have been oversimplified solutions to an immensely difficult problem. Scholars have sometimes selected one factor, for example, the barbarian invasions or the exhaustion of the soil, and have declared it to be the ultimate cause of the decline of the Roman Empire, or they have looked for one common denominator of decline to which they have reduced all other factors. We shall see, however, that the process of decline was due not to a single cause, but to a variety of interacting factors— political, economic, social, cultural, and psychological. To give priority to any one of them is virtually impossible, since each acted with and upon every other factor. At the outset, therefore, we should recognize the principle of multiple causation.

THE DISTINCTION BETWEEN CAUSES AND SYMPTOMS

A more common error arises out of the difficulty of distinguishing between cause and symptom. Many of the alleged causes are actually symptoms of decline due to antecedent causes or conditions, rather than ultimate causes in themselves. Some of the symptoms of decay are obvious: economic collapse, inadequate revenues, insufficient armed forces to defend the Empire, intellectual stagnation. Each of these factors, however, is itself in need of explanation. Each is a symptom of decline and at the same time a cause of further decline, in other words, an effect of an antecedent cause and a cause itself.

An example or two may illustrate the difficulty of differentiating between cause and symptom and between proximate and remote causes. We have seen how Romans or Romanized elements, those who had the largest stake in Roman institutions, came to form a dwindling minority in the army. The barbarization of the army and the civil service and Rome's dependence upon barbarian allies and mercenaries were undoubtedly one of the factors in the decline of Rome. But more and more Germans were admitted into the army and the civil service because Rome desperately needed men to help defend her frontiers and administer her empire. The barbarization of the Empire is, therefore, a symptom of decay, an indication that there was a shortage of manpower in relation to the tasks which had to be performed. What caused that? Was it a declining birth rate, high mortality in wars and epidemics, or increased requirements for men? Each and all may have been remote causes of the barbarization of the Empire, and the process of barbarization was itself both symptom and cause of decline.

Again, the insistent needs of the army and the bureaucracy imposed an enormous burden upon the treasury. The high cost of continuous warfare, the shrinking revenues which followed the loss of provinces, the dislocation of trade as a result of civil war, the depreciation of the coinage—all these had a ruinous effect upon the economic life of the Empire. The methods devised by the imperial government to meet soaring expenses reduced men to the level of slaves of the state, straining to support a costly machinery of defense and administration. Individual and municipal freedom was destroyed by the central government, and with the loss of that freedom initiative and enterprise were paralyzed. Was this a cause of decline? Or did the imperial government adopt the Draconian solution of bind-ing merchants and artisans to their callings, farmers to the land, and city officials to their posts because the emperors believed that only by mobilizing all their resources in this way could they save the Empire? Again we have symptoms of decline which are at the same time causes springing from other causes, each interacting upon the other, each an aspect of the whole causative process. Moreover, some factors, whether they are regarded as causes of symptoms, cannot be measured accurately. By tracing the deterioration of the coinage, we may describe with some precision such physical phenomena as the shrinking supply of precious metal, but we have no yardstick for measuring other aspects of the decline of the Empire, such as apathy or "loss of nerve." We can only infer that they existed both as causes and as symptoms of decline.

SOME UNFOUNDED THEORIES OF THE DECLINE

Some alleged causes may be rejected at once. Thus a major climatic change, an increasing drought caused by the diminution of rainfall, has been held responsible for the decline of ancient civilization. Long spells of dry weather are said to have led to the exhaustion of the soil, poor crops, abandonment of the land, impoverishment, famine, and depopulation. This remains, however, a hypothesis for which no valid evidence from the whole Empire has been adduced. A closely related physical factor, the exhaustion of the soil, has also been suggested. In certain districts, for example, in southern Italy, deforestation and other factors undoubtedly reduced the fertility of the soil, but there is no evidence for a general exhaustion of the soil throughout the Empire, despite primitive methods of fertilizing and farming. On the contrary, Gaul continued to produce bountiful crops in the late Roman Empire, and Egypt, largely dependent upon the flood waters of the Nile, had its fertility renewed annually.

Some scholars have explained the decline of Rome on the basis of biological factors. There are no scientifically acceptable data to support the argument that societies, like individuals, have a life-cycle—birth, growth, maturity, and death—and hence that civilizations like individuals are predestined to die. Nor can we accept the hypothesis that the "best" elements in Roman society were exterminated by wars and revolution or died out because of the disinclination of these members of society to reproduce. We are given neither a satisfactory definition of the "best," nor proof that only the "best" perished. Similarly, one may dispose of the related argument that Rome succumbed because of "race suicide" or "race mixture," that is, that the "superior Roman stock" was overwhelmed by "inferior races" who bred freely while the "best" failed to reproduce. Biologists and anthropologists have demonstrated that there are no superior or inferior races. The decline of Rome has also been attributed to malaria or to the great plague which occurred in the reign of Marcus Aurelius, but malaria was not endemic throughout the Empire, and the effects of the plague, however deadly, might have been overcome were it not for other factors which we shall analyze later. In any event, we cannot be sure that Rome would have been saved by a larger population.

Moralists have suggested that the decline was caused by a slackening of personal morality, but most of the evidence they have presented is from the flourishing years of the early Principate.

In the Later Empire, under the influence of the religious revival, morals may actually have been elevated. In any case, most people in both the earlier and the later period seem to have lived decent and sober lives. Even if moral standards had decayed, it would still be necessary to seek an explanation for such an historical phenomenon.

THE ROLE OF SOCIAL CONFLICT

The decline of ancient civilization has been attributed, by Rostovtzeff, to the failure of the upper classes to extend their culture to the rural and urban lower classes. In the end, according to this argument, there was a prolonged social conflict between the urban propertied classes and the rural masses who made up the bulk of the army. The masses put their leaders on the throne, absorbed the higher classes, and lowered standards in general. But there is little evidence that the army was made up of a class-conscious proletariat which hated the urban upper classes. On the contrary, in its greed the army plundered town and country alike. Yet so much of the argument must be granted: that Roman culture had not penetrated sufficiently into the masses, had not inspired them with devotion to a high ideal to which all alike were committed, and that now in a time of mounting difficulties it failed to evoke their active effort and cooperation in its defense.

Another unsatisfactory hypothesis is that the lack of any clear constitutional provision for the succession on the death of an emperor led to military usurpation of power, anarchy, and all its concomitant evils. The method of adoption of an heir to the throne by the incumbent, haphazard as it may have been, worked well during most of the Antonine period. Indeed, the choice of the ablest man available, regardless of family affiliation, worked better than Marcus Aurelius' solution of designating his own son Commodus as emperor.

Finally, the Empire was not suddenly destroyed by the barbarians, although their attack contributed to Rome's decline and eventually they took possession of the western half of the Roman Empire. The pressure of barbarians had been felt by the Romans from very early times, and the invasions of the fifth century were not much more formidable than previous ones which had been repelled. If Rome had not already been weakened internally and demoralized, she might have put up an effective resistance, as she had to earlier onslaughts.

POLITICAL FACTORS

We have rejected certain explanations of the decline of ancient civilization. What factors remain? Among the political factors may be counted the failure of the civil power to control the army. We have seen how the troops were preoccupied with making and unmaking emperors and how ambitious generals fought for the throne. The result was military disorganization, which facilitated the advance of the barbarians. We have observed both as a symptom and as a cause of decline the decay of civic vitality, as the emperors interfered more and more with municipal freedom and thus undermined a civilization which had been based upon an association of self-governing city-states. The municipal aristocracy, the backbone of that civilization, was crushed by a harsh and arbitrary despotism and old loyalties were weakened. Cities decayed and eventually many of them disappeared.

... Within the geographical limits set by the emperor Hadrian (117–138), Rome quickly attained the maximum possibilities of exploitation under existing techniques and economic stagnation set in. Since her wealth was no longer replenished by the plunder and resources of new provinces, there was a shift from an economy which had grown with the Empire to a static economy. Meanwhile pressures on the frontiers increased, and the government was compelled to maintain more armed forces and administrative officials than she could afford. Higher taxes, bureaucratic and autocratic controls, and the whole machinery of compulsion followed.

Further expansion, however, would have been neither feasible with the resources of manpower which Rome had available nor immediately profitable. As an alternative the Romans might have extended their domestic markets. But the purchasing power of the mass of the people was always limited, and the requirements of the rich were not sufficient to compensate for the limited demands of the majority of men. It has been suggested that an abundance of cheap slave labor prevented the invention and use of labor-saving machinery which might have produced cheap products and thus stimulated the economy by extending the internal market. Long before the fourth century, however, with the cessation of expansion, slaves were neither readily available nor cheap and there was, in fact, a labor shortage. A more valid explanation of the failure to produce a machine technology was the inability of the impoverished masses to purchase its products. The civil and foreign wars of the third century further dislocated the limited markets, and the economic structure of the Empire was badly shaken. The very measures taken by the government to preserve the Empire weakened and finally paralyzed initiative and enterprise.

THE DISINTEGRATION OF CENTRAL AUTHORITY

We have traced the growth of an inefficient and oppressive financial system which was both cause and result of economic decline. We have see how the normal requirements of defense and administration and the extraordinary costs of half a century of military anarchy led to higher taxes, depreciation of the coinage, extension of the system of compulsory requisitions and forced labor, and economic chaos. The enforcement of the system called for an ever larger and more elaborate machinery of government and more repressive measures. As men sought to escape the insatiable demands of the state, they were regimented and bound to their classes and callings. The heavy hand of a centralized bureaucracy lay upon everyone, but especially upon the townsfolk. Men lost public spirit as well as individual initiative, and the failure of both was a portent of the decline of ancient civilization. These are some of the aspects of decline, but it must be remembered that in taking these measures the emperors were trying to prop up a structure which was already tottering and that these measures were therefore symptoms as well as causes of decline.

Economic decentralization was another factor. The provincials either had their own industrial skills or quickly developed them. Soon they began to manufacture goods themselves for local and even for imperial markets, and the market for Roman and Italian products shrank as competition from new provincial industries increased. Although the Empire was linked by an excellent system of roads and seaways, the methods of transportation were relatively poor. The normal difficulties of movement from one region to another were intensified by the disorders of a century of crisis. Thus high costs and risks helped promote economic decentralization, and provincial autarchy in turn fostered political disintegration.

Related to these economic and political develments was the growth of large estates cultivated by slaves and semiservile *coloni*. The free peasantry, once a major element in the strength of the Roman Empire, sank to the status of dependents. As early as the time of the Gracchi (133–121 B.C.) this evil has been apparent; now the whole process was intensified. In the end it led to the development of more or less self-sufficient large estates which in turn advanced economic decentralization.

INTELLECTUAL AND PSYCHOLOGICAL ASPECTS OF DECLINE

It is extremely difficult to assess the intellectual and psychological aspects of decline, but certain characteristics may be noted. Gibbon and others considered Christianity a major cause of the decline of ancient civilization. To be sure, the Christian attitude of resignation to adversity and the Christian emphasis upon a life to come represented a surrender to the material difficulties which beset men rather than a struggle to overcome them. But this is only a phase of the changing intellectual interests of the ancient world. As a result of the chaos and dislocation of life, there was a growing note of pessimism and despair which led to apathy and inertia. A reflection of this was the shift of interest from the here to the hereafter. We have seen how, under the stress of political, economic, and social ills, men turned to other-worldly religions, the Oriental mystery cults and Christianity. As they lost confidence in the Empire and in their own power to alter conditions, they tried to find inner security as compensation for a world which was grim and uncertain. This groping for salvation in new religions is one aspect of the psychological change; another is the resignation to the misfortunes of this world: to a totalitarian regime, a collapsing economy, and the barbarian invaders themselves. There was a "loss of nerve," as it has been called, a breakdown of morale, a defeatist mentality. Even if they had the means, men no longer had the will to maintain the Empire against invasion and dissolution. An intellectual collapse accompanied and hastened the decline of the Roman Empire.

In the final analysis, it was interaction of many factors, some hidden, some only partly discerned, some obvious, which resulted in the decline of ancient civilization. A nexus of political, social, economic, and psychological factors, each both cause and symptom of decline, accounts for the phenomenon. In time we may have more evidence and other historical methods which may enable us to determine with a greater degree of precision and accuracy the causes of historical events. Meanwhile we may study the facts and seek to establish their meaning, but we cannot always say categorically and definitely how and why great historical phenomena, like the decline of Rome, occurred.

Our description of the maladies which beset Rome must not make us think that all was unrelieved gloom. The foundations of Roman civilization endured and on them mediaeval civilization was built. In the West the Germanic kingdoms inherited many elements of Roman civilization; while in the Byzantine East, ancient civilization, adapted to Christian purposes, flourished for a thousand years. Both in the East and West the Christian church assumed many of the functions of Rome. In the period of transition which we shall now consider much was preserved and much was salvaged from the ruin of the ancient world. A continuous thread linked the old and the new, and out of the chaos and confusion the mediaeval world slowly emerged.

NO
Arther Ferrill

THE FALL OF THE ROMAN EMPIRE: THE MILITARY EXPLANATION

Although [eighteenth-century historian Edward] Gibbon's explanation of the decline and fall of Rome has had its adherents to the present day, the twentieth century has produced many alternative versions. Indeed, there have been so many that the last generation of professional ancient historians has seemed bored by the recurrent problem. One major historian has recently dismissed the fall of Rome as simply 'inevitable' and another has ridiculed as 'simplistic' the historians of the fall who proceed 'as does a detective investigating a crime, pursuing the forces responsible for it, to arraign them before the bar of history'.

Perhaps the most popular approach to the period in the last generation has been to deny the fall altogether—to emphasize the continuity between Rome and the Middle Ages. Peter Brown in his book, *The World of Late Antiquity AD 150–750* (1971), generally ignores the fall and the barbarians (or at least the implications of the word, 'barbarians'). He concentrates instead on the transformation from Roman to Byzantine history in the East and to a certain extent from Roman to early medieval history in the West. On the whole the emphasis of the 'Late Antique' school is positive and up-beat—it is on change rather than collapse and cataclysm, on spirituality in religion rather than superstition. 'Savage barbarians' and 'Germanity' have little role to play in the world of 'Late Antiquity', and Brown's approach has attracted many followers.

It is not difficult to understand the ennui now felt by historians confronted with the fall of Rome. There is a feeling of hopelessness, that no one will ever find an answer that will satisfy the majority of scholars. Nor has there been any significant 'new evidence' since Gibbon's day. There have been relatively few important literary discoveries, and, although some interesting archaeological work on the Late Empire has been undertaken, archaeologists generally are more attracted to the romantic fields of Egypt and Mesopotamia, the Minoan and Mycenaean world, and Periclean Athens.

From Arther Ferrill, *The Fall of the Roman Empire: The Military Explanation* (Thames & Hudson, 1986). Copyright © 1986 by Thames & Hudson, Ltd., London. Reprinted by permission. Notes omitted.

Another reason for discontent with the 'problem' of Rome's fall is that many of the best-known explanations, even in some instances those offered by otherwise outstanding ancient historians, are frivolous or absurd....

Likewise some historians are undoubtedly troubled by the polemical or 'topical' nature of attempts at explanation: 'reflecting the problems of those who propounded them,' wrote F. W. Walbank, 'and designed to illuminate what was dark in contemporary life.' In the fifth century Christians blamed the pagans and pagans blamed the Christians. In the twentieth century writers concerned with growing bureaucracy or immorality in modern life commonly see bureaucracy or immorality as the cause of Rome's fall. The obvious absurdity of some of the arguments seems to make little difference. Morality, in the Christian sense in which the word is normally intended, was much greater in the fourth and fifth centuries than it had been before. If immorality contributed to Rome's fall, why did it take so long?

The main line of substantial scholarly research into the fall of Rome, however, particularly in England but elsewhere as well, has emphasized that the fall of the Western Empire in the fifth century was a cataclysmic event, a sharp break in European history, and that the invasion of the barbarians was the chief act in the story. In the last two hundred years, three works in particular stand out: Gibbon's *Decline and Fall*, J. B. Bury's two-volume *History of the Later Roman Empire, 395–565* (1923), and A. H. M. Jones' multi-volume *The Later Roman Empire, 294–602* (1964). All three emphasize the role played by the barbarians in the fall of Rome. Even in languages other than English, that view has been a significant one. One of the most respected accounts of the Late Empire in French, Andre Piganiol's *L'Empire Chrétien (325–395)* (2nd ed., 1972) concludes:

> It is too easy to say that upon the arrival of the barbarians in the empire 'everything was dead, it was a powerless corpse, a body stretched out in its own blood', or that the Roman Empire in the West was not destroyed by a brutal blow, but that it was 'sleeping'.
>
> Roman civilization did not die a natural death. It was killed.

In German scholarship the age of the barbarian invasions, the so-called *Völkerwanderung*, has understandably attracted somewhat more attention, and there is a kind of nationalistic bias in favour of change rather than continuity. The idea that 'Germanity' combined with Christianity to add a strikingly new dimension to Graeco-Roman classical civilization has naturally had a strong appeal and indeed has influenced scholars outside Germany.

In many ways A. H. M. Jones' panoramic treatment of the fall of Rome is most representative of the mainline tradition. One of his greatest contributions to the problem was an important and obviously correct distinction—the Roman Empire did not fall in the fifth century: it continued to survive in the East in what we know as the Byzantine Empire until the Turkish conquest in the middle of the fifteenth century. Therefore, when we speak of the fall of Rome, a perfectly legitimate expression as long as everyone understands exactly what is meant by it, we refer only to the western half of the Roman Empire, and any explanation of the fall of the West must take into account the survival of the East.

'These facts are important,' Jones wrote, 'for they demonstrate that the empire did not, as some modern historians have suggested, totter into its grave from senile decay, impelled by a gentle push from the barbarians. Most of the internal weaknesses which these historians stress were common to both halves of the empire.' If Christianity weakened the Empire internally, since the religion was stronger and more divisive in the East, why did the West fall and the East continue to stand? The evils of bureaucracy, of social rigidity, of the economic system, were all present in the East as well as the West.

The main difference, as Jones accurately saw it, was that 'down to the end of the fifth century' the East was 'strategically less vulnerable' and 'subjected to less pressure from external enemies.' In short, the barbarian invasion of the West was the main cause of the fall of Rome. The Western emperors of the fifth century could not stop attacks from both the Rhine and the Danube whereas the Eastern emperor more easily held Constantinople, a superbly fortified capital. Trouble with Persia threatened the East, but Romans for various reasons found the Persians easier to deal with than the barbarians. For one thing Persians were not migratory. They had their own internal problems, and they could be dealt with according to the well developed protocol of ancient diplomacy....

It is quite possible that many significant features of Roman life survived the overthrow of the last emperor in the West, Romulus Augustulus, in 476. Obviously they did in the East, and in the West too one would expect to see major Roman survivals in the economy, in society and in law. The advocates of change are much too strident in their insistence that the fall

of Rome destroyed everything Roman. Likewise, the advocates of continuity all too often ignore the obvious fact that not everything survived the barbarian invasions of the fifth century, that indeed dramatically significant changes occurred in the West from AD 400 to 500.

In fact the Roman Empire of the West did fall. Not every aspect of the life of Roman subjects was changed by that, but the fall of Rome as a political entity was one of the major events of the history of western man. It will simply not do to call that fall a myth or to ignore its historical significance merely by focussing on those aspects of Roman life that survived the fall in one form or another. At the opening of the fifth century a massive army, perhaps more than 200,000 strong, stood at the service of the Western emperor and his generals. In 476 it was gone. The destruction of Roman military power in the fifth century AD was the obvious cause of the collapse of Roman government in the West....

THE FALL OF ROME

When the adherents of the 'Late Antique' school use the word 'transformation' in describing the fall of Rome, they mean it as an explanation as well as a description. The transformation they see from Rome to the Middle Ages developed over centuries, not years. Yet the fall of Rome in the West was more than a process— it was also an event, one that occurred rather suddenly, in the same sense at least in which the fall of the British Empire after World War II required about a generation but can nevertheless be said to have been sudden.

If one takes 476 as the date of the fall, and looks back merely a hundred years to 376, one can see an empire still strong, still as large as the Empire of Augustus, still respected by its foes across the imperial frontiers. Furthermore, it was defended by an army that continued to fight effectively despite the catastrophe in Persia under Julian, a strategic blow that cannot be laid at the feet of the legions.

On the other hand, 376 was itself an important year in Roman history. It was then that the Visigoths, driven by the pressure of the Huns and the Ostrogoths, crossed the Danube with the emperor's permission to settle permanently in Roman territory. Thus began a series of invasions (for the crossing of the Danube soon turned into an invasion) that led in a hundred years to the fall of the Western Roman Empire. It is easy with hindsight to regard that fall as inevitable, to emphasize the vulnerability and fragility of the Roman Empire, to see in the fall of Rome what has been called, in another context, 'the weary Titan syndrome'. One cannot argue, as in the case of modern Britain, that the loss of empire 'cushioned' Rome's fall in the world. The Empire had been so inextricably identified with Rome itself that the fall of the Empire *was* the fall of Rome.

To see Roman history from Marcus Aurelius on, as the story of a troubled giant, as so many historians do, a decaying empire, the victim of 'cultural and world-political Angst', is to miss the point. Some historians, recognizing the common fallacy, turn the problem around and ask why the Empire survived so long. Both tendencies, however, have the same effect—to direct attention away from a consideration of the factors that led to the disappearance of the Western Roman Empire in the last half of the fifth century; one by seeking the causes in the much too distant past and the other by accepting the fact as inevitable.

The Roman Empire on the eve of Adrianople was not obviously on a downhill course. Nor had Roman citizens lost faith in their destiny to rule the world. The Empire was strong, despite a recent defeat in Persia, and it continued to show remarkable strength in the devastating thirty or so years between the defeat at Adrianople and the sack of Rome by Alaric. Since the days of the Punic Wars the strategic strength of Rome had consisted to a certain extent in the ability of the Empire to suffer tactical defeats in the field and yet mobilize new forces to continue the fighting.

Even after AD 410 some of that resilience remained, but there was one difference, particularly in the West. Rome had almost stopped producing its own soldiers, and those it did draw into military service were no longer trained in the ancient tactics of close-order formation though they tried to fight that way. Many historians have argued, either directly or more often by emphasizing other causes, that the fall of Rome was not primarily a military phenomenon. In fact, it was exactly that. After 410 the emperor in the West could no longer project military power to the ancient frontiers. That weakness led immediately to the loss of Britain and within a generation to the loss of Africa. One need not produce a string of decisive battles in order to demonstrate a military collapse. The shrinkage of the imperial frontiers from 410 to 440 was directly the result of military conquests by barbarian forces. To be sure, the loss of strategic resources in money, material and manpower compounded the mere loss of territory, and made military defence of the remainder of the Empire even more difficult. It is simply perverse, however, to argue that Rome's strategic problems in the 440s, 50s and 60s were primarily the result of financial and political difficulties or of long-term trends such as gradual depopulation.

The modern historian must keep in mind the fact that Rome in the East did not fall, and any explanation of the fall of Rome must also account for its survival in Byzantium. Why was the East to marshal its military resources, to survive the barbarian invasions and to emerge under Justinian in the sixth century with a burst of military power, sufficient to reconquer, at least temporarily, parts of the West? Some specifically military explanations can be set aside. Recruitment in the Late Empire was difficult, but too much has been made of imperial legislation on that score. Even in the great days of the Roman Empire, for example in the last years of Augustus, recruitment could be a problem during military crises. In the fourth and fifth centuries it was no greater a problem in the West than in the East, at least not until western difficulties were highly exacerbated by military and territorial losses. The strategic strength of the East behind the impenetrable walls of Constantinople is often emphasized as a factor in the survival of the Byzantine Empire, but one must look also at the elements of weakness in the West.

In fact, of course, the sack of Rome, the loss of Britain and of Africa, and parts of Gaul and Spain, dealt heavy blows to the military capacity of the Western emperor. If one begins the story of Rome's fall with the year 440, the collapse of the West and not of the East is easy enough to explain. By 440 western forces were much weaker than those of the East. That was not true, however, on the last day of the year 406, the day Vandals,

Suebi and Alamanni crossed the frozen Rhine and moved into Gaul. In 406, on paper, western power was as great as eastern. Stilicho had driven Alaric and Radagaisus out of Italy. Indeed on behalf of the West he had dealt more effectively with Alaric than eastern generals had done. Yet in the short period, 407–10, the West received an ultimately fatal blow. After 410 it was never again militarily as strong as the East. Barbarians were permanently established in Gaul and Spain, and Britain had been lost.

One could argue, as I am inclined to do, that even after 410 the emperor of the West had not lost all military options, that he might yet have restored Roman military power, if not in Britain, at least in the rest of the Western Empire. But military losses in 407–10 were sufficient to make a major difference between the strategic, projective military power of the Eastern and Western emperors. Those few years constitute a turning point after which it is no longer necessary to explain why the West fell and the East survived.

Why, then, did the West do so badly in 407–10? To a certain extent, as we have seen, the strategic strength of the East contributed to the fall of the West. Constantinople was heavily defended. No barbarian tribe could possibly hope to storm those walls. Furthermore, the emperor in the East was better able to afford the heavy subsidies barbarian leaders demanded in the years after Adrianople, though in fact the West also paid a heavy monetary price for peace.

Perhaps the most popular approach to the explanation of Rome's fall, if we can set aside the examination of those long-term causes such as depopulation, race mixture, political and economic deterioration, lead poisoning and other fashionable theories, has been to find a scapegoat, to see in an error or errors of human judgment the fatal mistake that caused the tragedy. Although this approach has often been ridiculed in recent times, it is not without merit. Leaders do matter. Strategic decisions produce successful or unsuccessful results. The weight of history, in the form of long-term trends, may impose limitations on the military mind, but a good general or political leader will bear the burden and solve his strategic problems one way or another.

The Emperor Honorius has been asked by ancient and modern historians alike to take far too much of the blame for Rome's fall. Partly that is because Rome suffered its great humiliation in 407–10 under his rule, and since he did not prevent it, he must undoubtedly be held responsible for it. As citizens we apply this kind of standard to our present leaders, and it is perhaps not unreasonable to do the same for leaders of the past. On the other hand, if it is possible to be right and still lose, Honorius may have done just that. He does not deserve the criticism he uniformly gets for doing nothing, since doing nothing was almost certainly, for him, an 'active' or conscious strategy, not simply negligence, a strategy that might in fact have worked if someone had not opened a gate to Rome for Alaric's Visigoths in August 410.

Stilicho's role in the fall of the West is harder to assess, and he has had vigorous attackers and defenders. That he was much too interested in affairs in Constantinople rather than in Italy is certain. Whether he can also be accused of having let Alaric escape on several occasions when the barbarian leader might have been crushed is impossible to determine on the basis of the inadequate surviving evidence. To those who see the fall of Rome as a matter of trends,

Stilicho's efforts are of no concern. Presumably if he had not left Alaric free to sack Rome, someone else would have sacked it. How can even Rome fight trends? But in fact the fate of the Western Roman Empire might have been very different had events in 407–10 taken another course. Insofar as human agency might have prevented them, the failure of Stilicho is significant. His inability to shape a better future for the Western Roman Empire was much more the result of actual mistaken judgment (leading to his execution in 408) than was the failure of Honorius. Stilicho was wrong; Honorius was unlucky.

It is also true, however, that the army itself underwent significant deterioration between 378 and 410, more so in the West than in the East. In the fourth century the western army had been the better one. It was the eastern army that had been defeated in Persia and at Adrianople, but at the Frigid River in 394 Theodosius had beaten the western army with the help of twenty thousand Visigoths, who attacked Arbogast and Eugenius in line of column suffering extraordinarily heavy losses (50 per cent). The loss at the Frigidus undoubtedly demoralized the western army to a certain extent, but it must have been much more humiliated by its treatment at the hands of Stilicho, who commanded it from 395 to 408.

At that time there was a reaction in the East against the use of Germans in the Roman army, but in the West Stilicho imposed the Theodosian policy of barbarization. First, with the western army in the Balkans he failed to crush Alaric on at least two occasions, and then, during the successful campaigns in Italy from 401 to 405 against Alaric (who got away again, twice) and Radagaisus, Stilicho relied heavily on barbarian troops. His use of barbarians became a matter of controversy and contributed to his downfall in 408. For that reason 'barbarization' in this period is often treated as a political problem (which it was), and little consideration has been given to the probable effect the policy had on the proud army of the West.

There is no way of knowing, unfortunately, to what extent the central, mobile army in Italy, by 408, was a traditional Roman army and to what extent it had become overwhelmed by barbarian influences. Possibly, if the resources of Britain and Gaul had been united with the army of Italy in the crisis of 408–10, it might have been possible to have defeated Alaric again, but the revolt of Constantine prevented that kind of cooperation, and Honorius decided to pursue a strategy of exhaustion rather than to bring Alaric to battle. Such a policy was extremely humiliating for the army. General Sir John Hackett has said: 'An army's good qualities are best shown when it is losing.' To fight on in the face of certain defeat requires much more than courage. But the army of the West in the crisis of 408–10 was not allowed to fight at all, and after what it had suffered earlier at the hands of Stilicho, this was the crushing blow. Never again was the emperor of the West the military equal of his eastern counterpart.

In the aftermath of 410 Constantius and Aëtius had done the best they could to maintain Rome's reduced position in the West. Constantius was the better strategist of the two, and his skillful use of naval power did give the regime, now in Ravenna, a new lease of life. Aëtius was unfortunately too interested in Gaul at the expense of Italy, Spain and particularly Africa. The loss of Carthage was a double blow to Rome since the emperor in the West had relied heavily on African grain and because the resources of the African city now strengthened the Vandal kingdom. Declining revenues and territory made recruitment difficult, and the true Roman contingent of the army that fought Attila at Châlons was the object of ridicule. In the last twenty years of the Western Empire, after the death of Valentinian III, the central government in Italy relied exclusively on barbarians until the latter finally, in 476, put one of their own officers in as king and abolished the emperorship in the West.

It is clear that after 410 the Roman army no longer had any special advantage, tactically, over barbarian armies—simply because the Roman army had been barbarized. Hans Delbrück has argued that Roman strength had always been strategic rather than tactical, that man for man Roman armies were no better than Germanic ones:

> Vis-a-vis civilized peoples, barbarians have the advantage of having at their disposal the warlike power of unbridled animal instincts, of basic toughness. Civilization refines the human being, makes him more sensitive, and in doing so it decreases his military worth, not only his bodily strength but also his physical courage.

Delbrück goes on to say that Roman tactical organization and training merely 'equalized the situation'.

This is stuff and nonsense, as careful reading of du Picq might have revealed. Rome's army had always been small, relative to the population of the Empire, because Roman training and discipline gave it an unparalleled advantage in tactically effective, close-order formation. By 451, to judge from the speech Attila gave to the Huns at the battle of

Châlons, the feeble remnant of the once-proud legions still fought in the ancient formation, but apparently without the training and discipline. Without them, close order was worse than no order at all. Romans could be expected to huddle behind their screen of shields; Visigoths and Alans would do the fighting. As the western army became barbarized, it lost its tactical superiority, and Rome fell to the onrush of barbarism.

POSTSCRIPT

Did the Roman Empire Collapse Under Its Own Weight?

As Ferrill points out, historians of the Roman Empire have recently chosen to emphasize the points of political and social continuity between Rome and its successor states, thereby removing much of the impetus from the debate over precisely why the Roman Empire fell. If the empire merely transformed itself into a different variant of social organization, the notion of a "fall" seems to lose all meaning. Peter Brown's *The World of Late Antiquity* (Thames & Hudson, 1971) remains the best statement of this thesis.

It is interesting to note the effect that the loss of Western European empires in the post–World War II era might have had on historiographical discussion of the fall of Rome. Certainly, the loss of will to maintain an empire, which afflicted both Britain and France in the late 1940s and early 1950s, had its counterpart in fifth-century Rome, as did the British and French decline of military power. Perhaps the loss of imperial pretensions by the Western European nations helps explain the concomitant loss of interest in—or the denial of—the fall of the Roman Empire 15 centuries earlier.

In any event, one of the liveliest contemporary writers on the Roman Empire is Michael Grant, whose *Fall of the Roman Empire* (Macmillan, 1990) forms an excellent overview of the subject. Classic interpretations may be found in J. B. Bury's *History of the Later Roman Empire* (Dover, 1958) and A. H. M. Jones's *Decline of the Ancient World* (Holt, Rinehart & Winston, 1966). Andre Piganiol, in *L'Empire Chretien* (Presses Universitaires, 1947), supports Ferrill's contention that the Roman Empire was, in fact, killed by barbarian invasions.

More specialized, and certainly more controversial, interpretations have been advanced by Michael Rostovtzeff, who asserts that the empire succumbed to a class war between the aristocracy and an alliance of soldiers and peasants in *Social and Economic History of the Roman Empire* (Clarendon Press, 1926), and Tenney Frank, whose essay "Race Mixture in the Roman Empire," *American Historical Review* (July 1916) puts forth the thesis that debilitating eastern influences sapped the will of Rome to survive.

ISSUE 7

Does the Ninth Century Mark the End of the Dark Ages?

YES: Kevin Reilly, from *The West and the World: A Topical History of Civilization* (Harper & Row, 1980)

NO: Joseph Dahmus, from *The Middle Ages: A Popular History* (Doubleday, 1968)

ISSUE SUMMARY

YES: Kevin Reilly, a world historian and textbook author, paints a portrait of the postclassical period as dark and bloody and argues that it established a tradition of violence in Western civilization.

NO: Joseph Dahmus, a professor of medieval history, portrays the period as a not-so-dark age filled with cultural, political, and religious advancement.

In the fifth century A.D., the slowly decaying empire of Rome finally collapsed. Subsequently, the Roman Empire in the West was divided up amongst various barbarian rulers: Visigoths to the west, Ostrogoths in the east, and Franks and Saxons in the north. The fall of Rome ushered in the beginning of what later was to be called the Middle Ages. In particular, the years from 476 to around 1000 have been popularly referred to as the Dark Ages, first, because we know so little about these chaotic years, and second, because of the bleak outlook and bloody nature of the period's politics and society.

It took several decades for the barbarian kingdoms of western Europe to consolidate, but nearly from the beginning one tribe, the Franks, came to dominate the others. Much of their success can be attributed to their first and most successful king, Clovis Merowech, founder of the Merovingian dynasty. After successfully defeating what remained of the Roman legions in Gaul, Clovis went on to defeat and incorporate into his empire the Lombards, the Visigoths, and the other lesser barbarian kingdoms. His conversion to Roman Catholicism ensured the survival of the last remaining institution of Rome, the Church; provided for the destruction of the Arian version of Christianity; and guaranteed the prominence of the pope as a spiritual leader in the West. The West might have been reunified at this time had Frankish tradition not dictated that Clovis divide his holdings amongst his numerous sons, who then fought each other to gain further riches and prestige. The years following Clovis were violent, chaotic, brutal, and bloody.

Adding to the turmoil of this time was the rise of expansionist Islam in Arabia. Muslim warriors, or Saracens, conquered Palestine, annexed North Africa, crossed over to Gibraltar, and came to dominate the Iberian Peninsula. Muslim raids were launched from North Africa and Spain, at one point sacking Rome and threatening the southern frontier of Frankish Europe north of the Pyrenees. In 732 a mayor of the palace of one of the Do-Nothing Merovingian warlords organized an army to resist the Muslim incursions and decisively defeated the invaders at the Battle of Poitiers, sometimes referred to as the Battle of Tours. This successful warrior leader, Charles Martel, became the founder of the Carolingian dynasty, whose most famous and successful member was Charles the Great, or Charlemagne. Some historians mark Charlemagne's reign as the end of the Dark Ages. Not only did Charlemagne complete the reunification of the Frankish Empire started by his father, Pepin the Short, but he also encouraged and patronized a cultural rebirth in architecture (Romanesque), political organization, learning, and letters. Known today as the Carolingian Renaissance, the period exhibited Charlemagne's self-conscious desire to establish himself and to be recognized as the restorer of the Roman Empire in the West.

Another aspect of the early Middle Ages that cannot be discounted is the overwhelming role played by the Church in its rise to spiritual and political dominion. The acceptance of Roman Catholicism by the Franks allowed for the adoption of uniform codes of morality among the rulers of western Europe, a shared sense of belonging to a common cause, and, consequently, a measure of stability that ultimately ended the Dark Ages.

However, the assumption that *Dark Ages* is an appropriate term for this period has been challenged by historians who see these times as dynamic and progressive intellectually and technologically. Undoubtedly, between the sixth and the ninth centuries enormous changes occured in the methods of agricultural production. The triennial system, whereby one-third of an estate's arable land would be left idle during each growing season, allowing for the restoration of depleted nutrients in the soil, increased crop yield. The increased availability of iron tools also facilitated the farmers' task, as did the crank, which allowed water and animal power to be used in the milling of grain. Along with this, the nailed iron horseshoe, the tandem harness, and the horse collar increased the use of animal power, allowing for larger cultivated fields and more food produced by fewer people. All of this had social consequences, since some were freed from agricultural production and given time to produce the artisanal products that became the foundation for a revival of trade, the establishment of permanent markets, and, eventually, the growth of towns.

In the following selections, Kevin Reilly and Joseph Dahmus focus on the two different views of the early Middle Ages. One, the establishment of a tradition of violence in Western civilization; the other, the development of political order and intellectual pursuit.

YES
Kevin Reilly

VIOLENCE AND VENGEANCE: BARBARIANS, KNIGHTS, AND CRUSADERS

CHILDREN OF ATTILA: THE BARBARIANS

All white Americans are descended (at least in good part) from the barbarian tribes that swept over Rome and Europe from the steppes of Asia. These ancestors were a pretty unruly bunch. The Roman gentleman Sidonius Apollinaris boasted that he would rather "have braved destitution, fire, sword and pestilence" than submitted to the Visigoths or Gauls. But when these tribes moved into Italy, he resigned himself to rub shoulders with their unkempt chieftains whose hair smelled of rancid butter and whose mouths emitted odors of onion and garlic and strange Germanic sounds.

One of the best of these chiefs, according to their own storytellers, was "good king Guntramn," a leader of the Franks (who settled in what is now France). Guntramn could be as jovial and lustful as the next guy but "when he was with his bishops he conducted himself like one of them." In fact he was made a saint by the early church. The only thing you might say against Guntramn is that he had a taste for murder. Among his many victims were two physicians who were unable to heal his wife.

The Lombard king Alboin, who brought the tribe from the Danube into Italy, killed the king of the Gepids and married his daughter. He might have created a unified Lombard state in northern Italy (in the sixth century) if he had been more sensitive. Paul the Deacon tells a story of Alboin offering his wife some wine in a goblet that was made from her father's skull. It seems she didn't get the joke. Paul tells us that the "silly woman" had the old jokester assassinated.

It is possible that Guntramn and Alboin were not unusual. One seventh-century historian of the tribal invasions has a mother of a barbarian king advise her son: "If you want to accomplish something and make a name for yourself, destroy everything that others have built and massacre everyone that you have conquered; for you are not able to build better monuments

From Kevin Reilly, *The West and the World: A Topical History of Civilization* (Harper & Row, 1980), pp. 206–214, 216–221. Copyright © 1980 by Kevin Reilly. Reprinted by permission of Addison Wesley Educational Publishers, Inc.

than those constructed by your predecessors and there is no more noble accomplishment for you to make your name." Whether or not any mother's son ever heard those words, they certainly express a part of the barbarian consciousness. The leaders of nomadic tribes were particularly sensitive to the issue of proving their abilities in war: courage, strength, and even cruelty must have ranked high among tribal values. The fortunes of these tribes, especially in hard times, was often a direct product of their capacities for destroying and taking. And throughout their lives they were trained to hunt, to wield a sword, to carry out lightning invasions on horseback, and to bring booty and slaves back to camp.

The tribes which penetrated deepest into the Roman Empire were probably less fierce than those which were pushing them from the steppes. (The earliest invaders closest to Rome were actually often semicivilized tribes "retreating" across the Alps.) Even the barbarians told stories about the greater cruelty of other tribes further away from civilization. The Huns, according to Ammien Marcellin were the least civilized and the most feared:

> Their ferocity knew no bounds. They branded their own children's cheeks so that they grew old beardless. These stocky, thick-necked creatures cooked no food, but gorged themselves on wild roots and the raw flesh of the first animal they saw. They had no shelters, no burials, and only rat skin clothing that they wore until it disintegrated. It was said that they were nailed to their horses. They did not dismount to eat or drink. Often they stayed mounted to sleep and dream.

Our tribal ancestors were certainly "barbarians." The word is appropriate.

They were barbarians in the sense that the Greeks and Romans used the word: they spoke strange "bar bar" like sounds. But, more significantly, they were barbarians in the two modern senses of the word: they were both violent and primitive (or, more precisely, at a preurban state of development). The brutality of their lives and their lack of the tools, knowledge, arts, or comforts of more advanced city societies are enough to warrant the description "barbarian."

We do not use the word "barbarian" in order to make moral judgments about these people. Some of the early Christians and Romans did. It was enough for some of the educated witnesses to the invasions to point out that the tribes were pagans or Germanic: that was just like saying that the invaders were morally inhuman. This attitude was particularly common in the Roman aristocracy and among the bishops of the church. But at least one monk in Marseilles around the year 440, who called himself Salvien, gives us a different view.

It is true, Salvien wrote in a book that has somehow survived, that the Saxon people are cruel, the Franks untrustworthy, and the Huns immodest. "But," he asks rhetorically, "are their vices any more sinful than our own? Is the lewdness of the Huns more criminal than ours? Is the treachery of the Franks to be blamed more than our own? Is the drunken German more reprehensible than a drunken Christian? Is a greedy barbarian worse than a greedy Christian? Is the deceit of a Hun or of a Gepid so extraordinary?"

The barbarians, Salvien reminds us, had no monopoly on brutality or sin. In fact, they were not much different from the Roman authorities that they displaced. Their invasion was successful because Roman society had become as violent and insecure as nomadic society. From the perspective of the poor in Roman society the barbarians were sometimes preferable masters:

> The castaway Roman poor, the grieving widows, the orphans under foot, even many of the well-born and educated Romans took refuge among their enemies. They sought Roman humanity among the barbarians so that they would not perish from barbarian inhumanity among the Romans. They were different from the barbarians in their manners, their language, and the smell of their clothes, but these differences were preferable to injustice and cruelty. They went to live among the barbarians on all sides, and never regretted it. They preferred to live free under the appearance of slavery, than to be slaves under the guise of liberty. Roman citizenship, once highly esteemed and bought at a high price, is today not only worthless, but despised. Those who did not flee were forced to become barbarians by the persecution of Roman law or the anarchy of Roman lawlessness. We call them rebels and lost men, but it is we who have forced them to become criminals.

Salvien says a lot. Rome had become as violent as the barbarian world. The invasions were accompanied by the revolt of the Roman oppressed and dispossessed. The Roman Empire wasn't assassinated. It committed suicide. At least (since civilizations are not mortal), the owners of Rome allowed their possession to be mangled beyond repair.

Europe was born in this marriage of settled barbarian and barbarized Roman poor. The barbarian had learned that you get from life only what you take from others. The Roman poor had learned that there is no peace or security when a few wealthy families take everything from everyone else. Neither the barbarian nor the Roman knew anything of freedom or the peaceful life. The only world they were allowed to have was chaotic and violent —and even that had to be taken by force.

Life meant very little in early European society. Few writers were concerned with the hardships of the common people, but a few examples taken at random give us an idea of what it must have been like in the first few centuries after the barbarian migration.

One writer, Gregory of Tours, tells a story about the people of Orléans and Blois looting and burning the houses of Chateaudun and Chartres, massacring many of the people, and then receiving the same treatment from the survivors. Another, Gregory I, writes of the tyranny of the tax collectors forcing the inhabitants of Corsica to sell their children and seek refuge among the "unspeakable Lombards." Another, the Venerable Bede, describes how after three years of drought and famine one group of forty or fifty people "exhausted by hunger, went to a cliff top above the sea and flung themselves over, holding hands."

The neutral language of the law codes expresses the cheapness of life: "the fine for cutting off someone's hand, foot, eye, or nose is 100 sous; but only 63 if the hand is still hanging; for cutting off a thumb 50 sous, but only 30 if it is still hanging; for cutting off an index finger the fine is 35 sous; two fingers together is 35 sous; three fingers together is 50 sous."

Written law (like the excerpt from the Salic code above) had little meaning if you fell into the hands of the enemies. When Saint Leger, the bishop of Autun, was captured by an enemy palace mayor in 677, they cut out his tongue; then they forced him to walk barefoot in a pool of sharpened rocks that cut like spikes; then they pierced his eyes. The stories are endless. Another tells of some unfortunate soul being tortured for three days and then tied to the rear of a vicious horse who was whipped until it bolted. Others were killed by being "drawn and quartered": attached to two horses who ran in opposite directions. Cruelty was limitless.

THE BARBARIANS CIVILIZE THEMSELVES

One thing that is indisputable is that the chaos of the barbarian invasions gradually abated. By the sixth and seventh centuries, the number of invasions declined and most of the nomadic tribes had settled down to an agricultural life. The Goths who had terrorized Roman legions had produced a fairly elaborate culture by the sixth century. One of them, Jordanes, an historian, could boast that the Goths had a king who was a philosopher and scientist and that they had enough professors of philosophy to rival ancient Greece. He exaggerates, of course, but these are not exaggerations that would please a real barbarian.

By the eighth century the sudden terror of barbarian life had given way to the stable regularity of farming, collecting taxes, and making laws. The Franks had established a kingdom with relatively fixed boundaries and laws that was healthy enough to ward off an invading Moslem army from Spain. By 800 Charlemagne had himself crowned by the pope as "Emperor of the Romans," and this was not a completely foolish analogy: his empire included all of France and a good part of current Germany, Austria, and Italy (including Rome). Though he himself could not write, he gathered many of the leading European intellectuals (monks) to his court. One of

them, Alcuin, could tell Charlemagne: "If your intentions are carried out, it may be that a new Athens will rise in Frankland."

A new series of invasions from the north (which we'll turn to soon) were to cut short the Carolingian summer of high culture and established law. But stability and prosperity had conditioned even the common peasant to demand "justice" where an ancestor may have needed "blood." The customs of the people were no longer those of barbarians.

Barbarian morality had been based on the need for vengeance. Tribal families were often ripped apart by feuds that continued indefinitely. When an affront was committed against one's family or tribe, honor required that it be avenged. It was impossible to sleep until the wrong had been righted with blood. Gradually, settled barbarian chiefs (and later, kings) were able to insist on a legal settlement of tribal disputes. Money or something of value became a symbolic substitute for blood vengeance. The excerpt from the Salic code (which we quoted disparagingly before) was actually a step toward a less violent society. "An eye for an eye" satisfied the basest human passions for vengeance, but (as the Christian monks taught) the motives of an assailant were also important. What was the point of blinding another merely to even the score? One life could not be brought back by the loss of another, and (as the tribal elder, king, or administrator well knew) the score was never even: the feud or vendetta meant continual warfare and prevented the rise of an orderly state.

Thus, the vendetta was gradually replaced by a system of "blood prices" for various kinds of mutilation and murder. These fines depended on the extent of the damage and the "blood worth" of the victim. The result, as the Lombard king

Rothbari explained at the end of his own list of fines, was that "for all of the above-mentioned wounds we have provided a higher compensation than our forebears, so that when such compensation is paid, all hostility will cease."

The blood price should be judged a step beyond barbarism as it made family feuds less frequent as they became more expensive. But even the notion of a blood price was barbaric from the perspective of the Christian church. It limited violence but withheld blame. As long as the price was paid, the matter was settled. The church welcomed the substitution of the blood price for the vendetta but still insisted that a moral issue was involved. Churchmen compiled books of God's punishments for acts of violence. These acts were seen as sins, not just temporary imbalances in the social order. Eventually, the Lombards and other tribes viewed the spilling of blood and taking of life as moral wrongs which should not be committed—even if compensation were possible. This more "moral" attitude toward violence was still not based on any modern humane faith in the sacredness of life. It was based only on the fear of God's punishment. Gradually, the barbarian indifference to death was replaced by a feeling of "shame" for committing antisocial acts. In turn, shame, which was only produced by social pressure, was eventually transformed into Christian feelings of personal guilt. The history of the human conscience has not yet been (and may never be) written, but it seems quite likely that as barbarians became settled, civilized, and Christian, they developed greater capacities for shame and then guilt. Even guilt became increasingly internalized. In medieval Europe guilt was little more than the verdict rendered by the Christian king or his judge. In modern society guilt is still the verdict of the jury, but it is much more: it is the massive internal regulator which responds to so much of what we do.

From indifference to shame to guilt, from vendetta to blood price to responsibility, as barbarian society became more settled, as the individual became more responsible for his or her behavior, as laws and procedure replaced the gut need for vengeance, European society became less violent. Certainly we have evolved in these directions since the Middle Ages.

We have not given up the old ways completely, however. The change has sometimes been agonizingly slow, and in many ways we have only begun to give up our barbarian past. The family feud was a way of life in Appalachian America only decades ago. The vendetta is still common in Italy, Eastern Europe, and other poor regions of the developed world. Banditry, secret societies (like the Mafia), and vigilantes are still more important than the law and the justices of the peace in some relatively "modern" areas. And besides these remnants of the old world in the new, the newest, most developed countries (like the United States) often display a considerable appetite for violence.

The remnants of old world barbarism are easier to understand. The Sicilian home of the Mafia has not changed all that much in the last thousand years, neither has the climate of Latin American revolutions and Indian massacres, nor has the culture of social oppression and natural catastrophe in much of the developing world. These examples remind us that this sort of violence—even in the barbarian period—was the natural life of "hardship society."

Charlemagne's empire was never able to overcome hardship. Its thriving culture and law were only a hint of what was possible. That possibility was shattered by a new series of invasions: Hungarian nomads from the steppes, Viking pirates from the north, and Moslem cavalry from the south.

CIVILIZED MILITARISM: KNIGHTHOOD AND FEUDALISM

The violence of the ninth-century invasions was met by the militarization of European society. We call it "feudalism" and recall images of knights in shining armor riding on large horses and jousting in tournaments with long lances. We don't normally think of medieval knighthood as a process of militarization. Nor do we usually think of it as a response to a particular threat in a particular period. We probably have Hollywood to thank for the image of King Arthur, Lancelot, Camelot, and European knighthood that emphasizes its romance and fun and overlooks the immediate military necessity for its rise. It should have become clear by now that medieval Europeans could not afford to create expensive social institutions for fun. Knighthood, or the existence of aristocratic heavy-armored cavalry, was a most expensive social institution. The armor and horses were expensive investments for the aristocracy, and the development of such an army was a considerable burden on the peasantry (who had to increase their own production to pay for these defenders). Knighthood developed as a response to the new invasions of Hungarians, Moslems, and Vikings....

Feudalism was the way to raise an armored cavalry. It involved the exchange of land for the military service of knights. Eventually, most of the chiefs, kings, and large landowners of Europe were forced to exchange portions of their land for such military service. Church lands were not enough. After particularly devastating invasions (like some of the Viking raids) new feudal relationships were the only means for both defense and food. Much of today's European aristocracy can trace its origins back to the land gifts of this period. The peasants, as always, marched on foot, but even they received the benefits of protection that the heavily armored aristocracy provided....

TRADING AND RAIDING: THE VIKINGS

The Vikings are one of the most colorful "warrior societies" of European history. Between the eighth and eleventh centuries Viking ships and soldiers terrorized village settlements from Ireland to Russia, fought and traded in the cities of the Byzantine and Moslem empires, and established European outposts across the Atlantic Ocean. Not too much was known about the origins of these Norse when they first struck out from Scandinavia to conquer the English island of Lindisfarne in 793. Their ancestors may have been the "German" tribe which the Roman historian Tacitus called the Suiones in the first century. Tacitus remarks that the Suiones "are strong not only in arms and men but also in their fleets," that their curious ships have "a prow at both ends" but no sail, and that they can be found with their slaves along the ocean and rivers in search of wealth. Apparently, the Suiones were more settled than the nomadic tribes that Tacitus described. We hear no mention of them after Tacitus until the sixth century when the Gothic historian Jordanes reports that the inhabitants of Scandinavia are unusually ferocious and tall. It was not until the end of the eighth century that the European tribes and descendants of the Romans had firsthand experience with the Norse. By that time the Scandinavians had improved their ships, added sails, and realized the potential plunder to be gained from a more settled Europe.

"Out of the north an evil shall break forth." The warning of the prophet Jeremiah must have rung in the ears of the Christian monks at Lindisfarne when the Norse sailed into history in 793. The English scholar Alcuin, who was staying in France at the court of Charlemagne, expressed the shock of European Christians at the sudden "pagan" attack. "Never before had such a terror appeared in Britain," he wrote, than the invasion of Lindisfarne by the Vikings. The Church of St. Cuthbert was robbed of its treasures and "spattered with the blood of the priests of God."

In a matter of decades the Vikings had conquered much of England, Scotland, and Ireland. They came usually as pirates. They murdered unarmed monks, looted sanctuaries, plundered the libraries that had preserved the literary heritage of the ancient world, and burned what they could not carry away. The booty they sought was more precious than the literary achievements of Charlemagne's civilization. They took gold and jewels, valuable objects that they might trade, and they raped and enslaved the wives and daughters of their victims. Sailing first from Norway, and then from Denmark and Sweden, these pirates terrorized the inhabitants of the British Isles especially throughout the ninth century.

In time, the terror of the Norse became modified or institutionalized. In 865 the English began paying a yearly ransom to their Scandinavian overlords which was kind of a "protection" payment called the *Danegeld* (money for the Danes). Much of central England was placed under the Danish king and administered as the *Danelaw*. Scandinavians established their own villages (like Dublin) in occupied territory or set up colonies in existing towns. These settlements were sometimes fortified encampments used for further pirate expeditions, but gradually became more like administrative and trading centers.

Perhaps there has always been a hazy line between raiding and trading, or maybe the sons of raiders are the ones who can afford to trade. Whatever the case, there is evidence for both continual piracy mixed with trading in Viking history and a gradually increasing emphasis on trade instead of raids. Piracy certainly continued throughout the Viking age, but the raids of the tenth and eleventh century up the rivers of France, along the coast of Spain, and into the Mediterranean Sea often became trading missions. This was especially true when the Vikings established fairly permanent colonies, as in Normandy in northern France and on the island of Sicily in the Mediterranean. It's safer to pillage distant ports than to plunder a neighbor.

Viking expansion was not all piracy and business, even in Western Europe, as the examples of colonization indicate. But colonization was usually a secondary activity in populated Western Europe. It was the major type of Scandinavian expansion in the east along the long rivers of Russia and in the west beyond the edge of the world.

Russia is, of course, the land of the Rus. The Rus were the Swedish colonists who began settling on the river trade routes between Scandinavia and the Byzantine capital at Constantinople in the ninth century. There the Swedes met some of the older inhabitants, Slavs (whose name reminds us that the Vikings took them as slaves) and Asians. The meetings must have often been violent, but eventually the Swedish towns at Novgorod and Kiev lost their Viking flavor and became the trading centers of the emerging Russian state. From these towns the Rus learned of the magnificence of the Byzantine Empire. The Rus were too weak to pose a serious threat to Constantinople, but Viking courage and military ability were famous enough for the Byzantine emperors to recruit these Rus for a special palace guard and as mercenaries in the Byzantine army. Meanwhile the Rus traded northern furs, honey, amber, wax, and captured slaves in exchange for the fine textiles, spices, wines, and luxuries of the Byzantine Empire at Constantinople and the Moslem Empire at Baghdad. According to a Moslem visitor, the Rus merchants would pray: "O Lord, I have come from distant parts with so many girls, so many sable furs.... Please send me a merchant who has many *dinars* and *dirhems*, and who will trade favorably with me without too much bartering."

While the Swedish Vikings turned piracy into colonization, and colonization into commercial activity in the vast eastern lands which were to be known as Russia, the Vikings of Norway explored the Atlantic Ocean. Since Viking society condoned piracy, its criminals and outcasts were not admitted to such a "respectable" calling. They were forced instead, like Erik the Red, to explore and settle in relatively unpopulated areas. Erik the Red had to leave Norway in a hurry "because of some killings" in the late 970s. He went to Iceland which Vikings had taken from Irish priests about a hundred years before. He got into trouble there also, and was outlawed around 980. With another Icelander he set sail westward, arriving finally at a bleak mountainous land which he called Greenland. He ran into more trouble on his return to Iceland so he was forced to make Greenland his permanent home. Soon a colonial settlement had been established on Erik's farm, a haven, probably, for the outcasts of "polite" Viking society.

Bjarni Herjolfsson discovered America about 985. Of course, Asians had arrived there by way of the Bering Sea over a thousand years before. It is also quite possible that the Irish priests who settled Iceland also "discovered" America before Bjarni. In any case, it was an accident (though less accidental than Columbus's later voyage). After a visit to Norway, Bjarni returned to his home in Iceland to find that his parents had left for Erik the Red's colony in Greenland. Bjarni set out to follow them. After a longer trip than expected, Bjarni and his crew finally saw land, but it lacked the mountains of Greenland.

Realizing they had gone too far, Bjarni and his crew did not land but sailed back until they found Greenland and Erik's colony. When they told the colonists of this discovery, Erik's sons Leif and Thorvald gathered a crew to explore the new land. They named part of it *Helluland*, and part of it they called *Vinland*, presumably because of its vine foliage. It's also reported that Thorvald lived there for two years until he was killed by the local inhabitants. The only certain Viking site that has been unearthed so far is at the northern tip of Newfoundland, but it is quite likely that further archeological exploration will yield other sites.

The important thing, of course, is that the colony did not last. That fact tells more about Viking society than the fact of discovery. Viking society was capable of vast oceanic explorations, but it possessed neither the will nor the capability of maintaining all of these far flung colonies for long. The Vikings did not even remain in Greenland. They stayed in Iceland because its climate and vegetation and animal life were much more inviting, and also because it was within relatively easy supply distance of Norway. They remained in Russia because their settlements were prosperous trading centers close to the junction of three thriving cultures: the Byzantine, the Moslem, and the European Christian. Perhaps Viking culture was always more attuned to raiding and trading than to isolated, peaceful settlement.

The causes of Viking failure, as well as success, lie in the character of its militaristic culture. It was a culture in which aggressiveness was channeled into long-distance trade and profit seeking or war. Its long-term success was in the revival of trade and the development of both feudal and capitalistic institutions in Europe. The warrior element in Viking society which was not "civilized" into economic aggression was defeated in battle. The usual closing date is 1066 since that was the year that Harald the Hard Ruler, king of Norway, was killed by the English. The death of King Harald is a fitting symbolic end to Viking ascendency. He represented Viking expansiveness at its zenith. As a boy he had fled from Norway to Kiev. To win back his father's Norwegian crown he prepared himself as a member, and then as the commander, of the Byzantine emperor's palace guard. He fought for the Greeks in Asia Minor, the Caucasus Mountains, and Jerusalem. He returned to Kiev as a seasoned victor, married a Russian princess, and lived to rule Norway, explore the Atlantic, and reconquer England. This "Thunderbolt of the North," an ultimate Viking ruler, was defeated, almost by chance, by Earl Harold Godwinson on September 25, 1066. The Vikings lost England, and gradually thereafter much more of their overseas empire.

The death of a universal Viking king like Harald was the proper symbol for the end of the Viking age. Except for the fortuitousness of his actual defeat, the event had all of the drama of final tragedy —almost the final Twilight of the Gods imagined in Viking legend. But despite the hopes of heroic culture, the death of a single individual never means the end of an age. Actually, Godwinson was killed a few days later by William of Normandy, a descendant of the Vikings who had conquered northern France. In a sense, 1066 marks the final victory, rather than defeat, of Viking culture. At the same time, Scandinavia became disorganized, European armies became better able to cope with pirate raids, and within a couple of hundred years new military techniques and gunpowder made Viking military tactics obsolete.

As a military culture, the Vikings were doomed to fail when their victims learned how to defend themselves. The weakness of Viking culture was that it remained largely militaristic. Only those elements of the raid which could be channeled into trade survived. Much of Viking beliefs and behavior could not. The trading outposts in Normandy, France, made it possible for Vikings sons to conquer England and parts of Italy. By the twelfth century they were engaged in a phase of European expansion called the Crusades.

NO

Joseph Dahmus

THE DARK AGES AND THE DAWN OF A NEW ERA

It now comes time to return to western Europe of the sixth century which we left in the hands of rough Franks, Angles and Saxons, Burgundians, Visigoths, and Lombards. From point of view of culture and intellectual life, this century ushered in the period known as the Dark Ages. As Gregory of Tours had lamented, "Woe to us, for the study of letters has disappeared from amongst us!" For most people, however, Gregory's lament would have been equally expressive of the times had he simply said, "Woe to us!" These centuries from the sixth to the close of the tenth were the most turbulent and misery-laden that Europe has ever experienced. It is not an accident that the three "greats" who lived during the period, Gregory the Great, Alfred the Great, and Charlemagne, earned most merit for having halted further deterioration of conditions during their lifetimes and for having achieved some improvement.

Nevertheless, the Dark Ages were not just a period of strife and turmoil, of renewed invasions and more plunder. Those were melancholy times to be sure, and there were many men who feared the very bases of society would dissolve before the terrifying onslaughts of the fierce Vikings, Saracens, and Magyars. Still, when the smoke from their widespread and pitiless pillagings had cleared, the outlines of a new aid vigorous Europe stood clearly to view. By the close of the eleventh century the new Western states that were aborning had even acquired sufficient strength and maturity to mount a powerful attack against the world of Islam. A large measure of the darkness of the Dark Ages was, therefore, relative, not unlike the unproductive years it requires to make a young man out of a boy....

In 768 Charles, the most renowned of all Frankish kings, perhaps of all medieval kings, followed his father Pepin to the throne. Time has been harsh with the title "Great," which a dozen men have borne from out of the past. Of the few remaining "Greats," Charles should be the last to relinquish his title, at least in the English-speaking world. There tradition has incorporated "the Great" into his name of Charlemagne. That two modern states, France and Germany, both count him their most heroic ancestor, will also prolong his fame. His dominion included all of France, western Germany and the lands to the east, as well as part of Spain and more of Italy. Across the Channel kings extended him tacit recognition as lord, and even proud Byzantium for a time acknowledged his title emperor.

The account of Einhard, Charlemagne's secretary, expresses some of the awe in which the king's contemporaries held him. "Charles was large and strong, and of lofty stature, though not disproportionately tall (his height is well known to have been seven times the length of his foot); the upper part of his head was round, his eyes very large and animated, his nose somewhat long, hair fair, and his face was bright and pleasant. Thus his appearance was always stately and dignified, whether he was standing or sitting.... His meals ordinarily consisted of four courses, not counting the roast which his huntsmen used to bring in on the spit.... While at table he listened to reading or music. The subjects of the readings were the stories and deeds of men of olden time: he was fond, too, of St. Augustine's books, and especially of the one entitled 'The City of God.'"

By temperament Charlemagne was a man of moderation, firm without being cruel, in his dealings with men frank and straightforward. Given his powerful position and his conviction that no human authority stood above his, he might have been arrogant or despotic, but he was not. His demeanor resembled that of an Old Testament patriarch, and he ruled his large household at Aachen with the paternalistic benevolence of a Jacob. Of his own children he was especially fond of his daughters, so much so that he would not permit them to marry. There were stories, as a consequence, of moral irregularity on their part which Charlemagne, if he knew, accepted without complaint. The fault may have been his, he might have argued, or he might have accepted such conduct with the same tolerance as he did the easy moral atmosphere that prevailed at Aachen. It would require several centuries more before Frankish mores would approach the moral level set by monastic reformers. After the death of his fourth wife, Charlemagne kept several mistresses of his own, although the austerities he practiced in his last years, it is said, were meant to atone for his earlier laxity.

Charlemagne remained nonetheless a dedicated Christian. Contemporaries, including churchmen, took little heed of his moral laxity. To them he was the great strong arm of God, the terror of the Infidel, the scourge of the pagan. Charlemagne too believed his foes were God's foes. His was a sacred responsibility to destroy these enemies to bring to pass in his own lifetime the City of God of which Augustine had written. His first major victory was over the Lombards, a people the papacy had never ceased to abominate despite its conversion to Catholic Christianity. Yet when Pope Hadrian begged him to come down to Rome to drive them off, Charlemagne at first hesitated. The daughter of their king Desiderius had once been his wife —that marriage had been annulled—and the Lombards had given him no provocation. When Desiderius refused to withdraw from territories the pope claimed and to accept lands elsewhere, however, Charlemagne marched across the Alps, captured Pavia, Desiderius' capital, placed him in a monastery, and put an end to Lombard history. He took over their iron crown for himself.

Against the Moslems in Spain he won a magnificent victory if one accepts the romantic tale in the *Song of Roland.* Actually he suffered a sharp, though not serious, setback. In this instance he had committed the one blunder of his career. He had permitted himself to accept the assurances of several Abbasid emirs that they would join him in an attack on the Umayyad emir of Cordova should he march an army across the Pyrenees. When he did come south, they failed to show, and the discomfited Charlemagne, after several reverses, returned to Gaul. On his retreat Basques attacked his rear guard as it was passing through a defile and "in the struggle that ensued, they cut them off to a man." Some years later Charlemagne avenged this earlier defeat and annexed the territory to the Ebro River.

The most stubborn of Charlemagne's enemies were the Saxons, the last of the powerful German tribes that had once harassed imperial Rome's northern frontier. Frankish kings before Charlemagne had won temporary victories over scattered groups of Saxons when these ventured west of the swamps and forests that covered their homeland. Charlemagne also gained victories, secured promises of subjection, and took hostages, yet to no avail. Once the summer was over and the Frankish army had returned home, the Saxons would revolt and massacre the officials, missionaries, and bishops Charlemagne had left behind. Year after year, for thirty-three summers so Einhard writes, Charlemagne fought the Saxons. Even his execution of 4500 of their leaders, following upon a particularly serious revolt, did not bring them to heel. What finally broke their indomitable spirit was the policy of deportation Charlemagne finally adopted, when he moved thou-sands who "lived on the banks of the Elbe and [settled] them with wives and children, in many different groups here and there in Gaul and Germany."

Charlemagne also extended his rule over the Bavarians, forced the Slavs between the Elbe and Oder to recognize his authority, then destroyed the barbarous Avar nation to the southeast. This brutal people had failed to acquire, during the two centuries since coming from Asia, even sufficient culture to make use of the horde of booty it had since accumulated. "All the money and treasure it had been years amassing was seized, and no war in which the Franks have ever engaged within the memory of man brought them such riches and such booty." Charlemagne also extended his rule over Brittany, but against the Danes who were just beginning their raids along the North Sea, he and his Franks could do little but throw up defenses and pray. As an old man, it is said, he wept over the misery these savage Northmen would cause his people after his death. The tale may be true, for the aged Charlemagne had lost his youthful vigor, his two ablest sons had died, and when his own death came in 814, his empire appeared on the point of disintegrating.

Historians attribute part of the ineffectiveness of most Frankish kings to the primitive administrative machinery with which they had to rule. Despite long contact with imperial Rome and Byzantine rule, the personal character of the Frankish government had remained almost unchanged from tribal times. Custom continued to expect the king to administer the kingdom from what revenues his own personal estates produced. Charlemagne did nothing to alter this custom, although among the most valuable documents from his reign is the detailed directive he sent to his stewards (Capitulary *de Villis*) concerning the efficient administration of his estates. Fortunately for Charlemagne and the peace of his realm, he possessed more extensive estates than his Merovingian predecessors, and he also captured more booty. His counts and margraves were also expected to bring gifts with them in the spring when they met and advised with him concerning matters dealing with the empire. It was at these Mayfields, as they were called, that he generally issued his capitularies after consultation with these men. In a country that had few roads and no postal system, no better opportunity presented itself for publicizing such proclamations. Charlemagne experienced little trouble from his counts. They held him in fear if not respect, and they also were wary of the *missi dominici,* the two royal inquisitors Charlemagne sent to each county each year "to report to him any inequality or injustice... and to render justice to all, to the holy churches of God, to the poor, to widows and orphans, and to the whole people."

What strikes the modern scholar who examines Charlemagne's capitularies as most unusual is the wide variety of problems he made his concern. He legislated on education, on roads and trade, on justice and military service as might be expected. But with equal freedom he issued decrees touching theology, the liturgy, and monastic reform. His father Pepin had cooperated with the papacy in fighting the pagan and in pushing church reform. Charlemagne did not cooperate so much as dictate. He did not follow the lead of the pope; he ignored or led him. He appointed bishops and abbots, convened synods to discuss doctrine and liturgy, and even lectured the pope on his failure to introduce the Filioque clause in the Nicene Creed. Still it was not arrogance but faith that drove him, not pride but love of God, as when he personally attended the baptism of thousands of pagans in the waters of the Elbe. Above all cities he loved Rome the most, the city made holy by Peter and Paul and so many martyrs. When he learned of the death of Pope Hadrian, "he wept as much as if he had lost a brother or a very dear son."

There was one occasion when the pope undertook to act without first securing Charlemagne's approval. That was on Christmas Day in the year 800. Charlemagne happened to be in Rome at the time. He had come there in answer to the pope's urgent plea for help against enemies who wanted to unseat him. Charlemagne confirmed the pope in his position; then some days later, on Christmas, as the king knelt in St. Peter's, Leo placed a crown on his head. The assembled faithful must have been aware of what the pope planned, for they promptly cried out: "To Charles Augustus, crowned by God, great and peaceful Emperor of the Romans, life and victory." Charlemagne, for his part, was so annoyed at the pope's action, so Einhard insists, that he declared he would not have gone near the church that day had he suspected what the pope had in mind.

Because of Einhard's testimony, historians have long puzzled over the incident. Surely Einhard must be in error, some have argued, for what man should not have been pleased with so noble a title. Scholars reason, furthermore, that Charlemagne should have appreciated the greater propriety of the title emperor over the tribal "king of the Franks" in dealing with his polyglot subjects. If Charlemagne was irritated as Einhard declared, scholars suggest that it was over the pope's own decision to do the crowning himself. Such action could be dangerous in an age which set such high store on precedent. Some years later, in 813, as if to undo this precedent, Charlemagne had his son Louis crowned emperor without benefit of any ecclesiastic. Charlemagne's coronation made official, incidentally, the alliance between the Latin church and the Frankish monarchy, while it severed by implication the pope's political subordination to Byzantium.

Among Charlemagne's other achievements was a revival of learning which he inspired. No doubt his personal interest in learning provided him strong motivation, although what aroused his greatest concern was the low level of learning among churchmen. The letters he received from monasteries which should have been penned in quite scholarly Latin, he found full of grammatical errors and "uncouth expressions. Hence we began to fear," he explained, "that being too little skilled in writing, there might also be far too little wisdom in understanding the holy Scriptures." He accordingly issued instructions to the bishops and abbots of his empire that they improve and expand their schools and libraries, and that they keep these schools not entirely to themselves but open them to the sons of the laity who had no intention of becoming monks. And "let them learn psalms, notes, singing, computus (arithmetic), grammar, and let the religious books that are given them be free of faults because often some desire to pray to God properly, but they pray badly because of faulty books. And let care be taken that the boys do not damage them [books] either when reading or writing."

As if to dramatize his efforts at elevating the level of learning in his kingdom and, at the same time, to provide himself

teachers and scholarly companionship, Charlemagne invited leading scholars of the day to come and make their home at Aachen. Alcuin, England's brightest light, came from York and spent fifteen years at Aachen. For a somewhat shorter time came the grammarians Peter of Pisa and Paulinus of Aquileia from Italy, Theodulf from Spain, the leading poet of the day (Glory, Laud, and Honor), and Paul the Deacon, who later composed a history of the Lombards. Charlemagne proved himself an apt scholar, learned to speak Latin "as well as his native tongue, but he could understand Greek better than he could speak it.... He most zealously cultivated the liberal arts, held those who taught them in great esteem, and conferred great honors upon them." His favorite teacher and mentor was Alcuin, with whom he "spent much time and labor...studying rhetoric, dialectic, and especially astronomy; he learned to reckon, and used to investigate the motions of the heavenly bodies most curiously, with an intelligent scrutiny. He also tried to write, and used to keep tablets and blanks in bed under his pillow, that at leisure hours he might accustom his hand to form letters; however, as he did not begin his efforts in due season, but late in life, they met with ill success."

Had the empire of the Franks remained at peace following Charlemagne's death, his encouragement of learning might have inaugurated an intellectual revival which would have anticipated that of the eleventh century. As it was, when Charlemagne died, so did peace; and within a century conditions in Frankland had sunk almost to the low level of the Dark Ages. Still some good lived on from the work of the great emperor. The bishops he had carefully selected for their learning and worthiness worked with his son Louis and the reformer Benedict of Aniane in effecting a general improvement in the condition of the church. Charlemagne's renaissance could also claim credit for a harvest of textbooks, principally by Alcuin, improved monastic schools, renewed attention to the collection of books and the copying of manuscripts, a much more legible script (Carolingian minuscule), an improved Vulgate (this had suffered considerable corruption), and a more scholarly Latin. What in particular assured his work endurance were the monasteries whose cultural life he had helped stimulate. "The great abbeys, such as St. Gall and Reichenau, Fulda, and Corbie, were not only the intellectual and religious leaders of Europe, but also the chief centers of material culture and of artistic and industrial activity. In them there was developed the traditions of learning and literature, art, and architecture, music and liturgy, painting and calligraphy, which were the foundations of medieval culture." ...

Two additional lands deserve attention during these formative centuries when western Europe struggled to establish new civilizations. These were the lands of Spain and Italy. Except for the mountainous region of the Asturias in the northwest, all the Spanish peninsula had fallen to the Islamic conquerors. Until 750 A.D., when the Abbasids seized the empire, an Umayyad emir ruled the land from Cordova. Then a new Abbasid emir took over and all seemed quite secure until Abd al-Rahman, one of the few Umayyad princes to escape the purge, appeared five years later and, after considerable fighting, took over the country. Five years of harassment, deprivation, and flight had made this Abd al-Rahman a tough, determined young man. When al-Mansur, who was

caliph back in Baghdad, sent his own governor to Spain, Abd al-Rahman had him decapitated, put his head in camphor and salt, and sent it back to the caliph wrapped in a black flag. The warning was not lost on the caliph. "Thanks be to Allah," he is said to have observed, "for having placed the sea between us and such a foe." Baghdad never bothered with Spain again.

Abd al-Rahman made Cordova his capital, then made it the rival of Constantinople and Baghdad in magnificence, while building an army and navy that were the most formidable in western Europe. Moslem power reached its zenith during the reign of Abd al-Rahman III (912–961), who was the first emir to assume the title caliph. The year 1031 marked the end of the ruling dynasty and the breakup of the emirate into smaller principalities based upon Toledo, Valencia, Seville, Cordova, and Saragossa. Meantime Spain under Moslem rule had become one of the wealthiest, most populated, and culturally advanced states in Europe. No Western state exported a greater volume or variety of agricultural and industrial products: olives, cotton, sugar, grapes, figs, wheat, oil, leather, glassware, metalwork, gold, and silver. Nowhere in Europe, except perhaps in Constantinople, could one find so many libraries, scholars, and artists. And it was principally by way of Spain that Moslem learning made its greatest impact upon the West.

Even before the breakup of the Cordovan caliphate, Christian states to the north had been slowly enlarging their holdings. León expanded from its base in the Asturias, then gave birth to Castile which later broke off to form a separate state. By this time the county of Barcelona, later Catalonia, had thrown off control of the Carolingians—it had constituted the Spanish march—while the Basque state of Navarre had come into existence. The first important Spanish conqueror was Ferdinand I, who extended his authority over most of the Christian princes and even forced tribute from several Moslem emirs. When his son Alfonso VI (1072–1109) annexed Toledo, the Moslems sought the assistance of the Almoravides, who had established a militant Moslem state in Morocco. Their appearance halted Christian expansion for a half-century, although not the fighting. This was the era when Rodrigo Diaz de Bivar, the renowned Spanish warrior, worked the spectacular feats that gained him immortal fame in *El Cid*, the best-known of Spanish epics. His name, El Cid Campeador (the champion), he earned from his Moslem soldiers. For Rodrigo, like occasional other Christian warriors, now fought on the side of the Infidel, now with the Christians, though always for himself. When he died in 1099 as ruler of Valencia, the First Crusade was already under way.

The Moslems were also active in Italy, the other land that merits attention during these centuries. To recapitulate the history of Italy during the years before the appearance of the Moslems: the Lombards who crossed the Alps shortly after Justinian's death had never been able to conquer the entire peninsula. They almost succeeded, however, during the reign of their most able monarch Liutprand (712–743). So close, indeed, did they come to attaining their objective that the pope in desperation called in the Franks. Pepin responded, drove them away from Rome, but left their destruction to his son Charlemagne. It was only a few years after Charlemagne's death that Saracens from Tunis began their attacks on Sicily, took Palermo in 831, then crossed over to Italy proper, and a few years later were plundering the churches of St. Peter and St. Paul outside Rome (that is, outside the Aurelian Wall). Louis II, son of Lothair, first slowed their progress, then after his death Basil I sent over troops and ships from Constantinople. Though Basil drove the Saracens from Italy, he could not prevent their overrunning the whole of Sicily....

Perhaps the most significant development in the history of the church during the seventh and eighth centuries had been the growing estrangement between papacy and Constantinople. Justinian had been sufficiently strong to force compliance upon Rome; his successors had not. Because of Byzantine involvement with the Lombards in Italy, with the Persians, then Moslems, in the east, and a series of dangerous enemies along the Danube, popes over in Rome discovered that they could resist, occasionally even defy, pressures from Constantinople. It was during these centuries, beginning with Gregory the Great, that there began to emerge what is commonly referred to as the temporal power of the popes, that is, the growing ability of the popes to exercise authority in civil and political matters. While Gregory the Great might deplore the nonreligious responsibilities this growing independence from Constantinople brought with it, his successors gradually came to regard the freedom this furnished them, for example in dealing with the iconoclastic emperors, as the *sine qua non* of the existence of the church. For that reason the allegiance of the popes to Byzantium always remained an unknown quantity, nor were they any more willing to accept Lombard hegemony instead when this threatened to become a fact. They never trusted these former Arians; for one reason they were too close. They preferred rather to accept the status of a protectorate under control of the distant Franks whose interests north of the Alps promised to keep them sufficiently engaged elsewhere to prevent their assuming too powerful a position in Italy.

This was not true of Charlemagne, however, who ruled Rome with an uncomfortably firm hand. Still Charlemagne was only human. When he died the situation might improve, and it did. Louis the Pious reversed, in fact, the relationship between king and pope. The pope directed him, not he the pope as Charlemagne had done. The resurgence of the papacy reached its height under Nicholas I (858–867), who interfered in the election of the patriarch of Constantinople and even ordered the Frankish king Lothair II to take back his divorced wife.

Yet Nicholas was premature in announcing that the day of king-priests and emperor-pontiffs was past. Almost overnight the grand prospect he had contemplated for the papacy faded and died. Instead of dictating to kings what kind of lives they should lead and to Byzantine emperors who should be and who should not be patriarchs, the papacy found itself the prisoner of factions within the city of Rome. Ambitious men and women now sat in judgment, and made and unmade popes as it pleased their sordid fancies. Never had the character and prestige of the papacy fallen to so low a point. Its deficiencies need not detain us except to point up the fact of how much the medieval church during these rough times stood in need of a protector....

The tenth century, which witnessed the general decline of the church through-out western Europe, also welcomed the first solid evidences of reform. Where the wellsprings of this reform movement were located is difficult to say. The very extensiveness of the movement suggests that its roots were widespread. Kings had their part in the movement; so did rough warriors whose consciences were touched, along with bishops and monks, not to forget the many commoners who found a new attractiveness about monastic life. So many abbeys sprang up from the labor of monks and the benefactions of non-monks, that the new style in which they were constructed, commonly called Romanesque, also bears the name monastic. Because of the widespread interest in reform one had best view the movement as a popular reaction to the low moral conditions of the times....

The man who traditionally receives credit for pushing through the reform program of the eleventh century was Pope Gregory VII. This may be doing an injustice to Gregory's predecessor Leo IX whose solid work in reorganizing the papacy made possible Gregory's achievement. Until Leo's time the papacy, following its degradation in the late ninth and early tenth centuries, had remained hardly more than a Roman institution. Leo reorganized the chancery, greatly expanded its activities by conducting correspondence with all the important men of Europe, and sent out legates everywhere to champion the cause of reform. He spent as much time traveling about western Europe as he spent in Rome, preaching reform, investigating monasteries and dioceses, even stopping long enough at Reims to censure its archbishop and several bishops of the vicinity for simony. He also laid the foundation for the important role the college of cardinals was to play by inaugurating the policy of bringing able men to Rome from all corners of Christendom, where they were to assist the pope in administering the church. This policy of appointing men from different countries as cardinals continued, incidentally, on down to the Great Schism. Then Pope Urban VI, in order to assure himself its loyalty, transformed the curia into an Italian institution. It has remained that up to the present time.

NOTES

1. Christopher Dawson, *The Making of Europe.* New York (1938), pp. 231–32.

2. Quoted in Hitti, *History of the Arabs*, p. 507.

POSTSCRIPT

Does the Ninth Century Mark the End of the Dark Ages?

What do historians mean when they speak of a "dark age"? In the study of ancient Greece, historians apply the term to the period between the fall of the Bronze Age's Mycenean civilization and the beginning of the rise of Hellenic culture in the seventh century B.C. During this time, the skill of writing was forgotten, the ruling elite disintegrated as a class, the central trading economy collapsed, and the cities were abandoned. The intervening years saw the population revert back to a nomadic society. As a result, accomplishment in the arts diminished, and culture and learning declined. If this period can be characterized as a "dark age," should the same term be applied to the postclassical era in European history?

Reilly certainly draws a bloody and brutal portrait of the era. He describes the barbarians as a people interested only in achieving power and glory through destruction and pillage. He points out that in its latter years, Rome also descended into the maelstrom of violence and barbarism. "Europe was born in this marriage of settled barbarian and barbarized Roman poor," he writes. When writing of the more stable times of Charlemagne, Reilly admits that "barbarian life had given way to the stable regularity of farming, collecting taxes, and making laws." Nevertheless, he emphasizes that violence was inherent even in the culture of the Carolingian Renaissance. The Middle Ages were a time when violence always remained just above the surface, even as it evolved from the chaotic bloodshed of vendetta to the more organized blood price to the establishment of the law courts. The militarization of early medieval society regularized the violence by institutionalizing it. With the introduction of the saddle and the stirrup, the armored cavalry soldier, or the knight—necessarily elitist due to the cost of armor, mount, and training—came to be the necessary protector in a battle-scarred world. In exchange for his warrior skill, he received political power, supreme social status, and land. The feudal system arose out of the need for security from violence through the successful application of violence, concludes Reilly.

The second wave of invasions began in the ninth century and continued into the eleventh century. Here the homicide and horrors continued, as Vikings "murdered unarmed monks, looted sanctuaries, plundered the libraries that had preserved the literary heritage of the ancient world, and burned what they could not carry away." In fact, it is hard to tell from Reilly's account when the Dark Ages ended because he places the Crusades in this continuum of Western violence.

"Nevertheless, the Dark Ages were not just a period of strife and turmoil, of renewed invasions and more plunder," writes Dahmus. He indicates that the rise of the Franks ensured that the postclassical era would not plunge into the darkness of a failed civilization. Clovis's conversion to Roman Catholicism confirmed the survival of the Christian Church, even when he was followed by a succession of incompetent heirs. The Carolingian patronage of the monasteries provided for the preservation of literacy and art despite the ravages of the Norsemen. Dahmus also points out that the civilization of the Romanized barbarians was not the only one on the European continent; the Muslims in Spain built a magnificent culture at Cordova, preserving much of the learning, philosophy, and science of the classical Greeks and Romans.

Several books are available in the continuing debate on how dark the Dark Ages really were. Michael Wood's *In Search of the Dark Ages* (Facts on File, 1987) is an engaging series of essays focusing on Britain in the early medieval era. More recently, the popular and amusing *How the Irish Saved Civilization* by Thomas Cahill (Doubleday, 1995) is a delightful read. For a more traditional scholarly approach, Joseph Reese Strayer's *Western Europe in the Middle Ages* (Prentice Hall, 1974) is recommended, as is *The Medieval Machine: The Industrial Revolution in the Middle Ages* by T. Jean Gimpel (Holt, Rinehart & Winston, 1976).

On the Internet . . .

http://www.dushkin.com

Archaeology Magazine
This is the home page of the Archaeological Institute of America's *Archaeology* magazine. It contains full texts of news briefs and abstracts of feature articles.
http://www.he.net/~archaeol/index.html

Civ Web from Providence College
This site is a guide to Internet resources related to the development of Western civilization. Information is available on Mesopotamia, Ancient Egypt, Ancient Palestine, Ancient Greece, Ancient Rome, the Middle Ages, and the Renaissance.
http://www.providence.edu/dwc/index.html

Military History
This is a good place to start exploring military history. The site includes a time line of major wars and links to military history by period.
http://www.cfcsc.dnd.ca/links/milhist/

MSANEWS Home Page
The world of Islam, past and present, is available at this Web site from the Muslim Students' Organization. It includes search mechanisms and a news service.
http://www.mynet.net/~msanews/

PART 2

The World in Transition

This section shows world civilizations building upon the world that the ancients created as they searched for a better life for themselves and their citizens. However, it also shows that some of the problems these civilizations faced early in their histories continued to plague them and that greater problems occurred for them as they began to have increased contact with other civilizations.

■ Does the Modern University Have Its Roots in the Islamic World?

■ Were Environmental Factors Responsible for the Collapse of the Mayan Civilization?

■ Were the Crusades an Early Example of Western Imperialism?

■ Did Women and Men Benefit Equally from the Renaissance?

■ Should Christopher Columbus Be Considered a Hero?

■ Did Calvinism Lay the Foundation for Democracy in Europe?

■ Did Tokugawa Policies Strengthen Japan?

■ Did Oliver Cromwell Advance Political Freedom in Seventeenth-Century England?

■ Did Indian Emperor Aurangzeb's Rule Mark the Beginning of Mughal Decline?

■ Did Peter the Great Exert a Positive Influence on the Development of Russia?

ISSUE 8

Does the Modern University Have Its Roots in the Islamic World?

YES: Mehdi Nakosteen, from *History of Islamic Origins of Western Education* A.D. *800–1350* (University of Colorado Press, 1964)

NO: Charles Homer Haskins, from *The Rise of Universities* (Great Seal Books, 1957)

ISSUE SUMMARY

YES: Professor of history and philosophy of education Mehdi Nakosteen traces the roots of the modern university to the golden age of Islamic culture (750–1150 C.E.). He argues that Muslim scholars assimilated the best of classical scholarship and developed the experimental method and the university system, which they passed on to the West before declining.

NO: The late historian Charles Homer Haskins (1870–1937) traces the university of the twentieth century to its predecessors in Paris and Bologna, where, he argues, during the twelfth and thirteenth centuries the first universities in the world sprang up.

In the seventh century A.D. the prophet Muhammad united the Arab world under the banner of a new monotheistic religion, Islam, which means "surrender" to Allah or God. In 622 Muhammad left the city of Mecca for the city of Medina. Since he was fleeing persecution, this flight is known as *Hijra,* or "breaking of former ties." Muslims, the followers of Islam, use that date as the first year in their calendar. Using that calendar, the year 2000 according to the Christian calendar will be 1378 A.H. (*anno Hegirae*). Christians began their calendar with the birth of Jesus, calling everything after that date A.D. for *anno Domini* (in the year of our Lord) and everything before that date B.C. (before Christ). Taking into account that much of the world is not Christian, Western scholars have begun to use the designations C.E. (for common era) to replace A.D. and B.C.E. (for before the common era) to replace B.C. You will find the A.H. and A.D. designations used in the following selections.

United under Islam, Arab warriors conquered the Persian Empire, took some Byzantine cities, crossed North Africa, and invaded Europe. Stopped at 732 in Tours, France, the Islamic conquest ushered in a "golden age" of learning centered in Cordoba, the capital of Muslim Spain. At that time the largest monastery library in Europe contained fewer than 100 books, while the library in Cordoba contained over 500,000 volumes. At a time when

Europe had lost much of its Greco-Roman intellectual heritage and learning was at a low point, Muslim scholars were translating Greek works from the Persian and Byzantine cultures into Arabic and commenting on them. This learning, along with their original contributions in mathematics, medicine, science, and philosophy, was passed on to the West when Islamic culture was conquered first by the Seljuk Turks and later by Genghis Khan and the Mongols of Central Asia.

The Western intellectual debt to Islamic scholars is undisputed. However, what about the college or university as an institution of higher learning? Were Western scholars able to take the world's heritage of learning and use it to fashion the modern world because they invented the university or because it, too, was borrowed from the Islamic world?

In the following selections, professor of history Mehdi Nakosteen argues that the language barrier and general inaccessibility of historical material to Western scholars, along with religious prejudice and the decline of Islamic culture, have made it easy for Europeans and Americans to assume credit for the modern university. In actuality, he maintains, the university is rooted in the Islamic world. Historian Charles Homer Haskins, however, sees the medieval European universities in Paris, France, and Bologna, Italy, arising spontaneously in response to an influx of new knowledge. Although he credits the Arab scholars of Spain with much of that new knowledge, he does not trace the roots of the university as an institution to the Arab world.

Haskins delivered the lectures on which his selection is based in 1923. The challenge put forth by Nakosteen is part of the revisionist process that has been going on in history for the last 30 or so years. Part of that process is challenging assumptions that have gone unchallenged for centuries. In 1937, the year Haskins died, Western historians often credited Europe and America with all that was worthwhile in modern life. Our heritage was Greek, and the line was assumed to be unbroken. Modern scholars, however, are examining the influence of Africa on the Greeks and considering the contributions from Asia and the Arab world with a new openness. This is all part of the ongoing refinement of historical knowledge and may be expected to continue as long as there are scholars.

YES

Mehdi Nakosteen

THE NATURE AND SCOPE OF MUSLIM EDUCATION, 750–1350

All dates refer to A.D. unless otherwise specified.

Europe was in its medieval period when the Muslims wrote a colorful chapter in the history of education. Many of their greatest contributions, particularly to Western education, have gone unnoticed because of religious prejudice, language barriers, the decline of Islamic culture, and inaccessibility of historic materials for Western historians of education. The Muslims assimilated through their educational system the best of classical cultures and improved them. Among the assimilated fields were philosophy and Hellenistic medical, mathematical, and technological sciences; Hindu mathematics, medicine, and literature; Persian religions, literature, and sciences; and Syrian commentaries on Hellenistic science and philosophy. By applying the classical sciences to practical pursuits, the Muslims developed the empirical-experimental method, although they failed to take full advantage of it. Later the method was adopted in Europe. They encouraged free inquiry and made available to the public the instruments of research and scholarship. They opened their public and even private libraries to public use, not only regionally but internationally. At a time when books were "published" only through the tedious labor of copyists, they made hundreds, even thousands, of copies of reference materials and made them available to all caring to learn from them. Often they allowed scores of books—sometimes more than a hundred per person—to be borrowed for an almost indefinite time for special studies and prolonged research. They provided food, lodging, and even incidental money for scholars from far away; they made their great teachers internationally accessible by encouraging the concept of the travelling scholar.

In the golden age (750–1150) of their cultural-educational activities they did not permit theology and dogma to limit their scholarship. They searched into every branch of human knowledge, be it philology, history, historiography, law, sociology, literature, ethics, philosophy, theology, medicine, mathematics, logic, jurisprudence, art, architecture, or ceramics. They respected learn-

From Mehdi Nakosteen, *History of Islamic Origins of Western Education* A.D. *800–1350* (University of Colorado Press, 1964), pp. 37–42, 52–53, 61–63. Copyright © 1964 by University of Colorado Press. Reprinted by permission. Some notes omitted.

ing; they honored the scholar. They introduced the science and philosophy of the Greeks, Persians, and Hindus to Western Christian schoolmen. But the story of Western education's debt to Islam is still to be written with fullness of knowledge and without prejudice and predetermination of results. What kind of education was responsible for so much in so short a time?

Muslim education went through two distinct periods. First was the period covering the ninth and tenth centuries, when schools developed spontaneously with private endowments interested in public enlightenment; and second the period beginning in the eleventh century and developing through the twelfth and thirteenth centuries, when education became the function of the state, and schools were institutionalized for purposes of sectarian education and political indoctrination.

MADRASAHS AND NIZAMIYYAS

A new type of school was conceived as a state institution to promote religious indoctrination of the Sunnite Islamic faith and political indoctrination of a Turkish-Persian style, aside from general learning and particular training. Nizam-al-Mulk (d. 1092; 485 A.H.), the founder and popularizer of these *madrasahs* (schools of public instruction), was a famous vizier (prime minister) in the administration of the Seljuq sultans in the eleventh century. He established the madrasah about the middle of that century, which, though not the first school in Islam, was the first system of special schools geared to that state and Sunnite Islam. The madrasahs had, aside from their zest for learning, both political and religious purposes— the moulding of public opinion in Sun-

nite orthodox Islam against the Shi'ah branch. Large sums of money were allotted for the establishment and maintenance of these schools with generous scholarships, pensions, and rations granted to all worthy students. In fact, Nizam arranged for regular stipends to all students. The schools were institutionalized under state control and support, and standardized madrasahs were established in all large cities within Islam, with the exception of Spain and Sicily. The greatest of these academies was the one established by Nizam in Baghdad, the famous *Nizamiyyah,* which opened for teaching in 1066–67 (459 A.H.) and continued as a center of learning for several centuries, motivated primarily by religious and literary pursuits. Altogether, Nizam-al-Mulk made the greatest single contribution to education in founding and extending an almost universal system of schools (madrasahs) throughout Eastern Islam.[1] He was one of the most learned men of his time, greatly versed in Muslim hadith, or tradition, and one of the great political theorists of Islam, as shown in his famous *Siyasat-Namah.* His passion for universal education was limited only by the means at his disposal. The schools he founded all over the empire were endowed generously. He supplied them with libraries, the best professors he could find, and a system of scholarships to aid all the students. Let us look into his educational enterprise in some detail.

NIZAM-AL-MULK AND MUSLIM EDUCATION

The opening of the first school carrying the name of the Persian statesman, Nizam-al-Mulk, took place in 1066 (459 A.H.). It marks the transition from the mosque schools and the beginning of a system of public schools, or madrasahs, throughout the vast area of the Muslim world, which was under strong Persian cultural and administrative influence. This influence continued, first under Arab political supremacy under the Abbassides from the middle of the eighth century to the ninth, and again during the long period of Turkish (Ottoman) politico-religious supremacy, to the early decades of the sixteenth century (1517). It is true that the earlier Turks had a simple culture and were given to warfare and conquest. But settling down to administer their empire, they learned from the superior cultures of the Persians and the Arabs, adopted the Arabic alphabet, and accepted Islam. In time they adapted the foreign cultures to their own needs and tastes, and encouraged the establishment throughout their empire of schools to perpetuate Sunnite Islam and Turkish politics and policies. Tarikh Zaidan, in his *Al-Tamaddun al-Islami (History of Islamic Civilization)*, states that the Turkish princes encouraged learning and increased the number of schools in their empire, guided by three motives: The type of heavenly reward; the fear of losing their fortunes to more greedy superiors or antagonists, so that they utilized their wealth in establishing schools; finally, but most important of all, the desire to indoctrinate religious beliefs of the founder and to combat opposing religious views.

It was the employment of the school for sectarian indoctrination and political influence and propaganda that led the famous Seljuk Sultan Saladin to found madrasahs and also to close the college of Dar al-Ilm (The House of Learning) in Cairo in order to eliminate its Shi'ite influence. In fact it was not uncommon to dismiss professors during this period from the madrasahs because of their religious beliefs, particularly Shi'ite. Muslim scholasticism (*Ilm al-Kalam*) developed in these sectarian colleges of Sunnite or Shi'ite beliefs.

The Sunnite belief received its most sweeping expression under Nizam-al-Mulk. Before his day, there were several institutions of learning in the Islamic world which resembled a college, such as Al-Azhar in Cairo, Egypt, in the last quarter of the tenth century; Dar al-Ilm and Dar al-Hikmah, also in Cairo, in the early decades of the eleventh; Bait-al-Hikmah in Baghdad during the reign of al-Ma'mun; and Baihaqiyyah at Nishapur in Khrasan, Persia. But to Nizam-al-Mulk goes the distinct credit for having founded an institution for instruction and indoctrination under government and religious control, for political and religious ends—a sectarian system of public education with secular emphasis and political motivation.

With these objectives in mind, Nizam-al-Mulk established schools in every city and village of Iraq and Khorassan. Even a small place, such as "Kharn al-Jabal near Tus... had its teacher and school." These schools were well distributed from Khorassan in the east to Mesopotamia in the west. These so-called madrasahs soon became standardized, and many of them were built after the example of the one in Baghdad, which was built by Nizam-al-Mulk himself, and named Nizamiyyah (or Nidhamiyyah) in his honor.

Nizamiyyahs... were founded not only in Baghdad, but in Nisabur, Balkh, Herat, Isfahan, Marw, Basrah and Mosul. Not only did Nizam-al-Mulk establish these academies or colleges, but he endowed them. It is estimated that $1,500,000 was spent annually on educational, semi-educational and religious institutions.

Nizamiyyah University, the most famous of the chain of madrasahs, was built in Baghdad in 1065 under the educator's personal supervision. The earliest account of this university is given by ibn Khaldun, the great Arab philosopher-historian, who says:

> Nizam-al-Mulk ordered that Abu Is'haq al-Shirazi should be its professor, but when the people were assembled to hear him he did not appear. He was searched for, but was not to be found; so Abu Nasir ibn-al-Sabbagh was appointed to the post. Later Abu Is'haq met his classes in his mosque, but his students showed their dissatisfaction with his action and threatened to go over to ibn al-Sabbagh unless he accepted the professorship at the Nizamiyyah. Finally he acceded to their wishes, and ibn al-Sabbagh was dismissed after having lectured for only twenty days.

The chief reason for Abu Is'haq's refusal to teach at the Nizamiyyah was, according to ibn Khallikan, that he was "informed that the greater part of the materials employed in the construction of the college have been procured illegally." But the foregoing quotation is of extreme interest for the information it gives us that the mosques were the chief places of learning before the foundation of universities. There were over one hundred such mosques in Baghdad alone.

The principal motive in founding the Nizamiyyah was religious. Its objective was the teaching of "The Shafi'ite (Sunni) school of law," its sole emphasis being upon the teaching of theology and Islamic law, and it stood as a university of Islamic theological learning for several centuries. The great mystic al-Ghazzali taught there twenty-five years after its founding. Al-Abiwardi (d. 1104;

498 A.H.) and ibn Mubarak (d. 1184; 580 A.H.) were associated with it. Ibn Jubair who visited the school about the middle of the fourteenth century, said of it: "And in the midst of Suq al-Thalatha (Tuesday market) is the wonderful madrasah Al-Nizamiyyah, whose beauty has become proverbial."

AIMS OF MUSLIM EDUCATION

The aims of Muslim education in "medieval" times may be defined as follows:

1. Religious aims, based on (a) *Qur'an* as source of knowledge, (b) spiritual foundation of education, (c) dependence upon God, (d) sectarian morals, (e) subordination of secular subjects to religion, (f) equality of all men before God and man, (g) supremacy of Muhammad over all other prophets, (h) belief in the six articles of Imam or Creed (God, angels, scripture, prophets, judgment, decrees) and (i) belief (and application) in A'amal or religious duties, including confession of faith (There is no God but God), prayers, alms, fasting, and pilgrimage.

2. Secular aims, the importance of which is well suggested by a Muslim tradition, attributed to Muhammad, which says, "The best among you are not those who neglect this world for the other, or the other world for this. He is the one who works for both together." Among these aims were pursuit of all knowledge, as the revelation of the nature of God; education open to all on equal terms, limited only by ability and interest; and guidance and teaching as essential to promote (initiate) knowledge and education.

The *Mutakallimun (Loquentes)*, the Muslim scholastic teachers (speakers of truths), stressed the importance of teachers whose knowledge may be traced back to relevation or may have been made manifest directly by intuition. This was the view of the theologian-philosopher-educator al-Ghazzali, who believed in three degrees of knowledge: (a) Common-sense knowledge, restricted by undisciplined sense-experience and dependent upon external authority; (b) scientific knowledge; (c) intuitive knowledge.

It is of interest to note that al-Ghazzali's concept of scientific knowledge includes seven basic principles or conditions: Stimulation of the search for scientific knowledge; application of scientific arts; advancement of applied sciences and extensive application of them; development of laboratory and experimental pursuits; encouragement of arts and crafts (It was Aristotle in particular, from among the Greeks, who appealed to Islam. This was because of the Greek master's application of philosophy and science to the arts and needs of everyday living and because of the adaptability of his philosophic and scientific concepts to the art of living and the necessities of individual and civic life); encouragement of individual initiative and academic freedom for both teachers and pupils (in the college of Baghdad an inquiring student, who greeted the great teacher with devoted *salams* [bows], often ended the day with an intellectual fist fight with his master in defense of some principles, refutation of others, or hairsplitting argument over insignificant details); attainment of excellence, to produce great men of learning and leaders in public affairs. The pragmatic spirit of their education is indicated by development of textile fabrics, of irrigation systems, of iron and steel products, of earthenwares, and leather products, by architectural innovations, weaving of rugs and carpets, manufacture of paper and gunpowder, maintenance of a merchant marine of a thousand ships, and advancement of commercial activity.

Although Muslim education aimed at practical training, such training was a rule based upon instruction in fundamental sciences. Thus, in the system, practice was sustained by theory; theory verified in practice. Even in commercial training, economics as a science was a foundational training.

It is of interest to note that as Islam began to decline after the end of the eleventh century, the number of its schools of higher learning increased and flourished. These colleges were, however, almost all denominational schools opened and supported by leaders of various Islamic religious factions. Each denominational college was open, with few exceptions, only to followers of a given sect. Religious and literary studies and Arabic language and grammar dominated the subject matter at the expense of philosophy, science, and social studies. The very abundance of these religious schools indicated the gradual decline which was under way. These colleges were intolerant of innovations, suspicious of secular studies, and aloof from creative scholars. Some of these colleges survived destruction by the Mongols in the thirteenth century and remained centers of dogmatic theological instruction to the fourteenth and fifteenth centuries.

There was competition among these denominational schools, particularly between the Shi'ite and Sunnite (Hanafite) religious factions. This competition proved healthy in the increase of these colleges and in their facilities, endowments, and the like, and would have been a tremendous educational power except for their limitations because of their religious nature.

It is of interest also to note that during this same period new universities were beginning to develop in western Europe, particularly in Italy, Germany, France, and England. But unlike the Islamic denominational schools, the Western universities were preserving the best intellectual elements that Islamic research and scholarship had developed during its creative centuries, from the ninth to the twelfth centuries. Islamic works were reaching Europe at about the same period (twelfth and thirteenth centuries) when secular learning was declining in Islam. The works of hundreds of translators not only enriched and created or enlarged many Western universities but brought about the Western Renaissance of the fourteenth and fifteenth centuries. One reason for this, of course, was the revival of secular interest and research in the West, which, though curtailed by religious passion until the seventeenth and eighteenth centuries, was left relatively free from then on to discover new knowledges and usher in the modern world. . . .

THE CURRICULUM OF MUSLIM SCHOOLS

The curriculum of Muslim education at that time reminds us in its extensive and intensive nature of curricular programs of modern advanced systems of education, particularly on higher levels of education. It was not unusual to find instruction in mathematics (algebra, trigonometry, and geometry), science (chemistry, physics, and astronomy), medicine (anatomy, surgery, pharmacy, and specialized medical branches), philosophy (logic, ethics, and metaphysics), literature (philology, grammar, poetry, and prosody), social sciences, history, geography, political disciplines, law, sociol-ogy, psychology, and jurisprudence, theology (comparative religions, history of religions, study of the *Qur'an*, religious tradition [*hadith*], and other religious topics). They offered advanced studies in the professions, for example, law and medicine.

Their vocational curriculum was varied and founded on the more general studies; in fact, it appears generally to have been as comprehensive as their education was universal. The extent and depth of Muslim curriculum can be detected by references to a number of encyclopedias of general knowledge and specific disciplines, among them the celebrated *Encyclopedia of the Ikhwan al-Safa* (the *Brethren of Purity* or *Sincerity*), which was known to and respected by European schoolmen.

Another indication of the extent of Muslim curriculum is manifested in the fact that one Arabic dictionary contained sixty volumes, with an illustration for each definition. Again, its richness may be determined by its practical and useful consequences, leading to such ventures as calculating the angle of the ecliptic, measuring the size of the earth, calculating the procession of the equinoxes, inventing the pendulum clock, explaining in the field of optics and physics such phenomena as "refraction of light, gravity, capillary attraction and twilight," using the globe in teaching the geography of a round earth, developing observatories for the empirical study of heavenly bodies, making advances in the uses of drugs, herbs, and foods for medication, establishing hospitals with a system of interns and externs, improving upon the science of navigation, introducing new concepts of irrigation, fertilization, and soil cultivation, discovering causes of certain diseases and developing correct diagnoses of them, proposing new concepts of hygiene, making use of anesthetics in surgery with newly innovated surgical tools, introducing the science of dissection in anatomy, furthering the scientific breeding of horses and cattle, and finding new ways of grafting to produce new types of flowers and fruits. In the area of chemistry, the curriculum led to the discovery of such substances as potash, alcohol, nitrate of silver, nitric acid, sulphuric acid, and corrosive sublimate. It also developed to a high degree of perfection the arts of textiles, ceramics, and metallurgy....

SOME MUSLIM CONTRIBUTIONS TO EDUCATION

Before concluding this brief summary of "medieval" Muslim education, it may be well to point out some of its basic contributions to educational theory and practice, and state also its basic shortcomings.

1. Throughout the twelfth and part of the thirteenth centuries, Muslim works on science, philosophy, and other fields were translated into Latin, particularly from Spain, and enriched the curriculum of the West, especially in northwestern Europe.
2. The Muslims passed on the experimental method of science, however imperfect, to the West.
3. The system of Arabic notation and decimals was introduced to the West.
4. Their translated works, particularly those of men such as Avicenna in medicine, were used as texts in classes of higher education far into the middle of the seventeenth century.
5. They stimulated European thought, reacquainted it with the Greek and other classical cultures and thus helped bring about the Renaissance.
6. They were the forerunners of European universities, having established hundreds of colleges in advance of Europe.
7. They preserved Greco-Persian thought when Europe was intolerant of pagan cultures.
8. European students in Muslim universities carried back new methods of teaching.
9. They contributed knowledge of hospitals, sanitation, and food to Europe.

The strength of the Muslim educational system lay in the following areas: It produced great scholars in almost every field. It developed literacy on a universal scale when illiteracy was the rule in Europe. It transmitted the best features of classical cultures to the West. It led the way in the development of libraries and universities. Its higher education in its creative centuries was open to rich and poor alike, the only requirements being ability and ambition. It held teachers and books in reverence, particularly on higher levels of instruction. The teacher, the book, the lecture, the debate—these were the nerve centers of its educational system.

The curriculum, which was in the early centuries balanced between sectarian and secular studies, became in the later centuries scholastic, making all or practically all secular studies subject to religious and theological approval. The curriculum became formal, fixed, traditional, religious, dogmatic, backward-looking. It encouraged static minds and conformity. It became authoritarian and essentialist.

Whereas in its early centuries Muslim education encouraged debates, experimentation, and individualism, in its later stages it encouraged formal methods, memorization, and recitation. A system which was in its early stages rather spontaneous and free, encouraging individuals to pursue learning and inspire others to enlightenment, lost in the later stages this sense of intellectual adventure and its direction became superimposed from the top (the state and church) rather than inspired by the people. This led in time to an elite and aristocratic concept of education, replacing its early democratic educational spirit. Muslim education did not, and with its scholastic disciplines could not, take advantage of the tools of science and experimentation which it had inherited and improved upon. Rather, it passed on these tools to European men of science, who utilized them effectively after the Renaissance and thus initiated and developed the modern world of science.

NOTES

1. Among the leading founders of schools in Islam should also be mentioned al Ma'mun (d. 833; 218 A.H.), who supported and endowed the first great Muslim educational center in Baghdad, the famous *Bait-al-Hikmah*, and was instrumental in having Greek, Persian, and Hindu translations made into Arabic by the greatest scholars of the time; Nur-al-Din (d. 1173; 569 A.H.), the Sultan of the kingdom of Syria who, after the dissolution of the Seljuq Empire, founded schools in Damascus and throughout his kingdom, including Egypt; Saladin (d. 1193; 589 A.H.), who extended the school systems in Syria and Egypt.

NO

Charles Homer Haskins

THE EARLIEST UNIVERSITIES

Universities, like cathedrals and parliaments, are a product of the Middle Ages. The Greeks and the Romans, strange as it may seem, had no universities in the sense in which the word has been used for the past seven or eight centuries. They had higher education, but the terms are not synonymous. Much of their instruction in law, rhetoric, and philosophy it would be hard to surpass, but it was not organized into the form of permanent institutions of learning. A great teacher like Socrates gave no diplomas; if a modern student sat at his feet for three months, he would demand a certificate, something tangible and external to show for it—an excellent theme, by the way, for a Socratic dialogue. Only in the twelfth and thirteenth centuries do there emerge in the world those features of organized education with which we are most familiar, all that machinery of instruction represented by faculties and colleges and courses of study, examinations and commencements and academic degrees. In all these matters we are the heirs and successors, not of Athens and Alexandria, but of Paris and Bologna.

The contrast between these earliest universities and those of today is of course broad and striking. Throughout the period of its origins the mediaeval university had no libraries, laboratories, or museums, no endowment or buildings of its own; it could not possibly have met the requirements of the Carnegie Foundation! As an historical text-book from one of the youngest of American universities tells us, with an unconscious touch of local color, it had "none of the attributes of the material existence which with us are so self-evident." The mediaeval university was, in the fine old phrase of Pasquier, "built of men"—*bâtie en hommes.* Such a university had no board of trustees and published no catalogue; it had no student societies—except so far as the university itself was fundamentally a society of students— no college journalism, no dramatics, no athletics, none of those "outside activities" which are the chief excuse for inside inactivity in the American college.

And yet, great as these differences are, the fact remains that the university of the twentieth century is the lineal descendant of mediaeval Paris and Bologna. They are the rock whence we were hewn; the hole of the pit whence we were digged. The fundamental organization is the same, the historic continuity is unbroken. They created the university tradition of the modern world, that common tradition which belongs to all our institutions of higher learning, the newest as well as the oldest, and which all college and university men should know and cherish. . . .

* * *

In recent years the early history of universities has begun to attract the serious attention of historical scholars, and mediaeval institutions of learning have at last been lifted out of the region of myth and fable where they long lay obscured. We now know that the foundation of the University of Oxford was not one of the many virtues which the millennial celebration could properly ascribe to King Alfred; that Bologna did not go back to the Emperor Theodosius; that the University of Paris did not exist in the time of Charlemagne, or for nearly four centuries afterward. It is hard, even for the modern world, to realize that many things had no founder or fixed date of beginning but instead "just grew," arising slowly and silently without definite record. This explains why, in spite of all the researches of Father Denifle[1] and Hastings Rashdall[2] and the local antiquaries, the beginnings of the oldest universities are obscure and often uncertain, so that we must content ourselves sometimes with very general statements.

The occasion for the rise of universities was a great revival of learning, not that revival of the fourteenth and fifteenth centuries to which the term is usually applied, but an earlier revival, less known though in its way quite as significant, which historians now call the renaissance of the twelfth century. So long as knowledge was limited to the seven liberal arts of the early Middle Ages, there could be no universities, for there was nothing to teach beyond the bare elements of grammar, rhetoric, logic, and the still barer notions of arithmetic, astronomy, geometry, and music, which did duty for an academic curriculum. Between 1100 and 1200, however, there came a great influx of new knowledge into western Europe, partly through Italy and Sicily, but chiefly through the Arab scholars of Spain—the works of Aristotle, Euclid, Ptolemy, and the Greek physicians, the new arithmetic, and those texts of the Roman law which had lain hidden through the Dark Ages. In addition to the elementary propositions of triangle and circle, Europe now had those books of plane and solid geometry which have done duty in schools and colleges ever since; instead of the painful operations with Roman numerals—how painful one can readily see by trying a simple problem of multiplication or division with these characters—it was now possible to work readily with Arabic figures; in the place of Boethius, the "Master of them that know" became the teacher of Europe in logic, metaphysics, and ethics. In law and medicine men now possessed the fulness of ancient learning. This new knowledge burst the bonds of the cathedral and monastery schools and created the learned professions; it drew over mountains and across the narrow seas eager youths who, like Chaucer's Oxford clerk of a later day, "would gladly learn and gladly teach," to form in Paris and Bologna those academic gilds which have given us our first and our best definition of a university, a society of masters and scholars.

To this general statement concerning the twelfth century there is one partial exception, the medical university of Salerno. Here, a day's journey to the south of Naples, in territory at first Lombard and later Norman, but still in close contact with the Greek East, a school of medicine had existed as early as the middle of the eleventh century, and for perhaps two hundred years thereafter it was the most renowned medical centre in Europe. In this "city of Hippocrates" the medical writings of the ancient Greeks were expounded and even developed on the side of anatomy and surgery, while its teachings were condensed into pithy maxims of hygiene which have not yet lost their vogue—"after dinner walk a mile," etc. Of the academic organization of Salerno we know nothing before 1231, and when in this year the standardizing hand of Frederick II regulated its degrees Salerno had already been distanced by newer universities farther north. Important in the history of medicine, it had no influence on the growth of university institutions.

If the University of Salerno is older in time, that of Bologna has a much larger place in the development of higher education. And while Salerno was known only as a school of medicine, Bologna was a many-sided institution, though most noteworthy as the centre of the revival of the Roman law. Contrary to a common impression, the Roman law did not disappear from the West in the early Middle Ages, but its influence was greatly diminished as a result of the Germanic invasions. Side by side with the Germanic codes, Roman law survived as the customary law of the Roman population, known no longer through the great law books of Justinian but in elementary manuals and form-books which grew thinner and more jejune as time went on. The *Digest*, the most important part of the *Corpus Juris Civilis*, disappears from view between 603 and 1076; only two manuscripts survived; in Maitland's phrase, it "barely escaped with its life." Legal study persisted, if at all, merely as an apprenticeship in the drafting of documents, a form of applied rhetoric. Then, late in the eleventh century, and closely connected with the revival of trade and town life, came a revival of law, foreshadowing the renaissance of the century which followed. This revival can be traced at more than one point in Italy, perhaps not first at Bologna, but here it soon found its centre for the geographical reasons which, then as now, made this city the meeting-point of the chief routes of communication in northern Italy. Some time before 1100 we hear of a professor named Pepo, "the bright and shining light of Bologna"; by 1119 we meet with the phrase *Bononia docta*. At Bologna, as at Paris, a great teacher stands at the beginning of university development. The teacher who gave Bologna its reputation was one Irnerius, perhaps the most famous of the many great professors of law in the Middle Ages. Just what he wrote and what he taught are still subjects of dispute among scholars, but he seems to have fixed the method of "glossing" the law texts upon the basis of a comprehensive use of the whole *Corpus Juris*, as contrasted with the meagre epitomes of the preceding centuries, fully and finally separating the Roman law from rhetoric and establishing it firmly as a subject of professional study. Then, about 1140, Gratian, a monk of San Felice, composed the *Decretum* which became the standard text in canon law, thus marked off from theology as a distinct subject of higher study; and the pre-eminence of Bologna as a law school was fully assured.

A student class had now appeared, expressing itself in correspondence and in poetry, and by 1158 it was sufficiently important in Italy to receive a formal grant of rights and privileges from Emperor Frederick Barbarossa, though no particular town or university is mentioned. By this time Bologna had become the resort of some hundreds of students, not only from Italy but from beyond the Alps. Far from home and undefended, they united for mutual protection and assistance, and this organization of foreign, or Transmontane, students was the beginning of the university. In this union they seem to have followed the example of the gilds already common in Italian cities. Indeed, the word university means originally such a group or corporation in general, and only in time did it come to be limited to gilds of masters and students, *universitas societas magistrorum discipulorumque*. Historically, the word university has no connection with the universe or the universality of learning; it denotes only the totality of a group, whether of barbers, carpenters, or students did not matter. The students of Bologna organized such a university first as a means of protection against the townspeople, for the price of rooms and necessaries rose rapidly with the crowd of new tenants and consumers, and the individual student was helpless against such profiteering. United, the students could bring the town to terms by the threat of departure as a body, secession, for the university, having no buildings, was free to move, and there are many historic examples of such migrations. Better rent one's rooms for less than not rent them at all, and so the student organizations secured the power to fix the prices of lodgings and books through their representatives.

Victorious over the townsmen, the students turned on "their other enemies, the professors." Here the threat was a collective boycott, and as the masters lived at first wholly from the fees of their pupils, this threat was equally effective. The professor was put under bond to live up to a minute set of regulations which guaranteed his students the worth of the money paid by each. We read in the earliest statutes (1317) that a professor might not be absent without leave, even a single day, and if he desired to leave town he had to make a deposit to ensure his return. If he failed to secure an audience of five for a regular lecture, he was fined as if absent —a poor lecture indeed which could not secure five hearers! He must begin with the bell and quit within one minute after the next bell. He as not allowed to skip a chapter in his commentary, or postpone a difficulty to the end of the hour, and he was obliged to cover ground systematically, so much in each specific term of the year. No one might spend the whole year on introduction and bibliography! Coercion of this sort presupposes an effective organization of the student body, and we hear of two and even four universities of students, each composed of "nations" and presided over by a rector. Emphatically Bologna was a student university, and Italian students are still quite apt to demand a voice in university affairs. When I first visited the University of Palermo I found it just recovering from a riot in which the students had broken the front windows in a demand for more frequent, and thus less comprehensive, examinations. At Padua's seventh centenary in May 1922 the students practically took over the town, with a programme of processions and ceremonies quite their own and an amount of noise and tumult which almost broke up the most solemn occasions and did break the windows of the greatest hall in the city.

Excluded from the "universities" of students, the professors also formed a gild or "college," requiring for admission thereto certain qualifications which were ascertained by examination, so that no student could enter save by the gild's consent. And, inasmuch as ability to teach a subject is a good test of knowing it, the student came to seek the professor's license as a certificate of attainment, regardless of his future career. This certificate, the license to teach (*licentia docendi*), thus became the earliest form of academic degree. Our higher degrees still preserve this tradition in the words master (*magister*) and doctor, originally synonymous, while the French even have a *licence.* A Master of Arts was one qualified to teach the liberal arts; a Doctor of Laws, a certified teacher of law. And the ambitious student sought the degree and gave an inaugural lecture, even when he expressly disclaimed all intention of continuing in the teaching profession. Already we recognize at Bologna the standard academic degrees as well as the university organization and well-known officials like the rector.

Other subjects of study appeared in course of time, arts, medicine, and theology, but Bologna was preeminently a school of civil law, and as such it became the model of university organization for Italy, Spain, and southern France, countries where the study of law has always had political and social as well as merely academic significance. Some of these universities became Bologna's competitors, like Montpellier and Orleans as well as the Italian schools nearer home. Frederick II founded the University of Naples in 1224 so that the students of his Sicilian kingdom could go to a Ghibelline school at home instead of the Guelfic centre in the North. Rival Padua was founded two years earlier as a secession from Bologna, and only in 1922, on the occasion of Padua's seven-hundredth anniversary, I saw the ancient feud healed by the kiss of peace bestowed on Bologna's rector amid the encores of ten thousand spectators. Padua, however, scarcely equalled Bologna in our period, even though at a later age Portia sent thither for legal authority, and though the university still shines with the glory of Galileo.

* * *

In northern Europe the origin of universities must be sought at Paris, in the cathedral school of Notre-Dame. By the beginning of the twelfth century in France and the Low Countries learning was no longer confined to monasteries but had its most active centres in the schools attached to cathedrals, of which the most famous were those of Liège, Rheims, Laon, Paris, Orleans, and Chartres. The most notable of these schools of the liberal arts was probably Chartres, distinguished by a canonist like St. Ives and by famous teachers of classics and philosophy like Bernard and Thierry. As early as 991 a monk of Rheims, Richer, describes the hardships of his journey to Chartres in order to study the *Aphorisms* of Hippocrates of Cos; while from the twelfth century John of Salisbury, the leading northern humanist of the age, has left us an account of the masters.... Nowhere else today can we drop back more easily into a cathedral city of the twelfth century, the peaceful town still dominated by its church and sharing, now as then,

> the minister's vast repose.
> Silent and gray as forest-leaguered cliff
> Left inland by the ocean's slow retreat,
> .... patiently remote
> From the great tides of life it breasted once,
> Hearing the noise of men as in a dream.

By the time the cathedral stood complete, with its "dedicated shapes of saints and kings," it had ceased to be an intellectual centre of the first importance, overshadowed by Paris fifty-odd miles away, so that Chartres never became a university.

The advantages of Paris were partly geographical, partly political as the capital of the new French monarchy, but something must be set down to the influence of a great teacher in the person of Abelard. This brilliant young radical, with his persistent questioning and his scant respect for titled authority, drew students in large numbers wherever he taught, whether at Paris or in the wilderness. At Paris he was connected with the church of Mont-Sainte-Geneviève longer than with the cathedral school, but resort to Paris became a habit in his time, and in this way he had a significant influence on the rise of the university. In an institutional sense the university was a direct outgrowth of the school of Notre-Dame, whose chancellor alone had authority to license teaching in the diocese and thus kept his control over the granting of university degrees, which here as at Bologna were originally teachers' certificates. The early schools were within the cathedral precincts on the Ile de la Cité, that tangled quarter about Notre-Dame pictured by Victor Hugo which has long since been demolished. A little later we find masters and scholars living on the Little Bridge (Petit-Pont) which connected the island with the Left Bank of the Seine —this bridge gave its name to a whole school of philosophers, the Parvipontani —but by the thirteenth century they have overrun the Left Bank, thenceforth, the Latin Quarter of Paris.

At what date Paris ceased to be a cathedral school and became a university, no one can say, though it was certainly before the end of the twelfth century. Universities, however, like to have precise dates to celebrate, and the University of Paris has chosen 1200, the year of its first royal charter. In that year, after certain students had been killed in a town and gown altercation, King Philip Augustus issued a formal privilege which punished his prévôt and recognized the exemption of the students and their servants from lay jurisdiction, thus creating that special position of students before the courts which has not yet wholly disappeared from the world's practice, though generally from its law. More specific was the first papal privilege, the bull *Parens scientiarum* of 1231,[3] issued after a two years' cessation of lectures growing out of a riot in which a band of students, having found "wine that was good and sweet to drink," beat up the tavern keeper and his friends till they in turn suffered from the prévôt and his men, a dissension in which the thirteenth century clearly saw the hand of the devil. Confirming the existing exemptions, the Pope goes on to regulate the discretion of the chancellor in conferring the license, at the same time that he recognizes the right of the masters and students "to make constitutions and ordinances regulating the manner and time of lectures and disputations, the costume to be worn," attendance at masters' funerals, the lectures of bachelors, necessarily more limited than those of fully fledged masters, the price of lodgings, and the coercion of members. Students must not carry arms, and only those who frequent the schools regularly are to enjoy the exemptions of students, the interpretation in practice being attendance at not less than two lectures a week.

While the word university does not appear in these documents, it is taken for granted. A university in the sense of an organized body of masters existed already in the twelfth century; by 1231 it had developed into a corporation, for Paris, in contrast to Bologna, was a university of masters. There were now four faculties, each under a dean: arts, canon law (civil law was forbidden at Paris after 1219), medicine, and theology. The masters of arts, much more numerous than the others, were grouped into four "nations": the French, including the Latin peoples; the Normans; the Picard, including also the Low Countries; and the English, comprising England, Germany, and the North and East of Europe. These four nations chose the head of the university, the rector, as he is still generally styled on the Continent, whose term, however, was short, being later only three months....

It is, then, in institutions that the university tradition is most direct. First, the very name university, as an association of masters and scholars leading the common life of learning. Characteristic of the Middle Ages as such a corporation is, the individualistic modern world has found nothing to take its place. Next, the notion of a curriculum of study, definitely laid down as regards time and subjects, tested by an examination and leading to a degree, as well as many of the degrees themselves—bachelor, as a stage toward the mastership, master, doctor, in arts, law, medicine, and theology. Then the faculties, four or more, with their deans, and the higher officers such as chancellors and rectors, not to mention the college, wherever the residential college still survives. The essentials of university organization are clear and unmistakable, and they have been handed down in unbroken continuity. They have lasted more than seven hundred years—what form of government has lasted so long?

NOTES

1. H. Denifle, *Die Enstehung der Universitäten des Mittelalters bis 1400*, vol. I (Berlin, 1880).
2. H. Rashdall, *The Universities of Europe in the Middle Ages*, 2 vols. in 3 (Oxford, 1895); rev. ed., 3 vols. (Oxford, 1936)....
3. Trans. by L. Thorndike, *University Records and Life in the Middle Ages* (New York, 1944), pp. 35–39.

POSTSCRIPT

Does the Modern University Have Its Roots in the Islamic World?

It is tempting to think that all modern institutions, especially those that we find admirable, have come down to us in a direct line from our intellectual forebears, the Greeks. To take the university as a case in point, however, we cannot trace its origins to Greece. As Haskins points out, the Greeks and Romans had no universities. Higher education was a much less organized enterprise of student-teacher interaction. There were no diplomas, courses of study, examinations, or commencements—at least not as we understand these terms today. Agreeing that we cannot trace the Western university to the Greeks, Haskins and Nakosteen part company on where its roots actually lie. Haskins finds universities springing up in Bologna, Paris, Salerno, and Oxford in response to an infusion of new knowledge brought about by the restoration of trade routes after the Crusades. Nakosteen finds an unbroken line from the eighth-century Arab world to the late European Middle Ages. The university system, he argues, was formed in an Arab context and made its way unchanged into a European one.

If we begin a history of education from within the Islamic world, new patterns will emerge. For an introduction to Islam as a cultural system, *Islam and the Cultural Accommodation of Social Change* by Bassam Tibi (Westview Press, 1991) offers a clear introduction to the Sunni/Shi'a split in Islam, which persists today, and a discussion of language (in this case Arabic) as the medium in which cultural symbols are articulated. Students may also be interested in Francis Robinson, ed., *The Cambridge Illustrated History of the Islamic World* (Cambridge University Press, 1996), especially chapter 7, "Knowledge, Its Transmission, and the Making of Muslim Societies." In chapter 9, "The Iranian Diaspora: The Edge Creates a Center," of *Islam: A View from the Edge* (Columbia University Press, 1994), Richard W. Bulliet describes the role of Iranian scholars in the spread of *madrasa*, or Islamic colleges.

For additional background on European universities of the Middle Ages, see *The Medieval University* by Helene Wieruszowski (Van Nostrand Reinhold, 1966) and *The Scholastic Culture of the Middle Ages: 1000–1300* by John W. Baldwin (D. C. Heath, 1971). The movie *Stealing Heaven* tells the story of Heloise and Abelard. Set in twelfth-century France, it also offers a very realistic portrayal of the emerging European university system of disputation between professors and students. Finally, Norman F. Cantor's *The Civilization of the Middle Ages* (HarperCollins, 1993) has a chapter entitled "Moslem and Jewish Thought: The Aristotelian Challenge," which summarizes the influence of Islamic thought on Europe.

ISSUE 9

Were Environmental Factors Responsible for the Collapse of the Mayan Civilization?

YES: Richard E. W. Adams, from *Prehistoric Mesoamerica,* rev. ed. (University of Oklahoma Press, 1991)

NO: George L. Cowgill, from "Teotihuacan, Internal Militaristic Competition, and the Fall of the Classic Maya," in Norman Hammond and Gordon R. Willey, eds., *Maya Archaeology and Ethnohistory* (University of Texas Press, 1979)

ISSUE SUMMARY

YES: Professor of anthropology Richard E. W. Adams argues that although military factors played a role in the Mayan demise, a combination of internal factors was more responsible for that result.

NO: Professor of anthropology George L. Cowgill contends that although there is no single explanation for the Mayan collapse, military expansion played a more important role than scholars originally thought.

A notable civilization from long ago wrote in hieroglyphs, developed an accurate calendar, built pyramid-like structures to honor its gods, practiced polytheism with gods represented by animal imagery, and advanced in areas such as mathematics and astronomy. These characteristics could describe the ancient Egyptians. But here they are used to describe the Mayas of Mesoamerica, who established a New World civilization a millennium before the arrival of Europeans. Before this invasion, this Amerindian civilization was in a state of decline. The Spanish conquistadors completely destroyed what remained, causing it to disappear until it was uncovered in the nineteenth century by explorers seeking to find the lost civilization of the Mayas.

Within the last 100 years, work by archaeologists, linguists, and scientists of all sorts have not only exposed what remains of Mayan grandeur but, by deciphering their language, have uncovered the secrets of their advanced civilization. The continuing discoveries have inspired regular reassessments of earlier theories. It was once thought, for example, that Mayas were peaceful people, with little interest in war as a means to achieving ends. We now know that this was not true. As far as the Mayas are concerned, today's theory is only as good as the latest archaeological discovery or linguistic decipherment.

In spite of the wealth of information that scholars have on the Mayas, there are still questions about them that have not been definitively answered. One of the most important questions is, What caused the decline of the Mayan civilization? Scholars and scientists who have spent their lives studying the Mayas have developed theories about the decline of that civilization using the best evidence that is presently available. In spite of this, a definitive answer seems to be lacking.

This issue seeks to explore the two major theories involving Mayan decline: (1) It occurred because of internal factors that the Mayans could not or would not control; and (2) the demise was brought about by excessive militarism.

Both of these theories are considered by Richard E. W. Adams and George L. Cowgill, two noted Mayan scholars, in the selections that follow. Adams considers internal stresses—overpopulation, agricultural scarcities, disease, and natural disasters—to be the major factors responsible for the collapse of the city-states of the Southern Maya Lowlands. Cowgill uses the Teotihuacan civilization, centered in the Mexican Highlands, as a "contrastive example" as to what may have happened to the civilization of the Southern Maya Lowlands. He claims that because the two histories "exhibit a similar developmental trajectory," the military factors that caused the collapse of the former may have also been responsible for the demise of the latter.

Future archaeological work in Central America is likely to shed more light on the fate of the Mayan civilization.

YES

Richard E. W. Adams

TRANSFORMATIONS

THE CLASSIC MAYA COLLAPSE

According to what we now know, Maya civilization began to reach a series of regional peaks about A.D. 650. By A.D. 830, there is evidence of disintegration of the old patterns, and by A.D. 900, all of the southern lowland centers had collapsed. An understanding of the Maya apocalypse must be based in large part on an understanding of the nature of Maya civilization. During the Terminal Classic period, A.D. 750 to 900, cultural patterns of the lowlands can be briefly characterized as follows. Demographically, a high peak had been reached at least as early as A.D. 600 and perhaps earlier. This population density and size in turn led to intensive forms of agriculture and the establishment of permanent farmsteads in the countryside. Hills were terraced, swamps were drained and modified, water impoundments were made by the hundreds, and land became so scarce that walls of rock were built both as boundaries and simply as the results of field clearance. These masses of people were also highly organized for political purposes into region-state units, which fluctuated in size. These states were more than simple aggregations of cities and were characterized by hierarchical and other complex relationships among them.

Society was organized on an increasingly aristocratic principle by A.D. 650. Dynasties and royal lineages were at the top of the various Maya states and commanded most of the resources of Maya economic life. Most of the large architecture of the cities was for their use. Groups of craft specialists and civil servants supported the elite, with the mass of the population engaged in either part-time or full-time farming. Trade was well organized among and within the states. Military competition was present but was controlled by the fact that it had become mainly an elite-class and prestige activity which did not greatly disturb the economic basis of life. Thus, Maya culture at the ninth century A.D. seems to have been well-ordered, adjusted, and definitely a success. Yet a devastating catastrophe brought it down.

Characteristics of the Collapse

It sometimes seems that the accumulation of weighty theoretical formulations purporting to explain the collapse of Maya civilization will eventually, instead, cause the collapse of Maya archaeology. A refreshingly skeptical and clear-sighted book by John Lowe reviews the major theories and tests them as well. We will not be as thorough in the following section but, it is to be hoped, just as convincing. A brief characterization of the collapse includes the following features:

1. It occurred over a relatively short period of time: 75 to 150 years.
2. During it the elite-class culture failed, as reflected in the abandonment of palaces and temples and the cessation of manufacture of luxury goods and erection of stelae.
3. Also during the period there was a rapid and nearly complete depopulation of the countryside and the urban centers.
4. The geographical focus of the first collapse was in the oldest and most developed zones, the southern lowlands and the intermediate area. The northern plains and Puuc areas survived for a while longer.

In other words, the Maya collapse was a demographic, cultural, and social catastrophe in which elite and commoner went down together. Drawing on all available information about the ancient Maya and comparable situations, the 1970 Santa Fe Conference developed a comprehensive explanation of the collapse. This explanation depends on the relatively new picture of the Maya summarized above. That is, we must discard any notion of the Maya as the "noble savage" living in harmony with nature. Certainly, the Maya lived more in tune with nature than do modern industrial peoples, but probably not much more so than did our nineteenth-century pioneer ancestors. As we shall see, some dissonance with na-

ture was at least partly responsible for its failure. More than this, however, data have been further developed since the conference which strengthen some assumptions and weaken others. Therefore, the explanation which follows is a modified version of that which appears in the report of the Santa Fe Conference.

Stresses

Maya society had a number of built-in stresses, many of which had to do with high populations in the central and southern areas. Turner's and other studies indicate that from about A.D. 600 to 900 there were about 168 people per square kilometer (435 per square mile) in the Río Bec zone. The intensive agricultural constructions associated with this population density are also found farther south, within 30 kilometers (19 miles) of Tikal. They are also to be found to the east in the Belize Valley, and there are indications elsewhere to the south that high populations were present. According to Saul's studies of Maya bones from the period, the population carried a heavy load of endemic disease, including malaria, yellow fever, syphilis, and Chagas's disease, the latter a chronic infection which leads to cardiac insufficiency in young adulthood. Chronic malnutrition is also indicated by Saul's and Steele's studies. Taken altogether, these factors indicate the precarious status of health even for the elite. Average lifespan in the southern lowlands was about thirty-nine years. Infant mortality was high; perhaps as many as 78 percent of Maya children never reached the age of twenty. Endemic disease can go epidemic with just a rise in malnutrition. In other words, the Maya populace carried within itself a biological time bomb which needed only a triggering event such as a crop failure to go off.

With population pressing the limits of subsistence, management of land and other resources was a problem, and one which would have fallen mainly on the elite. If food were to be imported, or if marginal lands were to be brought into cultivation, by extensive drainage projects, for example, then the elite had to arrange for it to be done. There were certain disadvantages to this arrangement. Aristocratic or inherited leadership of any kind is a poor means to approach matters that require rational decisions. One need only consider the disastrous manner in which seventeenth-century European armies were mishandled by officers whose major qualifications were their lineages. There is a kind of built-in variation of the Peter Principle in such leadership: one is born to his level of incompetence. Maya aristocracy apparently was no better equipped to handle the complex problems of increasing populations than were European aristocrats. There were no doubt capable and brilliant nobles, but there was apparently no way in which talent could quickly be taken to the top of society from its lower ranks. Lowe's model of the collapse of Maya civilization emphasizes the management-administrative aspects of the problem and essentially considers the collapse as an administrative breakdown.

There are also signs in the Terminal Classic period of a widening social gulf between elite and commoners. At the same time, problems were increasing in frequency and severity. The elite class increased in size and made greater demands on the rest of Maya society for its support. This created further tensions. Intensive agriculture led to greater crop yields, but also put Maya food production increasingly at hostage to the vagaries of weather, crop disease, insects, birds, and other hazards. Marginal and complex cultivation systems require large investments of time and labor and necessitate that things go right more often than not. A run of bad weather or a long-term shift in climate might trigger a food crisis. Recent work on tree rings and weather history from other sources indicates that a Mesoamerica-wide drought may have begun about A.D. 850. In addition, there are periodic outbreaks of locusts in the Maya Lowlands.

These stresses were pan–Maya and occurred to a greater or lesser degree in every region. No matter whether one opts for the city-state or the regional state model, competition over scarce resources among the political units of the Maya resulted from these stressful situations. The large southern center of Seibal was apparently taken by a northern Maya elite group about A.D. 830. Evidence is now in hand of military intrusions from north to south at Rio Azul, at the Belize sites of Nohmul, Colha, and Barton Ramie, and at Quirigua in the Motagua Valley. At least at Rio Azul and Colha a period of trade preceded the raids, presaging the later Aztec *pochteca* pattern. The patterns and nature of the intrusions indicate that the raids were probably from the Puuc zone and that a part of the motivation, as suggested by Cowgill, was to capture populations. Warfare increased markedly along the Usumacinta River during the ninth century A.D., according to hieroglyphic texts and carved pictures from that area.

There are also hints that the nature of Maya warfare may have changed during this last period. A lintel from Piedras Negras appears to show numerous soldiers in standard uniforms kneeling in ranks before an officer. In other words, organized violence may have come to involve many more people and much more effort and therefore may have become much more disruptive. Certainly competition over scarce resources would have led to an increasingly unstable situation. Further, the resultant disorganization would have led to vulnerability to outside military intervention, and that seems to have been the case as well.

There were also external pressures on the Maya. Some were intangible and in the form of new ideas about the nature of human society as well as new ideologies from the Gulf Coast and Central Mexico. The northern Maya elites seem to have absorbed a number of these new ideas. For example, they included the depiction of Mexican Gulf Coast deities on their stelae as well as some Mexican-style hieroglyphs. Altar de Sacrificios was invaded by still another foreign group from the Gulf Coast about A.D. 910. These people may have been either a truly Mexican Gulf Coast group or Chontal Maya, who were non-Classic in their culture.

A progressive pattern of abandonment and disaster in the western lowlands is suggestive. Palenque, on the southwestern edges of the lowlands, was one of the first major centers to go under; it was abandoned about A.D. 810. The major Usumacinta cities of Piedras Negras and Yaxchilan (Bird-Jaguar's City) were the next to go. They put up their last monuments about A.D. 825. Finally, it was Altar de Sacrificios's turn about A.D. 910. Clearly, there was a progressive disintegration from west to east, and it seems likely that it was caused by pressures from militaristic non–Maya groups. These peoples, in turn, were probably being jostled in the competitive situation set up after the fall of Teotihuacan and may

have been pushed ahead of peoples such as the Toltecs and their allies. Perhaps the Epi-Classic states discussed above were involved, as well as some mercenary groups. In any case, it appears certain that these groups were opportunists. They came into an area already disorganized and disturbed and were not the triggering mechanism for the catastrophe but part of the following process.

At any one Maya city or in any one region, the "mix" of circumstances was probably unique. At Piedras Negras there is evidence that the elite may have been violently overthrown from within. Faces of rulers on that site's stelae are smashed, and there are other signs of violence. Invasion finished off Altar de Sacrificios. Rio Azul was overrun by Maya groups from the north, perhaps including Toltec allies, as were a number of Maya centers along the Belize coast and down to Quirigua. At other centers, such as the regional capital of Tikal, the elite were apparently abandoned to their fate. Without the supporting populations, remnants of the Maya upper classes lingered on after the catastrophe. At Colha and Seibal, northern Maya acting as new elites attempted to continue the southern economic and political systems, but they abandoned these attempts after a relatively short time. The general demographic catastrophe and disruption of the agricultural systems were apparently too great to cope with.

In short, ecological abuse, disease, mismanagement, overpopulation, militarism, famines, epidemics, and bad weather overtook the Maya in various combinations. But several questions remain. What led to the high levels of populations which were the basis of much of the disaster?

The Maya were much more loosely organized politically during the Late Formative than during the Classic period. The episodes of interstate competition and of Teotihuacan's intervention seem to have led them to try new, more centralized political arrangements. These seem to have worked well for a time, in the case of the Early Classic expansion of Tikal. After the suggested civil wars of the sixth century there seems to have been a renewed and still stronger development of centralized states, which were probably monarchical.

Using general historical and anthropological experience, Demitri Shimkin observed that village-level societies approach population control very differently than do state-level societies. Relatively independent villages are oriented plainly and simply toward survival. There are many traditional ways of population control, female infanticide being a favorite practiced widely even in eighteenth-century England. Use of herbal abortion, late marriage, ritual ascetisicism, and other means keep population within bounds for a village. A state-level society, on the other hand, is likely to encourage population growth for the benefit of the directing elite. The more manpower to manipulate, the better. In the case of the Maya, we have noted a certain megalomania in their huge Late Classic buildings. Unfinished large construction projects at Tikal and Uaxactun were overtaken by the collapse. Such efforts required immense manpower reserves and a simultaneous disregard for the welfare of that workforce. The Maya appear to have shifted gears into a more sophisticated and ultimately maladaptive state organization.

Another question to be considered is, Why did the Maya not adjust to cope with the crises? The answer may lie in the nature of religiously sanctioned aristocracies. Given a crop failure, a Maya leadership group might have attempted to propitiate the ancestors and gods with more ritual and more monuments. This response would have exacerbated the crisis by taking manpower out of food production. Inappropriate responses of this sort could easily have been made, given the ideology and worldview that the Maya seem to have held. On the other hand, if the crisis were a long-term drought, with populations dangerously high and predatory warfare disrupting matters even more, perhaps any response would have been ineffectual.

The rapid biological destruction of the Maya is an important aspect of the collapse. From a guessed-at high of 12 million, the population was reduced within 150 years to an estimated remnant of about 1.8 million. The disease load and the stress of malnutritional factors indicate that a steady diminishment of Maya population probably started by A.D. 830 and rapidly reached a point of no recovery. An average increase of 10 to 15 percent in the annual mortality rate will statistically reduce 12 million to 1.8 million in 75 years. Obviously there was not anything like a steady decline, but the smoothed-out average over the period had to have been something of that order, or perhaps the decline began earlier, at A.D. 750, when Maya civilization reached its peak.

The disruptive nature of population declines can be easily understood if one considers the usual effects of epidemics. In such catastrophic outbreaks of disease, those first and most fatally affected are the young and the old. Even if the main working population survives relatively untouched, the social loss is only postponed. The old take with them much of the accumulated experience and knowledge needed to meet future crises. The young will not be there to mature and replace the adult working population, and a severe manpower shortage will result within fifteen to twenty years. Needless to say, much more work on population estimates and studies of the bones and the general health environment of the ancient Maya needs to be done to produce a really convincing statement on this aspect of the collapse.

A last, although not by any means final, question concerns the failure to recover. This feature may involve climatic factors. If shifts of rainfall belts were responsible for triggering the collapse, then the answer might be the persistence of drought conditions until there were too few people left to sustain the Classic cultural systems. As now seems probable, the Maya were confronted with the situation of having overcultivated their soils and having lost too much surface water. Temporary abandonment of fields would have led to their being rapidly overrun by thick, thorny, second-growth jungle, which is harder to clear than primary forest. Thus, a diminished population may have been faced with the problem of clearing heavily overgrown, worn-out soils, of which vast amounts were needed to sustain even small populations. Second-growth forest springs up overnight and is even today a major problem in maintaining archaeological sites for tourists.

Another possible answer to the question of recovery is that the Maya may have been loathe to attempt the sort of brilliant effort that had ultimately broken them. Just as they preferred to revert to swidden agriculture rather than main-

tain intensive techniques, they probably found it a relief to live on a village level instead of in their former splendid but stressful state of existence.

The above is an integrated model of the Maya collapse. It explains all the features of the collapse and all the data now in hand, but it is not proved by any means, and in some respects is more of a guide to future research than a firm explanation. If the model is more or less correct, however, it should be largely confirmed within the next ten years of research. Indeed, this process of confirmation has already begun. The 1970 conference which developed the model could explain certain features of the archaeological record only by assuming much higher levels of ancient population than were otherwise plausible at the time. The 1973 Rio Bec work of Turner and Eaton turned up a vast amount of data which indicate that higher levels of ancient populations indeed had been present. Recent work at Colha and Rio Azul has indicated the importance of militarism in the process. All of these findings lend credibility to the model.

Delayed Collapse in the North

The vast and very densely distributed centers of the Puuc area survived for a time. These Puuc cities, possibly a regional state with a capital at Uxmal, appear to have turned into predators on the southern cities. As noted before, part of the motivation may have been for the capture and enslavement of southern populations. Even so, it seems that large centers such as Uxmal, Kabah, Sayil, and Labna lasted only a century longer than the southern cities. Northern Maya chronology is much more disputed than that in the south, but it now seems likely that outsiders, including Toltec, were in

Yucatan by A.D. 900 and perhaps earlier, and there are clear indications that Uxmal was absorbing Mexican ideas much earlier. Certain motifs, such as eagles or vultures, appear on Puuc building facades late in the Classic period.

We are now faced with at least three possible explanations of the Puuc collapse: they may have succumbed to the same combination of factors that brought down the southern Maya centers; the Toltec may have conquered them; or a combination of these factors may have been at work. At this time, it appears that the northern florescence was partly at the expense of the southern area.... [E]vidence for Toltec conquest now appears even stronger, and this is presently the favored explanation for the Puuc collapse.

Chichen Itza, in north central Yucatan, is a center which was culturally allied with the Puuc cities in architecture and probably politically as well. Puuc centers have been found even in the far northeast of the peninsula. At Chichen Itza, Puuc architecture is overlaid and succeeded by Toltec architecture. Unmapped defensive walls surround both Chichen and Uxmal. The data available now make it likely that the Toltec and other groups may have appeared in Yucatan by A.D. 800 and thereafter, perhaps brought in as mercenaries, as so often happened later in Maya history. In whatever capacity they arrived, they appear to have established themselves at Chichen Itza by A.D. 950 as the controlling power. As has happened in history elsewhere, the mercenaries became the controlling forces. Toltec raids, battles, and sieges, combined with the internal weaknesses of Classic Maya culture and perhaps with changing environmental factors, brought about a swift collapse in the Puuc.

The aftermath of the collapse was also devastating. Most of the southern Maya Lowlands have not been repopulated until the last fifty years. Eleven hundred years of abandonment have rejuvenated the soils, the forests, and their resources, but modern man is now making inroads on them. Kekchi Maya Indians have been migrating into the lowlands from the northern Guatemalan highlands as pioneer farmers for the past century, and the Mexican government has colonized the Yucatan, Campeche, and Quintana Roo area with dissatisfied agriculturists from overpopulated highland areas. The forests are being logged and cut down. Agricultural colonies have failed in both Guatemala and Mexico, and some zones are already abandoned. In other areas, the inhabitants have turned to marijuana cultivation. Vast areas have been reduced to low scrub jungle, and large amounts of land are now being converted to intensive agriculture. One looks at the modern scene and wonders. Fortunately, in 1988 a movement began to set aside the remnants of the once immense monsoon forests, and it may be that a series of protected zones in the form of contiguous national parks will soon be in existence in Guatamala, Mexico, and Belize.

NO

George L. Cowgill

TEOTIHUACAN, INTERNAL MILITARISTIC COMPETITION, AND THE FALL OF THE CLASSIC MAYA

In very broad terms, the Teotihuacan civilization, centered in the Mexican Highlands, and the Classic civilization of the Southern Maya Lowlands exhibit a similar developmental trajectory. That is, both enjoyed a period of development, flourished for a time, and then collapsed. But as soon as one looks beyond these gross generalities, the evidence from each region shows striking differences in the pace and timing of events. These differences are of interest in their own right, and one of my objectives is to call attention to them. In addition, however, they help to direct our attention to some of the distinctive features of the Maya trajectory which are relevant for understanding the functioning of Late Classic Maya society and for explaining its collapse. My main concern is to point out difficulties in some recently proposed explanations... and to suggest that escalating internal warfare may have been more a cause than a consequence of serious trouble for the Maya. I do not suggest warfare as a mono-causal explanation for the Maya collapse, but I do think it may have been an important contributing factor, and old evidence should be re-examined and new evidence sought with this possibility in mind.

Emphasis on Maya warfare is part of a widespread recognition that the Maya were not the gentle pacifists that some archaeologists would have them be. But there is a difference between sporadic raiding, with occasional enslavement or sacrifice or captives, and what David Webster calls *militarism*: institutionalized warfare intended for territorial aggrandizement and acquisition of other capital resources, with military decisions part of the conscious political policy of small elite, semiprofessional warriors, and lethal combat on a large scale. Webster and I both argue that the Late Classic Maya may have become militaristic in this sense, but we differ about the probable dynamics and consequences of Maya militarism.

Although it is clear that there were important contacts between the Highlands and the Southern Maya Lowlands, I should stress that I am *not* arguing that either Teotihuacan intervention or the withdrawal of Teotihuacan

From George L. Cowgill, "Teotihuacan, Internal Militaristic Competition, and the Fall of the Classic Maya," in Norman Hammond and Gordon R. Willey, eds., *Maya Archaeology and Ethnohistory* (University of Texas Press, 1979). Copyright © 1979 by University of Texas Press. Reprinted by permission. References omitted.

contacts played a decisive role in the Maya collapse. Direct or indirect contacts with Teotihuacan are important and extremely interesting, but I doubt if they explain much about either the rise or the fall of the Lowland Maya. In any case, my use of the Teotihuacan data here is purely as a contrastive example.

It is often assumed that Teotihuacan developed rather steadily up to a distinct peak somewhere around A.D. 500 to 600, after which it soon began a fairly rapid decline.... [L]argely through the data obtained by the comprehensive surface survey and limited test excavations completed by the Teotihuacan Mapping Project, under the direction of René Millon, evidence for a very different pattern has emerged....

Briefly, it appears that the city of Teotihuacan enjoyed an early surge of extremely rapid growth, followed by a four-to-five-century "plateau" during which growth was very much slower or may even have ceased altogether. Then, probably not before the eighth century A.D., the city collapsed, apparently rather rapidly. This pattern is most clearly suggested by the dates of major monumental construction in the city, but it is also suggested by the demographic implications of quantities and areal spreads of ceramics of various periods, both in the city itself and in all parts of the Basin of Mexico which have been systematically surveyed. Further support comes from data on Teotihuacan obsidian industry.

In contrast, the Maya site of Tikal was settled at least as early as Teotihuacan but developed more irregularly to a modest Late Preclassic climax, followed apparently by something of a pause. There seems to have been a second peak in Early Classic times, and then a distinct recession for a century or so.

Then there was a relatively brief burst of glory in the seventh and eighth centuries, immediately followed by rapid decline and very drastic population loss. Tikal population may have been relatively stable from about A.D. 550 until after A.D. 800, or it may have shot up rapidly during the 600's to a short-lived maximum in the 700's. In either case, however, it seems clear that the Late Classic population of Tikal was larger than that at any previous time. Other major sites in the Southern Maya Lowlands had rather different trajectories, but they also generally peaked during the Late Classic and collapsed during the ninth or tenth centuries.

There are also striking contrasts in spatial patterns. The early growth of Teotihuacan is concomitant with rapid and marked decline in the number and size of other settlements in the Basin of Mexico. Teotihuacan quickly achieved, and for several centuries maintained, a size probably twenty or more times larger than any other known Basin of Mexico settlement. Even Cholula, in the Valley of Puebla some ninety kilometers away; does not seem to have covered more than a sixth of the area of Teotihuacan, and other settlements in the Tlaxcala–Northern Puebla area were much smaller. In the Southern Maya Lowlands there were other major centers comparable in size to Tikal, and below these there was a hierarchy of other sites ranging from fairly large secondary centers to small hamlets and individual households. (In contrast to Marcus, Hammond argues that present evidence is insufficient for assigning specific sites to specific hierarchical levels, although hierarchies probably existed. The very fact of the controversy points up the contrast with Teotihuacan, where there is no dispute at all about its primacy in the settlement hierarchy.) There is no suggestion that Tikal or other major centers ever drew people away from other sites or monopolized power to anywhere near the extent that Teotihuacan did in central Mexico....

IMPLICATIONS OF THE TEOTIHUACAN EVIDENCE

Several implications of the Teotihuacan pattern suggest themselves. The long duration of Teotihuacan seems unreasonable unless economic and political power were quite strong and quite effectively centralized in the city, and much other evidence also suggest this. In contrast, both the more or less concomitant development of many Lowland Maya centers and the dynastic evidence so far gleaned from inscriptions indicate that no single Southern Lowland Maya center ever gained long-term firm political or economic control of any very large region, although there is plenty of evidence for brief domination of one center by another, and of political alliances often bolstered by dynastic marriages.

The obvious next step is to suggest that Teotihuacan was long-lived and highly centralized because it was a "hydraulic" state, based on intensive irrigation agriculture in a semiarid environment, while the Southern Maya Lowlands was politically less centralized and enjoyed a much briefer climax because of critical deficiencies in its tropical forest environment. I do not think that environmental considerations are unimportant, but I do feel that there are extremely serious difficulties with these explanations.

Discussions of Teotihuacan irrigation usually do not deal adequately with its *scale*. Evidence for pre-Toltec irrigation in the Teotihuacan Valley remains circum-

stantial rather than direct, but it seems quite likely that canal irrigation there does date back to Patlachique or Cuanalan times. But the maximum area available for permanent canal irrigation is less than four thousand hectares. This is not a very large area, nor does it call for large or complex canals, dikes, or flood-control facilities. Assuming a peak population of 125,000, there would have been about one irrigated hectare for 30 people. It is clear that the city grew well beyond any population limits set by irrigation agriculture, and a substantial fraction of its subsistence must have come from other sources, including riskier and much less productive alternative forms of agriculture, and collecting and hunting wild plants and animals. Faunal analyses and paleoethnobotanical studies provide evidence that Teotihuacanos ate a wide variety of wild as well as domesticated plants and wild animals.

It seems unlikely that there were any environmental or purely technical factors which would have made it impossible for the Teotihuacanos to have practiced intensive chinampa agriculture in the southern part of the Basin of Mexico. Chinampas were an important subsistence source for the Aztec population, which was much larger than the Teotihuacan population. Yet there is no evidence for extensive use of chinampas in Teotihuacan times. It is tempting to speculate that technical difficulties in assembling food for more people in one place may be at least part of the reason that Teotihuacan grew so little after Tzacualli times (a point also made by J. R. Parsons). If indeed there were environmental reasons, such as a change in lake levels, which prevented extensive chinampa exploitation in Teotihuacan times, then Teotihuacan is an instance of a population which expanded until it approached a perceived subsistence limit and then stabilized, rather than disastrously exceed that limit. If, as seems more likely, there was no environmental reason why the Teotihuacanos could not have fed more people by simply moving part of the population down to the chinampa area and investing in chinampa developments, their apparent failure to do so must have been for social or political reasons. If so, Teotihuacan population growth in the Basin of Mexico halted at a level well below the number of people it would have been technically possible to feed.

Teotihuacan's behavior has particular significance for the Maya because Culbert suggests that the Maya collapsed because they were unable to control runaway expansion which caused them to "overshoot" disastrously the productive limits of their environment.

Whether or not I am right in suspecting that Teotihuacan population growth leveled off before environmental limits were approached, it is logically inescapable that it was biologically possible for Teotihuacan population to have continued to expand until it "overshot" all technically feasible subsistence possibilities. If it were simply the case that rapid development tends to acquire a sort of momentum which carries it beyond environmental limits and into disaster before it can be stopped, then the ability of the Teotihuacanos to slow down and stop short of disaster would be puzzling.

An extended discussion of Teotihuacan's eventual collapse is not possible here, but I should add that I do not know of any convincing evidence that even the end of Teotihuacan was primarily due to climatic deterioration or other environmentally generated subsistence difficulties. Growing competition from other Highland centers was probably important, and I suspect that Teotihuacan may have collapsed for political, economic, and military reasons, rather than purely ecological reasons.

Proponents of either "population pressure" or "hydraulic" explanations for early states may perhaps argue that Teotihuacan "plateaued" instead of overshooting because the power of the state was very much stronger and more centralized than in the Maya cities, so that when the disastrous consequences of further expansion of the city became evident, the state had the power to intervene effectively and halt further population growth. Possibly this may be part of the explanation, but I do not think this explanation is required. The main reason may have been that there was simply no advantage in further expansion that would have offset attendant inconveniences. There is much evidence that population growth rates are very responsive to shifts in other variables. Assuming the Southern Lowland Maya did indeed "overshoot" their environment, even in the face of growing subsistence difficulties, it is the Maya behavior which is puzzling—far more puzzling than Culbert assumes—and it is the Maya "overshoot" rather than the Teotihuacan "plateau" which is most in need of explanation.

Culbert's "overshoot" explanation of the Maya collapse is one of the least unsatisfactory suggestions made so far. Culbert himself cogently disposes of most previous explanations. And archaeological evidence for the Southern Maya Lowlands in the eighth century does suggest a population so large that, in spite of evidence for terraces, ridged fields, and tree and root crops in addition to swidden, a subsistence crisis seems a real possibility. Nevertheless, there are serious problems with Culbert's explanation. He speaks of many causal factors, but inspection shows that excessive population growth plays a central role in his model. And, in his 1974 book, he offers no particular explanation for the population growth itself. More recently he has attributed population growth to economic development. But the question remains: what would have driven the Maya to expand population and/or environmental exploitation to the point where a subsistence crisis was produced? And if, instead, there was little population growth after about A.D. 550, as Haviland (1970 and personal communication) argues, then the postponement of collapse for some 250 years seems even more puzzling.

A different explanation for the Maya collapse suggests that the eighth-century Maya "florescence" was not, in fact, a time of Maya prosperity at all, but instead an attempt to cope with already serious troubles. This theory, if I understand it correctly, suggests that ability to obtain foreign goods by trade was critical for elite Maya prestige, for the power that derived from that prestige, and as a means of providing incentives for local production. Exclusion of central Peten elites from developing Mesoamerican trade networks supposedly precipitated a crisis for these elites, in which they attempted to offset their sagging prestige by even more ambitious monumental construction projects. But clearly nothing indispensable for subsistence was lacking, and prestige games can be played with whatever one defines as status markers, as Sanders points out. Goods need not be obtained by long-distance trade in order to be scarce and valuable. Furthermore my guess is that

the decline of Teotihuacan, if anything, expanded the possibilities for profitable trade by Southern Lowland Maya elites. Webb's postulated development of new Mesoamerican trading networks following the decline of Teotihuacan seems, in very broad outline, a reasonable possibility. But I am much less persuaded than either Webb or Rathje that, at least at first, the Southern Lowland Maya were unable to participate in these new developments. The scale and substance of Late Classic Maya material civilization argues that they *were* able to profit from the situation, at least for a time. To be sure, there is some evidence for poor nutritional status for some Lowland Maya, but the same was probably true for much of the English and Western European population at the height of rapid economic growth in the early decades of the Industrial Revolution. It may well be that Late Classic Maya wealth was very unevenly distributed, and it also may be that the Late Classic Maya of the Southern Lowlands were increasingly "living off ecological capital," but this does not mean that the elites were already badly off, or were doing what they did in order to cope with resource pressures or an unfavorable balance of trade. The argument that the Late Classic Maya were already in serious trouble in the seventh or eighth centuries is unconvincing. Exclusion from trade networks does seem a good explanation for nonrecovery after the collapse, but not for the collapse itself....

It seems likely that in Late Classic times there was general economic development in a number of regional centers in the Southern Maya Lowlands, perhaps at least in part because of the weakening of Highland states such as Teotihuacan and Monte Alban. More speculatively, the elites of the individual centers may have increasingly seen it as both feasible and desirable to extend strong control over a relatively large surrounding area —a control based more on conquest and annexation than on political alliance and elite intermarriage. Population growth may well have been a concomitant of this economic and political development. My argument here and previously is not that population growth rarely occurs, nor that population growth does not have important reciprocal effects on other variables. My objections, instead, are to the idea that population can be counted on to increase for no reason except human procreative proclivities, and to the idea that competition and militaristic warfare would intensify mainly as a response to subsistence shortages. Instead, I suggest that if population was increasing, it was because it was useful either to elites, to peasant households, or to both. And I suggest that intensified militaristic competition is a normal extension of intensified economic competition.

Mayanists are accustomed to assuming that the political institutions of the Classic Maya Lowlands were marginally statelike. I suggest that we should seriously consider the possibility that by the seventh and eighth centuries the combination of economic development, population growth, and social changes was leading to the emergence of more highly developed and more centralized governmental structures—the kinds of structures which would make the incorporation of many small states into a single reasonably stable empire seem a realistic possibility. I would not venture to make further conjectures about the specific forms of these new political and economic developments. However, archaeological and epigraphical evidence promises not only to test the general proposition, but also to shed a great deal of further light on the precise forms of Maya political and economic organization.

What I suggest, then, is that eventually the major Maya centers may have begun to compete for effective political mastery of the whole Southern Lowlands. This postulated "heating up" of military conflict, for which there is some support in Late Classic art and inscriptions, may have played a major role in the Maya collapse. If, indeed, population growth and/or utilization of the environment expanded beyond prudent limits, the spur may have been provided by militaristic competition. And even if population and production did not expand beyond feasible steady-state values (under peaceful conditions), intensified warfare may have precipitated disaster through destruction of crops and agricultural facilities and through disruption of agricultural labor cycles. Clearly, internal warfare is not "the" single cause of the Maya collapse, but I believe it deserves renewed consideration as a contributing factor.

Webster also places new stress on the role of warfare in Maya history, but our views and emphases differ in several important ways. First, he is mainly concerned with Preclassic and Early Classic warfare as one of the causes of the *rise* of Maya civilization. This is a topic I have not discussed here. My feeling is that Webster makes some good points— there is certainly clear evidence for some Maya warfare quite early—but he probably overestimates the explanatory importance of early warfare. Second, Webster tends to see warfare largely as a response to shortages in land or other subsistence resources. I believe that this underestimates other incentives for warfare, especially for large-scale militaristic warfare.

Third, Webster places much less stress than I do on Late Classic economic development, and he differs sharply on the matter of political integration. He feels that even the largest autonomous political units were never more than forty to sixty thousand people and that incorporation of further large increments of population, especially at considerable distances, proved unworkable. Presumably, although Webster does not explicitly discuss the matter, he would assume that serious attempts to incorporate many more people and more land and other resources within single states did not play a significant role in Maya history. He does feel that warfare may have contributed to the Maya collapse, but he explains intensified warfare mainly as a consequence of the manipulation of militarism by the Maya elite for bolstering their control of their own subject populations, rather than for any extensive conquests of other states. He says that conflicts may also have intensified over strategic resources, especially capital improvements for intensified agriculture, in the intermediate zones between major centers, but he does not suggest that there may have been major attempts to expand beyond the intermediate zones to gain control of the other centers as well. He does not suggest, as I do, that an important contributory element in the Maya collapse may have been a struggle—violent, protracted, and unsuccessful—to bring into being something like the kind of polity Teotihuacan had succeeded in creating several centuries earlier.

POSTSCRIPT

Were Environmental Factors Responsible for the Collapse of the Mayan Civilization?

In studying the decline of civilizations, it is generally easy to see that, in most instances, both internal and external factors were responsible for their demise. This is certainly true for the Mayas. Both Adams and Cowgill would agree that there is no single explanation for the Mayan collapse; the question seems to be, Which set of factors was more responsible for the demise? Complicating the search for answers to the Mayan collapse are the regional and individual differences that existed within the myriad of city-states that provided the civilization with its political base. It should be noted that the reasons for their collapse could differ due to regional or local conditions. Today's research seems to bear out the existence of this dichotomy.

Simon Martin and Nikolai Grube, in "Maya Superstates," *Archaeology* (November/December 1995), lean toward militarism as a cause of Mayan decline. Others have speculated that the Mayas may have simply lost their will to rule. It is unlikely that this issue's question will ever receive a definitive answer. But future discoveries will keep the interest alive and generate more interest in this civilization, which has captured historians' imaginations at the end of the twentieth century just as the Egyptian civilization did at the beginning.

There are many highly recommendable books on the Mayas. A good starting point is *The Classic Maya Collapse* edited by T. Patrick Culbert (University of New Mexico Press, 1983), which contains a series of essays by Mayan scholars, each covering an aspect of the civilization's demise. Charles Gallenkamp's *Maya: The Riddle and Rediscovery of a Lost Civilization* (Penguin Books, 1987) offers a short, readable account of the civilization's history. And *A Forest of Kings: The Untold Story of the Ancient Maya* by Linda Schele and David Friedel (William Morrow, 1990) offers a contemporary and exciting account of all aspects of this great civilization.

A videotape on the Mayas entitled *Central America: The Burden of Time*, from Michael Wood's *Legacy* series, gives thorough coverage to the Mayas and sets them in the context of their Mesoamerindian neighbors.

ISSUE 10

Were the Crusades an Early Example of Western Imperialism?

YES: Hugh Trevor-Roper, from *The Rise of Christian Europe* (Harcourt, Brace & World, 1965)

NO: Marcus Bull, from "The Pilgrimage Origins of the First Crusade," *History Today* (March 1997)

ISSUE SUMMARY

YES: Historian Hugh Trevor-Roper looks to the secular motivation of the knights of the Crusades and argues that they represented another example of Western imperialism.

NO: Marcus Bull, a lecturer in medieval history, stresses the continuity that the First Crusade had with the pilgrimage tradition in medieval Europe.

Nineteen ninety-five marked the 900th anniversary of the start of the First Crusade. One of the hinges on which the door of history swings, the failure of the Christian crusaders to achieve their immediate aims—namely, to permanently recapture the Holy Land from the Muslims, convert the populace, and reunite the Eastern Orthodox and Roman Catholic Churches—hardly obscures the consequences of this series of wars, which lasted from 1095 until 1291. The reopening of the Mediterranean to trade between Asia and Europe led to the rise of the fabulous Italian city-states and stimulated the growth of an influential middle class. In the ensuing two centuries, the continued growth of international trade and an ongoing rivalry with the Muslims encouraged countries such as Portugal and Spain to look for alternative trade routes around Africa and westward across the Atlantic, resulting in the discovery of America. Arab and Byzantine learning and scholarship infiltrated the borders of feudal Europe, inspiring medieval Scholasticism and stimulating the beginnings of the European Renaissance. Even beyond the resulting ramifications of the Crusades, the romantic image of the knightly crusader selflessly going to face danger in foreign lands, fighting against a ruthless enemy for the highest ideals, has shaped the chivalric ideal of the West and influenced its own self-image.

Over the centuries the Crusades have been subject to romanticization, revision, and counterrevision. Who were the crusaders? What European factions did they represent? What were their aims? What were their hopes? What were their actions? And what were the results of those actions? All of these questions have been asked by a myriad of analysts within a climate of moral judgment. Historians of the Crusades tend to either condemn the episode as one of a hidden imperialism behind hypocritically religious language or apologize for the era in which the events occurred as being deeply and self-righteously religious and, therefore, quite foreign to our own time. Most recently, some journalists and historians have looked to the Crusades as the origin of today's animosity between the Muslim world and the West.

On the surface, the Crusades began as a response to the rising power of the Seljuk Turks, a community of devout and militant Sunni Muslims who came to control the Abbasid Empire and threatened the borders of the Byzantine Empire. As a result, the patriarch of Constantinople appealed to Pope Urban II in Rome for military aid to stem the encroaching Muslim tide. Despite the fact that Muslims had controlled the Christian Holy Land around Jerusalem for the previous 300 years, the pope's appeal called for the liberation of Palestine from a heathen people prone to torturing Christians by, among other atrocities, circumcising them and pouring their blood upon the church altars. Also within Pope Urban's appeal were promises of new and fertile land, opportunities for social mobility, increased wealth, and enhanced political power. Revenge, duty, and the assurance of salvation can all be found in the pope's speech, which marks the starting point for any student who wants to interpret the motives of the crusaders. It also points to the complexities of the motives of the soldiers and their followers who, in the First Crusade, journeyed for over a year through treacherous and difficult territory before they finally arrived to fight their enemy in Jerusalem.

The first crusaders recognized that their motives were not always purely spiritual, and many blamed their lack of success on this impurity. Of all the Crusades, only the first achieved the aim of conquest. Those following primarily consisted of Christian military responses to the Islamic revival of the twelfth and thirteenth centuries. Nevertheless, the Crusades struck a powerful chord in the minds of the powerful and the not-so-powerful during the Middle Ages and formed an ancillary background to the internal developments within the growing nations of medieval Europe.

In the following selections, Hugh Trevor-Roper and Marcus Bull come to very different conclusions regarding the motives of the crusaders.

YES

Hugh Trevor-Roper

THE CRUSADES

The Crusades, that extraordinary series of holy wars, that long struggle in the Levant [the countries that border on the east Mediterranean] between East and West, Christendom and Islam, which began so theatrically in the eleventh century and petered out so ignominiously in the thirteenth, were described by Gibbon as 'the World's Debate'. The world has debated about them a good deal since and will no doubt go on debating. I intend to debate about them now.

At first, the view was clear enough. The simple crusaders, who paused to chronicle their violent but holy deeds, and ended each chapter of carnage with devout scriptural ejaculations, questioned their own motives no more than the Spanish conquistadors of the sixteenth century. To them, the Turks were the infamous, accursed unbelievers, 'God's enemies and ours', while the Christians who perished in battle went up to Heaven to be robed in white and receive the palm of martyrdom. After the Reformation, some Protestants ventured to express doubt. The only gainer by all this great adventure, wrote Thomas Fuller in the reign of Charles I, was the pope; 'all other princes of Europe, if they cast up their audit, shall find themselves losers'; the Crusades, he argued, were both the fruit and the cause of superstition; the pope, for his profit, 'made all Jerusalem *Golgotha*, a place for skulls, and all the Holy Land *Aceldama*, a field of blood'. But good Catholics were not dismayed. At the court of Louis XIV, if the Abbé Fleury walked warily, his rival, the fashionable Jesuit Louis Maimbourg, brandished his pen boldly. To him the Crusades were still holy wars, whose every barbarity was justified by their high spiritual aim; and he described with relish how the Christians, once in possession of Jerusalem, 'used to their full extent the rights of victory.... Everywhere one could see nothing but heads flying, legs hacked off, arms cut down, bodies in slices... they killed the very children in their mothers' arms to exterminate, if possible, that accursed race, as God formerly wished should be done to the Amalekites.'

Then, in the mid-eighteenth century, came a change. It was the time when religious controversy was giving way to 'philosophy'. All the great 'philosophical historians' of the Enlightenment turned their minds to the problem of the Crusades. The more incomprehensible it seemed to those cool, rational spirits, the more they felt the necessity of comprehending it. What had hitherto seemed perfectly right and natural did not seem right at all to them. The example of Saul and the Amalekites provided them with neither explanation nor justification. But they were not content to denounce or even to doubt. Believing that all men are fundamentally similar, and their actions ultimately explicable, they sought for psychological or social keys, and to find those keys they asked secular questions. What force could have launched this strange series of migrations in which, in the words of the astonished Byzantine princess who had witnessed it, Europe was loosened from its foundations and hurled against Asia? What was the real historical significance of those incredible adventures? What were the ultimate consequences for Europe and for Asia?

In their answers to these questions, the eighteenth century historians sometimes differed in detail or in emphasis, but in general they agreed. On a superficial view, unquestionably, the Crusades were a deplorable outburst of fanaticism and folly. They were contrary to justice and common sense. With what justice, asked Voltaire, could the barbarian princes of Europe claim for themselves provinces which had been seized by the Turks not from them but from the Emperor of the East? By what rule of sense, asked Gibbon, did those descendants of German, Frankish and Norman conquerors assume that time had consecrated their own acquisitions in Europe but not those of the Moslems in Asia? If the eighteenth-century historians allowed any credit to Christian princes, it was not for enthusiasm but for scepticism

in the holy cause. The only virtue of our William Rufus, said Hume, was his intelligent immunity from that epidemical folly. The only fault of St Louis, King of France, said Voltaire, was his liability to it. Voltaire's heroes were the Emperor Frederick II, who negotiated instead of fighting with the Sultan and found himself the victim of a papal crusade as a result, and the great enemy of the crusaders, Saladin, who having beaten the Christians in battle, bequeathed his wealth impartially to the Moslem, Jewish and Christian poor.

But causes are distinct from consequences. If the cause of the Crusades was human fanaticism, what was the result? It was not, certainly, the permanent establishment of Christian kingdoms in the East. The Christian kingdom of Jerusalem continued for less than a century. The Christian virtues, such as they were, evaporated in the East. The Christian dynasties ran out. The fathers might slaughter the Jews of Germany and the infidels of Palestine, catapult the heads of their prisoners into besieged cities, and wade through holy massacres singing Te Deums with tears of joy; but the sons—or rather the successors, for there was a dearth of sons—settled down to a life of luxurious co-existence in which feudal bonds were rotted and oriental tastes indulged. By the end of the thirteenth century all was over. The adventure was finished.

And what, if any, had been the profit of it? Voltaire wrote that Asia Minor was a gulf in which Europe was swallowed up, the tomb of over two million Europeans. Its only gift to Europe, he said, was leprosy. Gibbon added silk, sugar and windmills (but it seems that he may have been wrong about the windmills). If Europe gained anything, both agreed, it was very indirectly. The crusading nobles dissipated their estates and extinguished their families in those costly expeditions. But this dissipation and this extinction led to unexpected advantages for society. In order to equip themselves, the nobles were obliged to sell charters of freedom 'which unlocked the fetters of the slave, secured the farm of the peasant and the shop of the artificer, and gradually restored a substance and a soul to the most numerous and useful part of the community. The conflagration which destroyed the tall and barren trees of the forest gave air and scope to the vegetation of the smaller and nutritive plants of the soil.'

Some of the eighteenth-century historians allowed more direct advantages. Wilham Robertson, the great Scottish historian, who was a minister of the Presbyterian Kirk and Moderator of its General Assembly, allowed that the Crusades were 'a singular monument of human folly', but he saw them also as 'the first event that roused Europe from the lethargy in which it had long been sunk', and he ascribed to them certain 'beneficial consequences which had neither been foreseen nor expected'. The Italian cities, which conveyed, financed and exploited the Crusades, grew in wealth and created the lay culture of Europe; even the crusaders themselves were improved by contact with Moslem civility; and so, ultimately, 'to these wild expeditions, the effect of superstition or folly, we owe the first gleams of light which tended to dispel barbarism and ignorance'. But even here Gibbon dissented. 'Great', he admitted, 'was the increase and rapid the progress, during the 200 years of the Crusades, and some philosophers have applauded the propitious influence of those holy wars, which appear to me to have checked rather than forwarded the maturity of Europe. The lives and labours of millions which were buried in the East would have been more profitably employed in the improvement of their native country; the accumulated stock of industry and wealth would have overflowed in navigation and trade; and the Latins would have been enriched ... by a pure and friendly correspondence with the climates of the East.'

So the historians of the eighteenth century debated. Since then, the material for debate has vastly grown. We know, or can know, far more than they did about the politics and the property transactions and the theological discussions of the Crusades. But these additional details, though they may add depth and complexity to historical problems, do not of themselves solve them; to think that they do is a common mistake of scholars. The great problems remain the same. What was the cause and function of the Crusades? Did they advance or retard the progress of Europe, and if so, how? Why did they occur when they did? Why did they break out in the eleventh century? And why did they end in the thirteenth? For although Crusades continued to be preached, and even occasionally launched, after the middle of the thirteenth century, the taste for them had gone by then. When the warriors of the Fourth Crusade had turned aside from the Moslem East to sack the Christian city of Constantinople, and popes were preaching crusades not against the infidel, or to recover the holy places from the Turks, but against Christian kings and Christian preachers who had the misfortune to differ from them on points of jurisdiction or theology, it was difficult to rouse that popular enthusiasm which had once caused clergy and laity alike to respond to Pope Urban II's preaching of the First Crusade at Clermont and had drawn thousands after the barefoot Peter the Hermit, as he rode on his donkey through France and Germany, calling for volunteers. By the second half of the thirteenth century the idea of the Crusade might linger on, for popes to abuse, but its captivating power was extinct.

What I wish to do is to place [the Crusades], if I can, in some historical context and perspective: that is, first to set the whole movement against the secular background of the time, and secondly to see it in relation to other episodes in the expansion of Europe. For the historians of the Crusades have too often treated them in isolation. In fact, I believe, they should be seen as part of a larger social process which was characteristic of these two centuries. Moreover, behind their medieval, archaic, theological romantic colouring, the Crusades—I suggest—are remarkably similar to certain other stages in the expansion of Europe which, since they occurred in later times, wore other, less medieval, less archaic, perhaps less theological, but no less romantic colours.

What, then, was the secular background of the Crusades?... [R]ural Europe, in its utter pulverization in the eighth century, possessed two social cells —if I may use that metaphor—in which its vitality could be preserved and defended. One was the monasticism of St Benedict, based originally on a simple, self-contained economy, sustained aid sanctified by a religious impulse, and proof against all but total destruction. The other was the feudalism which found its distinguishing character in the time of Charles Martel: the social and military unit based on the heavily armed, well-mounted, stirruped horseman, sustained by grants of land and military tenures. Both of these units, obviously, were capable of great abuse. Monasticism, in its abusive form, would counterbalance all the temporal advantages of Christianity. It would be the means by which every corruption entered the Church. Feudalism would become a repressive, anarchical system, stifling economic growth, and leading to perpetual military faction. But these were corruptions of the original ideal. In their ideal form both monasticism and feudalism had a sense of purpose. To achieve that purpose they only needed organization. If the monastic units could be organized as a system, if the feudal units could be co-ordinated for action, and if the two systems could work together, then it was possible that the combination of ideology and military technique might, as it has done since, carry through a revolution and alter the balance of the world.

In the eighth century, when Charles Martel and his successors laid the foundations of knighthood and brought the monks of the Far West into France, Germany and Switzerland, this new organization, this new unity, already seemed at hand. In fact it was not, as yet. The Carolingian dawn was not followed by full day, and in the later ninth and tenth centuries the increasing splendour of Arabic civilization was set off by the continued darkness of Europe. Why this was so, I cannot say. Perhaps the economy of Europe could not yet sustain an effective feudalism: Charles Martel, after all, had had to confiscate laid to found it: he had based it on capital, not income. Perhaps every new institution needs time to be digested; and the ninth and tenth centuries were anyway troubled times, with renewed invasions, by the Magyars on land and by the Vikings and Saracens at sea. At all events, in the tenth century neither monasticism nor feudalism showed much capacity to re-create the society of Europe. Emperors could not continue the work of Charlemagne, nor popes the work of St Gregory. Indeed the tenth-century popes have caused some embarrassment to devout historians who have to record that the papal crown was bestowed by or upon the successive lovers of one accomplished Roman courtesan and the successive descendants of another (thus justifying the medieval fable of the female Pope Joan, so dear to Protestant enthusiasts), and that the gallantries of one of them—I leave you to guess whom I am quoting—'deterred the female pilgrims from visiting the tomb of St Peter lest, in the devout act, they should be violated by his successor.'

But these times passed and in the eleventh century a great change came over Europe: a change which began north of the Alps. Exactly what that change was we can hardly say. Only one thing is certain in history, and that is that no historical process, or historical change, has a single cause: all depend not on simple mathematical logic but on a complex chemistry of causes. But one element in the chemical change of the eleventh century was undoubtedly a great, though to us unmeasurable, increase in population, and one cause, or at least concomitant, of this increase of population was a series of technical improvements which increased the productivity of the land.

One such improvement, which has been a topic of vigorous historical controversy, was probably in the method of ploughing. The original plough used in the Middle East and the Mediterranean was a light 'scratch-plough', a downward-pointing spike drawn by two oxen, first in one direction, then crosswise, over a square plot of land. This was sufficient for those light, dry soils. But

on the damp, heavy soil of northern Europe such a plough was inadequate except for light, well drained uplands. Consequently agriculture was at first applied only to very limited areas. But gradually, in the Dark Ages, a new type of plough became general in northern Europe. This was a heavy plough with a coulter and ploughshare set to cut into the earth and a 'mouldboard' to turn the sod sideways and form a ridge and furrow, thereby draining as well as digging the ground. This heavy 'German' plough was often set on wheels and drawn by a team of oxen; it therefore ploughed a long strip rather than a square field. The team of oxen required communal ownership and therefore entailed, with strip-farming, a new social unit. The ultimate result of its use was greater agricultural productivity and greater social cohesion. But of course it could not be adopted all at once. In fact it seems to have become general in northern Europe by the tenth century, and to have coincided with several other changes, such as the use of modern harness, the replacement of oxen by horses for traction, and the three-field system of crop rotation, all of which increased both the area and the productivity of cultivable land.

These agricultural innovations could sustain a certain increase of working population. But an increase in population is never nicely calculated, and in fact, in a generation of opportunity, the larger families which survive infant mortality will always, when they grow up, press too heavily even on expanded means of production. In the eleventh century Europe north of the Alps could not sustain the whole increase of its population, and so, on every frontier, the pressure grew. At the same time, those two preservative and aggressive institutions which Europe had found for itself discovered a new vitality, a new unity. The reforming zeal of the English and Irish monks was taken over by the monks of Cluny in France, who sought to colonize and, by colonizing, to rescue and control the Church. Where the Benedictine abbeys had been equal, independent foundations, the Cluniac houses were a disciplined, organized system, controlled from the top, from the abbey of Cluny itself, and so capable of a united policy in the Christian world. The institution of feudalism was taken over by the Norman invaders of France who used it to conquer kingdoms and fiefs for themselves and their followers in Italy and England.

It was in Italy that the two forces, always ahead in society, met in politics. In 1059 the papacy, already influenced by the ideas of Cluny, allied itself with the Norman adventurers in South Italy. Seven years later it was with the blessing of a reforming pope that William of Normandy, with his small band of invincible, horsed, stirruped knights, conquered in one day the un-feudal kingdom of England. A generation later it was the same alliance of a reformed papacy and Norman feudal knights from France, England and South Italy, which sought to create new kingdoms in the East. The pressure of population forced the pace; the new institutions provided the ideology, the technique, the leadership. And in the end the ideology, as always, was adaptable: what was constant was the expansion, the conquest. The crusaders who justified their aggression against the Moslems by their virtuous detestation of the false prophet, Mahomet, did not falter when that pretext failed. The Anglo-Saxons were Christian; so were the Irish;

indeed Anglo-Saxons and Irish, in the past, had been among the makers of Christian Europe. That did not save the former from William the Conqueror nor the latter from Strongbow. The Greeks of Constantinople were Christians too. That did not save them from those terrible Franks, that army of land-hungry younger sons and superfluous peasants who swarmed out, to the West as well as to the East, in search of earthly as well as spiritual salvation.

Everywhere it is the same. Let us turn from the eastern to the western Mediterranean, from the north to the south Atlantic coast of Europe. In the ninth and tenth centuries, Moslem Spain, like the rest of Islam, enjoyed its golden age. While the caliph of Córdoba built the magnificent mosque there, the relics of independent Spanish Christendom cowered in northern pockets of the peninsula, worshipping in low, cavernous churches, barrel-vaulted like crypts. But in the next century, here too, we find a new Christian pressure; and once again it comes from outside, from the north. It was the monks of Cluny and the knights from France who gave form and spirit to the movement. It was the monks of Cluny who organized the pilgrimages to the great shrine of Santiago de Compostela on the remote north-west tip of Spain. They turned Santiago—the apostle St James, the brother of Jesus—into the military, crusading, patron saint of Christian Spain, and made the road to Compostela one of the great pilgrim routes of Europe; and from the beginning it was Frenchmen who ran the hotels along the route. The petty kings of Christian Spain welcomed these enterprising immigrants, gave them lands, made them bishops in Spain. Wide the monks and the *hôteliers* came the feudal knights, Normans and Burgundians, to animate the 'Re-conquest'—that is, the war to recover the rest of Spain from its Moorish conquerors. Ten years before the First Crusade, it was with Burgundian soldiers that the Christians had captured Toledo; and a Frenchman was made bishop of it. It was with Norman soldiers that they twice captured the great Aragonese fortress of Barbastro. And other foreigners came too. Fifty years later a party of English and Flemish crusaders, sailing towards the Mediterranean to join the Second Crusade, arrived at the mouth of the river Douro. They were easily persuaded that there was no need to sail farther. There were infidels in Portugal, and lands as rich as any in Palestine. The crusaders agreed. They stayed. Instead of Edessa they captured Lisbon; and having massacred the Moslem inhabitants and installed themselves on their lands, they forgot about the Christian kingdom of Jerusalem and founded —with immense, undreamed-of consequences—that of Portugal.

Italy, England, Palestine, Spain, Portugal: in all directions the frontiers of Christendom are being pushed forward. In Germany, too we can see it. In the eighteenth century, the Englishman St Boniface had converted the Germans by preaching to them, and Charlemagne had converted the Saxons by knocking them on the head; but beyond the Elbe lay the world of the Prussians and the 'Slavs', those conveniently heathen submen who hitherto had passed through the pages of history, as they passed through the Christian kingdoms, only as long coffles of marketable eunuchs and slaves, heading for Moslem lands. In the early tenth century we find German colonists and missionaries pressing forward into the land of the Slavs and new

bishoprics being founded on the Elbe; but fifty years later the Slavs have risen in revolt and all the work is undone. In the East, as in the West, the effort of Carolingian times cannot be sustained. Advance is followed, at least temporarily, by retreat.

Yet, in the next century, the advance is resumed. And, once again, it is barons and churchmen who lead the way, confident that from the pressing population behind them they will always have hands for the task. Soon they will have another instrument too. The Germans who have gone as crusaders to the Holy Land have been formed into a military order, the Order of St. Mary's Hospital at Jerusalem, known as the Teutonic Knights. When opportunities in the Holy Land run short, the Teutonic Knights will be transferred to this northern theatre and will end as a rich, colonial aristocracy, a master race on the shores of the Baltic. The crusading movement is indivisible—against Moslems in the Mediterranean, pagans in eastern Europe, schismatic Christians in Byzantium, heretical Christians in the south-west of France, orthodox Christians in England and Ireland. It is indivisible because the real causes are not religion; religion only consecrated and canalized a great movement of social expansion.

But if Europe, swollen by an increased population, inspired by the Church and armed with feudal institutions, is everywhere pressing forward its frontiers, what are the means of colonization? What organization occupies and exploits the land? In part, it is the abbeys. The monastery, that cell into which the rural economy of Europe withdrew from the wrack of the Roman Empire, is now expanding again; and everywhere, under the protection of feudal institutions, it is being carried forward as an essential part of advancing Christendom. But as times have changed, the monastery too has changed, both in form and in function. In the new age of expansion the monastery is no longer a receptacle for fugitive civilization, retreating on to its narrowest base to preserve something of life, something of culture, from advancing barbarism. Far from it. It is now a pioneering, colonizing institution, the economic organism of a conquering society. And as such it has changed its form. Always, at every stage of civilization, old organs are adjusted or replaced and new movements either take over the machinery of the past or build afresh. In the darkening, defensive days of the sixth century, the Benedictine monastery had been the cell of Christendom: every cell independent, so that if one failed, another might survive. In the iron years of resistance, in the tenth century, the Cluniac monasteries have worn another form, a disciplined hierarchy. In the new, expansive era of the Crusades, yet other orders appeared: and they appeared, naturally enough, not in Italy, the Italy of St Benedict, the heart of the old Roman Empire whose extremities were failing; but in the centre and source of the new expansion, the power-house of the Crusades, the lands north of the Alps.

The greatest of these new monastic orders was the order of Cîteaux, the Cistercian order. Its effective founders were Stephen Harding, the English abbot of Cîteaux, and—appropriately enough—St Bernard, preacher of the Second Crusade. The success of the new movement was immediate. All over Europe, in the twelfth century, its abbeys sprang up. Moreover these new abbeys were not like the old abbeys. The old Benedictine abbeys, like all old foundations, had become lax and comfortable. The new Cistercian abbeys—and others, like the Premonstratensian, which followed their pattern—were stricter and more puritan. They were also up-to-date in economy and purpose. They were organized for advance, for colonization. They were centrally controlled, and yet flexible: each house sent out its own colony, and that colony would then send out another, always pushing forward in the wake of feudal power, opening up new lands. The Cistercian monks are essentially great agricultural exploiters, great cattle-raisers, and, in forward areas, colonizers of the waste. We find them in Bradenburg and Pomerania and on the Baltic coast, where the Slavs were yielding to the Germans; we find them in the wake of the German *Drang nach Osten* in Poland, Bohemia, Hungary; and we find them—at Rievaulx and Jervaulx, Fountains and Furness, Melrose and Dundrennan Tintern and Strata Florida—in the Yorkshire valleys and on the Scottish and Welsh borders: wherever there was waste to cultivate and forest to clear.

But if abbeys were one organ of colonization, another, ultimately far more important, was towns. Those towns, which had almost disappeared from western Europe with the decline of the Roman Empire, began again, with the Crusades, a sudden development. They did not begin because of the Crusades. Indeed, at the beginning, the Crusades were a positive setback to the Italian towns which lived by innocent commerce with Constantinople and the Moslem cities of the Mediterranean. The Norman conquest ruined Amalfi and damaged Bari. Venice was at first a reluctant crusader. But as the Crusades went on, requiring constant sea-transport and financial refreshment, the coastal towns of Italy saw their opportunity. They provided the transport, they invested the funds, they secured payment in concessions of every kind—their own quarters in captured seaports, privileges and monopolies of trade, farms of taxes —until, in the end, they became the living, thriving link whereby Europe was once again in regular contact with the East. First on the coast of Italy—Venice, Genoa, Pisa, Naples—then behind the coast—Florence, Milan—then along the trade-routes which ran into Central and Northern Europe—over the Alps into Switzerland and South Germany, down the Rhine to Flanders, the economic capital of the North—a vivifying impulse ran through the cities of Europe. Because the cities of Italy were enlivened by the touch of the East, they were able to stretch out their tentacles to the north also; Venice reached northwards, through the Alps into Austria, and Milan into Switzerland; Bohemia and Germany found themselves in distant touch with the Mediterranean; and Italian factors in Bruges and Ypres would buy wholesale, for Florentine manufacturers, the wool grown by the new Cistercian monasteries of England.

Moreover, thanks to the trade of the Mediterranean, and an industry financed by it, the Italian towns drew back into Europe the essential motor of such commerce: gold. Since the time of Charlemagne, as we have seen, gold had been scarce in Europe, and the western European rulers had minted no regular gold coins. The few exceptions to this rule only prove it: they were the half-arabized princes of Sicily and Spain on the borders of Islam, the Viking grand dukes of Kiev who supplied Islam with slaves, and the Anglo-Saxon King Offa who copied Arab models. But after the Crusades, all this changed. Once again the gold of Africa found its way copiously into Europe. From the Sudan it was brought by the caravans of the Sahara to the Barbary ports and thence traded to the Italian cities. Or it was sucked by trade or conquest from Constantinople, Syria, Egypt. From these new supplies the European States, after 500 years, could now mint their own gold coins. Florence led the way, minting the gold *florin* in 1252; then the other cities of Italy and France followed. In 1284 the duchy of Venice minted the *ducat*. In the next century the whole continent was once again using gold coins, the essential means of long-distance trade and high civilization.

The Italian cities profited by the Crusades; but the long-distance trade which they handled would not have reached such proportions, or had such effect, had it not been for the larger movement which lay behind the Crusades: the growth of European population and the colonization of new lands or waste lands by feudal conquest or agricultural settlement; and this larger movement also led directly to another and different farm of urban development: the growth of old towns at home and the foundation of new towns beyond the old frontiers of settlement. For the European advance in the crusading period is not merely conquest and exploitation. (In some places it is. It is in the Levant. That is why the Levantine conquests were so short-lived. The crusaders were a numerically feeble ruling class, always liable to be absorbed or evicted by the more numerous natives over whom they ruled.) But elsewhere conquest is followed by settlement: the settlement not merely of new landlords imposed on a native peasantry, but of a whole society in depth; and that new society needed, for its supply and cohesion, new towns. In Spain, the advancing Christian kings everywhere set up new towns. Sometimes the kings themselves, or abbots or lay lords organize the repopulation; sometimes it is left to the old towns to create new ones in their own image. In Germany, the old towns of the west, which began as settlements of miscellaneous population taking advantage of the protection of a castle or a bishop's palace, acquire a new wealth, a new mercantile spirit and civic independence: the lord and the bishop shrink, the city government asserts itself. And behind the eastern advance the towns follow. The feudal lords want to set up new towns, as in Spain. The old towns send out urban colonies to supply them, just as the Cistercian monasteries also send out monastic colonies. Cologne founded Freiburg. Regensburg restored the desolate Roman city of Vienna. Lübeck planted a string of German towns on the Baltic coast and islands to open up and control the fur trade of Russia. In Brandenburg, Pomerania and Rugen alone, one hundred new towns had been founded by 1300.

My point is that the Crusades were not just a religious movement—whether we regard them as a heroic movement or an 'epidemical folly'. They were not even, by themselves, the cause of the European break-through. They were part of a much larger, much wider process: a process which can be seen all over Europe and on all the frontiers of western Christendom: beyond the Pyrenees, beyond the Elbe, on the Scottish border, in Ireland. This process is essentially a north European process. It is based on a new population-growth and new techniques, agricultural, social, military. The heavy German iron plough drives the wooden Slav plough before it beyond the Elbe, just as the

heavy, stirruped, Norman knights drive the Anglo-Saxon or Celtic footmen before them in England and Ireland, and the new Cistercian monasteries press forward against the empty wastes of the Welsh and Scottish borders, the Pomeranian plain and the Baltic seashore. The towns, and the rising prices which accompany the growth of trade, do more than the Crusades to dissolve the 'feudal' power of rural knights. Perhaps, as Gibbon wrote, the Crusades were a diversion of this great expansion into the sideline of unprofitable imperialism; perhaps the imperialism was inseparable from the expansion. That is another question.

Moreover, when we look at this movement in the perspective of time, we see another thing. The Crusades were no more isolated in time than in substance. They are not a unique, unrepeatable episode. In particular combination of detail of course they are unrepeatable. No historical situation is ever exactly repeatable. But in general character they are a social phenomenon which has occurred often in history and will occur again, very shortly, even in European history. We only have to look closely to see it. The adventurers who carved out estates for themselves in the Levant, and whose grim castles still dominate the hills of Syria and scowl, impossibly alien, down the romantic valleys of Greece; the sugar plantations which the Venetians and Genoese established in the conquered islands, and the slave-labour by which they worked them; the monopolies thereby created and the spectacular fortunes of the Italian maritime cities which rested thereon—are not all these familiar at another time too?

We think of the later conquest of America. It too was a crusade. Just as the monasteries of Cluny directed the conquest of the Levant, so the great Jeronymite monasteries of Spain directed the conquest of America. For that conquest too was to be a 'spiritual conquest'. Monks and friars would accompany it and animate it, preaching down the false gods, smashing down their temples, and studding the New world with gigantic convents, granaries for the new harvest of souls. If the discovery of the Holy Lance and the True Cross inspired the crusaders in the East, Santiago on his white horse would appear to encourage the conquistadors in the West. He was 'Santiago Matamoros'—St James the Moor-killer—but he would do to kill Red Indians too. To America also Spaniards and Portuguese would transplant all the techniques which had been developed four centuries before in the Levant. Hernán Cortés would bring to Mexico the sugar-industry which had been practised since the Crusades in the Venetian Genoese colonies of the eastern Mediterranean. Slave-labour on the plantations and in the mills, first applied in those Levantine conquests, would become the 'peculiar institution' of the new continent. In many ways the islands of the eastern Mediterranean, now abandoned to the Turks, must have served their purpose as experimental farms for the vaster exploitations in the western hemisphere. And in the two movements, the colonization of the East in the twelfth century and the colonization of the West in the sixteenth, the spiritual and economic motives would be equally mixed. We came to America, wrote Bernal Díaz del Castillo, the companion of Cortés, as he rested on his conquered estates in Guatemala, 'para servir a Dios y hacernos ricos'—to serve God and become rich. The inducement to the earlier crusades had been exactly the same.

Come to the East, cried the Norman conqueror Bohemond, take the cross, save the tottering principality of Edessa for Christ, and get yourselves strong castles and rich cities and lands. And in Germany, at a great gathering at Merseburg in 1108, the same rewards were offered to those who would cross the Elbe and make war on the pagan Slavs: 'the country is excellent, rich in meat, honey, feathered game and flour. Therefore come hither, you Saxons and Franconians, Lorrainers and Flemings, for here two things can be won together: salvation for your souls and settlement on the best lands.'

Even the literature of the two periods is similar. The crusaders of the eleventh and twelfth centuries lived, intellectually, on the high-strung, heroic melodramas of the Chansons de geste—the Song of Roland, the Song of the Albigensian crusaders: melodramas which would be brought down to earth by the pedestrian, common-sense Spanish author of the Poem of the Cid. The conquistadors of the sixteenth century lived on the equally high-strung, heroic melodramas of the 'romances of chivalry': Amadis of Gaul, Palmerín de Ohva, Sergas de Esplandián: melodramas which would be brought down to earth by the exquisite Spanish irony of Cervantes. Some of the results were the same too. If the crusaders presented Europe with leprosy, the conquistadors, not to be outdone, presented it with syphilis.

That, however, was long in the future. No one could have predicted it in the thirteenth century; less still in the fourteenth. For before the close of the thirteenth century Europe's first essay in expansion was over: over, it might seem, for ever. The wonderful generation of the Cistercians was over. The colonization of the waste had begun to slacken.

Population, or at least the rate of its increase, was falling off. The world, once again, was the world of the nomads, as it had been in the seventh century; and as for the conquered empire and conquered kingdoms in the Levant, they had all gone. In Gibbon's famous phrase, 'a mournful and solitary silence prevailed along the coast which had so long resounded with the World's Debate'.

NO
Marcus Bull

THE PILGRIMAGE ORIGINS
OF THE FIRST CRUSADE

On November 27th, 1095 at Clermont in central France, Pope Urban II delivered the sermon which launched the expedition now known as the First Crusade. He called on the faithful, in particular the lords and knights who formed society's military élites, to relieve the oppression of Eastern Christians and to liberate the Holy Places by means of an armed pilgrimage, participation in which would earn remission of one's penances because of the great hardships which would be faced. The pope's message was bold and challenging, and it received an enthusiastic response; according to Robert the Monk, one of the chroniclers who described the scene, everyone shouted 'God wills it!' once Urban stopped speaking.

Why was this speech important? Urban was a good communicator, but what he said was as much a briefing as a piece of oratory. His audience mostly comprised bishops and abbots who had assembled some days earlier for a church council. Not many lay people were present, and only a small minority of those who went on the crusade could claim that they had heard the Clermont speech. Nor was Urban's message a one-off, for it was repeated many times in the following months by the pope himself and by other churchmen. Many people learned about the crusade from popular preachers and through other unofficial channels. So the pope's initial speech was just one small part of a much wider recruitment effort. None the less, contemporaries soon came to remember Urban's sermon as a great defining moment; the myriad complexities of the preaching and organisation of an expedition which involved tens of thousands of people from many parts of Europe could be understood more easily by focusing on the rousing events at Clermont and the emotions they released.

This makes it all the more frustrating for historians that it is impossible to know precisely what Urban said. A number of accounts of his speech survive, some of them by members of his audience, but they were written a decade or more later and were influenced by the authors' knowledge of how events unfolded after Clermont, in particular how the crusaders captured Jerusalem in 1099 after a remarkable three-year campaign. The best way to

From Marcus Bull, "The Pilgrimage Origins of the First Crusade," *History Today*, vol. 47, no. 3 (March 1997). Copyright © 1997 by *History Today*. Reproduced with kind permission from *History Today*.

reconstruct Urban's message, therefore, is to examine the ideas and images which he used to excite his audience. After all, the crusade needed careful presentation. Urban was proposing a novel idea to a generally conservative society. He was also asking people to volunteer to do something which was very expensive, time-consuming, arduous and dangerous. What he told them, then, had to be direct and vivid.

Two ways to win over an audience are to conjure up bold, easily visualised images and to tap into deep-seated emotions. Urban used both techniques skillfully. He described a state of crisis in the eastern Mediterranean: the Byzantine Empire was in retreat; churches were being defiled and polluted by infidels; Christians were being subjected to horrible persecutions including rape, torture, mutilation and murder. The Muslim aggressors were portrayed as wantonly cruel: according to Robert the Monk, Urban claimed that Christians were being tied to stakes so that they could be used for archery target practice. The particular villains of the piece were the Turks, nomadic warrior bands with roots in central Asia who had been extending their power into Asia Minor, Syria and Palestine since the 1070s. Of particular concern was their treatment of Jerusalem, which Urban reminded his listeners was the holiest place known to Christians.

Urban had almost certainly never been to the Holy Land himself, and what he said owed more to rhetoric than reality. His depiction of the sufferings of Christians, with its lurid details of torture and pain, resembled contemporary ideas about what it was like to suffer in Hell. It is possible that the Turks, as newcomers to the western Fertile Crescent and its complicated religious history, were

sometimes hostile to the Christians living in their domains. But their treatment seldom, if ever, amounted to the sort of horror stories which Urban recounted. Nor was the composition of the Muslim world as straightforward as the pope's message implied. In fact the Turks lost control of Jerusalem to the Egyptians in 1098, a year before the crusaders arrived: it is a curious irony that the enemies faced at the climax of the crusade were not those whom Urban had originally envisaged.

Most Westerners' understanding of the politics and peoples of the Middle East was vague at best, and Urban exploited this. His aim was to instill the feeling that there was something gravely wrong, dirty and dishonourable about the plight of the Holy Land. This was a substantial achievement: such a sense of urgency comes through in the accounts of Urban's speech that it is easy to lose sight of the fact that Christians had not controlled Jerusalem since the Arabs captured it from the Byzantines in 638. Yet Urban was able to present a long-term fact—457 years of uninterrupted Muslim rule—in terms of a pressing injustice against God and His people. This was the key reason for the success of his message. Why?

An important clue is contained in the version of Urban's speech written by the contemporary chronicler Guibert of Nogent. Having described at length the important role which Jerusalem had played in history and would play at the Last Judgement, the pope asked his audience to consider the plight of those who went on pilgrimage to the Holy Land. The richer among them, Guibert has Urban say, were subjected to violence at the hands of infidels; they were also forced to pay heavy tolls, taxes, entry fees to get into churches, and bribes. The poorer pilgrims were badly mistreated by locals trying to get money off them at any cost. 'Remember, I urge you', the pope said, 'the thousands of people who have died horribly and take action for the Holy Places'. This is rhetorical exaggeration, but there is also an underlying idea that Jerusalem meant something very real to Western Europeans.

Perhaps Urban did not actually dwell on the troubles of Westerners going to the Holy Land as much as this —other accounts of the speech focus more on Eastern Christians—but Guibert was right to suppose that mentioning pilgrimage was an excellent way to evoke a sympathetic response in an audience. Jerusalem was a distant, exotic place, but it was also within the bounds of many people's experience. Monks sang about it daily in their psalms. Relics of the True Cross and other physical reminders of the Holy Places were to be found in many European churches. And significant numbers of people had been to the East themselves. Jerusalem was, paradoxically, both far away and familiar.

By linking his crusade message with Jerusalem pilgrimage Urban was cleverly tapping into a long-established feature of Christian religious practice. Some churchmen had reservation about the value of pilgrimage, doubting whether the faithful could earn greater spiritual merit in some places rather than others. It was also argued that travelling to the actual Jerusalem was less important than striving through prayer and good works to enter the celestial Jerusalem, the community of the blessed in Heaven. But such detached attitudes were a minority view. Enthusiasm for relics and sites associated with saints was widespread among both clergy and lay people. More specifically, interest in

the humanity of Christ—an emerging feature of eleventh-century spirituality and devotion—focused attention on the Holy Land, which was in a sense one huge relic sanctified by Christ's presence.

The emotional appeal of Jerusalem in particular could be enormous. This is clearly illustrated by the behaviour of Richard of Saint-Vanne, an abbot who arrived on pilgrimage on Palm Sunday 1027. Throughout Holy Week he busied himself visiting places associated with Christ's life, Passion and Resurrection. He would regularly throw himself on the ground in prayer, sobbing and crying. According to his biographer, seeing the pillar where Christ was scourged and Calvary where he was crucified reduced Richard to floods of tears. So strong was his attachment to the Holy Sepulchre that when an Arab threw a stone which bounced into the shrine, Richard kept it as a treasured relic.

Richard was able to find and be moved by the scenes of the Passion and other holy places largely because of building work done by the Byzantines many centuries earlier. Interest in Jerusalem had blossomed in the fourth century, when Constantine the Great (306–37) recognised Christianity as an official religion of the Roman Empire, Sites familiar from the Gospels were identified by drawing on the traditions of Christian communities in Palestine and through architectural detective work: for example, Christ's tomb was reckoned to be beneath a pagan temple built in the second century by Emperor Hadrian.

As the holy topography of Jerusalem became established, Constantine began an ambitious construction programme, the centre piece of which was a collection of buildings containing Calvary and the Holy Sepulchre. To these was later added the site of where Constantine's mother Helena was believed to have found the cross used at the Crucifixion. Over the next 300 years emperors and other rich benefactors continued Constantine's work, turning the city and nearby places into an impressive complex of churches, monuments and shrines. Jerusalem was not an important mercantile or industrial centre, and its agricultural hinterland was not particularly rich. Much like Rome in later centuries, its prosperity came to be based largely on its churches and the visitors attracted by them, among whom were Western Europeans.

The flow of Western pilgrims to the Holy Land was disrupted by the Arab conquests in the seventh century and later by unsettled conditions within Europe as political conflicts and the depredations of Vikings, Arabs and Magyars made long-distance travel difficult. But interest in Jerusalem survived, and the journey there was still made by some hardy souls such as the Anglo-Saxon St Willibald in the 720s and a Breton monk named Bernard in about 870. The fact that Jerusalem was never forgotten was important, because it meant that the numbers of pilgrims grew quickly once conditions became more favourable in the years either side of 1000.

Hungary was converted to Christianity, and the Byzantines extended their power in the Balkans and Asia Minor. This meant that travelling to Jerusalem entirely by land, slower than going some of the way by sea, but cheaper and open to more people, became a practicable proposition. What had earlier been a pious adventure for an élite few could now exert a wider appeal. This important change is memorably described by the Burgundian chronicler Ralph Glaber. Writing of the time around the millennium of the Passion (1033), Glaber reports that an 'innumerable multitude from all over the world began to flock to the Saviour's sepulchre in Jerusalem': swept up in the excitement, he says, were men and women, lowly people, those of middling status and also nobles and bishops.

By the time that Glaber's pilgrims were going to Jerusalem, the city had changed a great deal from its Byzantine heyday. In 1009 the Fatimid caliph al-Hakim, who was possibly mad, ordered that the church of the Holy Sepulchre and other Christian places in and around Jerusalem be razed to the ground. There was widespread destruction: when the crusaders arrived ninety years later they found many churches still deserted or ruinous. But the worst of the damage was eventually halted. After al-Hakim died in 1021 his successors were more moderate. The Muslims could sympathise with the idea of pilgrimage because of their experience of the *Hajj*, the journey to Mecca. And Jerusalem was a holy place in Islamic tradition: the Dome of the Rock had been built in the late seventh century on the site from where it was believed Muhammad had ascended into Heaven.

On a more practical level, pilgrim traffic was an important economic resource which could be exploited through tolls, taxes and markets. Consequently the Byzantines were allowed to restore some of the major Christian sites. The complete reconstruction of Constantine's precinct was out of the question, so the rebuilding effort was concentrated on the *Anastasis*, the rotunda containing the shrine built over Christ's tomb. This structure was later incorporated within the imposing church of the Holy Sepulchre which the Franks constructed in the twelfth century, and parts of it are what pilgrims see today (though extensive rebuilding was undertaken after a serious fire in 1808).

It is impossible to know how many Western pilgrims went to the Holy Land in the decades before the First Crusade. Certainly there were fewer than during the eighty-eight years (1099–1187) when Jerusalem was in Frankish hands: this was a boom period when many tens of thousands made the journey. But the numbers of eleventh-century pilgrims were none the less substantial. There seem to have been peaks of activity once or twice in every generation, but there would also have been departures every year. We have most information about pilgrimages by members of the aristocracy. They could most easily afford the expense of a long journey, and they were less tied to the land than the majority of the population. One notable pilgrim was Count Fulk Nerra of Anjou (987–1040) whose nickname, 'the Black', belies the fact that he was a great enthusiast for Jerusalem, going there at least three and probably four times.

A good illustration of the appeal of Jerusalem pilgrimage to the European nobility is how closely it touched the lives of the three leading figures in the well-known events of 1066. King Harald Hardrada of Norway, whom Harold of England defeated and killed at Stamford Bridge less than three weeks before the Battle of Hastings, had been to the Holy Land many years before while serving the Byzantines as a Varangian mercenary. One reason why Harold Godwinson was the foremost English contender for the throne in 1066 was the fact that his elder brother Swein had died some years earlier. A violent and unstable man with many sins to repent, including the murder of his cousin Beorn, Swein had gone barefoot on a penitential pilgrimage

to Jerusalem in 1052 and had died on the return journey. Accounts of how he met his end vary: he may have been waylaid by bandits, or he may have died of exposure in Asia Minor.

The life of William the Conqueror, too, was affected by Jerusalem pilgrimage. His father, Duke Robert I of Normandy, travelled to the Holy Land in 1035 and died at Nicaea in Asia Minor on the journey home. His heir William, was only a young boy, and the weakening of ducal authority plunged Normandy into years of turmoil. The obstacles which William encountered in restoring order and the enormous dangers he faced— many of those close to him were cut down —seem to have had a profound impact on his character and political education. It may not be an exaggeration to say that Robert's death on pilgrimage helped to create in his son the sort of determined and ruthless leader who was capable of undertaking the conquest of England.

Robert was only about twenty-six years old when he went to Jerusalem. Though many people travelled to the East intending to spend their last days there, it is unlikely that he had this in mind. (Indeed, the story later circulated that he had been poisoned.) None the less, simply by going he was taking an enormous risk, as many of the Norman barons and clergy were quick to point out when he announced his plan. Their fears proved well-founded. But in the longer run, once people knew that William had more than reversed the damage to ducal authority caused by his troubled minority, it was difficult to criticise Robert for his actions. The story of his pilgrimage, pieced together from the memories of his companions and heavily embroidered by epic motifs, became the stuff of legends.

By about 1100 people told of how Robert, as he approached Constantinople, ordered golden horseshoes for his mount in order to impress the Byzantines. This and other tales were developed by the twelfth-century poet-historian Wace to turn the duke into a larger-than-life figure. For example, the story went that when Robert fell ill on the outward journey he hired some Muslim peasants to carry him on a litter, enabling him to joke to a passing Norman pilgrim that he was being carried to Paradise by devils. It is a telling indication of the prestige and respect attached to Jerusalem pilgrims that Robert was not remembered as an irresponsible dynast and ruler, but as a heroic blend of penitent and adventurer.

A good deal of Wace's account of Robert's journey is fanciful, of course, but one detail which has an element of truth is the sight which greeted the duke when he arrived at Jerusalem: crowds of destitute pilgrims were stranded outside the city walls because they could not pay the entry toll levied by the Fatimid authorities. Running out of money was but one of the many hazards faced by pilgrims. Robbers and wild animals were often a serious problem. Language differences made travellers vulnerable, and strangers were often mistrusted and abused by the communities they encountered. It is significant that however much Robert of Normandy's pilgrimage was decked out as an epic adventure in Wace's telling, something of the harsh reality still comes through. Long-distance pilgrimage was a grim business in the eleventh century. Its physical and mental rigours made it effective as a penance. A cemetery just outside Jerusalem, Akeldama, contained the bodies of many pilgrims who died there. And the accounts of pilgrims like Richard of Saint-Vanne being swept up in outpourings of emotion on their arrival in the Holy City read like the explosive release of tension and anticipation after months of suffering.

One way to cope with the dangers and stresses was to seek safety in numbers. Groups of pilgrims sometimes formed around a prominent noble or prelate. Richard of Saint-Vanne, for example, is reported to have had 700 companions whom he supported with money given him by Duke Richard II of Normandy (Robert I's father). The most remarkable instance of a mass pilgrimage was that undertaken by a group of Germans in 1064–65 under the leadership of a team of bishops and nobles. Figures of 7,000 and 12,000 are given by chroniclers; even the lower number is probably inflated, but even so this was the largest movement of Western Europeans to Jerusalem before the First Crusade. Interest seems to have been generated by the fact that in 1065, for the first time in over seventy years, Easter Sunday fell on March 27th, the date commonly ascribed to the historical Resurrection. The large numbers may also have been encouraged by the leaders because in recent years some pilgrims had found their journeys disrupted by unsettled conditions in the Holy Land. In 1055, for example, Bishop Lietbert of Cambrai had been refused permission to proceed by the governor of Latakia, the Byzantines' border outpost in northern Syria, because of fears for his safety. The pilgrims of 1064–65 must have hoped to overcome any problems by sheer weight of numbers.

With large numbers, however, came a problem which was to dog the whole enterprise. The leaders had to provide substantial amounts of supplies. One of the most practicable ways to do this was to carry, in addition to cash, luxury items which could be sold or exchanged en route. Contemporary chronicles describe the bishops' lavish tent hangings and gold and silver vessels: these represented good forward planning as well as aristocratic display. But so much wealth slowly on the move made the pilgrims very vulnerable. Robbery began to be a serious problem as the party passed through the Balkans, and it became worse in Palestine. About two days' journey from Jerusalem they were ambushed by Arab bandits. Some of the pilgrims fled to a deserted village, organised resistance and managed to keep their attackers at bay. The Arab leaders were lured into a parley, where they were overpowered by followers of Gunther of Bamberg, the most dynamic of the bishops. Soon afterwards there arrived a relief force sent by the Fatimid authorities, mindful of the value of keeping the pilgrimage route open. A fortnight later the remnants of the party were taken under armed escort to Jerusalem.

This remarkable episode has often caught the imagination of historians looking for precursors of the First Crusade. In particular attention has focused on the fact that some of the pilgrims fought back even though this was contrary to the centuries-old principle that pilgrims should renounce violence. The willingness of the German pilgrims to break this powerful taboo has seemed to anticipate the First Crusade, which was conceived as a fusion of warfare and pilgrimage. But perhaps historians have exaggerated the significance of what happened. The pilgrims did not set out from Germany armed. When they were attacked they at first fought back with stones and whatever else was to hand before using weapons snatched off their opponents. The fighting was an exceptional episode born of desperation and intense pressure, and it was only made possible by the unusually large numbers involved.

What is more significant about the 1064–65 pilgrimage is what it demonstrates about the conditions faced by pilgrims generally in the years before Urban's speech at Clermont: the great expense, the physical effort, the constant dangers, and the fact that poorer travellers relied heavily on the resources and leadership of nobles and senior clergy. All these features are also to be found, magnified, in the story of the First Crusade.

It is clear that crusading owed a great debt to pilgrimage, and Urban II realised this when he set about creating his crusade appeal. His use of scare stories, exaggerations, and stereo-typing of the enemy was effective because he knew that Western European society had formed a strong attachment to Jerusalem. Pilgrimage to the Holy Land was an important reason for that sense of attachment, and it was one of the firm foundations upon which the popularity of crusading came to be built.

POSTSCRIPT

Were the Crusades an Early Example of Western Imperialism?

Exotic, distant, and complex, the Crusades offer the student of history a fascinating assortment of topics to explore, from the mystical to the monetary. Bull focuses on the historical and ideological connections that western Europeans of the Middle Ages possessed with the eastern city of Jerusalem. In describing the atmosphere of attitudes, he illustrates the power that Pope Urban II's appeal had on his audience as he masterly tapped into the passions and desires of western Christendom. On the other hand, Trevor-Roper comments on the imperialist nature of the Crusades, focusing on the secular causes behind the religious rhetoric. With Europe experiencing population expansion as a result of the medieval agricultural revolution and with merchants willing to exploit conquered lands for materials and markets, Trevor-Roper concludes that all the ingredients were present for a classic imperialist enterprise.

Interesting to note, however, is the emphasis both authors put on the continuity that the Crusades maintained with the historical trends leading up to the end of the eleventh century. As Bull points out, Jerusalem and Palestine were not foreign worlds to the Christians of medieval Europe. Pope Urban's concept of a pilgrimage in arms was one that would have appeared to his contemporaries as consistent with their own experiences with travel in this time. Journeys of any type were fraught with danger, whether they were military, mercantile, or missionary. The medieval devotion to holy relics also helped facilitate the concept of a war with the distant Saracens. Jerusalem came to be seen as the consummate relic of relics. Pope Urban tapped into a current of experience and attitudes that already existed amongst the clergy and commanders that he wished to reach. Trevor-Roper accentuates the view that the Crusades were a logical extension of an already expanding western Europe. To him, the Crusades were simply a continuation of an imperialism that was already an inherent aspect of Western civilization.

For various essays on the Crusades and their origins, Thomas Patrick Murphy's edited book *The Holy War* (Ohio State University Press, 1976) provides a variety of authors' views, while *What Were the Crusades?* by Jonathan Riley-Smith (Rowman & Littlefield, 1977) is a good text with which to begin. And Steven Runciman's work, including his three-volume *History of the Crusades* (Cambridge University Press, 1987) is always scholarly and well written.

ISSUE 11

Did Women and Men Benefit Equally from the Renaissance?

YES: Mary R. Beard, from *Woman as Force in History: A Study in Traditions and Realities* (Collier Books, 1946)

NO: Joan Kelly-Gadol, from "Did Women Have a Renaissance?" in Renate Bridenthal, Claudia Koonz, and Susan Stuard, eds., *Becoming Visible: Women in European History*, 2d ed. (Houghton Mifflin, 1987)

ISSUE SUMMARY

YES: Historian Mary R. Beard contends that during the Renaissance, Italian women of the higher classes turned to the study of Greek and Roman literature and committed themselves alongside men to developing well-rounded personalities.

NO: Historian Joan Kelly-Gadol argues that women enjoyed greater advantages during the Middle Ages and experienced a relative loss of position and power during the Renaissance.

In 1974 Joan Kelly-Gadol published a pathbreaking essay that challenged traditional periodization. Before that, virtually every publication on the Renaissance proclaimed it to be a great leap forward for everyone, a time when new ideas were everywhere discussed and the old strictures of the Middle Ages were thrown off. The difficulty for Kelly-Gadol was that her own work on women during the medieval and Renaissance periods told a different story. She was one of the first to raise this troubling question: Are the turning points in history the same for women as they are for men? Kelly-Gadol found that well-born women lived in a relatively free environment during the Middle Ages. The courtly love tradition allowed powerful, property-owning women to satisfy their own sexual and emotional needs. With the arrival of the Renaissance, however, the courtly love tradition was defined by powerful male princes who found it desirable for women to be passive and chaste in order to serve the needs of the rising bourgeoisie.

Mary R. Beard is considered the original pathfinder. Her stunning 1946 book *Woman as Force in History* was written, she said, to "destroy the myth that women have done and are suited for little else than bearing and rearing children." Beard, like Kelly-Gadol, studied women of the upper classes. She was eager to find a place for women in history to counter the prevailing view of male historians that by studying the "great man" we could understand the age he created. Beard began looking for the "great woman" and found traces of her throughout human history. After Beard's book was published, it became much more difficult for historians to treat women as passive victims of history.

The field of women's history has a history of its own. Beginning with the pioneering work of historians such as Beard, scholars first engaged in what Gerda Lerner has called "compensatory history"—compensating for past omissions by researching and writing about the great women of history. In a second phase, women's history moved to "contributory history." Looking past the great women, historians took all the traditional categories of standard male history and found women who filled them—women who spent their lives as intellectuals, soldiers, politicians, and scientists. The current phase of women's history parallels more general trends in social history, concentrating on the ordinary people who lived during historical epochs. In this more fully mature phase, the emphasis is on women's culture—how women saw the world from within their own systems and ways of doing things. If Beard was doing compensatory history, Kelly-Gadol might be said to be engaging in contributory history. The women she writes about led lives similar to those of men in their class during the Middle Ages, but Kelly-Gadol contends that they had a different experience during the Renaissance.

One caution to keep in mind is that people are not aware of the times in which they live in terms of the historical periods that scholars later use for identification. People of the past, like people today, are more concerned with their personal lives and fortunes than with historical trends. Periodization, or the marking of turning points in the past, can be useful. It can help to identify broad trends and forks in the road as we explore the past. What women's history has taught us, however, is that looking at the experiences of men may or may not tell us what the experiences of women were like during the same time periods.

Mary Beard collaborated with her husband Charles Beard on many widely read history books. When she wrote *Woman as Force in History*, which is excerpted in the following selection, her aim was to demonstrate that women "have been a force in making all the history that has been made." Her book and the field of women's history that it inspired made possible the work of later scholars such as Kelly-Gadol. Mary Beard challenged traditional notions about the role of women in history; Kelly-Gadol challenged history itself. If what has been said about certain turning points in human history is true only for men or much more true for men than for women, then the whole field of history must be reconceptualized. Although both of the selections that follow were written some time ago, the questions they raise remain lively today.

YES

Mary R. Beard

EVIDENCES IN MEDIAEVAL EDUCATIONAL AND INTELLECTUAL INTERESTS

HUMANIZING EDUCATION—INDIVIDUAL, CIVIC, AND PHILOSOPHIC

Many things conspired to give leadership and acclaim in education and letters to the women of Italy, earlier than to women of other countries. Italy was the original home of the revival of the Latin classics and it was to Italy that the choicest of Greek classics were brought from Byzantium, before and after the fall of Constantinople to the Turks in 1453. To Italy came able scholars and tutors straight from the Near East; and at their hands, or under their influence, Greek and Latin grammars and texts of the classics were issued in profusion.

With the revival of classical learning came the humanizing of intellectual interest, knowledge, and public measures; that is, thought and action were directed by this learning to human concerns, as distinguished from the divine, and to the human race in general, as distinguished from individual salvation and particular peoples. Now educated men and women in Italy had at their command, for example, the great histories written by Greek and Roman authorities in antiquity and were attracted by the difference between these human and secular works and the monkish chronicles which, besides being fragmentary, twisted the story of the past to fit theological conceptions of the universe. Now Italian men and women were in possession of literary and philosophic works dealing entirely with the great human and nature subjects, without regard for those "ultimate causes" with which theologians occupied themselves on the basis of theories and convictions respecting the nature and designs of God. Moreover, instead of the degraded Latin so often employed by monkish chroniclers, Italian men and women now had models of writing by Greek and Roman thinkers and stylists, inviting them to lofty aspirations

From Mary R. Beard, *Woman as Force in History: A Study in Traditions and Realities* (Collier Books, 1946). Copyright © 1946 by Mary R. Beard; copyright renewed 1974 by William Beard and Miriam Vagts. Reprinted by permission of Simon & Schuster.

and lucid expressions whether in poetry, letters, the arts, history, philosophy, or politics.

In the promotion of the new learning, two tasks had to be carried out. The first included the recovery of additional classical works, the preparation of critical editions, the reissue of the best in manuscript form and, after the invention of printing, in book form, and critical study of the new texts. The second was the dissemination of the knowledge derived from the critical study.

The number of women who devoted themselves to scholarship was by no means as large as the number of men, for reasons other than the lack of talents; but in the fifteenth century and early sixteenth century many Italian women displayed the highest technical competence in the study, interpretation, and exposition of the revived humanist learning. Some of them, for example Isotta Nogarola, we are told by Dr. G. R. Potter in *The Cambridge Mediaeval History* (Volume VIII, Chapter XXIII), "could hold their own in matters of scholarship with the best of their male contemporaries and... were accepted and even acclaimed everywhere."

According to Dr. H. J. Mozans' *Women in Science*, women took "an active part in the great educational movement inaugurated by the revival of learning" and won "the highest honors for their sex in every department of science, art, and learning.... The universities, which had been opened to them at the close of the middle ages, gladly conferred upon them the doctorate, and eagerly welcomed them to the chairs of some of their most important faculties.... Cecelia Gonzaga, pupil of the celebrated humanist, Vittorino da Feltre, read the gospels in Greek when she was only seven years old. Isotta and Ginevra Nogarola, pupils of the humanist, Guarino Verronese, likewise distinguished themselves at an early age by their rare knowledge of Latin and Greek.... Livia Chiavello, of Fabriano, was celebrated as one of the most brilliant representatives of the Petrarchian school.... Cassandra Fidele, of Venice, deserved, according to Poliziano, the noted Florentine humanist to be ranked with that famous universal genius, Pico de la Mirandola. So extensive were her attainments that in addition to being a thorough mistress of Latin and Greek, she was likewise distinguished in music, eloquence, philosophy, and even theology.... But for the extent and variety of her attainments, Tarquinia Molza seems to have eclipsed all her contemporaries. Not only did she excel in poetry and the fine arts, she also had a rare knowledge of astronomy and mathematics, Latin, Greek and Hebrew. So great was the esteem in which she was held that the senate of Rome conferred upon her the singular honor of Roman citizenship, transmissible in perpetuity to her descendants."

In nearly every great intellectual center of Italy women were lecturing on literature and philosophy, and religious faith could not escape impacts of the new knowledge. They were studying medicine and natural science in the light of pagan learning in these subjects. Great Italian women teachers of the awakening "sent forth such students as Moritz von Spiegelberg and Rudolph Agricola to reform the instruction of Deventer and Zwoll and prepare the way for Erasmus and Reuchlin."

Some of the women crossed the Alps themselves, as the ancient learning was said to do when Erasmus and other returning students bore back to outlying countries the knowledge gleaned in Italy. One of the most distinguished classical scholars of the age, Olympia Morata, for example, meeting difficulties as Renée's court where the duchess and all her friends were persecuted by the Duke for their religious independence, fled to Germany, with a young Bavarian student of medicine and philosophy, and was planning to continue her teaching of the classics in Heidelberg, to which she had been invited, when an untimely death closed her career.

In the dissemination of the new learning among the Italian people, especially among the rich but including some not as well off in this world's goods, five methods were widely and intensively employed: tutoring and self-directed study in families, education in schools, humanist lecturing, conversations in small private groups and larger coteries, and correspondence.

As soon as the Renaissance had got under way, Italian women in the rich commercial cities and at ducal or princely courts, such as Ferrara and Urbino, turned with avidity to the study and discussion of Greek and Roman literature.

While men of the governing class were away from their castles fighting in wars, women and girls of their families thus "improved their minds" and displayed their accomplishments to the warriors when they came home on furloughs. French officers and Spanish ambassadors who were guests in the great houses from time to time were so impressed that they let their own women relatives and friends know how backward they were and how advisable it would be for them to catch up with Italian women. When Erasmus, Grocyn, and Colet joined in the student pilgrimage to

Italy early in the sixteenth century, they found women immersed in the ancient languages and lore, surrounded by poets, artists, scholars, and writers from near and distant places as companions in the new intellectual movement.

This linguistic and literary development was not confined to the ruling circles, however. Classical schools for girls and boys were opened in Italian cities, giving to the business and professional circles, as well as to patricians, opportunities to acquire knowledge of the ancient languages and the natural, or secular, philosophies embodied in Greek and Latin literature. Here entered the insurgent bourgeois influence which Henry Adams, looking back from the twentieth century and his vantage point within it, concluded was an invincible menace to the throne of Mary, Queen of Heaven.

Among the outstanding Italians of the fifteenth century who promoted education, letters, and arts were Gian Francesco Gonzaga II and his wife, Paola Malatesta, who brought to Mantua in 1425 the exceptional humanist, Vittorino da Feltre, and established him there as the teacher of their sons and daughters. The Gonzagas took it as a matter of course that their daughters should have the same kind of instruction as their sons —in an age when women, according to a tradition of our time, were supposed to have no education at all. It was with the full support of both patrons that Vittorino was to devise and execute a program of education that made his school one of the most creative in the Italy of the Renaissance.

In Chapter XVI, Volume I, of *The Cambridge Modern History*, Sir R. C. Jebb describes the new type of civic education created by Vittorino at his school in Mantua under the patronage of Gian and

Paola Gonzaga in 1425 and carried on until his death in 1446: "His aim was to develop the whole nature of his pupils, intellectual, moral, and physical; not with a view to any special calling, but so as to form good citizens and useful members of society, capable of bearing their part with credit in public and private life. For intellectual training he took the Latin classics as a basis; teaching them, however, not in the dry and meagre fashion generally prevalent in the mediaeval schools... but in the large and generous spirit of Renaissance humanism. Poetry, oratory, Roman history, and the ethics of Roman Stoicism, were studied in the best Latin writers.... By degrees Vittorino introduced some Greek also.... He provided for some teaching of mathematics, including geometry... arithmetic, and the elements of astronomy. Nor did he neglect the rudiments of such knowledge as then passed for natural philosophy and natural history. Music and singing also found a place.... With great insight and tact, Vittorino saw how far social education could be given in a school with advantage to morals and without loss to manliness; he inculcated a good tone of manners, and encouraged the acquirement of such social accomplishments as the age demanded in well-educated men."

It was not only as scholars, tutors, lecturers, members of coteries, participants in the work of academies, and patrons of schools that Italian women led and cooperated in the dissemination of the humanist learning. They carried on extensive correspondence with men and other women engaged in spreading humanist knowledge and doctrines in Italy and throughout Western Europe. Of Olympia Morata, we are told that she "corresponded on equal terms with the most learned men of the day."

All these free, wide-reaching, and influential activities of Italian women in the promotion of humanist learning were in keeping with the very spirit of the Renaissance. In the third chapter of *Die Kultur der Renaissance*, Jacob Burckhardt, a renowned authority, says: "In order to understand the higher forms of social intercourse during the Renaissance, it is necessary to know that woman was regarded as in a position of perfect equality with man. One should not allow one's self to be deceived by the cunning and in part malicious researches respecting the presumptive inferiority of the beautiful sex.... Above all, the education of the woman among the higher classes is essentially the same as that of the man. There was not the slightest hesitation among the Italians of the Renaissance in according the same literary and even philological instruction to sons and daughters; for as they saw in this new classical culture the highest possession of life, so they assumed gladly that girls were welcome to it.... There was no question of a conscious 'emancipation' of woman or anything so out of the ordinary, for the situation was understood to be a matter of course. The education of the woman of rank, just as well as that of the man, sought the development of a well-rounded personality in every respect. The same development of mind and heart that perfected the man was necessary for perfecting woman."

Men of the Renaissance not only accepted as a matter of course this free and easy association with women in the advancement of learning and the civic spirit. Many writers of the period made a point of paying special tributes to women, if frequently in exaggerated form. Take, for example, Boccaccio (1313–1375), the fervent humanist, poet, story-teller, and friend of Petrarch. Besides writing *De Casibus Virorum Illustrium,* dealing with the troubles and vanities of illustrious men from the time of Adam to the fourteenth century, he wrote illustrious women, *De Claris Mulieribus,* starting with Eve and coming down to Giovanna, queen of Naples; included were Cleopatra, Lucretia, Portia, Semiramis, and Sappho. This work passed through many editions and is esteemed as among the important texts of the Renaissance. It was translated into Italian by Joseph Betussi who "in the ardor of his zeal enriched it by fifty new articles."

About a hundred years later, Henry C. Agrippa (1486–1525), German writer, soldier, physician, architect, historiographer, doctor of law, and traveler in many lands, outdid Boccaccio. In 1509 Agrippa published a work on the nobility and superexcellence of women (*De nobilitate et praecellentia feminei sexus*), dedicated to Margaret of Burgundy. In this volume of thirty chapters, Agrippa employed the writings of fable-makers, poets, historians, and the canon law in efforts to prove the case, and resorted to theological, physical, historical, moral, and even magical evidences to support his argument. He declared that he was moved to write the book by his sense of duty and obligations to duty.

Many men wrote paeans to women, as Lucian the Roman had done and as men were to continue to do in the mood of the Renaissance, in many countries, for centuries. Finally, in 1774, just two years before the Declaration of Independence at Philadelphia, an account of such hymning of women was published at Philadelphia. This was a work in two volumes: *Essay on the Character, Manners, and Genius of Women in Different Ages* —enlarged from a French work of M. Thomas by Mr. Russell, an Englishman. It included a section on the "Revival of Letters and the Learning of Women, Of the Books written in Honour of Women, and on the Superiority of the Sexes, and the subject continued."

After giving an account of the work by Boccaccio and Betussi, the author of the *Essay* continued: "Philip de Bergamo, an Augustine monk, published a volume in Latin OF ILLUSTRIOUS WOMEN. Another performance on the same subject was published by Julius Caesar Capacio, secretary to the city of Naples; one by Charles Pinto, in Latin, and in verse; one by Ludovico Domenichi; one by James Philip Tomassini, bishop of Venice; and one by Bernard Scardioni, a canon by Padua, OF THE ILLUSTRIOUS WOMEN OF PADUA.

"Francis Augustine della Chiesa, bishop of Saluca, wrote a treatise on THE WOMEN FAMOUS IN LITERATURE; Lewis Jacob de St. Charles, a Carmelite, wrote another on THE WOMEN ILLUSTRIOUS BY THEIR WRITINGS; and Alexander Van Denbushce, of the Low Countries, wrote one on THE LEARNED WOMEN.

"The celebrated Father le Moine published a volume under the title of GALERIE DE FEMMES FORTES; and Brantome wrote THE LIVES OF ILLUSTRIOUS WOMEN. But it is to be observed that Brantome, a French knight and a courtier, speaks only of queens and princesses....

"After Brantome, Hilario da Costa, a Minim, published two volumes in quarto, each volume consisting of eight hundred pages, containing, as he tells us, the panegyrics of ALL the women of the fifteenth and sixteenth centuries, distinguished by their valour, their talents, or their virtues.

But the pious ecclesiastic has, in fact, only given us the panegyrics of the CATHOLIC women of that period. He does not say a word, for example, of queen Elizabeth. . . .

"But all must yield to the indefatigable Italian, Peter Paul de Ribera, who published in his own language, a work entitled 'The Immortal Triumphs and heroic Enterprises of Eight hundred and forty-five women.' . . .

"Besides these large compilations dedicated to the honour of the whole sex, many of the writers of those times, men of taste and gallantry, addressed panegyrics to individuals, to women who were the living ornaments of their age. This practice was most common in Italy, where every thing conspired to favour it. . . . The courts of Naples, of Milan, of Mantua, of Parma, of Florence, and several others, formed so many schools of taste, between which reigned an emulation of glory and of talents. The men distinguished themselves by their address in war, or in love; the women, by their knowledge and accomplishments."

From Italy zeal for classical learning fanned out like rays from a sun. Queen Isabella of Spain became interested in it through her acquaintance with Vittoria Colonna and brought Italian men and women to Spain to instruct her courtiers and students in the universities. She studied the classics herself. She established a school of the classics in her palace. She attended examinations of students and watched with eagle eyes and sharp ears the progress of this education among her retinue. She collected texts for the courtiers to read and for students to use in the universities. One woman was commissioned to lecture on the classics at Salamanca; another on rhetoric at Alcalá. Later Philip II enriched this Spanish Renaissance by his patronage of Italian

artists. He encouraged Spanish women to paint portraits as well as write letters, by inviting the Italian women portrait painter, Sophonisba Anguisciola, to his court. Of this portrait painter Van Dyck long afterward was to say that he learned more from her, even in her blind old age, than he had learned from many seeing men.

In France enthusiasm for classical learning was stimulated by Christine de Pisan—Italian in background—who grew up at the court of Charles V, in the late fourteenth century, where her father was installed as an astrologer. After the visit of Petrarch to France in quest of Greek and Latin texts possibly among the monastic treasures, monarchs began to accumulate a library for the French court. But Christine de Pisan did more than read texts there. She studied Plato and also Arab scientific learning in some books in the library. She shared Dante's interest in the State and urged the French to come to grips with their problem of national survival so seriously menaced by the invading armies of the English King. By coming to grips she meant more than war; she meant coming to realize the necessity of granting privileges to the middle class without which, she contended, France could not get up on its feet. Before Christine died, Jeanne d'Arc took the field as commander of French troops—her actual leadership financed by the great capitalist, Jacques Coeur, her will to lead inspired by her "voices," her acceptance as leader facilitated by French adoration of the Virgin.

Christine de Pisan tried to offset the influence of Jean de Meung's stereotype of the perfect lady in his *Roman de la Rose* by her *Le Livre des trois Vertus* (*The Book of the Three Virtues*) addressed especially to women. She hoped to arouse and develop political consciousness among French women. To this end she defended the spirit of the freer-thinking Italian women of her day in her *Cité des Dames* and awakened such interest that she was invited to the English court. She did not accept the invitation on the ground that her supreme duty lay in France, but this book was translated into English as *The City of Women*.

NO

Joan Kelly-Gadol

DID WOMEN HAVE A RENAISSANCE?

One of the tasks of women's history is to call into question accepted schemes of periodization. To take the emancipation of women as a vantage point is to discover that events that further the historical development of men, liberating them from natural, social, or ideological constraints, have quite different, even opposite, effects upon women. The Renaissance is a good case in point. Italy was well in advance of the rest of Europe from roughly 1350 to 1530 because of its early consolidation of genuine states, the mercantile and manufacturing economy that supported them, and its working out of postfeudal and even postguild social relations. These developments reorganized Italian society along modern lines and opened the possibilities for the social and cultural expression for which the age is known. Yet precisely these developments affected women adversely, so much so that there was no renaissance for women—at least, not during the Renaissance. The state, early capitalism, and the social relations formed by them impinged on the lives of Renaissance women in different ways according to their different positions in society. But the startling fact is that women as a group, especially among the classes that dominated Italian urban life, experienced a contraction of social and personal options that men of their classes either did not, as was the case with the bourgeoisie, or did not experience as markedly, as was the case with the nobility.

Before demonstrating this point, which contradicts the widely held notion of the equality of Renaissance women with men, we need to consider how to establish, let alone measure, loss or gain with respect to the liberty of women. I found the following criteria most useful for gauging the relative contraction (or expansion) of the powers of Renaissance women and for determining the quality of their historical experience: 1) the regulation of *female sexuality* as compared with *male sexuality*; 2) women's *economic* and *political roles*, that is, the kind of work they performed as compared with men, and their access to property, political power, and the education or training necessary for work, property, and power; 3) the *cultural roles* of women in shaping the outlook of their society, and access to the education and/or institutions necessary

From Joan Kelly-Gadol, "Did Women Have a Renaissance?" in Renate Bridenthal, Claudia Koonz, and Susan Stuard, eds., *Becoming Visible: Women in European History*, 2d ed. (Houghton Mifflin, 1987). Copyright © 1987 by Houghton Mifflin Company. Reprinted by permission. Notes omitted.

for this; 4) *ideology* about women, in particular the sex-role system displayed or advocated in the symbolic products of the society, its art, literature, and philosophy. Two points should be made about this ideological index. One is its rich inferential value. The literature, art, and philosophy of a society, which give us direct knowledge of the attitudes of the dominant sector of that society toward women, also yield indirect knowledge about our other criteria: namely, the sexual, economic, political, and cultural activities of women. Insofar as images of women relate to what really goes on, we can infer from them something about that social reality. But, second, the relations between the ideology of sex roles and the reality we want to get at are complex and difficult to establish. Such views may be prescriptive rather than descriptive; they may describe a situation that no longer prevails; or they may use the relation of the sexes symbolically and not refer primarily to women and sex roles at all. Hence, to assess the historical significance of changes in sex-role conception, we must bring such changes into connection with all we know about general developments in the society at large.

This essay examines changes in sex-role conception, particularly with respect to sexuality, for what they tell us about Renaissance society and women's place in it. At first glance, Renaissance thought presents a problem in this regard because it cannot be simply categorized. Ideas about the relation of the sexes range from a relatively complementary sense of sex roles in literature dealing with courtly manners, love, and education, to patriarchal conceptions in writings on marriage and the family, to a fairly equal presentation of sex roles in early Utopian

social theory. Such diversity need not baffle the attempt to reconstruct a history of sex-role conceptions, however, and to relate its course to the actual situation of women. Toward this end, one needs to sort out this material in terms of the social groups to which it responds: to courtly society in the first case, the nobility of the petty despotic states of Italy; to the patrician bourgeoisie in the second, particularly of republics such as Florence. In the third case, the relatively equal position accorded women in Utopian thought (and in those lower-class movements of the radical Reformation analogous to it) results from a larger critique of early modern society and all the relations of domination that flow from private ownership and control of property. Once distinguished, each of these groups of sources tells the same story. Each discloses in its own way certain new constraints suffered by Renaissance women as the family and political life were restructured in the great transition from medieval feudal society to the early modern state. The sources that represent the interests of the nobility and the bourgeoisie point to this fact by a telling, double index. Almost all such works—with certain notable exceptions, such as Boccaccio and Ariosto —establish chastity as the female norm and restructure the relation of the sexes to one of female dependency and male domination.

The bourgeois writings on education, domestic life, and society constitute the extreme in this denial of women's independence. Suffice it to say that they sharply distinguish an inferior domestic realm of women from the superior public realm of men, achieving a veritable "renaissance" of the outlook and practices of classical Athens, with its domestic imprisonment of citizen wives. The courtly Renaissance literature we will consider was more gracious. But even here, by analyzing a few of the representative works of this genre, we find a new repression of the noblewoman's affective experience, in contrast to the latitude afforded her by medieval literature, and some of the social and cultural reasons for it. Dante and Castiglione, who continued a literary tradition that began with the courtly love literature of eleventh- and twelfth-century Provence, transformed medieval conceptions of love and nobility. In the love ideal they formed, we can discern the inferior position the Renaissance noblewoman held in the relation of the sexes by comparison with her male counterpart and with her medieval predecessor as well.

LOVE AND THE MEDIEVAL LADY

Medieval courtly love, closely bound to the dominant values of feudalism and the Church, allowed in a special way for the expression of sexual love by women. Of course, only aristocratic women gained their sexual and affective rights thereby. If a knight wanted a peasant girl, the twelfth-century theorist of *The Art of Courtly Love*, Andreas Capellanus, encouraged him "not [to] hesitate to take what you seek and to embrace her by force." Toward the lady, however, "a true lover considers nothing good except what he thinks will please his beloved"; for if courtly love were to define itself as a noble phenomenon, it had to attribute an essential freedom to the relation between lovers. Hence, it metaphorically extended the social relation of vassalage to the love relationship, a "conceit" that Maurice Valency rightly called "the

shaping principle of the whole design" of courtly love.

Of the two dominant sets of dependent social relations formed by feudalism—*les liens de dépendence*, as Marc Bloch called them—vassalage, the military relation of knight to lord, distinguished itself (in its early days) by being freely entered into. At a time when everyone was somebody's "man," the right to freely enter a relation of service characterized aristocratic bonds, whereas hereditability marked the servile work relation of serf to lord. Thus, in medieval romances, a parley typically followed a declaration of love until love freely proffered was freely returned. A kiss (like the kiss of homage) sealed the pledge, rings were exchanged, and the knight entered the love service of his lady. Representing love along the lines of vassalage had several liberating implications for aristocratic women. Most fundamental, ideas of homage and mutuality entered the notion of heterosexual relations along with the idea of freedom. As symbolized on shields and other illustrations that place the knight in the ritual attitude of commendation, kneeling before his lady with his hands folded between hers, homage signified male service, not domination or subordination of the lady, and it signified fidelity, constancy in that service. "A lady must honor her lover as a friend, not as a master," wrote Marie de Ventadour, a female troubadour or *trobairitz*. At the same time, homage entailed a reciprocity of rights and obligations, a service on the lady's part as well. In one of Marie de France's romances, a knight is about to be judged by the barons of King Arthur's court when his lady rides to the castle to give him "succor" and pleads successfully for him, as any overlord might. Mutuality, or complementarity, marks the relation the lady entered into with her *ami* (the favored name for "lover" and, significantly, a synonym for "vassal").

This relation between knight and lady was very much at variance with the patriarchal family relations obtaining in that same level of society. Aware of its incompatibility with prevailing family and marital relations, the celebrants of courtly love kept love detached from marriage. "We dare not oppose the opinion of the Countess of Champagne who rules that love can exert no power between husband and wife," Andreas Capellanus wrote (p. 175). But in opting for a free and reciprocal heterosexual relation outside marriage, the poets and theorists of courtly love ignored the almost universal demand of patriarchal society for female chastity, in the sense of the woman's strict bondage to the marital bed. The reasons why they did so, and even the fact that they did so, have long been disputed, but the ideas and values that justify this kind of adulterous love are plain. Marriage, as a relation arranged by others, carried the taint of social necessity for the aristocracy. And if the feudality denigrated marriage by disdaining obligatory service, the Church did so by regarding it not as a "religious" state, but an inferior one that responded to natural necessity. Moreover, Christianity positively fostered the ideal of courtly love at a deep level of feeling. The courtly relation between lovers took vassalage as its structural model, but its passion was nourished by Christianity's exaltation of love.

Christianity had accomplished its elevation of love by purging it of sexuality, and in this respect, by recombining the two, courtly love clearly departed from Christian teaching. The toleration of adultery it fostered thereby was in itself not so grievous. The feudality disregarded any number of church rulings that affected their interests, such as prohibitions of tournaments and repudiation of spouses (divorce) and remarriage. Moreover, adultery hardly needed the sanction of courtly love, which, if anything, acted rather as a restraining force by binding sexuality (except in marriage) to love. Lancelot, in Chrétien de Troyes's twelfth-century romance, lies in bed with a lovely woman because of a promise he has made, but "not once does he look at her, nor show her any courtesy. Why not? Because his heart does not go out to her. . . . The knight has only one heart, and this one is no longer really his, but has been entrusted to someone else, so that he cannot bestow it elsewhere." Actually, Lancelot's chastity represented more of a threat to Christian doctrine than the fact that his passion (for Guinevere) was adulterous, because his attitudes justified sexual love. Sexuality could only be "mere sexuality" for the medieval Church, to be consecrated and directed toward procreation by Christian marriage. Love, on the other hand, defined as passion for the good, perfects the individual; hence love, according to Thomas Aquinas, properly directs itself toward God. Like the churchman, Lancelot spurned mere sexuality—but for the sake of sexual love. He defied Christian *teaching* by reattaching love to sex; and experiencing his love as a devout vocation, as a passion, he found himself in utter accord with Christian *feeling*. . . .

In his handbook for the nobility, Baldassare Castiglione's description of the lady of the court makes [the] difference in sex roles quite clear. On the one hand, the Renaissance lady appears as the equivalent of the courtier. She has the same virtues of mind as he, and her education is symmetrical with his. She learns everything—well, almost everything—he does: "knowledge of letters, of music, of painting, and ... how to dance and how to be festive." Culture is an accomplishment for noblewoman and man alike, used to charm others as much as to develop the self. But for the woman, charm had become the primary occupation and aim. Whereas the courtier's chief task is defined as the profession of arms, "in a Lady who lives at court a certain pleasing affability is becoming above all else, whereby she will be able to entertain graciously every kind of man" (p. 207).

... The Renaissance lady is not desired, not loved for herself. Rendered passive and chaste, she merely mediates the courtier's safe transcendence of an otherwise demeaning necessity. On the plane of symbolism, Castiglione thus had the courtier dominate both her and the prince; and on the plane of reality, he indirectly acknowledged the courtier's actual domination of the lady by having him adopt "woman's ways" in his relations to the prince. Castiglione had to defend against effeminacy in the courtier, both the charge of it (p. 92) and the actuality of faces "soft and feminine as many attempt to have who not only curl their hair and pluck their eyebrows, but preen themselves... and appear so tender and languid ... and utter their words so limply" (p. 36). Yet the close-fitting costume of the Renaissance nobleman displayed the courtier exactly as Castiglione would have him, "well built and shapely of limb" (p. 36). His clothes set off his grace, as did his nonchalant ease, the new manner of those "who seem in words, laughter, in posture not to care" (p. 44).

To be attractive, accomplished, and seem not to care; to charm and do so coolly —how concerned with impression, how masked the true self. And how manipulative: petitioning his lord, the courtier knows to be "discreet in choosing the occasion, and will ask things that are proper and reasonable; and he will so frame his request, omitting those parts that he knows can cause displeasure, and will skillfully make easy the difficult points so that his lord will always grant it" (p. 111). In short, how like a woman—or a dependent, for that is the root of the simile.

The accommodation of the sixteenth- and seventeenth-century courtier to the ways and dress of women in no way bespeaks a greater parity between them. It reflects, rather, that general restructuring of social relations that entailed for the Renaissance noblewoman a greater dependency upon men as feudal independence and reciprocity yielded to the state. In this new situation, the entire nobility suffered a loss. Hence, the courtier's posture of dependency, his concern with the pleasing impression, his resolve "to perceive what his prince likes, and ... to bend himself to this" (pp. 110–111). But as the state overrode aristocratic power, the lady suffered a double loss. Deprived of the possibility of independent power that the combined interests of kinship and feudalism guaranteed some women in the Middle Ages, and that the states of early modern Europe would preserve in part, the Italian noblewoman in particular entered a relation of almost universal dependence upon her family and her husband. And she experienced this dependency at the same time as she lost her commanding position with respect to the secular culture of her society.

Hence, the love theory of the Italian courts developed in ways as indifferent to the interests of women as the courtier, in his self-sufficiency, was indifferent as a lover. It accepted, as medieval courtly love did not, the double standard. It bound the lady to chastity, to the merely procreative sex of political marriage, just as her weighty and costly costume came to conceal and constrain her body while it displayed her husband's noble rank. Indeed, the person of the woman became so inconsequential to this love relation that one doubted whether she could love at all. The question that emerges at the end of *The Courtier* as to "whether or not women are as capable of divine love as men" (p. 350) belongs to a love theory structured by mediation rather than mutuality. Woman's beauty inspired love but the lover, the agent, was man. And the question stands unresolved at the end of *The Courtier*—because at heart the spokesmen for Renaissance love were not really concerned about women or love at all.

Where courtly love had used the social relation of vassalage to work out a genuine concern with sexual love, Castiglione's thought moved in exactly the opposite direction. He allegorized love as fully as Dante did, using the relation of the sexes to symbolize the new political order. In this, his love theory reflects the social realities of the Renaissance. The denial of the right and power of women to love, the transformation of women into passive "others" who serve, fits the self-image of the courtier, the one Castiglione sought to remedy. The symbolic relation of the sexes thus mirrors the new social relations of the state, much as courtly love displayed the feudal relations of reciprocal personal dependence. But Renaissance love reflects, as well, the actual condition of dependency suffered by noblewomen as the

state arose. If the courtier who charms the prince bears the same relation to him as the lady bears to the courtier, it is because Castiglione understood the relation of the sexes in the same terms that he used to describe the political relation: that is, as a relation between servant and lord. The nobleman suffered this relation in the public domain only. The lady, denied access to a freely chosen, mutually satisfying love relation, suffered it in the personal domain as well. Moreover, Castiglione's theory, unlike the courtly love it superseded, subordinated love itself to the public concerns of the Renaissance nobleman. He set forth the relation of the sexes as one of dependency and domination, but he did so in order to express and deal with the political relation and its problems. The personal values of love, which the entire feudality once prized, were henceforth increasingly left to the lady. The courtier formed his primary bond with the modern prince.

In sum, a new division between personal and public life made itself felt as the state came to organize Renaissance society, and with that division the modern relation of the sexes made its appearance, even among the Renaissance nobility. Noblewomen, too, were increasingly removed from public concerns—economic, political, and cultural —and although they did not disappear into a private realm of family and domestic concerns as fully as their sisters in the patrician bourgeoisie, their loss of public power made itself felt in new constraints placed upon their personal as well as their social lives. Renaissance ideas on love and manners, more classical than medieval, and almost exclusively a male product, expressed this new subordination of women to the interests of husbands and male-dominated kin groups and served to justify the removal of women from an "unladylike" position of power and erotic independence. All the advances of Renaissance Italy, its protocapitalist economy, its states, and its humanistic culture, worked to mold the noblewoman into an aesthetic object: decorous, chaste, and doubly dependent —on her husband as well as the prince.

POSTSCRIPT

Did Women and Men Benefit Equally from the Renaissance?

Once we begin to consider the experiences of women in history as separate from those of men, we meet a new set of challenges. Women are not a universal category, and their experiences throughout history are as varied as their race, social class, ethnicity, religion, sexual orientation, and a host of other categories make them. In recent years historians have begun to consider both the ways in which women's historical experiences are more or less the same and the ways in which one woman's experience differs radically from another's. There are instances in which being a woman is the most important variable (with regard to childbirth, access to birth control or lack of it, and female sexuality, for example), times when race is what matters most and women feel more attuned to men of their own race than to women of different races, and times when social class is the key factor and both racial and gender differences seem less significant than a common class experience or approach to life.

The periodization question remains a fascinating one. Following Kelly-Gadol, other scholars began to look at historical periods with which they were familiar with an eye to using women's experiences as a starting point. For example, in *Becoming Visible* (from which Kelly-Gadol's selection was excerpted), William Monter poses this question: Was there a Reformation for women? Beginning with women's experience, this anthology offers a number of good points of departure for exploring the issue of periodization. For a fuller explanation of the differences among compensatory, contributory, and women's culture approaches, see Gerda Lerner's essay "Placing Women in History," in *Major Problems in Women's History*, 2d ed., edited by Mary Beth Norton and Ruth Alexander (D. C. Heath, 1996). This book also contains Gisela Bock's "Challenging Dichotomies in Women's History"—which explores nature versus culture, work versus family, public versus private, sex versus gender, equality versus difference, and integration versus autonomy—and "Afro-American Women in History," by Evelyn Brooks Higginbotham, which questions the concept of a universal womanhood by exploring the varying experiences of African American women.

For a Marxist analysis of women in history, see the chapter entitled "Four Structures in a Complex Unity" in Juliet Mitchell's *Woman's Estate* (Pantheon Books, 1972). In it, Mitchell argues that production, reproduction, sexuality, and the socialization of children must all be transformed together if the liberation of women is to be achieved; otherwise, progress in one area can be offset by reinforcement in another. This links the question of women's roles in history to economic forces such as production and social forces such as sexuality and childrearing.

Another good way to start is to explore our understanding of gender—what it has meant to be a woman (or a man) at a specific time in human history. Historian Joan W. Scott considers how gender and power designators construct one another in "Gender: A Useful Category of Historical Analysis," *American Historical Review* (December 1986). She sees in the categories "man" and "woman" a primary way in which social relationships are defined and power is signified. Linda Nicholson, in "Interpreting Gender," *Signs: Journal of Women in Culture and Society* (Autumn 1994), explores the question of biological foundationalism—the extent to which physicality influences gender construction. In this analysis, the body becomes a historically specific variable whose meaning changes or is capable of changing over time.

ISSUE 12

Should Christopher Columbus Be Considered a Hero?

YES: Paolo Emilio Taviani, from *Columbus: The Great Adventure, His Life, His Times, and His Voyages,* trans. Luciano F. Farina and Marc A. Beckwith (Orion Books, 1991)

NO: Basil Davidson, from *The Search for Africa: History, Culture, Politics* (Times Books, 1994)

ISSUE SUMMARY

YES: Italian television writer and biographer Paolo Emilio Taviani defends the traditional view of Christopher Columbus as a hero of the West.

NO: British journalist Basil Davidson, a longtime popularizer of African history, lays the blame for slavery and racism on Columbus.

From the very start Christopher Columbus inspired controversy. Initially, the court of King John of Portugal found his plans for westward travel unfeasible, not because they thought the world was flat but because they believed that Columbus had inaccurately calculated the distance from Europe to Asia. His visit to the court of King Ferdinand and Queen Isabella of Spain brought further controversy because his grandiose demands for title and wealth bordered on the impudent. Immediately after Columbus's epic first voyage of 1492, the debate centered on whether his discovery was a new world or merely a part of the much older world of Cathay (China) or Cipango (Japan). Even after he was named governor of Hispaniola (the island currently shared by Haiti and the Dominican Republic), Columbus became the focus of contention, this time over the treatment of the native inhabitants of the West Indies, the Taino people. On one hand, the Franciscan missionary Bernardino de Las Casas wrote of Columbus's ill treatment of the native peoples; on the other hand, the colonists criticized him for not expelling the missionaries who called for the Indians' protection. Eventually, after sailing four times to the Americas (never proving his own tenacious contention that he had found a new route to Asia), Columbus was arrested, replaced, and sent back to Spain. Although he was vindicated and acquitted of any wrongdoing while governor of the first Spanish colony in the Americas, Columbus died dissatisfied and disconsolate.

Five hundred years after his death, the controversies surrounding Columbus—Cristóbal Colón in Spanish—continue. The year 1992, the 500th anniversary of Columbus's first voyage, saw much point and counterpoint made by a wide range of commentators, including pundits on talk radio, television anchors, prestigious scholars, and writers in popular magazines. The numerous books published for the occasion described a vast assortment of Columbuses, from the heroic mariner to the ecologically unsound enemy of man. *Eurocentrism* became an everyday word in the debate over Columbus's true character, and its evils were discussed in grade schools and graduate seminars alike. Few took the middle ground over this sailor. Even his skill as a navigator was called into question, challenging the classic account of his journey by Samuel Eliot Morrison, which was written earlier but republished for the occasion. Columbus came to be seen as the scourge of the Native American, the destroyer of the ecosystem, a pillager of property, and the founder of racism.

The arguments for and against Columbus and his accomplishments seldom focus on the man himself and generally are more concerned with the consequences of Western expansion and its effects on the non-Western world. The trouble for the historian is in remaining fair to his subject in the context of his time while remaining sympathetic to the victims of the now-antiquated attitudes of the fifteenth and sixteenth centuries. The conundrum is whether or not the historian can ever write about imperialism outside of a moral framework that condemns the actions of his subjects. Does objectivity necessarily demand insensitivity or moral relativism?

The two authors featured in this issue both feel very strongly about their subject. Paolo Emilio Taviani admires Columbus and defends his reputation as an explorer, a Roman Catholic, and an Italian. Basil Davidson finds his sympathies lying with the victims of Columbus's legacy and attacks the explorer's personal reputation.

YES
Paolo Emilio Taviani

COLUMBUS THE MAN, PROTAGONIST IN THE GREAT UNDERTAKING

There are no true portraits of Christopher Columbus. There are, however, over eighty statues or paintings, each quite different from the others because the artists were inspired by their own imagination, sometimes taking into account the few but essential descriptions about the physical appearance of the Genoese left to us by those who knew him. These descriptions are four.

The first is given to us by his son Don Ferdinand, born when Christopher was thirty-seven or thirty-eight years old. In the *Historie della vita e dei fatti di Cristoforo Colombo,* he writes as follows:

> The Admiral was well formed, taller than average with a long face and rather high cheeks, neither fat nor skinny. He had an aquiline nose, light eyes, fair skin, and a healthy color. In his youth he had blond hair, but when he reached thirty it all turned white.

The second description is by Las Casas, who saw Columbus in person at Santo Domingo in 1500, when the latter was about fifty. Las Casas writes as follows in the *Historia de las Indias,* chapter 2:

> Concerning his person and outer appearance, he was tall, above average, his face long and authoritative, his nose aquiline, eyes blue, and complexion clear, tending to ruddy. His beard and hair were blond when he was young, but they turned white almost overnight from his travails.

The third description is by Oviedo, who met him when Columbus was about forty. The following passage is from the *Historia general y natural de las Indias:*

> A man of good stature and a fine appearance, taller than average and strong. His eyes were bright and his other features were well proportioned. His hair was very red, his visage reddish and freckled.

The last description is that of the Venetian Angelo Trevisan, chancellor and personal secretary to the Venetian ambassador to Spain. Trevisan probably saw the Genoese navigator when the latter was fifty: "Christopher Columbus, a Genoese, a tall man of distinguished bearing, reddish, with great intelligence and a long face." The word here translated "distinguished" *(procera)*

From Paolo Emilio Taviani, *Columbus: The Great Adventure, His Life, His Times, and His Voyages,* trans. Luciano F. Farina and Marc A. Beckwith (Orion Books, 1991). Translation copyrighted © 1991 by ERI. Reprinted by permission of Orion Books, a division of Crown Publishers, Inc.

in fifteenth-century Italian meant "tall," but it could also be used in its Latin sense of "aristocratic."

Face long, cheeks rather high without being fat (Don Ferdinand); long face (Las Casas); long face (Trevisan). His high, wide forehead gave him an appearance considered aristocratic by Trevisawn and authoritative by Las Casas. His nose was aquiline, as Don Ferdinand and Las Casas attest. His eyes were light (Don Ferdinand), blue (Las Casas), or lively (Oviedo), indicative of great intelligence (Oviedo and Trevisan), and of eloquence and pride (Las Casas and De Barros).

There remains the problem of his coloring. We can be certain of some elements. His hair was white after he was thirty. Don Ferdinand, Las Casas, Oviedo, and Trevisan—the four who saw him in person—knew him when his hair had already turned white. This explains why they differ on the color of his hair in his youth. According to Don Ferdinand and Las Casas it was *rubios*, which in Castilian means "blond"; one is at a loss to explain why some English speakers have translated it "red." Perhaps they were influenced by Oviedo, who speaks of his "very red hair," and by the color of his face, which all say tended toward ruddy. Dario Guglielmo Martini was justified in saying he had red cheekbones. in fact, Don Ferdinand, in the *Historie*, says "white, burning with a vivid color"; Las Casas, "complexion clear, tending to ruddy"; Oviedo, "reddish and freckled face"; Trevisan, "red." I tend toward the theory that the young Columbus's hair was more red than blond, as Don Ferdinand and Las Casas say, perhaps being more attracted to blond.

More important than his appearance were the great Discoverer's sensory abilities. He had an exceptional sense of smell; that is the most undeniable fact about his physical characteristics. All his writings indicate that. Many who knew him extolled his extraordinary olfactory ability and left accounts of his acute sensitivity to odors. Some have considered it affectation, but it was simply a highly developed sense that was a fundamental and determining component of his sixth sense, his sense of the sea.

Just as extraordinary were his sight and hearing. He ruined his sight during the crossing of the third voyage (1498), when he spent twenty-seven afternoons in July on deck, staring into the sun to make out the course from east to west. He developed ophthalmia, but he did not lose the outstanding, incredible maritime abilities he had acquired in his youth in the waters of Liguria and the Mediterranean and perfected in the Atlantic.

So much for his physical appearance and abilities. The discussion must be much longer and more complex when considering his character, psychology, and moral qualities. On these subjects hundreds, perhaps thousands, of essays and articles have been written over the last five centuries. There have been many novels, plays, and even lyric operas. Among the literary works, bound not by historical facts but only poetic inspiration, two stand out: Paul Claudel's *Le livre de Christophe Colomb* and Alejo Carpentier's *El harpa y la sombra*. These two authors interpret reality in a completely distorted fashion, at times altering history and at others scrupulously respecting it. Both books are unparalleled works of art, sufficient to ensure their place in world literature. They make a perfect antithesis: Claudel's Columbus hears voices like St. Joan of Arc, whereas Carpentier's is a fraud, a liar, a thief, and a womanizer. Two artistic interpretations, they are to be read without concern for the real Columbus, without regard for any myths of glorification or attempts at defamation.

On the level of scrupulous, rigorous historicity, Columbus was neither a saint nor a shrewd politician. His misfortunes cannot be explained as simply bad luck, caused by the maliciousness of his enemies and the envy of those who could not abide a foreigner of modest origins being granted such privileges and high honors. He was neither inept nor inefficient, but he lacked the two essential gifts of a politician: the capacity to make firm decisions for the long run and a keen knowledge of human nature, indispensable for putting the right people in the right position.

Some have called Columbus a man of the Middle Ages, while others have claimed him for the Renaissance, saying that his soul was superior to the century in which he lived. In reality he bestrode the two ages: his theoretical approach to philosophy, theology, and even science was medieval, whereas his zeal for scientific investigation, keen interest in nature, and capacity for accepting phenomena previously unobserved or unexplained were peculiar to the Renaissance. Renaissance too ... was his economics, typically mercantilistic and capitalistic, at least until the confused developments of the third voyage at Santo Domingo.

Psychologically he was a modern man. Concrete and pragmatic to the point of being overmeticulous, he elaborated his projects only after he had acquired direct experience, and from it sprang the conception for his grand design. In short, he had a modern psychology but roots in the Middle Ages.

The same can be said about his spirituality. He was a Christian and Catholic in the modern sense yet influenced by medieval teachings. His faith was strong, sincere, and inexhaustible, pure at all times and untainted by superstition and hypocrisy in the most demanding of circumstances. He was at times a fanatic or, as we would say today, a true believer. But his fanaticism never violated the eternal principles of the Christian and Catholic worldview. He was never particularly fond of the clergy. In defense of true Christianity, he quarrelled with priests, friars, and bishops, but by the same token a few friars and bishops gave him their friendship throughout his life, among them the Franciscan Father Antonio de Marchena. Marchena was also a leading figure in the greatest adventure in the history of discovery.

Confronted with the incredible mystery of a fourth continent, Columbus did not locate the Transcendent (purgatory) in the Immanent (the southern hemisphere), as Dante had done. Instead, he resorted to the idea of the earthly paradise, of which even a skeptic like Amerigo Vespucci had to admit, "if ever it existed it could have been only in these places."

When beset by mortal danger in storms he turned to the Madonna and saints as practicing Catholics have done throughout time—in the Middle Ages, the Renaissance, and the modern era. When he was wounded by jealousy, meanness, greed, and human wickedness, and especially when he was misunderstood or suffered what he considered injustice from the Spanish monarchs, the Admiral always reacted with Christian humility and with the resignation of the believer who looks beyond the limits of earthly life.

He was especially devoted to the Madonna and St. Francis. He knew to perfection the New Testament and many passages of the Old. Faced with the most terrible danger he had ever seen in his daily experience of love and war with the sea, and realizing that there was no hope left in the natural order, Columbus called directly on the Creator, the Word, reciting the first verses of the Gospel of St. John. This incident is important, because it shows that the cults of the Madonna and St. Francis were not the fruit of superstition but part of a systematic and rigorous religious nature.

Finally, it must be repeated that his continuous, obsessive search for gold and riches was always directed toward a very definite goal: a crusade to reconquer the Holy Sepulcher. This crusading spirit was not medieval. It was new, revived by the psychological trauma of the fall of Constantinople, the capital—along with Rome—of Christianity. The spirit of the new crusade aspired not only to reconquering the Holy Land but to much more, to rejoining that which had been divided, to bringing the world back to the unity it had had under the Roman eagle and which continued with the conversion to Christianity. All the barbarians—Germans, Slavs, even Vikings and Tartars—had found a place in Christianity, but Islam had disrupted the world, splitting Christianity. The subsuming of his plans into the religious ideal of a new crusade also had its roots in Genoa, where the desire for a crusade was felt at the beginning of the second half of the fifteenth century; it was strengthened when he came to the Iberian Peninsula, where he met Christians who had escaped the oppression of Islam.

The Christian and Catholic conception of the world constituted the essential and primary pillar of Columbus's personality. There is no contradiction between his assertion and the equally categorical one that he was no saint. For that status his faith, though unshakable, was not enough, nor were his humility, resignation, and occasional generosity, for he also demonstrated pride, avarice, suspiciousness, almost meanness, partiality for friends and relatives, and indifference to and direct participation in the horrendous institution of slavery. He was above all proud; his mystical conception of himself and his mission carried him in the last years of his life to the belief that he was the man who would open the door to the third age, that of the Holy Spirit, prophesied by Joachim of Floris. His faith was as strong as his charity was weak and intermittent; he was not a major or even a minor saint; he was—and it is not a small achievement—a convinced, profound, and constant defender of the faith.

The image of Columbus as a mere "adventurer" is false. There was adventure in his life, certainly. He never refused it but sought it repeatedly, living with a contempt for danger, with the daring and courage of one confident of his own powers and sure of divine aid. The first transatlantic voyage was without doubt a fabulous adventure, but in a certain sense his early voyages to Chios, Iceland, and Guinea were too. The third voyage was also an adventure, voluntarily pursued in the torment of the doldrums and the incessant, torrid heat of the tropics. But his greatest feat—or rather series of feats—was the fourth voyage, undertaken, when his star was setting, with the intention of circumnavigating the globe. it concluded with two worm-eaten vessels beached for a whole year at Santa Gloria, Jamaica, on a beach as open as one could find anywhere in the world.

Nor were all his adventures at sea. Was not his leaving Portugal for Spain and persisting for seven years—never admitting defeat—in his effort to gain support of his grand design an adventure? His expedition in the Vega Real and the founding of San Tomaso in the center of a land as unknown as the ocean was another daring feat. His whole life was a marvelous adventure, albeit a mixture of joy, unhappiness, and anguish. But those who call him an "adventurer" do so to diminish his merits, trying to credit sheer luck and chance with his success. In this sense Columbus was anything but an adventurer. His merits are indeed tied to his successes, but they were the cause, not the effect.

History would be distorted if we ignored one particular aspect of Columbus's character: his exceptional gift as a sailor. I have many times had occasion to linger on facts, episodes, and judgments that amply prove my assertion. Columbus not only discovered America, he discovered the routes between Europe and the Gulf of Mexico. During the days of sail, ships leaving from Spain, Portugal, France, or Italy for Mexico, the mouth of the Mississippi, any island of the Caribbean, or Colombia or Venezuela followed the route Columbus took on the first voyage. To return they went north of the Sargasso Sea on the parallel of the Azores. Even today, anyone who wants to cross the Atlantic by sail chooses the route of Columbus's second voyage, from the Canaries to Guadeloupe.

The discovery of the routes is tied to the discovery of the trade winds, [and] Columbus was the first to face the Sargasso Sea without fear, to have an inkling of the Gulf Stream, and to discover the western magnetic declination. But above all he was the one to begin, in the modern era, navigation in the open sea: first and determined, he dared to go out of sight of land for long periods of time.

I have already said that he possessed to an exceptional degree the physical gifts of the mariner. Michele da Cuneo writes as follows: "Just by seeing a cloud or a star at night he could tell what was coming up and if there would be bad weather. He commanded and stood at the helm, and when the storm was over he raised the sails himself while the others slept."

There is a spectacular proof of these extraordinary, almost magical, maritime abilities. During the fourth voyage Columbus found himself off Santo Domingo. He learned that thirty Spanish ships were about to sail for Europe with a large shipment of gold. He immediately sent word that they should wait because a tremendous storm was about to break. There seemed, however, to be no obvious sign to support his prediction. Sea and sky did not appear menacing, and the wind blew favorably for sailing east. The Spanish laughed at his worries, and the powerful armada set sail. But before it reached the eastern end of Hispaniola, the sky grew dim, the sea flat and dark, and the air suffocating. Thus did the storm announce itself, but the flat calm allowed no turning back. The heavily whirling hurricane shook masts and keels and smashed everything on board. The greater part of the fleet was lost with all hands and an enormous amount of gold. Only four ships managed to limp back to Santo Domingo. Others, badly battered, took refuge in the bays and roadsteads of the southeastern coast.

A single ship, the smallest and worst of them all, the *Guecha*, was unscathed. It continued to Spain, oblivious of the fate of the other ships. Aboard it was Columbus's agent, Alonso Sánchez de Carvajal, who was carrying about four thousand gold pesos surrendered by Bobadilla on orders from the monarchs for Columbus. That was the only gold of the great quantity shipped on that occasion from Santo Domingo that arrived in Spain, where it was consigned to Columbus's son Don Diego. Besides the surprising fact that only Columbus's gold was saved from the hurricane there was another, equally surprising. All four of the Discoverer's ships, even the *Santiago de Palos*, which he had wished to trade, managed to save themselves.

The haughty foreigner was now also a seer, a witch able to conjure up a hurricane and make it sink his enemies' ships while leaving his untouched. Obviously, Columbus was not a witch, and it is just as apparent that through mere chance the only ship that managed to save itself and reach Spain was the one carrying his gold. But it is not obvious that Columbus sensed the approach of a hurricane, a phenomenon completely unknown in the Old World. He had experienced only one before, seven years earlier. Thus, he demonstrated yet again his matchless reading of the sea.

Among the greatest Columbus scholars, Thacher, Harrisse, Caddeo, De Lollis, Revelli, Morison, Ballesteros Beretta, Madariaga, and Nunn fully confirm Las Casas's judgment: "Christopher Columbus surpassed all his contemporaries in the art of navigation." Just a handful disagree with that assessment. The most drastic critic of Columbus's sailing skills was Vignaud, whose nautical experience seems to have been limited to outings on passenger steamers on the Seine River. The great French explorer Charcot calls Columbus "a mariner who had 'le sens marin,' that mysterious and innate ability that allows one to pick the right course in the middle of the ocean.... The dogs have barked and will continue to do so, but the caravels have sailed into history. The achievement of Christopher Columbus is so great it moves one to the point of rapture." Such is one great sailor's judgment of another, of the man who, except for Cook, has no peer among the sailors of all time.

Columbus was also a geographer, mostly self-taught. It is not surprising or unimportant—as some say quite thoughtlessly that he was born in Genoa. In his childhood there he learned the first elements of navigation, and in Genoa and Savona he acquired that familiarity with the problems of the sea and navigation that was second nature in the traditions of the republic. Genoa was a leader in navigation not only in the Mediterranean but in all of Christendom. Then, with his first voyages and especially the prolonged Atlantic experiences, Columbus developed an acute sense for geography and unveiled many of its problems. He demonstrates in his writings how inclined he was toward geography and how cleverly he often solved problems related to it.

Alessandro Humboldt points out Columbus's quick grasp of natural phenomena. Once in a new world and under a new sky he studied closely the land and vegetation, the habits of the animals, the variations in temperature and in the earth's magnetism. The entries in his *Journal* touch on nearly all the subjects of interest to science in the late fifteenth century and early sixteenth. Although he lacked a solid preparation in natural history, Columbus's instinct for observation developed in many ways from his contact with exceptional physical phenomena. A self-taught man without formal education, he nevertheless became a great geographer.

Columbus was a genius in the full sense of the word. He had not only a sense of the sea and an acute sensibility for geography but an unshakable faith and a limitless desire for glory, a character strong willed and tenacious almost to the point of foolhardiness. He was courageous, patient, imaginative, and possessed an excellent memory. in crises he usually managed to use his intuitions and many abilities for effective action as only geniuses can.

All of this explains how he could conceive of the grand design to reach the Orient by sailing west. This explains how he could give up family, gain, and the main component of his dreams, the sea, for the best years of his life, the ages thirty-four to forty-two. This explains how he was able to carry out the four great Atlantic voyages: directing, commanding, resisting, showing clear perception, and making prompt decisions when faced with the fury of the elements and the rebellions of men.

Firm and unshakable in his convictions and judgments, Columbus dealt with the king of Portugal, the Spanish monarchs, and the Genoese, Florentine, and Jewish bankers almost as an equal. He was not conceited but perfectly aware of his own merits and of the strength of his ideas. Had he been conceited he would not have gained the friendship of Father Antonio de Marchena and Father Juan Pérez. Had he been conceited he would not have won so many friends, protectors, and admirers at the Spanish court; he would not have obtained the sympathy and trust of Queen Isabella, a woman of exceptional intelligence and rare virtue. Had he been conceited he would not have convinced Martín Alonso Pinzón, that shrewd and expert Paleñan captain who shares credit and glory for the success of the first voyage; through him Columbus recruited most of his men for the first voyage. Had he been conceited he would never have had, even in the most vexing situations, the respect of the sailors, most of whom obeyed him even under the trying conditions of the tragedy at Santa Gloria.

Columbus's success was not a product of chance. He was not, as is so often repeated, the navigator who left in search of new lands without knowing precisely where they were. True, he found America on his way, but it is also true that he was a discoverer and the inventor of a new idea, or a new perspective, until then unknown to the Old World and its civilizations—Greco-Roman-Christian, Arabic-islamic, Indian, Chinese, and Japanese.

The Columbian discovery was of greater magnitude than any other discovery or invention in human history. Europeans realized that in the sixteenth century. In the centuries since then, the importance of Columbus's discovery has continued to swell, both because of the prodigious development of the New World and because of the numerous other discoveries that have stemmed from it. It was after Columbus's voyages that the task of integrating the American continents into Greco-Roman-Christian —European—culture was carried out. Notwithstanding errors, egoism, and unheard-of violence, the discovery was an essential, in many ways the determining, factor in ushering in the modern age. It was brought about first and above all by the Spanish and then by the Portuguese, French, English, Italians, Irish—to some extent by all the peoples of Europe. But this recognition cannot diminish the value of the inception of that task, which was Columbus's discovery....

Columbus gave the Old World two great revelations. One was foreseen by some scholars and expected by some sailors, but no one had the courage to verify it: beyond the Ocean was not the abyss but more land. Columbus landed there on 12 October 1492, beginning a new era. The other revelation, fabulous and fantastic until then, Columbus received at the mouth of an immense river, the Orinoco. That evening, 15 August 1498, he wrote in his *Journal:* "I think that this is a vast mainland, unknown till today." A few years later he would write, "Your Highnesses are masters of these vast lands, which are another World." "Another world, a new world": only with Columbus's undertaking did Europe, Islam, India, China, and Japan learn of the existence of a New World. And that changed the course of human history profoundly.

What would human history have been without the great discovery of that year? The question is fruitless, for no valid history is based on *ifs*. It is also silly, because there is no doubt that if the Genoese had not realized his fantastic plan in 1492, some other navigator from Christendom, caught up in the fever for voyages and exploration of those decades at the end of the fifteenth century and the beginning of the sixteenth, would have revealed to the Old World the existence of the New.

There remain, then, three solid facts:

1. It was the genius of Christopher Columbus that conceived the plan of crossing the Dark Sea, opening the way for the enlargement of the world.
2. It was coincidence that Genoa—home of the Vivaldis, of Lanzarotto Maroncello, Antoniotto da Noli, and Nicoloso da Recco, of the best cartographers of the Mediterranean, of vic-

torious fleets in the Tyrrhenian, Adriatic, Aegean, and Black seas and in the Crusades—gave birth to the man that the world would recognize as the mariner par excellence, one of the two greatest sailors of all time (the other being Cook).

3. Columbus was not the only genius in fifteenth-century Italy. True, Italy was not yet a state; it had not yet achieved political unity. Nor had it attained unity in a spoken language. We have seen that when Columbus left Liguria he knew Genoese and some rudiments of the Latin of the time. He learned Italian, that is, Tuscan, in Spain while discussing his plans with Monsignor Geraldini, from Umbria, and organizing his voyages with Berardi, Vespucci, and other Florentines. Italy did not yet have a unified spoken language, but it did have a unified literary language, from the Veneto to Sicily, from Puglia to Liguria, from Calabria to Ticino, today a Swiss canton.

There was already an Italian culture. And Columbus was not an isolated product of fifteenth-century Italian culture, of which Genoa was an essential part. Christopher Columbus of Genoa was the greatest and most spectacular actor at the beginning of the modern age. Beside him, enlarging the boundaries of geography, philosophy, politics, science, art, and music, stand a host of Italian geniuses, his contemporaries. Columbus was born about 1451: six years earlier Botticelli; two years earlier Lorenzo de' Medici and Ghirlandaio; a year later Leonardo da Vinci and Savonarola; two years later Giuliano de' Medici; three years later Amerigo Vespucci, Pinturicchio, and Politian. While Columbus was having his first nautical experiences in the Ligurian and Tyrrhenian seas, Pico della Mirandola (1463) and Machiavelli were born (1469). While he was conceiving the idea of reaching the Orient through the west, Ariosto (1474), Michelangelo (1475), and Titian (1477) were born. While he was reaching San Salvador (1492), Piero della Francesca was dying. While he was searching for the strait to circumnavigate the globe, Benvenuto Cellini was born (1500). The year before he died, Raphael was born. The year he died Mantegna died. A few years later Pier Luigi da Palestrina was born, who opened the boundaries onto new musical spaces.

If these names were omitted from history the Italian Renaissance would disappear. Without the Italian Renaissance there would have been no modern age. Christopher Columbus symbolizes the creative genius of Italy shaping the beginning of the modern age.

NO

Basil Davidson

THE CURSE OF COLUMBUS

The man himself seems to have been driven by an overweening personal ambition and a truly monstrous greed, as strange and violent in character as the ends he sought and the adventures he invited. His cautious biographer in the *Encyclopaedia Britannica* explains that the "discoverer" of the Caribbean possessed a mind that was "lofty and imaginative, and so taut that his actions, thoughts and writings do at times suggest a man just this side of the edge of insanity." But not, perhaps, so very far "this side," while in behavior this Cristóbal Colón, as he usually called himself (being in any case of dubious Genoese extraction), may stand in history as a worthy leader of the plunderers and tyrants who hastened to follow him across the seas. All this is well known, even while one need not be surprised that the five hundredth anniversary of his initial voyage should have become an occasion for rejoicing in some parts of the Americas. Here I want to look "behind Columbus" at what our world today may more widely regard as his greatest achievement: his first opening of a "New World" to be "developed" by the merciless use of chattel slaves.

Chattel slavery has to be seen from the start as inseparable from the Columbus project, and certainly in Columbus's own mind. He himself insisted that it was. "He raised crosses everywhere," recalls his encyclopaedic biographer, "but he kept his eye on the material value of things even to the extent of seeing men as goods for sale." He lost little time, moreover, in getting into the business of sending Caribbean captives back for sale in Spain. The dates on the calendar tell the essential story and deploy its ferocious implications. Aside from the enslavement of Caribbean peoples, the enslavement of imported Africans in the Caribbean, and soon elsewhere, was in full swing within a dozen years or so. The Spanish government's earliest proclamation of laws concerned with the export of enslaved captives to the other side of the ocean —mainly, at this date, to the island of Hispaniola (Haiti and Santo Domingo) —came as early as 1501, only nine years after Columbus's first voyage. Some of these earliest victims were white: but already how many were black— were African—may be glimpsed in a complaint of 1503 sent back to Spain by the governor of Hispaniola, Nicolá's de Ovando. He told the Crown that fugitive "Negro" slaves were teaching disobedience to the "Indians," and

From Basil Davidson, *The Search for Africa: History, Culture, Politics* (Times Books, 1994). Copyright © 1994 by Basil Davidson. Reprinted by permission of Times Books, a division of Random House, Inc. Notes omitted.

could not be recaptured. It would, therefore, be wise for the Crown to desist from sending African captives; they would only add to troubles already great enough. But the Crown, naturally, did no such thing. Even by now, there was too much money at stake.

These early slaves, like others later on, proved incurably rebellious. Huge African revolts shook island after island, and the records are copiously eloquent on the incapacity of settlers and garrisons to put them down. Never mind—the project set moving by Columbus continued to prosper. In 1515 there came the first shipment of slave-grown West Indian sugar back to Spain, and three years later, another date to be remembered, the first cargo of captives from Africa to be shipped to the West Indies, not by way of Spain or Portugal (then under the same Crown), but directly from an African port of embarkation. With this, the long-enduring and hugely profitable "triangular trade" had its inception: trade goods from Europe to Africa for the purchase of captives from African merchants; purchased captives sold into enslavement across the ocean; and sugar (chiefly, sugar) back to Europe. Such was the potent value of this trade that millions of African captives would be dispatched along that via *dolorosa*, and centuries would pass before it could be stopped.

In this perspective, then, Columbus was the father of the slave trade to the Americas; and this trade, far more than any other consequence attached to his name, may be seen—it seems to me without the least manipulation of the evidence—as composing the true and enduring curse of Columbus. Should Columbus then be seen, as well, as the father of the racism which was to excuse or justify this massive work of enslavement? Was this racism of the slave trade in any case a new thing, or was it simply an elaboration of earlier justifications for medieval forms of bondage? When can one say, with some solidity of judgment, that racism in the modern sense—the plain and directly instrumental sense of crude exploitation —actually began? The argument here is that it began with the early consequences of Columbus.

Of course, slavery was nothing new in Europe; far from it. In medieval Europe it had long depended on supplies of captives from pre-Christian Slav lands and then from Muslim lands in northern Africa or farther east; and, at least in Mediterranean Europe, a trade in captives was both permanent and pervasive. Papal prohibitions on the enslaving of Christians made little difference, and the Genoese were not the only Europeans in the business to shrug off excommunication for persisting in the trade of selling Christians. It remains that none of this slavery was chattel slavery, mass slavery, plantation slavery; rather, it took the form of what may perhaps be called "wageless labor"—coerced, but in no way subject to any kind of "market law." Slaves were bought and sold after their capture, and prices varied with the times, but a market in wages had still to come into existence. Demand was overwhelmingly for domestic labor of one kind or another and, in general, only the rich and privileged could afford to buy and maintain this labor. This was a slavery that could involve great pain and misery, but rather seldom was it a hopeless Calvary: the relatively high cost of slaves helped to limit the persecutions they were otherwise liable to suffer.

The point is worth emphasis. Throughout the High Middle Ages (roughly, the tenth through the thirteenth centuries), in S. D. Goitein's authoritative summary, slavery "was neither industrial nor agricultural. With the exception of the armies, which were largely composed of mercenaries who were legally slaves, it was not collective but individual. It was a personal service in the widest sense of the word, which, when the master served was of high rank or wealthy, carried with it great economic advantages as well as social prestige.... In and out of bondage, the slave was a member of the family." No doubt there were exceptions, but I am not concerned with exceptions here; I am concerned with the general run of things. I have read quite a few accounts of plantation slavery in the Caribbean, most lately the horrible and revolting memoirs of Thomas Thistlewood, and I have found in them nothing that remotely resembles the domestic slavery of medieval times.

If that was the general situation in lands around the Mediterranean, it was just as true of tropical African lands farther south. Absorbed into extended-family structures, slaves in Africa—and, here again, the records are copious and unequivocal—could expect with a fair confidence to accede to full family rights without long delay. They could marry into their owner's families. They could inherit their owner's wealth. They could make careers in the public service; and wherever slaves acquired military training, armaments, and corresponding disciplines or connections, they could (and quite often did) seize state power, govern as kings, and even found dynasties of kings. I am not here putting in a good word for slavery, any more than for dynasties of kings. I am only emphasizing the differences between modes of enslavement. Not surprisingly, these different modes gave rise to different ways of

thinking about slaves—to different ideologies, as the academics would say.

In Spain and Portugal, for example, there was also a large number of slaves before the New World was discovered by Columbus. But there were very few chattel slaves, and no sensible owner would have considered that his or her slaves were of a naturally and inherently inferior kind of human being. There was, in short, no ideology of instrumentalist racism. By the fifteenth century most such slaves in Iberia were from North Africa. They lived hard lives, and yet, so far as the evidence goes, a good deal less hard than the "free workers" who toiled alongside them. "Slaves—as all servants—of wealthy and powerful men were [in those times] better off materially, and before the courts, than were free labourers. If their work was not domestic"—tied to the home, that is—"they might travel the country or live apart from their masters"; sometimes they could benefit, if they wished (and it is not at all clear that many would have wished), from early manumission. The point here, may I be allowed to insist, is that this was a servitude, however much otherwise to be deplored, which did not foster, because it did not have to foster, the ideology that slaves were slaves because they belonged to an inherently inferior humanity, to a humanity, as it was going to develop in the mentality of the slave trade, that could be "set apart" as being barely human at all. To grasp the nature of the medieval relationship of bondage, as it appears generally to have been, one can usefully study the medieval iconography of slaves, including slaves from Africa. They are seen and shown as servants like other servants, but valuable servants, costly servants, even cherished servants.

They were no more inherently inferior than they were easily expendable.

* * *

Was there, then, no racism before the major onset of the Atlantic slave trade? It is a teased issue because the words in general use are vague, but overall the answer is in the negative. There was vast misunderstanding, gross abuse, bewildered superstition. But there was no racism in the instrumentalist sense in which the term is rightly used today. Broadly, in those days when the "known world" was so very small and narrow, human deviation from the norm was believed to grow with physical distance (yet is it, really, so very different today?). Neighbors were entirely "normal" and "nondeviant," even if distrusted or disliked. Near-neighbors might also be fairly normal. But peoples far away began to become exceedingly strange until, as imagined distance widened, they altogether ceased to be human like you and me. The locus classicus of this view of life is probably a passage in the histories of Herodotus (ca. 450 B.C.) where he relates that "Aristeas, son of Caystrobius, a native of Marmora" in nearby Asia Minor (Turkey today) "journeyed to the country of the Issedones." These lived a long way off, but were still reasonably human. Yet "beyond the Issedones live the one-eyed Arismaspians," clearly deviant in having only one eye apiece, "and beyond them the griffins who guard the gold"; and the griffins, whatever exactly they may have been, were obviously much more than deviant. So it was, in medieval times, that distant peoples were confidently reported as "having heads that grow beneath their shoulders," or a single eye in the middle of their chests, or, if they were women—as the Florentine Malfante was

reporting back from the central Sahara in 1447—as being able to habitually produce up to five children at a birth. In those times, when the earth was so flat that you could risk falling off the edge, anything was possible.

Such beliefs seem to have been universal in one form or another, and they long persisted among peoples beyond the reach of the "known world." Less than half a century ago, for instance (but the instances are many), the Lugbara of Uganda (numbering then some 200,000 souls) were found to believe in all good faith that people became hostile, strange, and "upside down" in the measure that they dwelt farther away or far from the Lugbara homeland. Of the most distant strangers known to the Lugbara, even if known only by hearsay, there were creatures who habitually walked on their heads or hands, and indulged in other habits which the Lugbara thought perverse and wicked. Distance multiplied deviation; and all this bespoke customary superstition, distrust of foreigners, various onslaughts of xenophobia, and so on. But it did not bespeak racism.

The transition from beliefs such as this to all that superstructure of instrumentalist justification of mass enslavement, of racist enslavement, which began with the Columbian voyages was an often complex and contradictory process in the European mind. But it can first be seen at work in the case of the Portuguese, if only because their active involvement in mass enslavement, plantation enslavement, came at least half a century, or even longer, before that of other European peoples (in some degree with the exception of the Spanish). Beginning with the import of a few hundred trans-Saharan captives (mostly Berbers of the desert) in the 1440s, they found a home market which rapidly demanded more. These early African captives were sold on the open Iberian market for the most part as domestic servants who would also, if they revealed a talent for learning and literacy, serve as clerks and trusted commercial agents. Their small numbers in the fifteenth century were merely added to the much larger number already in the country and in Spain, and their arrival called for no rethinking of Portuguese attitudes to the status and condition of slavery.

But all this changed after 1500, and so did much else. The earth would soon cease to be flat, the stars no longer hang fixed immutably in space, and even the sun would stop revolving and stand still, until much that yesterday had seemed sacred and unquestionable was due to be thrust aside, forgotten, or derided. Ferocious times lay ahead such as even the Middle Ages, with its racks and thumbscrews, had not envisaged, and whole continents would feel their impact and bleed from their destructions. This is the context of that elusive ideological transition to the mentalities of the slave trade and plantation slavery. It is reported, for example, that the first auction of African captives imported into Portugal in the 1440s "was interrupted by the common folk, who were enraged at seeing the separation of families of slaves." All such attitudes were rapidly swept away, and every humanist reaction was engulfed in a rising tide of greed. On all this the records are unrelievedly grim. Of the Portuguese who were looting India, wrote in 1545 the Christian missionary who was to become St. Francis Xavier, "there is here a power which I may call irresistible, to thrust men into the abyss where, besides the seductions of gain and the easy chance

of plunder, their appetites for gain will be sharpened by having tasted it."

The New World, beginning with the Caribbean, already lay in the pain of that abyss by 1545, and there were men in Europe, peering over its edge into what they saw below, who were shocked into protest. Merchants in Portugal and Spain —and, afterward, merchants elsewhere as well, above all in England and France —had now to deal with the pricks of an uneasy conscience at the consequences of their booming trade in chattel slaves. The polemics of the time are clear on that; but they are also clear that ideological balm was quickly found and applied. And in this process, in this "transition," one may see how and where the bedevilments of racism now began....

A. C. de C. M. Saunders is entirely right when he says in his most useful book (to which I would like to draw attention here) that "the introduction of black slaves into Portugal marks a turning point in the history of slavery." It marks this turning point not because that introduction, in itself, brought anything new to the scene. It does so because it led directly, and within a handful of years, to the massive export of captives from Africa for chattel enslavement in the Americas. And this was made possible, in turn, because Christopher Columbus had "discovered America." That is why this "history of slavery" is, no less, the history of modern imperialism, for without the slave trade, the "conquests" across the Atlantic must soon have withered for lack of the labor to exploit them. Without mass enslavement, in short, there would have been no transatlantic European empires save for the initial looting and sacking of material wealth. The track followed by the maturity of capitalism would have been a different one, and very conceivably a less ruthless and destructive one.

Anyone who cares to toil through the archives of the partition of Africa, and its consequences after 1900, when that partition was made more or less complete, will soon find reason to ponder all this. For the partition of Africa and other such activities in the history of modern imperialism all lead back to the birth of an instrumentalist racism. The dead hand of Columbus, clutching in its icy grasp the "certainties" of white superiority in one guise or another, and therefore the destinies of black subjection, is there to shake its ghastly warning as surely as did Banquo's ghost at Macbeth's triumphal feasting and to evoke Macbeth's response:

> Avaunt, and quit my sight! Let the earth hide thee!
> Thy bones are marrowless, thy blood is cold ...

And yet we know with what malignant power the bones and blood of this racism could operate. Calling up this Banquo's ghost at the festivities in celebration of Columbus may be tactless, even in poor taste. Yet I have the hope that some awareness of the curse that Columbus labored to lay upon humankind may occur at this time, and induce—what shall I say—a certain sobriety, even a sense of shame.

POSTSCRIPT

Should Christopher Columbus Be Considered a Hero?

After reading these two accounts, students may believe either that Davidson and Taviani are using completely different sources or that Columbus was an early Jekyll and Hyde. Undoubtedly, the truth lies somewhere in between. Each historian has his own particular agenda, both of which are barely concealed behind the essays.

Davidson is clearly concerned about the lack of recognition that is given to the negative consequences of Columbus's discoveries, in particular the legacy of racism that he asserts developed as a result of the trans-Atlantic slave trade. Other than a personal attack on Columbus's sanity, however, Davidson rarely looks directly at the individual explorer. Because black slaves were recorded as first appearing in the Caribbean within 12 years of the first voyage, Davidson brands Columbus the father of the slave trade and, consequently, the father of modern racism. He also blames the nineteenth-century "partition of Africa" amongst the European colonial powers on the "dead hand of Columbus, clutching in its icy grasp the 'certainties' of white superiority."

Taviani, on the opposite end, sees Columbus as a kind of extraordinary superman. Not only was he tall, dark, handsome, "strong, sincere, and inexhaustible" in his religious faith, intrepidly brave, and unshakable of conviction, but he was also an insightful geographer, a Renaissance man, and a transcendental genius who founded the modern age. Clearly, Taviani wishes to counteract the opinions held by revisionists such as Davidson and Kirkpatrick Sale, the author of *The Conquest of Paradise* (Alfred A. Knopf, 1990), and return to the more traditional view of Columbus as a hero.

It is often useful for historians to engage in extreme arguments if only to allow for the truth of history to appear somewhere in the center. For the traditional view of Columbus's maritime accomplishments, read Samuel Eliot Morrison's classic *Admiral of the Ocean Sea* (Little, Brown, 1991). For a balanced and scholarly examination of the question of Columbus, see Felipe Fernandez-Armesto's biography simply entitled *Columbus* (Oxford University Press, 1991).

ISSUE 13

Did Calvinism Lay the Foundation for Democracy in Europe?

YES: Kenneth Scott Latourette, from *A History of Christianity, vol. 2:* A.D. *1500–*A.D. *1975,* rev. ed. (HarperSanFrancisco, 1975)

NO: Owen Chadwick, from *The Reformation* (Penguin Books, 1964)

ISSUE SUMMARY

YES: Kenneth Scott Latourette, a professor of missions and Oriental history, asserts that Protestantism—Calvinism, in particular—contributed to the development of individualism and democracy in Western culture and politics.

NO: Owen Chadwick, a professor of ecclesiastical history, states that there was little democracy in Calvin's political ideal.

On October 31, 1517, in the city of Wittenberg, Germany, Augustinian monk and theologian Martin Luther nailed his celebrated Ninety-five Theses to the door of the chapel, inviting those who were interested to discuss the issues that would eventually come to be accepted as the basic tenets of the Protestant faith. Luther argued that the only basis for religious authority came by reference to biblical Scripture. From that point he argued that the Roman Catholic belief in the necessity of ritual acts such as pilgrimage, the repetition of prayer, and the acquisition of papal indulgences were unnecesary. He asserted that salvation was achieved only through faith and the grace of God, not through any penitent action, good work done by the Christian, or action carried out by a priest. Congruently, Luther denied the authority of the pope as the unerring interpreter of Scripture and determined that every believer was responsible for reading and interpreting the Bible for himself or herself. Consequently, Luther was excommunicated by the pope in 1521, but he was protected by the duke of Saxony and continued to minister to a congregation that included former priests, monks, and nuns who were sympathetic to his views. These first Lutherans were also the first successful Protestants. However, the consequences of Luther's arguments were not limited to the realm of theology. In the sixteenth century, the vocabulary of religion also served as the language of authority, politics, and society. Luther's diminution of the priesthood and his concept of "the priesthood of all believers" threw into question the spiritual justification of the feudal order. As a result, various classes that resented their powerlessness in the medieval system found Luther's doctrine to be a powerful catalyst to social action and protest. In 1524–1525, a peasant revolt broke out within the German states. Luther, fearing the violence of the outbreak and basically disinterested in social reform, called on the German princes and nobility to crush the rebellion with brutal force. Needless to say, this attitude was seen as a betrayal by those who looked to Luther as a leader of social reform. Yet, at the same time, it opened the door for the expansion and development of the Protestant Reformation because new leaders with new ideas attracted the various segments of society to their call.

Amongst this next generation of Protestant leaders was John Calvin. Born in France in 1509, he authored what can arguably be seen as the single most influential book of the Protestant Reformation, *The Institutes of the Christian Religion*. In essence, Calvin's work clarified and organized Protestant thought in a systematic framework that justified the ideas of the reformers in a rationalistic and scholarly fashion. Calvin basically instilled order out of what had been a rather disorganized movement up to that point. Forced to seek protection in Switzerland, Calvin found a following in Geneva, where the situation for the city fathers in the 1530s was both ecclesiastically and politically chaotic. Here Calvin's theological ideas were translated into secular practice: both the church and the state were organized (with some compromise and discussion) in accordance with a model of his own design.

In essence, the polity established in Geneva from 1541 to 1555 can be described as theocratic republicanism. Distrusting monarchs, both those found in the Scripture and those ruling during his own time, Calvin advocated a system whereby church congregations elected their own leadership (elders, or "presbyters") who, in turn, elected representatives to serve as secular magistrates. These magistrates elected members to an ecclesiastical council known as the consistory. The political and social ramifications of this system were immediately perceived. Calvin argued that the organization established by the Genevans was more appropriate to that described by the early Christians. The feudal hierarchy, then, was not an inherently godly system. James VI and I of Scotland and England put it bluntly: "No bishop, no king." Calvinism was seen as a threat to monarchy, aristocracy, and the traditional order.

Historian and sociologist Max Weber proposed that Calvinism was instrumental in the development of capitalism in Europe during the sixteenth century because its political and theological doctrines appealed to and justified the lives of the developing middle class. What he described as the Protestant work ethic was based on the Calvinist belief that since all occupations were holy (as long as they did not conflict with the morality of the Christian faith), then working hard and achieving success in one's endeavors demonstrated that one was in particular favor with God.

The question as approached by Kenneth Scott Latourette and Owen Chadwick in the following selections is one of whether or not the concepts of Protestant Calvinism evident in Calvin's Geneva provided the justification and the impetus for a movement toward political democracy in Europe over the centuries that followed.

YES
Kenneth Scott Latourette

A HISTORY OF CHRISTIANITY

PROTESTANTISM: A PAUSE FOR PERSPECTIVE

At first sight Protestantism seemed a confused medley of sects which warred with one another and the Roman Catholic Church. Moreover, its sources were not purely religious. They included political, national, social, and personal factors. Peoples and monarchs shared, somewhat confusedly, a common desire to be freed from the administrative control of the Papacy and from the diversion of their revenues to the support of the Holy See and of those who, basking in its favour, as absentees battened off benefices to the exclusion of native sons. In some of the cities many from the growling middle class found Protestantism congenial. Extreme forms, such as Anabaptism, flourished among the proletariat.

Yet the core of the Protestantism was a strong religious impulse expressing itself in convictions which were common and central in all the varied forms. Protestantism sprang up in many different places and countries, seemingly almost independently, and had numerous creative leaders. However, common to all its forms, but not always equally stressed, was what had been emphasized by Luther, salvation by faith. As a corollary, even when not acknowledged in practice, was a principle, also formulated by Luther, the priesthood of all believers. Since salvation by faith meant the faith of the individual, by implication Protestantism entailed the right and the duty of the individual to judge for himself on religious issues. This was vividly demonstrated in Luther's dramatic refusal at the Diet of Worms to regard Pope or general council as infallible. Yet, so Luther and other Protestants held, this did not mean ungoverned, rampant individualism. To them the Christian was bound by his allegiance to God. Protestants acknowledged authority, the authority of the word of God as recorded in the Scriptures. The Scriptures must be interpreted by reason, the reason of the individual. On that memorable occasion Luther had declared, and in this he was enunciating a basic characteristic of Protestantism, that he would not renounce any of his beliefs unless "convicted by Scripture and plain reason." He had said: "My conscience is captive to the Word of God. I cannot and I will not recant anything, for to go against conscience is neither right nor safe." In this, whether they knew or did not know of Luther and his words, Protestants of otherwise diverse views were to share. This was true of Cranmer, the ranking bishop in the Church of England, who, holding to much of the Catholic tradition, slowly worked his way to clarity of insight and in his last hours repudiated the authority of the crown which he had regarded as set over him by God and went to the stake. At the other extreme was George Fox, who rejected all sacraments and inherited ecclesiastical traditions and forms.

Their distinctive convictions, Protestants declared, were of the essence of the Gospel and therefore were not new. They insisted that theirs was the primitive and therefore the true Christianity and that it was not they, but the Roman Catholics who were innovators and heretics. They had much in common with some of the pre-Reformation movements which the Catholic Church had denounced. [Bohemian religious reformer Jan] Hus had been burned because he was convinced that to bow to Pope or council was to be disloyal to Christ, and the remnants of the Waldensees had found the Reformed Churches sufficiently congenial to associate themselves with them. Yet in its emphasis upon salvation by faith alone, *sola fide*, Protestantism was distinct from other movements which had been cast out of the Catholic Church.

Salvation by faith alone and the attendant insistence of the individual that his conscience must not be surrendered to the authority of state or Church seemed to violate the sense of community so prominent in the Scriptures which the Protestants professed to revere and appeared to lead to anarchy. It is true that here was a sharp contrast between Protestants and

Catholics and especially between Protestants and Roman Catholics. In principle Catholics submitted their consciences to the authority of the Church. They were not yet agreed on where that authority was finally lodged, whether in general councils or the Bishop of Rome, but "holy obedience" to ecclesiastical superiors was demanded of monks and clergy and in questions spiritual and moral the laity were under the direction of the clergy. Were salvation by faith alone and the priesthood of all believers to be carried to what seemed their logical conclusion, endless division and eventual rejection of beliefs inherited from previous generations of Christians would seem to follow. This, indeed, Roman Catholics have declared to be inevitable. At times their prediction has appeared to be proved by the event. Organizationally Protestantism, especially among those who sought to carry out its principles in thoroughgoing fashion, became more and more divided. Minorities went over to a rationalistic Unitarianism and, moving still further, ceased to believe in God, at least in any such sense as most Christians had conceived Him.

However, the vast majority of Protestants retained a sense of community. Their individualism was not irresponsible but submitted itself to the divine sovereignty. Luther, Zwingli, and Calvin and those who followed them were profoundly impressed with the majesty of God. It was that which was to a large degree the sustaining element in their individualism. They held themselves to be accountable to God and believed that to submit their conscience to Pope or council was to put another authority above Him. They remembered that Christ had made love to one's neighbour a corollary to the primary command of love to God.

Luther had expressed it in the seeming paradox: "A Christian man is the most free lord of all, and subject to none; a Christian man is the most dutiful servant of all, and subject to everyone." The fashion in which, in increasing measure, in the nineteenth and twentieth centuries Protestants devised fresh ways of giving organizational forms to a sense of community reaching out to all who called themselves Christians was evidence that they were not atomistic.

It was no accident, moreover, that out of Protestantism arose democratic movements in Church and state. Such extreme Protestant groups as the Independents and Baptists were in theory pure democracies, with each member of the local church on an equality with every other. Luther, conservative in many ways, had stopped short of pushing the priesthood of all believers to its extreme implications. However, Calvin and others in the Reformed Churches moved in that direction. Puritans, Independents, and others on the far edge of Protestantism reinforced the principle that there is a body of law which the king must obey, and used as an instrument Parliament, inherited from the pre-Protestant Middle Ages, to curb the power of the monarch and to give a major impetus to the kind of democracy which was seen in the United States and in the nineteenth and twentieth century Britain.

In Protestantism the "exceeding greatness of the power" found fresh expression. Although mixed with alien and even contradictory elements, it gave rise to currents of life which were increasingly to mould human culture in art, literature, thought, government, economics, morals, and religion. . . .

THE EXPANDING EFFECT OF CHRISTIANITY. . .

Christianity and Political Life and Structure

In spite of the control of the Church by the state, the influence of Christianity on the political life of Europe was striking and was exhibited in both old and new ways. With the exception of the Turks, the monarchs professed to be Christian. Claiming absolute power, they did so on the theory of divine right. Hence n principle they held themselves accountable to God. This was old.

Here and there after 1500 ecclesiastics held high political office and exerted a striking influence over governments. As in the Middle Ages when the chief ministers of monarchs were often bishops, this did not necessarily mean that Christianity was potent in determining their actions. Indeed, as in earlier centuries, in political office clergy were usually as un-Christian in their advice and action as though they had been frankly pagans. Outstanding in this period were Wolsey in England, Richelieu, Mazarin, and Fleury in France, and Alberoni in Spain. All cardinals of the Roman Catholic Church, they were as avid for power and as little governed by Christian principles in their policies of state as though they had not borne the Christian name. It is doubtful whether even Nikon in the days when he controlled the tsar was an exception to this generalization.

Some of the lay rulers were as intent upon exercising their power as Christians as had been any of the monarchs of the Middle Ages. Examples can be found among both Roman Catholics and Protestants. To mention only a few, they include Philip II of Spain, Mary of

England, Gustavus Vasa and Gustavus Adolphus of Sweden, William the Silent of the Netherlands, and Oliver Cromwell of England.

Partly old and partly new were the efforts to bring order into what threatened to be destructive chaos in the relations between the nation-states ruled by absolute monarchs into which Europe was divided. War among them was chronic. The power of the Papacy over their relations had been declining since the thirteenth century and, except for Italy, had virtually disappeared.

The Christian faith and conscience inspired and constrained Christians to formulate principles for regulating the relations between states. What came to be known as international law was developed. Some of its basic ideas went back to pre-Christian philosophy, but the courage to give them actuality came chiefly from the Christian Gospel. The family of nations envisaged by international law was at the outset made up of professedly Christian states....

Christianity also had important effects upon the political theories which governed individual states. As we have suggested, it was called upon to reinforce the absolute monarchies which characterized the period. Generally monarchs were believed to hold their office by divine appointment. They were usually crowned with a ceremony which was a religious service designed to symbolize their dedication to their high office as Christians responsible to God.

When carried to its logical conclusion, Protestantism made for democracy. Its basic principles, salvation by faith and the priesthood of all believers, issued in governments in which each citizen had a voice and possessed rights and responsibilities equal with those of all his fellows. The majority of Protestants did not go as far as this. Most Lutheran states were monarchies. The Reformed Churches moved further towards democracy. Calvin disliked monarchies, but held that if God ordains governments we must obey them. He was not an egalitarian or a leveller. He taught liberty and fraternity but not equality. He shrank from revolution and desired an elective aristocracy. Yet under his leadership Geneva became a firmly established republic. The organization of the Reformed Churches had in it much of democracy. That was especially true of the Presbyterians. Still more democratic were the "gathered" churches, including the Independents, the Baptists, and the Quakers. The seventeenth century struggle in England in which Puritanism and the Independents were prominent and even more radical groups had a voice, contributed immeasurably to the democratic trend in the government of that country.

In the Thirteen Colonies the aristocratic patterns of the mother country were weakened and the radical groups— Puritans, Congregationalists, and Quakers—were much stronger than in England. Because of that fact, democracy flourished earlier and more vigorously in the Thirteen Colonies than in the British Isles. Sometimes the democracy of the United States is attributed to the westward-moving frontier, for it is said that conditions on it made for individual initiative and for the belief that one man is as good as another and that any one, regardless of birth, is competent to occupy any post. Yet the frontier was a constant factor in the Spanish, Portuguese, and French possessions in America and in none of them did democracy and the democratic dream develop in the form prized in the United States. The difference seems in large part to have been due to contrasts in religion. In the Spanish, Portuguese, and French colonies Roman Catholicism was the only religion permitted. In the Thirteen Colonies, so far as the population adhered to any religion, it was to one form or another of Protestantism, and in that Protestantism the Reformed and radical wings were n the majority. In the Thirteen Colonies John Locke (1632–1704) had more immediate influence than in England. From a Puritan home and educated in a Puritan atmosphere, Locke was widely read and quoted by those who, after 1750, shaped the nascent United States. In Locke, for example, was the assertion that men are "by nature, all free, equal, and independent. No man can be put out of his estate without his full consent." This was to be echoed, partly in the identical words, in the Declaration of Independence of the Thirteen Colonies.

In contrast, the Roman Catholic Church did not make for democracy as the Anglo-Saxon world understood that term. In France, reinforced by that church in his effort to make the crown supreme, Louis XIV sought to crush out the Protestant minority. That minority, it will be recalled, was of the family of Reformed Churches, from which issued much of Anglo-Saxon democracy. Bossuet, the most famous preacher of France in the age of Louis XIV, supported with his eloquence the power of the crown and inveighed against the theory propounded by such Protestants as Hugo Grotius that there is a law higher than the state and which the king must obey.... Those who created French democracy drew their inspiration partly from Christian sources, but in doing so denounced the Christian faith, identified as that was for them with the Roman Catholic Church.

NO

Owen Chadwick

CALVIN

In the summer of 1536 Calvin passed through Geneva on his way from Paris to Strasbourg, the haven of Protestant refugees fleeing from France. Born at Noyon in 1509, he studies Latin and theology at the University of Paris and law at Orleans. He published in 1532 a reputable edition of Seneca's *De clementia*. Unsafe in Paris, he retreated to Basle, and in 1536 issued a lucid handbook of Protestant theology, *The Institutes of the Christian Religion*. Passing by chance through the city of Geneva, he was persuaded by [William] Farel to stay. The city council offered him employment as a teacher of Scripture.

Farel was no organizer. The Reformation in Geneva consisted of little but broken statues and more sermons. Calvin, who was trained as a lawyer, had been employed at Geneva for some four months when he confronted the city council with a programme of desirable reforms. He had a tidy mind in practical affairs as well as on paper, and one of the consuming passions of his life was a hatred of public mess. He began to seek an organization of the Church and ministry which should ensure decency and order. Like all other Reformers he assumed that this could be achieved by a systematic reproduction of the practices of the primitive Church as history and the New Testament disclosed them.

His first efforts to organize the Church were stopped by exile, from 1538 to 1541, for Geneva never wished to be organized altogether as Calvin preferred. But the moment he was recalled, triumphantly, he persuaded the city council to establish a series of regulations known as the *Ecclesiastical Ordinances*. Even when these regulations were revised twenty years later by a Calvin firmly in the saddle, they still failed to represent his precise ideal of an ecclesiastical polity. But from 1541 the outline of his programme as being put into practice. . . .

There was little that was democratic in Calvin's ideal constitution. The pastors chose the pastors, though the city council could reject the choice. They were to meet once a week for the common study of the Scriptures, and this meeting was not voluntary. They chose the teachers, who were responsible

From Owen Chadwick, *The Reformation* (Penguin Books, 1964). Copyright © 1964 by Owen Chadwick. Reprinted by permission of Viking Penguin, a division of Penguin Books, Ltd.

for the teaching of the Scripture and for education generally, though again the council insisted that the choice should be ratified by themselves. The elders—the most characteristic of Calvin's institutions—were disciplinary officials. It was their duty to survey the morals of their congregations, to ensure that notorious sinners were not permitted to receive holy communion, and to make reports to the 'Venerable Company' of the pastors. These elders were appointed by the councils of the city government, after consultation with the pastors. Every Thursday they were to meet with the pastors in consistory and consider whether there was any disorder in the church requiring a remedy. They were to summon before themselves heretics, parishioners who failed to attend their churches or who treated the ministers with contempt. They were to admonish; and if the sinner was still impenitent they might excommunicate him and inform the magistrate.

This control over the morals of the population was not new. For centuries bishops' courts and city councils had decreed rules which a later generation would think an intolerable tyranny over the liberty of the citizen. Calvin wanted to give this right and duty to the authorities of the Church, not of the State; and where the Church authorities delivered a sinner to the civil power, the civil power would punish him.

Like the councils of Basle, Berne, Zurich, and other Swiss cities, the council of Geneva had no desire to give the power of excommunication to their clergy. At every turn they sought to add provisos in the Ordinances ensuring that the pastors might act only after reference to the council. They added a note to the final text of the Ecclesiastical Ordinances which stated: 'These arrangements do not mean that the pastors have any civil jurisdiction, nor that the authority of the consistory interferes in any way with the authority of the magistrates and the civil courts.'

The addition betrayed an uneasiness. In a measure the magistrates had already been forced to allow the right to excommunicate, as a condition of Calvin's return from exile. They sought to restrict it not only by these ambiguous additions but by insisting that a civil magistrate preside at the consistory, baton in hand, as a sign that he was acting as a civil magistrate and not simply as a lay elder. Calvin at last succeeded in removing the baton in 1561.

The council always retained more control of the elections to the consistory than he wholly approved, and they often interpreted the above clause on jurisdiction in a way which he vehemently disapproved.

The minutes of the consistory after 16 February 1542 are extant. The offences are mainifold, and not all are as interesting as the following. A woman knelt upon the grave of her husband and cried Requiescat in pace; others saw her and started to copy her. A goldsmith made a chalice. Someone said that the arrival of the French refugees had put up the cost of living. A woman tried to cure her husband by tying round his neck a walnut containing a spider. Another danced. Another possessed a copy of the lives of the saints, the Golden Legend. A woman of sixty-two married a man of twenty-five. A barber gave the tonsure to a priest. Another blamed Geneva for executing people for their religious opinions.

Calvin saw danger lurking behind the trivial in moral behaviour. An ordinance of 1547 renewed an older decree of 1535 against the wearing of slashed breeches. But 'we see that, by the loopholes of the breeches, they wish to bring in all manner of disorders'. He was inclined to take a grim view of offences. When several distinguished citizens were imprisoned for holding a dance in a private house, he became (for him) emotional, and declared his intention of uncovering the truth 'even at the cost of my life'.

In 1550 the magistrates authorized the clergy to make an annual visit to the home of each parishioner, with a view to examining whether the household was keeping the rules of the Church.

The Reformation had set out to remedy the corruption, superstition, and immorality of the Church and of society. The pendulum had swung. The remedy was beginning to work with an effectiveness beyond expectation.

The consistory was indefatigable in its maintenance of the moral order. Its members tried to suppress fortune-telling and sorcery, were pitiless towards merchants who defrauded their clients, denounced short measures, excessive rates of interest, a doctor who exacted high fees, a tailor who overcharged a travelling Englishman. They once compared themselves to dogs which bark when their master is attacked. They thought of themselves as charged with the protection of old people, orphans, widows, children, the sick. They attempted to educate the public conscience and somewhat resembled Hebrew prophets, with their courage, their power, and their unpopularity.

The boundaries between the jurisdiction of Church and State had never been easy to define, and they were not easy to define in Geneva. Calvin, the practised lawyer, drafted a revision of the city code for the council, a plan for a watch, a cleaner mode of dispersing refuse. It was not easy to distinguish whether he was offering these suggestions as an interested layman or as the chief pastor of the city. There is a story that when the first dentist arrived in Geneva, Calvin personally satisfied himself that the man was reputable before he allowed to practise; and though the story is probably apocryphal, it represents a truth about the entanglement of Church and State. The consistory gave its opinions on the bank rate, on the level of interest for war loan, on exports and imports, on speeding the law courts, on the cost of living and the shortage of candles. On the other hand the council, even during Calvin's last years, may be found supervising the clergy and performing other functions which logic would have allotted to the consistory. The council was not backward in protesting against overlong sermons, or against pastors who neglected to visit the homes of the people; they examined the proclamations by the pastors even if the proclamation called the city to a general fast, sanctioned the dates for days of public penitence, agreed or refused to lend pastors to other churches, provided for the housing and stipend of the pastors, licensed the printing of theological books.

It is correct to speak neither of magistrates dominated by pastors nor of pastors dominated by magistrates. Some people served on both council and consistory, and were perhaps not always clear in their own minds whether they were acting as Church or as State. A pastor who dominated the consistory could not help being one of the rulers of State as well as of Church. That was one reason why Calvin worked successfully with a constitution which was not quite faithful to his own ideas.

For Calvin was not the absolute ruler of Geneva pictured by legend and his enemies. There were many matters on which he could not achieve all that he wanted. He wanted the pastors to take the first steps in choosing the pastors, and the council insisted on being associated with the work of selection from the beginning. He wanted the pastors to be present when the council elected the elders, and succeeded in achieving this during his last few years, though the old practice was restored eight years after his death. He wanted the punishment of harlots to be severe, and it was never so severe as he thought proper. In October 1558 the council at last decreed that anyone guilty of a second offence should be marched through the city with a cap on her head, heralded by a trumpeter; but even then the council refused to apply the penalty with rigour. In 1546 Calvin persuaded the council to abolish taverns and establish cafés instead. Stringent regulations determined conduct in these cafés, banning indecorous conversation or bawdy songs, decreeing that no meals should be served unless grace were said before and after the meal, and that a French Bible should be available for consultation on the premises. The cafés proved unsuccessful, for the people preferred taverns, and the taverns perforce were reopened. In 1546 there was an act against the use of non-Biblical Christian names, and again the people were too strong. He wanted the pastors to be ordained with the laying-on of hands, and the council would permit only prayers and a sermon. Nor was he able to persuade the council to return all the ecclesiastical revenues which they had appropriated, like so many cities or princes, at the first rush of reform. This was no matter of principle for him, and he made no strenuous efforts. The question how often the Lord's Supper should be celebrated was nearer to his heart. He believed that frequent, weekly, communion was practised by the primitive Church and ought to be practised by the Church in Geneva. Laymen in the Middle Ages had been accustomed to such infrequent communion that all the Reformers found this change one of the most difficult for the laity to accept. In the Ordinances of 1541 he restrained his request to a monthly communion, and was refused even that. It was to be administered 'for the present' four times in the year....

The true source of Calvin's authority was in himself. Uncompromising though he might be, he pursued with a single mind what he believed to be the truth; he extorted that reluctant admiration and discipleship which is given to consistency, to courage, and to decisiveness. He always spoke and wrote with a magisterial force, knew what he wanted and where he was going, was as devoid of pomp or cant as of sentimentality. He impressed Geneva with the stamp of his mind; and therefore the Calvinists, whereever they went, shared a coherence and clarity of outlook not shared by Lutherans, Anabaptists, or Anglicans.

POSTSCRIPT

Did Calvinism Lay the Foundation for Democracy in Europe?

Did Protestantism foster a commitment to democratic movements in the West? Certainly, Latourette makes a strong case for the Protestant emphasis on individualism. He also demonstrates how that individualism was seen by the reformers not as a devisive force in society but as a unifying force for community among Christians who were unwilling to put any other ruler above God. The question was how such a community should be organized. Calvin's *Ecclesiastical Ordinances* provided that order in a semirepublican format. Latourette asserts that Western democratic movements were consequently led by leaders who were raised in a Calvinist tradition—Puritan and Independent—and that these movements saw the most success in countries that came to accept the various forms of reformed Protestantism. Particularly convincing is his argument concerning the development of democracy in the United States as opposed to the authoritarian regimes that are prevalent in the history of Latin America, countries that sprang from a Roman Catholic tradition. However, Latourette must admit that Calvin's own image of God's kingdom on earth shunned a society of equals and looked toward an elective aristocracy.

Chadwick makes much of this point when he writes, "There was little that was democratic in Calvin's ideal constitution." He argues that Calvin desired to form a community ruled by the Protestant pastors. What stood in Calvin's way was the town council of Geneva, whose unwillingness to follow Calvin blindly forced him to compromise. It can then be argued that it was not Calvinism that fostered democracy but something that already existed in the European tradition. This seems to fit in with the current view among medieval historians that individualism began early in the Middle Ages when a market economy developed and most families began to limit their numbers. Chadwick suggests that it was this movement toward individualism during the Middle Ages that fostered the Protestant Reformation; he rejects the idea that Protestantism fostered individualism and, therefore, democracy. One must admit, however, that Lutheranism did provide the theological justification for individualism, as Calvinism did for representative government.

Alister McGrath of Oxford University is an exceptional authority on Christianity and Protestantism, and his works *Christian Theology: An Introduction* (Basil Blackwell, 1993) and *Reformation Thought: An Introduction*, 2d ed. (Basil Blackwell, 1993) are scholarly and student-friendly. W. Stanford Reid's edited book *John Calvin: His Influence in the Western World* (Zondervan, 1982) continues the debate in a much more expansive style.

ISSUE 14

Did Tokugawa Policies Strengthen Japan?

YES: Marius B. Jansen, from "Tokugawa and Modern Japan," *Japan Quarterly* (vol. 12, no. 1, 1965)

NO: Milton W. Meyer, from *Japan: A Concise History,* 3rd ed. (Littlefield Adams, 1993)

ISSUE SUMMARY

YES: Historian Marius B. Jansen asserts that the Tokugawa emperors' policies, which were designed to restore order and stability to Japan, paved the way for Japan's remarkable rise to world power in the twentieth century.

NO: Historian Milton W. Meyer contends that the imperial Tokugawa conservatism preserved outmoded political and social institutions, closed off attractive trade opportunities, and turned Japan into an authoritarian nation.

Sixteenth-century Japan was a time of tremendous political disorder. The Ashikaga shogunate (Japan's military government), founded in 1338, had disintegrated, leaving Japan without any effective central government. De facto political authority devolved upon the *daimyo*, the feudal lords who controlled vast landed estates and who hired bands of armed retainers—*samurai* —to defend them. Incessant conflicts between ambitious daimyo ravaged the land and disarranged commerce, severely depressing the Japanese economy.

To make matters worse, Europeans arrived in Japan for the first time in 1542, when Portuguese traders visited the islands. The Portuguese brought with them firearms—hitherto unknown to Japan—and Christianity. Both of these novel forces disrupted Japanese society even further, as the daimyo attempted to use the Europeans, their weapons, and their religion to their own advantage.

Disorder ended only when a succession of powerful daimyo managed to pacify and unite Japan. The process of unification was completed by Tokugawa Ieyasu, an iron-willed aristocrat skilled in warfare and the subtle arts of diplomacy. Ieyasu subsequently introduced a policy of seclusion, or *sakoku* —literally, "the closed country." Convinced that, after a century of civil war, Japan required stability above all else and that foreigners necessarily introduced elements of instability, Ieyasu and his successors (known as the Tokugawa emperors) cut off Japan from all foreign contact. Japanese nationals were forbidden to leave the country, and foreign traders and priests were prohibited from entering Japan. The sole exception was a tiny Dutch trading factory at the port of Deshima. This Tokugawa policy of isolation and stability had the effect of freezing Japanese society and culture for nearly 250 years.

In the following selection, Marius B. Jansen argues that the Tokugawa emphasis upon authority and order was a positive accomplishment because it laid the foundation for the establishment of a modern state that necessarily placed group and collective goals above those of individuals or the family. Moreover, Jansen praises the Tokugawa rulers for fostering the sort of paternalistic government measures that subsequently helped Japan to build a modern industrial economy in a remarkably short time in the late nineteenth and early twentieth centuries. In short, Jansen believes that Tokugawa Japan's "closed society" promoted the intellectual and institutional developments that allowed the nation to adapt to the rapidly changing conditions that Japan has encountered in the twentieth century.

In an excerpt from his history of Japan, Milton W. Meyer argues that the Tokugawa period both strengthened and weakened Japan. Meyer acknowledges that Tokugawa policies achieved their primary objective of restoring order and stability but only at a tremendous cost to the Japanese national character. Independence, freedom, and a willingness to question established norms were crushed beneath the overbearing authority of a regimented state. Moreover, Japanese commercial contacts—save for those with China and Korea—were cut off at precisely the time that China was withdrawing into a shell of its own. Had the Japanese continued to expand their trade, Meyer suggests, they might have provided an effective challenge to the western European imperialist powers in East Asia.

YES

Marius B. Jansen

TOKUGAWA AND MODERN JAPAN

The increased awareness in recent years of the complexities of the process of modernization has had as one result a new interest in Japan's nineteenth-century transformation. Japan was after all the first, and remains the most successful, Asian country to respond dynamically to the impact of the West, to make successful use of imported technology, and to combine this with its own institutional intellectual traditions.

Just now we are probably in a better position to view this process dispassionately than ever before. The failures of institutions of constitutional government imported into other countries provide useful perspectives for consideration of the problems of parliamentary government in Japan. Military and authoritarian assaults on political party government, which are denounced as "corrupt" and "self-seeking," have now become a dreary pattern. As a result, Japan's prewar failures no longer look so unique and startling.

On the other hand, it is also possible that America's close and successful relationship with postwar Japan may tend to produce an overly optimistic view of Japan's modernization. It is worth remembering that for some time the political difficulties with militarist Japan made many Western writers concentrate on the militaristic and undesirable features of Japan's recent history. In those days, Japanese writers did their best to assure a skeptical West that their society was not really based upon oppression and aggression. And now our Japanese colleagues temper our enthusiasm for Japan's recent transformation with warnings against overestimation of the new democracy. Perhaps we are fated to disagree. Nevertheless, the changes in perspective at least help to balance the picture of all of us.

Yet no one, optimistic or gloomy, can deny that postwar Japan provides one of the most striking instances of economic and social change in the modern world. Today [1965] per capita income stands at U.S.$510. Farming population is 34 percent of Japan's total; of farm families, one in four own power tillers, and other agricultural machinery is widespread. Modest appliances like automatic rice cookers have revolutionized domestic economy in the most remote areas; in the urban areas, 91 percent of Japanese homes have television, in rural, 69 per cent. In TV sales, preferences have changed from

From Marius B. Jansen, "Tokugawa and Modern Japan," *Japan Quarterly*, vol. 12, no. 1 (1965). Copyright © 1965 by *Japan Quarterly*. Reprinted by permission.

12" sets, which led a few years ago, to 14" (1962), 16" last year, and 19" this year. Durables like iceboxes, washing machines, and automobiles, enter the scale of expectation of more families each year. A recent article refers to pianos, room coolers, and automobiles as the "three sacred treasures" of today. Small wonder that one reads sentiments like Irene Tauber's comment, "Feelings of wonder merge into awe as one watches this transformation in an Asian country." (*Foreign Affairs*, July 1962.)

It was tempting for some to credit all of this to the success and foresight of the Occupation authorities. But however great the changes which the Occupation introduced, it is clear that they could have taken root only to the degree that they were appropriate to the setting into which they came. It required, at the very least, readiness—in terms of willingness, know-how, literacy, and organization— to make a go of them. The successes of recent years thus make it necessary to look again at the background, and to seek the real well-springs of Japan's most recent transformation.

For a decade and more most American study of Japan has focused on changes and personalities involved in the Meiji Period. These were the years when Japan's authorities, who inherited most of the same handicaps of unequal treaties with the West that plagued China, sought "Wisdom throughout the world" in the words of the Imperial Declaration of 1868, and managed to create a modern nation state. They maintained political stability, built a mass education network, an industrial order, and achieved political strength and empire. By the end of the Meiji Period, Japan was one of the world's great powers, the envy of some of her neighbors, and master of others.

These achievements were questioned and downgraded by some. Dr. Hu Shih, for instance, argued persuasively that changes so fast and so carefully directed had to be superficial. Others pointed to contingencies like the collapse of the Chinese and Russian empires, and suggested that the Japanese had in reality been lucky in having prostrate neighbors, on whose backs they had stepped to wealth and power. I doubt this, for it is at least as likely that Japan would have been better off if she had enjoyed stable trading partners as neighbors. The opportunities on the mainland provided profits, to be sure, but even more temptations and diversions—incitations to domestic disorder and confusion, and encouragement for malcontents to question their leaders' priorities and patriotism.

But if the MacArthur changes rested on the developments that came before, so did the Meiji Restoration. What was new in the nineteenth century was the Western impact. But this was experienced by other countries, including China. What responded was there long before the West came. And so, necessarily, Western scholarship is now giving more and more attention to the pre-Meiji picture to see what the preconditions for modernization were. This study was slow in coming for a number of reasons. After the color and excitement of modern Japan, the Tokugawa scene seemed dull and static—a Ming Dynasty, as it were. (And, it is interesting to note that Ming studies and appreciation have risen together with Tokugawa studies.) It must also be granted that the Meiji Japanese did nothing to disabuse us of the unflattering image which we held of the Tokugawa scene. They were so glad to be out of it that they had nothing good to say for it. [Japanese educator] Fukuzawa [Yukichi] could, as Carmen Blacker tells us, remember chiefly the dead hand of the past "I hated the feudal system," he recalled, "as though it were my father's murderer." Poverty, boredom, and social ritual and discipline in personal experience were combined with the consciousness of weakness and humiliation at the hands of the West.

Nor was this without foundation in fact. One has to grant that on one level Tokugawa Japan had been a closed society in a very special sense of the word; a series of garrison states, or a system so warrior-dominated that the sociologist Andrejewski establishes it as a special type, for which he has coined the adjective "bookayan." Tokutomi Sohō pointed out that it was custom, and not Emperor, shogun, or samurai, who ruled. That is why the system seemed so moribund and dull to the Meiji men who looked back on it.

But a system that changed so rapidly had to have internal sources of dynamics and momentum, and however galling the early nineteenth-century conventions may have been for the Meiji leaders, they themselves were the products and beneficiaries of much of the change that had taken place in Japan between 1600 and 1868. And so more and more study is being devoted to the Tokugawa period— its institutions, personalities, its culture and values. And a good many of the papers produced for seminars of the Conference on Modern Japan... have centered on the Tokugawa period. It becomes more and more difficult to speak of abstracts like "traditional Japanese society" without going on to explain what part, what period, and what aspect of the premodern scene is meant.

On the other hand, it is equally necessary to define terms like "modern" and "modernization." The definitions popular in Japan today make important inclusion of political values and "democracy," itself by no means easily defined, and those who use them reject much of even postwar Japan as non-modern on these grounds. Studies in the West, on the other hand, have preferred to shy away from this because it leads too easily into an ideological quagmire, and to focus instead on those aspects of the modern world that unite and relate societies whose ideologies would otherwise divide them. To relate, that is, but not to equate, such systems in terms of values—for it obviously makes a great deal of difference what the goals and values of the elites are.

Ambassador Reischauer and other historians have pointed out that the elements which, in combination, characterize modern societies developed first in the Western world. No two countries have them to the same, or perhaps even to the desired, degree, and certainly no East Asian country was at any time without some of them. But if it is the combination that counts, then the presence in Japan of many of them, and of some of them in particularly striking degree, proves of importance for what followed the Western entry.

I propose to concentrate this discussion on two related aspects of the Tokugawa scene, each of which seems to me to have a significant bearing on Japan's rise as a modern state. The first is the clear consciousness of, and allegiance to, the national unit of political organization. A second is the existence of a literate population, capable of articulation and activation into political and economic processes of its society. For reasons of space I will say nothing of many other aspects that might be discussed, although some of what follows will overlap with points of modernity put forth by other writers. Without in any way suggesting that Tokugawa Japan was really very "modern," or without arguing that it was a far more jolly place than Fukuzawa remembered its being, I want only to discuss some ways in which it provided extraordinarily promising preconditions for the modernization movement of the nineteenth century.

NATION AND NATIONALISM

If we begin with the ways in which Tokugawa Japan contributed to the rise of modern nationalism, it is convenient to begin with the uses of Confucianism. Tokugawa Japan has often been called the most Chinese of Japan's historical eras. A complex bureaucratic structure was developed; Chinese was the main fare of scholars, the production of poetry, as of essays, in Chinese was very large, and the inspiration from China in fields of art and literature was important. One might have expected many of the aspects of Confucian thought that operated to slow or divert modernization in China to have shown themselves in Japan, and some of them certainly did. But on the whole the story was one of contrasts, and it reminds us how different the effect of a body of thought can be in different settings.

Confucianism in China produced the view of a Chinese cultural oecumene, which was probably the reverse of modern nationalism. This view was held also in Japan, but with the clear consciousness that Japan was somehow on its fringe. Their feelings might range from adoration to resentment, from emulation to rejection, but the Tokugawa scholars seldom forgot that they did not live in China. "Although ours is a small island" many began their essays, an unspoken reminder of the Chinese colossus on the mainland. Consider the consequence of some of the problems that arose. Yamazaki Ansai asked his students what their duty would be if an army led by Confucious and Mencius were to attack Japan. (The answer was to fight, and to capture them alive in the service of the country. In due course his successors rephrased the problem to show that Japanese armies were going to China to rescue Confucious and Mencius from democracy and communism.) A century later Ogyū Sorai (although he spoke of himself as an "Eastern barbarian") developed an operational definition of "sage" as dynasty founder and suggested that the "Way" might best be realized in Japan. Nichiren had done the same for Buddhism earlier, and Uchimura Kanzō would approach it for Christianity later. One senses in this strain to indigenize the import an effort to particularize the universal, to identify it and to claim it for Japan. Of course there were also men willing to abase themselves before China as a sacred country, and they were greeted with the eighteenth-century equivalent of the American "If you like it so well, why don't you move there?" It was really the same speech: Arthur Wright cites Ise Sadatake, an eighteenth-century Japanist, who condemned "wicked Confucians" who "while eating Japanese rice, wearing Japanese clothes, and living on Japanese soil," praised China and scorned Japan. They were, he thought, "of no use to this country. Let them cease eating Japanese rice and starve to death, the sooner the better." Insularity made for national consciousness. Allied with the resurgence of Shinto, it also made for a very strident self-assertion.

Tokugawa Confucianism, whatever its school, was not nearly as "Chinese" as it tried to be. As many writers point out, in a setting in which political, and not family, loyalties were paramount, its thrust was quite different. Chu Hsi's emphasis on loyalty, the practicality of the old text school, and the reformist tendencies of Wang Yang-ming, were all equally remarkable for the way they pointed to political service in Japan rather than speculative or ethical reflection. There is a striking contrast here with much of the Confucian thought of Ch'ing China, which tended increasingly toward interiorization and ethical introspection. In good measure this must have been because application of Confucian learning in China was constrained by the examination system with its official orthodoxy, all in the service of a particular political system. Confucianism in Manchu China was embodied in a concrete political structure and emperor, whose moral and philosophical injunctions were the subject of regular indoctrination even in the villages. Tokugawa Confucianism on the other hand, however compatible with the feudal regimes that encouraged its study, led ultimately to a system not in being, to an emperor not in power, and to goods not yet actualized. Clearly the total impact would be entirely different.

The slogans of nineteenth-century nation building were drawn from the Chinese tradition. "Rich country, strong army"; *fukoku-kyōhei*; these operated as national goals in quite the same way that "peace" and "democracy" did in the years after World War II (until they were temporarily replaced by the Olympics). But Benjamin Schwartz's thoughtful study of Yen Fu (*In Search of Wealth and Power*, 1964) reminds us that these ideas, while Chinese, were not in the heart of the Confucian tradition. They derive from the Han dynasty history's explanation of the way the Ch'in legalists had united the empire by policies of wealth and strength. Until the collapse of dynastic order that followed foreign imperialism in nineteenth-century China, there was some doubt about the propriety of such ideas there. But the Japanese in Tokugawa times were less concerned with distinguishing between parts and nauances of the Chinese intellectual tradition. *Fukoku-kyōhei*, was already a slogan in Tokugawa times well before Perry's appearance, as a policy line for the several fiefs. The principals of maximizing income and restricting consumption in the interests of the political unit had unquestioned currency, and they lay ready at hand for the nineteenth-century reformers. Everything—in politics, in economics, in education, in literature—was to be done "for the sake of the country," and it was with some alarm that leaders noted on the part of their contemporaries in the early twentieth century a readiness to ask what the country might do for them instead. To be sure, most commoners were outside all of this, and farmers showed no particular emotion when the Imperialists bombarded Shimonoseki and Kagoshima in the 1860's. But it is enough that one numerous class did; and that this class was later to instill its views into the masses.

Institutionally, as well as intellectually, Tokugawa Japan served as surprisingly good preparation for the modern world. Competition between the domains resulted in something of a multi-state system, with many invigorating consequences. Ambassador Reischauer and others draw on this to suggest that there may well be a significant relationship between feudalism and successful modernization. Whether or not one chooses to carry it this far, it is nevertheless clear that there was a kind of fief, or domain, nationalism—*han* nationalism, to use Albert Craig's term—in which leaders and activists were determined that their area should not be left behind in wealth or power or influence. One sees it particularly clearly in the maneuvering of the activists in the 1860's, in the desperate urgency with which they warned their superiors and contemporaries that leadership for a competing domain in the politics of exclusion or restoration would bring shame and disgrace to their own realm. These views were the product of generations of contact, and rivalry, between men of many ranks and areas. The rivalry was orderly, for regionalism was tempered—for the ruling class—by the uniformities of life in Edo and castle town.

In a variety of ways the experience of the multi-domain system prepared Japan for its future existence in a multi-state world. There were negotiations of complexity in terms of trade, finance, and above all, politics, which combined to provide a better learning process for the modern world than life in a unitary state could have. Feudal Japan could also afford experimentation. The Restoration activist Nakaoka Shintarō, when he stopped to ask himself whether feudalism was a good thing for Japan or not, concluded that the experimentation with small-scale antiforeignism in Satsuma and Chōshū had been invaluable; it had provided object lessons for the country as a whole, and it had also forced those realms to reorganize and modernize their defense structures after the European guns had knocked them down.

But what of the recollections of the Meiji statesmen of the stagnant politics, in which rank determined office, which they had found so frustrating? Even this, however depressing, provided opportunities, for the very arbitrariness of rank and inherited importance meant that other, lower, and more numerous ranks, came to do the work and learn the lessons.

The reasons for this were very simple. Despite the nominally absolute and autocratic role of the daimyo, the likelihood of an able individual's inheriting the realm seems to have been rather slight. In fact most able daimyo were adopted sons, and quite often the top post was all but vacant. The domain of Fukuoka, for instance, had virtually no daimyo for a century. With the shogun maintaining the peace, this made no difference in terms of national political stability. Nor was the next higher level, of *karō*, limited as it was to three to give families, much more likely to have the time (considering residence in Edo) or ability to do very much. Despite nominal authority at the top, then, each realm found itself with men of considerably lower rank, of whom there were far more, having the exercise (though not the recognition) of power. The pool of talent was constantly larger, and the opportunity for importance consequently greater. Adoption added further openings. Participation in politics was constantly on the increase. So was education for politics, and emphasis on ability and preparation. The 300-odd fiefs needed, used, and trained thousands more than a centralized state might have. This trend reached its peak in the mid-nineteenth century, when men too low on the table of organization for even this sort of eminence began to participate on their own, on a do-it-yourself basis.

This participation, however non-modern and irrational it seemed a generation later, had another very significant aspect. This was the abstract view of authority and authorities that developed. Separated from a daimyo increasingly less important, less in evidence, and less a personality, feudal loyalty shifted to the *concept* of daimyo and authority. What was needed in the nineteenth century was a way of bringing such regional and particular loyalties into central focus and relationships. The symbol of this new attachment, the even more remote and abstract Emperor, served perfectly. The Japanese samurai had had enough of their authorities, but not of authority. And this helped them to change allegiance from one sovereign, seldom seen, to another, without breaking ranks or losing discipline.

It is intriguing to try to estimate the importance of some of these Tokugawa precedents of organization and participation for the development of modern Japan. I think that no one will question the positive values of this sense of authority, related as it was to the unquestioned priority of group and collective goals over those of the individual or family, for the guided modernization of Meiji times. In many ways the continuities outnumbered the discontinuities. The domain governments were strongly paternalistic. Feudal statesmen worked for a kind of autarchy, or perhaps mercantilism, in which they would be less dependent upon "foreign" trade and purchases that might deplete their dwindling stock of money. They instituted monopolies in whatever was profitable for export. It is no accident that one of the great modern firms, that of Mitsubishi, had its origins in such an administrative arrangement; the administrator simply inherited the enterprise.

Merchants and administrators also came to think in terms of a national market and economy. The enforced residence at Edo, and the national market for agricultural products at Osaka where transactions in rice and debts determined many feudal houses' future, and whose merchants invested in land reclamation as far away as northern Japan, made this inevitable.

Government leadership also meant strongly paternalistic measures that foreshadowed the government's leadership in economic development later. In Tosa, to name one example of many, one finds forestry regulated to guarantee a sustained yield as early as the seventeenth century, one finds government orders to farmers (through headmen) instructing them on what they can plant, wear, and do, assigning tasks for the idle months, and warning against consumption of superfluities like tea and tobacco. Thus in 1643: "A farmer... who does not keep his rice in stock until spring... or who brews *sake*... is to be punished. Headmen will report breaches of this rule, and if it is kept secret, they will be punished. No one is to buy and drink *sake*. No one should be a late riser. Violators will be fined in silver for laziness.... A useless tree should never be planted.... Tea trees, paper mulberry trees, other trees that help in paying tax should be planted...." And in 1662: "Each farmer's behavior should be examined monthly, and his deeds during the month reviewed on the fifth day of the following month.... Each village will do this in one unit, and the officials will give rewards where edicts are well observed.... During winter, notices reading 'As this is a leisure month for farmers, they should do such and such work and produce such and such an amount' should be posted...." In general, the administrators acted as though they had read about the need for maximizing investment and minimizing consumption in periods of economic development. (That they consumed this themselves, instead of putting it into industrial plants, is for the moment beside the point.) The path to the pilot plants, agricultural testing stations, foreign consultants, and market supervision of the modern period was clearly indicated.

At the last, one has even the daimyo agreeing that his interest and that of the domain may not be identical. When the Tosa daimyo instituted a new and more intensive monopoly and marketing organization in the 1860's, his proclamation, read to his retainers, assured them that the measures proposed were not designed to benefit the Yamauchi house itself, but the entire province.

And then, a final note on the subordination of inferiors to superiors. Professor Maruyama has pointed out that in the sixteenth century, when violence made missteps perilous and fatal, the relation of samurai to lord was far from one of total and abject surrender. The good retainer reproved and argued with his superior. This found echo in some of the Confucian censorate role of retainers in Tokugawa times, but by and large the subordination, if more abstract, became also more absolute. The penalty for daimyo error was no longer so deadly. But in the Restoration decades of the nineteenth century, with danger and action once again in the air, samurai assertion came to the fore again, albeit without the personal relationship between lord and vassal that had conditioned these in the sixteenth century. Hence the striking insubordination of vassals, like those of Chōshū, who knew what was good for their lord's house and provinces, regardless of what he might think himself.

The Meiji period, in which the emperor and a group of consultants and servants worked together in times of danger and tension, reproduced, I suggest, the conditions of the sixteenth century on a larger scale. When one reads of talks between the Emperor and his genrō, there is an abundance of trust, responsibility, and a rather sturdy independence. The genrō, by the way, also rotated in office, much as the Tokugawa retainers had earlier. What the Emperor thought counted for something, although we will probably never know how much. Thereafter the Emperor became ever more abstract and sacred. The Shōwa emperor of the 1930's was much more like the daimyo of late Tokugawa Japan; he was an idealization, an abstraction seldom seen and never allowed to express an opinion. He could be, and was, dismissed and ignored by young men who knew what was good for Japan, whether he himself did or not, just as their grandfathers and great-grandfathers had ignored their daimyo in the 1860's. He could even be treated with condescension. General Sugiyama, paragon of official rectitude and patriotism as Chief of Staff, is said to have referred to the Emperor as "Tenchan" ("Empie"?) to his subordinates. This remoteness surely had its role to play in the ease with which ideas of imperial sovereignty could be set by the MacArthur shogunate.

EDUCATION AND AMBITION

One of the impressive things about modern Japan is the deep commitment to education. Japan has long been known for its mass literacy, and it has one of the world's highest proportions of college-age young people in college. Ninety-nine point nine per cent of all children, the

Education Ministry now reports, complete nine year's schooling. One might be inclined to put the enormous proliferation of educational opportunities in recent decades to the success of the economy, but actually Japan began the Meiji Restoration with a proportion of literacy (some estimate it above 35 per cent) which put it close to the most developed parts of the Western world. It is difficult to exaggerate the advantages which this high literacy rate gave the government in its efforts to spread information, make administration uniform, and cajole the nation into doing its will. Novels, prints, official newspapers, opinion journals, all were at hand to be developed and used. The early Meiji government could send out directives which provincial authorities were required to have *in print* within a set and short time.

All this owed everything to Tokugawa institutions and pressures. The two-and-a-half centuries of peace and order made of an unlettered warrior class a class of bureaucrats. Ronald Dore points out that in Ieyasu's time a literate samurai was unusual, and that a century later Saikaku spoke of an illiterate samurai as badly behind the times. By 1850 he would have been behind a good number of his inferiors as well. Beginning with the shogunate, each fief had established a school for its retainers, and thousands of private schools as well as universally available parish schools had made literacy widely available. On all levels, education grew steadily. As affects the samurai, school building really hit its stride in the latter half of the eighteenth century (only 28 of the 227 domain schools ultimately established were in being in 1750); the early Meiji rush to the schools was a continuation

and centralization of existing trends, and not something new.

Learning of some sort had become necessary for the increasing complexity of life for all groups in Tokugawa Japan. Villages had problems of tax computation and allocation, and they were visited by traveling book vendors and lenders. Townsmen, as the literature makes clear, were in constant need of literacy. And the samurai could get nowhere without it. It provided the key, or at least a chance, for success in the competitive pool of manpower from which officials were chosen. All the pressures of modern times were already there; many were born to rank, but few chosen; of those few many were selected arbitrarily, thus increasing the pressure on the others.

Ronald Dore points out another important feature: the authorities approved and promoted education, and had none of the fears of its diffusion which their counterparts in Europe showed. Part of this relates to the fact that there was surprisingly little class hostility, however great the class distinctions. Even more important is the fact that "learning" meant practical tools, and a pattern of morals and ethics (drawn from Confucian classics) which could only make the students better rulers or ruled. The wisdom of the sages was applicable to all branches of society, and no one had to fear its diffusion. In content, as in manner of transmission, it instilled discipline and humility. Every word that fell from the master's lips was true: teachers often exacted a pledge of conformity and obedience before accepting a student. This kind of training certainly did not encourage rash, individual experimentation by men who thought they understood, but really did not. Perhaps it is true, as Dore suggests, that many more boilers and machines would have been wrecked if the Tokugawa educators had stressed initiative and independence of thought.

It is not to this kind of training, in which the manner and the incidental were taken as seriously as was the core, that we should credit some of the tremendous influence of the Western educators? How else account for the oracular position of men like Clark and Janes? The painstaking, careful notes taken on every occasion by students overseas? Here is what a guide for students abroad, written in the 1870's, had to say: "You must take down everything you see and send it back immediately. What you do not send home you must note carefully in order to report it later." Travel was for the good of the larger unit, and not for personal development.

The main business of tokugawa higher education was political economy and morality, and this played its role in the fixation with politics and national survival. Dore provides Yamaji Aizan's expression of enthusiasm: "Politics is my mistress. I love politics. I adore politics. I live and breathe politics. My fate is bound up with the fate of the Japanese nation. The governance of the nation, the bringing of peace to the world, have been my study since youth."

These attitudes, expressed in education, had the further assumption that there was some point to it. Not only the learner, but the object, the State, could be improved by application of mind to problem. It was essential for the individual to master himself and to guide others. The path to the early Meiji outlook is a simple one; when the Education Act was issued in 1872, it said flatly that "learning is the key to success in life, and no man can afford to neglect it." And it went on to say, everyone should subordinate all other matters to the education of his children." Again, the preamble to the new school regulations: "Henceforth, throughout the land, without distinction of class and sex, in no village shall there be a house without learning, in no house an ignorant person." Characteristically, Kume Kunitake, the chronicler of the Iwakura Mission in 1872, noted that the problem of the former slaves in America could be solved only if they devoted themselves assiduously to education and self-improvement.

Tokugawa education, however formalistic, had important connotations for the development of abilities and ambition. The note of ambition seems out of consonance with feudal society, and the Meiji leaders complained that one could not have any under the system that had produced them. As Sakamoto Ryōma put it, "In a place like home you can't have any ambition. You waste your time loafing around, and pass the time like an idiot." But the cult of education suggests this is only half the story, or perhaps even less than half. In fact, there was a lot of ambition, a burning desire to bring honor to one's name, and a desire to excel. It is suggested by some that since status was inherited, it became all the more important to achieve success in one's proper status—whether farmer, merchant, samurai, high or low. Whatever the case, ambition was everywhere. The cult of commercial success permeates the novelists' tales of wealth and prudence. The most important folk-god of the times was neither Buddhist nor Shinto, but a curious figure, grotesquely represented, holding sheaves of rice, and usually identified as the God of Wealth. But *Shusse Daikokuten*, to give him his name, should be translated as the God of Success, and his votaries were numerous. Surely it is to this kind of value and obsession that we have to relate the astonishing religion of success that came into Japan in Western form; Samuel Smiles' *Self Help*, nearly the Bible of a generation; its title the inspiration for the first political society, the *Risshisha* in Tosa; Clark's winged words urging his boys to "Be Ambitious" in Hokkaido, and the national pursuit of wealth and strength.

Nor is the story over. If national goals are temporarily out of favor in Japan, individual desire and ambition grow apace. A best-seller..., a multivolume fictionalized biography of the first Tokugawa shogun, is credited with its success because of the way it shows how Ieyasu emerged victorious in an age of warring lords and unified the nation. The Japanese Consulate General newsletter explains in a matter-of-fact tone that "The book provides valuable lessons to businessmen and industrialists who are facing in this modern world competition that is comparable to the time Ieyasu was alive. This historical novel proves that victory or defeat between two opposing armies with equal number of men depends largely on the capability of the commanders-in-chief. The same thing can be applied to the current competition among businessmen and industrialists today."[1] Modern moralists deplore this as callous and materialistic, and the President of Dōshisha responds that the cult of success means "pushing others aside to win fame and high position, and is a manifestation of egotism.... Today's college students, I believe, are no longer aiming at standing above others. They should not. Their goal should be, rather, to 'be with and among fellow men, to live in harmony with others as responsible members of the community.' " He would have had a position in the shogun's Confucian academy without difficulty. But even there, as in Dōshisha, his students would be striving to enter, to excel, and to win.

More traditional is the spirit, admittedly extreme in its archaism, of a mountain school described by Nagai Michio in 1961. The "Spartan Academy," as it was called, began each day with a pledge of allegiance to its head and a resolve for the utilization of natural gifts to achieve greatness. Frankly aiming at university entrance examinations, the grammar school boys recited in unison their founder's vow: "What someone else reads once, I will read three times; what someone else reads three times, I will read five times. Taking examinations is the student's battle. From this day forth I vow that I will study with the intensity of a madman or like a lunatic in order to achieve my goal." And, lest anyone think this an isolated relic of Tokugawa days, one might quote from recent applications for admission to American universities: "I am determined to kill myself studying if necessary to enter your university." The logic may be imperfect, but the continuity of spirit is clear.

Tokugawa education, then, was less than modern, but it was widely diffused, it produced a fiercely competitive determination to succeed, and it bred a confidence that the individual could improve himself and his society. These were important aids when Japanese authorities called their countrymen to a new challenge in the name of nationalism and progress.

CONCLUSION

Although the attitudes and institutions of Tokugawa Japan were far removed from the torpor that was later attributed to them, there were nevertheless also respects in which the doubts of Hu Shih deserve consideration; the very rapidity of the change magnified the dislocations, and the aptness of the traditional carryovers guaranteed future strains for modern Japan.

The burst of enthusiasm for national goals helped account for the striking successes of the Meiji reform. But it also carried with it a single-mindedness, an intensity, that could lead to extremism. So long as the national goals were clear and unambiguous, and so long as the politically articulate felt involved and committed to such goals, the problems were relatively few. But the achievement of those same goals—great power status —coincided with an acceleration of social change, economic inequality, shortage of land, and alienation among intellectuals. How pleasant it could be to return to simple goals, and to use them as substitutes for thought, is shown by the psychological function of nation-building that Manuchukuo offered, or of empire building that the Greater East Asian Co-prosperity Sphere provided.

NOTES

1. An American book about executive politics also prefaces its discussion of tactics with a quotation from Field Marshal Montgomery.

NO

Milton W. Meyer

TOKUGAWA JAPAN

In a new era, the Tokugawa restored order to the country. They reversed the trend toward political and economic disintegration that had accelerated during the Ashikaga period, which had caused the loss of effective central control and the persistence of widespread and chronic strife in many forms. In these previously chaotic times, social and economic lines had been rearranged. Estates changed hands, land-holdings grew or shrank, lords won and lost power, villages assumed importance as semi-autonomous administrative units, cities sprang up, and guilds formed. Commerce and trade registered gains at home and abroad. Cultural vitality was maintained. The Japanese practiced popular arts, appreciated impressionistic-type paintings, developed early dramatic forms, wrote poetry, and erected architectural gems. But Buddhism had seen its heyday, and it was checked as a potent political force. Oda Nobunaga dealt the blow, and his two military successors continued the policies of eliminating the divisive forces in the land. Because of their cumulative campaigns, Japan once again achieved political reunification by the advent of the seventeenth century....

* * *

Tokugawa Ieyasu and his immediate successors were faced with the fundamental choice of resisting or accepting change. Recalling the previous periods of political disunity and of the terrible civil wars, they chose as their foremost policies those of political stability and national isolation. They resisted change, tried to control and freeze society in a number of ways, and suppressed many of the creative tendencies in the land. In these goals they were successful, for Japan was to enjoy two and a half centuries of social tranquility and domestic seclusion. But these ends were achieved only at great costs, for the shoguns retained anachronistic forms of government and administration at a time when Western countries in these same centuries were breaking their binding medieval shackles and were forging ahead in domestic programs and foreign explorations. Some of the later shogunal advisers endeavored to introduce policies of limited modernization, but their short-term attempts to come to grips with changing times proved abortive.

From Milton W. Meyer, *Japan: A Concise History*, 3rd ed. (Littlefield Adams, 1993). Copyright © 1993 by Rowman & Littlefield Publishers. Reprinted by permission.

SOCIETY

As Nobunaga and Hideyoshi had ruled from bases near their own sources of power, so did Ieyasu as shogun rule from his new military stronghold at Edo (present-day Tokyo) on the fertile Kanto plain. Just as the Minamoto and the Hojo regents had also previously ruled at Kamakura some distance from Kyoto, so did the Tokugawa establish themselves in familiar territory away from the imperial capital. From their great fortress complex, the fifteen Tokugawa shoguns governed Japan. Protected by wide moats, great embankments, and stone walls, the shogunal fortress was arranged in a series of concentric structures with an overall diameter of more than two miles. The inner circles of the great fort now constitute the imperial palace in the center of Tokyo where the emperor and court, having remained in Kyoto for almost eleven centuries, moved in 1868. Augmenting this impressive physical symbol of shogunal rule was the centralized administration at Edo, composed of a variety of positions and organs to serve the shogun. At the top of the political structure was a prime minister (tairo), a post sometimes left vacant by the shogun. A council of state of half a dozen elders (roju) advised the Tokugawa on weighty political matters, while a similar number of junior elders (wakadoshiyori) managed the affairs of the petty vassals. A large bureaucracy implemented the civil administration, and a corps of secret police (metsuke) spread out from Edo throughout the countryside to ferret out subversives and malcontents.

Located three hundred miles from Kyoto, the Tokugawa nonetheless kept rigid controls over the emperor and the court, which, as sources of potential trouble, were isolated from the daimyo. All previous shoguns had accepted the concept of the divinity of the emperor as the sole source of political authority, and the Tokugawa continued this tradition. In theory, shogunal powers derived from the emperor, and Edo rulers effected measures through the Kyoto imperial channels. But they stationed representatives at the capital to keep a watchful eye on royal affairs. All visitors, prior to making appointments at the court or with the emperor, had to clear with these deputies. Although emperors were the sources of theoretical political power, in reality they continued to be weak. The practice of abdication returned, and of the fifteen sovereigns (including the last empress) during the Tokugawa shogunate, ten left office before death.

The Tokugawa also imposed controls over the daimyo, or feudal lords, who were grouped into three categories. First and highest were shimpan, collateral families of the shogunal line itself. Outside of Edo, the major branches were centered in three strategic areas in central Honshu: at Mito, east of Edo; at Nagoya, near the geographical center of the Tokugawa lands; and at Wakayama, south of Osaka in the west. Then there were the so-called fudai (inside) lords, who had been allies of, or were friendly to, Ieyasu prior to the fateful battle of Sekigahara of 1600. They were given some liberties and a degree of autonomy in local affairs. Finally, there were the tozama (outside) lords, who had been enemies of the Tokugawa before Sekigahara, and who always remained a potential source of trouble. Located mainly in western areas, they resented their subordinate position; in the 1860s, some of them proved instrumental in the downfall of the shogun.

Through the principle of *sankin kotai* (alternate attendance), all daimyo were required to spend some time at Edo. Most spent every other year there, and they left their families behind as hostages in Edo when they returned to their *han*, or fiefs. Others spent only part of a year in residence. Reminiscent of a similar policy of Louis XIV in France, this double residence proved costly to the lords (a deliberate consideration on the part of the shogun to keep the lords in financial hardship); the practice usually claimed about a quarter of annual daimyo income. Rank and status heightened obligations, and, as a more extreme example, one rich lord maintained, besides his home quarters in northwest Honshu, four costly residences at Edo staffed by 10,000 retainers. The trains of these lords and their followers to and from the shogunal capital represented an economic boon to the country. Roads were extended and improved. Towns sprang up in locations where merchants, hostelries, and service professions benefited directly from these endless processions on the shogunal roads. Edo itself reached a population of more than a million before the end of the era.

All daimyo also were ranked according to the assessed value of their rice land production, the major economic factor in Japanese life. To attain rank and daimyo, the landlord had to record an annual minimal assessed yield of 10,000 *koku* (about 50,000 bushels) of rich on his land. In the early seventeenth century, Japan produced an estimated annual 24.5 million koku from daimyo fiefs of 10,000 koku or more. On this total, the Tokugawa possessed over a third, or 8.5 million koku. They controlled as fiefs most of the fertile rice lands of central Honshu, as well as that island's most important cities of Nagoya, Kyoto, and Osaka (in addition to Edo). Some 150 fudai lords held about 6 million koku. The remaining 120 tozama lords, and others with holdings in miscellaneous categories, reaped 10 million koku. The most extensive daimyo holdings, which were tozama, exceeded 1 million koku, although the average lord had 100,000 koku. The size of the lands and the number of daimiates varied in the course of the Tokugawa period as families became extinct or as fiefs were amalgamated or divided by the shogun. Because of this economic factor, one based on assessed rice land yields, stringent social and military hierarchical arrangements, rights, and privileges arose.

Not only were the lords ranked, but all society was divided into occupational groups, who were intended to remain hereditary. Drawing on precedent from both Hideyoshi, to whom the Tokugawa owed much, and from hierarchical Confucian doctrines that once again became important during this period, the Tokugawa froze Japan's population into four classes. The highest class, numbering some 10 percent of the population, were military administrators drawn from the daimyo and their samurai (now a generic term loosely applied to the military class as a whole). As members of the hereditary aristocracy, the samurai were permitted two swords, a long one for warfare and a short one for harakiri. Second in rank were the peasants, the primary producers, probably constituting about 85 percent of the populace. Rated high in theory but in reality treated with disdain, the peasant in the Tokugawa structure, as in earlier Japanese times and in traditional Chinese society, lived poorly. Attention was paid to agriculture but not to the agriculturist, who bore the brunt of taxes and agrarian rents. The third and fourth social ranks consisted of the artisans and the merchants, respectively, who, as secondary or tertiary producers, according to Confucian thought, bordered on economic parasitism. Despite their real intellectual and cultural status, merchants were placed last because theoretically they were an unproductive class. There was to be no change in class for any individual, and distinctive dress, habits, and symbols were prescribed for each class.

A multitude of codes governed Tokugawa life. In Japanese history, each political era (*jidai*) or shogunal dynasty has had its own codes, and in this respect, the Tokugawa were no exception. Ieyasu started the codification process, and his successors elaborated it. There were several basic types of decrees. One group of laws governed royal affairs. Consisting mainly of moral maxims, they enjoined the court to study diligently, to observe proper protocol, to follow regulations on dress and etiquette, and to behave discreetly. Other laws were directed at the feudal nobility. Also embracing moral and educational tenets, these stipulated that the daimyo and their military followers, in the absence of any campaigns to fight, were to redirect their efforts to intellectual pursuits, to the study of literature, and to the practice of frugality. Public laws, posted on notice boards to be read to the illiterate populace, also were predicated on ethical bases, which were important foundations for Japanese legal and administrative life. Finally, overall and comprehensive codes, such as the Hundred Regulations of 1742, applied to all. These covered criminal and civil behav-

ior, procedures to follow in filing suit, and sentences to be imposed. Decapitation was decreed for adultery; banishment to peripheral areas, such as Hokkaido, was imposed; and confession by torture through four progressively more horrible stages was permitted. The continuing rain of edicts sought to stabilize the populace. Augmenting the social measures were others that closed Japan to foreign influences.

ISOLATION

Westerners, initially welcomed by Hideyoshi and Ieyasu, were subjected to increasingly restrictive measures in the early decades of the seventeenth century. By the inception of the Tokugawa shogunate, a Dutch factory... had been constructed in Hirado. In 1641, the Dutch were forced to move to Deshima, a small artificial island in Nagasaki harbor. The English came last to Japan and left the earliest. They maintained an unsuccessful factory in Hirado from 1612 until 1623, when they abandoned it to concentrate their commercial efforts in India and Southeast Asia. The French had no trading interests in Japan.

... In the Tokugawa zeal for maintaining the status quo, the doors were closed to most commercial contacts, and, at this time, foreigners were in no position to retaliate. Although the English left Japan voluntarily, the Spanish were expelled in 1624, and the Portuguese were ejected in 1638, because of suspected complicity in the Shimabara rebellion. When a Portuguese mission returned a few years later in an effort to reopen trade links, its envoys were summarily executed. Only the Dutch trading post at Deshima, established in 1641, was permitted to operate, but the merchants of the Dutch East India Company were kept in virtual year-round imprisonment. Under close supervision, Chinese merchants also were permitted to visit and to trade at the port. Some foreign contacts were additionally maintained with China by individual daimyo who controlled the Tsushima Islands in the Korean straits and the Ryukyus to the south. The Tokugawa shoguns did not cut off all contact with foreign countries, but their policy of limited, controlled trade contributed to the later downfall of the bakufu, because modern foreign ideas continued to seep into Japan through Deshima.

Aliens were not allowed to enter the country, so in 1637, the Japanese were forbidden to leave it. Those abroad were not permitted to return, because the Tokugawa feared that they might return with subversive ideas. Another decree prohibited the construction of large ships that might be used in overseas trade. As a result, the indigenous merchant marine was restricted to small vessels engaged in limited coastal commerce among the home islands. The overseas expansion of Japanese trade and commerce came to an abrupt end. Many Japanese abroad were permanently cast adrift from their homeland, to be absorbed by the native population of the cities of Southeast Asia. The dynamic quality of Japanese international relations, noticeable during the Ashikaga era, was thwarted, and the country closed at a time when Europeans were beginning to expand. Had the process of Japanese overseas expansion been permitted to continue, in the concurrent absence of similar drives in China, Southeast Asia, or India, it is intriguing to speculate just where and how the Japanese would have encountered and reacted to Western forces of expansion in Asia.

The Occident left little immediate and appreciable impact during Japan's "Christian century." Christian theological ideas were difficult to comprehend, and the social doctrine of individuality conflicted with vassal-lord relationships. There were political reasons for leaders to fear the faith, for the shogunate could reasonably project a possible alliance among the daimyo converted to Christianity, who then would also enjoy special relations with Western powers. Some religious opposition to Christianity existed in the central government, but this opposition was based mainly on political grounds and was not basically different from Nobunaga's bloody suppression of Buddhist orders. Not viewing their policies for the eradication of Christianity as peculiar or unique, the leaders of a reunified Japan treated the alien faith as a domestic issue. But in spite of the suppression of their religion, Westerners bequeathed some secular legacies to Japan. Firearms began to play an important part in Japanese military campaigns. Castle construction on a grand scale with massive stone walls and moats received impetus. The Portuguese contributed a few words to the Japanese vocabulary. Some new plants, such as tobacco and potatoes, were introduced. The more fundamental Western secular effects were not immediately discernible, because modern political and economic ideas were to enter Japan in later years through the Dutch base at Deshima.

EFFECTS OF ISOLATION

In its aim of securing national political stability, the isolationist policy of the Tokugawa proved successful. For two centuries or more, no major revolution, strife, serious disturbances, or grave incidents threatened their rule. Japan slumbered fitfully on its ocean-protected, semi-isolated cocoon. The peace of the land was broken only by occasional and sporadic eruptions of man or nature such as fires in Edo, earthquakes, rice riots by impoverished country or city dwellers, and, in 1707, the last eruption of Mt. Fuji. Nothing occurred on a national scale to threaten the existing Tokugawa structure.

A good example of the carefully imposed political stability of the time was reflected in the true story of the forty-seven ronin that illustrated the potential stresses that could arise between samurai obligations to the ruling shogun and to their own lord. In 1700, a lesser feudal lord of Ako, insulted by a higher lord within the shogun's palace, drew his sword and wounded his antagonist. Because the act of drawing a sword within the palace was an offense that carried a death sentence, the Edo authorities ordered the lesser lord to commit harakiri and appropriated his domains. His loyal feudal retainers (*Ako-gishi*) lost their samurai status and became dispossessed men. Forty-seven of these ronin vowed to avenge themselves upon the daimyo who had caused their master's disgrace. To quiet the suspicions of the police, who were anticipating such an act of revenge, they bided their time. Their leader assumed a life of debauchery to cast off suspicion. Finally, one winter's night, two years later, they reassembled at Edo and took vengeance by beheading their lord's old enemy and several of his retainers at his abode. By taking justice into their own hands, they had defied shogunal authority, but they became heroes through their self-sacrificial act of loyalty to their lord. Caught in cross-currents, the bakufu debated the case for over a year, when finally it permitted the ronin to commit harakiri. Today, the simple graves of the forty-seven ronin lie side by side in a Tokyo temple compound that has become a national shrine.

The centuries of stability, seclusion, and conformity left their mark on the Japanese. The adventurous, spirited people of earlier centuries were transformed by the nineteenth century into a regimented nation. On all issues they looked to their leaders for guidance, and without dissent they obeyed authority. Patterns of social intercourse were firmly set. Society became structured and rigid, but the crowded Japanese managed to live together on their small islands in peace and with few outward signs of friction. Yet the feudal outlook and structure were preserved long after they had become outdated. On the other hand, in part because of the attitudes formed in the Tokugawa period, Japan accepted Western norms more easily than any country in Asia. After being opened by the Western powers, it forged ahead of its continental neighbors. Paradoxically, the Tokugawa legacy proved to be both a boon and a bane.

POSTSCRIPT

Did Tokugawa Policies Strengthen Japan?

In the end, Jansen and Meyer modify their conclusions about the effects of the Tokugawa policies of isolation and stability. Like Meyer, Jansen expresses qualms about the long-term effects of the single-minded Tokugawa pursuit of national goals. Indeed, it was precisely this obedience to authority and the popular adherence to collective goals that led the Japanese people to acquiesce in the government's aggressive policies in the 1930s and early 1940s—policies that eventually led to defeat and ruin in 1945.

Yet the same qualities produced the so-called "economic miracle" of Japan, the industrial resurgence of 1948–1989 that restored Japan to economic supremacy in Asia. Recently, however, tensions have appeared within Japanese society, signs that the younger generation will demand greater individual freedom apart from collective obligations and corporate allegiances.

Readers who wish to explore various facets of Tokugawa society may wish to consult the essays in *Tokugawa Japan: The Social and Economic Antecedents of Modern Japan* edited by Chie Nakane and Shinzaburo Oishi (University of Tokyo Press, 1990); W. Scott Morton's *Japan: Its History and Culture* (Thomas Y. Crowell, 1976); and *Early Modern Japan* by Conrad D. Totman (University of California Press, 1993).

ISSUE 15

Did Oliver Cromwell Advance Political Freedom in Seventeenth-Century England?

YES: Peter Gaunt, from *Oliver Cromwell* (Blackwell Publishers, 1996)

NO: John Morrill, from "Introduction," in John Morrill, ed., *Oliver Cromwell and the English Revolution* (Longman, 1990)

ISSUE SUMMARY

YES: Peter Gaunt, a lecturer in history and president of the Cromwell Association, argues that Oliver Cromwell's religious convictions led him to promote policies of "liberty of conscience."

NO: John Morrill, a lecturer in history and a former president of the Cromwell Association, maintains that Cromwell can best be described as a religiously devoted libertarian but a political authoritarian.

Charles I (1600–1649), king of England, Scotland, Wales, and Ireland, and representative of the Stuart dynasty of Great Britain, was the first king ever to be tried and executed for treason. Instrumental in his demise was a prominent member of an obscure western country family whose rise to power was nothing short of meteoric. This was Oliver Cromwell, whom the duke of Wellington referred to as "our chief of men."

Cromwell was brought to Parliament by the oligarchical electorate of the time, and he developed into a devout Puritan, as did many of his class. When compelled to call a parliament as a result of the invasion of England by a force of disgruntled Scottish Presbyterians, Charles found himself faced with a rebellious parliament disenchanted with the king's religious and economic policies. Cromwell stood with those who criticized the king, and when discontent led to civil war in 1641, he immediately raised a troop of cavalry for the parliamentary army.

Cromwell's skill as a military leader became increasingly apparent as the war dragged on in a series of inconclusive battles over the next four years. Finally, the army of Parliament reformed and reorganized into a force of committed veterans known as the "New Model Army," and Cromwell, though not the titular leader, took command. In 1645 the king and his forces were decisively defeated at the battle of Naseby. Over the next four years, the king, as an on-again, off-again prisoner of Parliament, played a dangerous game of intrigue that eventually alienated Cromwell from any support he may have held for the establishment of a constitutional monarchy. In 1648, leading a parliament purged of any moderate members, Cromwell directed the prosecution of the king and, along with some 30 other regicides, signed the death warrant of the hapless monarch. On January 30, 1649, Charles was beheaded on a scaffold before Whitehall Palace.

With the backing of the army, Cromwell now found himself the leader of the English government. Before he could establish a new polity, however, he needed to defeat his opponents in Ireland and Scotland. He did this through a series of ruthless campaigns and the establishment of oppressive laws. He has been particularly condemned by Irish historians and popular sentiment for his intentional massacre of the men, women, and children of Drogheda, an atrocity that has lived on in Irish folk memory.

The reign of Cromwell from 1649 until his death in 1658 has been known variously as the Interregnum or Commonwealth and Protectorate. It consisted of a series of failed experiments in republican government and ended in a virtual military dictatorship.

In 1653 Cromwell called a parliament consisting of members elected by the Independent (Puritan) congregations. This came to be known as the Barebones Parliament, after one of its particularly fanatical members, colorfully named Praise-God Barebones. This body attempted to pass laws that were too radical for Cromwell's taste, including threats to private property. As a result, he disbanded the assembly in much the same way the Stuart monarchs had done before. After one more attempt to construct a legislative parliament, Cromwell was offered by its more moderate leaders the Instrument of Government (England's first written constitution), which established him as Lord Protector. As such, Cromwell divided Britain into military governorships, established Puritanism, and, at the same time, allowed religious toleration of all Protestant sects. He even accepted the Jews' return to England in 1656 (they had been expelled by Edward I in the thirteenth century). Cromwell was offered the crown in 1657, but he refused. Upon his death, his mantle of power was taken up by his son Richard Cromwell. However, Richard had neither the political support nor the political prestige of his father. Under the instigation of George Monck, the commanding general in Scotland, the son of Charles I was invited to return as monarch of Great Britain, which he did in the Restoration of 1660.

Historically, from the very inception of Cromwell's rise to power, opinions have diverged about him personally and politically. Contemporaries and historians have considered and interpreted him variously, from tyrant and titan to genius and hypocrite. In the following selections, Peter Gaunt defends Cromwell's career as a soldier and a politician as one devoted to "liberty of conscience" without compromising the peace of the realm. John Morrill argues that although Cromwell may not have been a deliberate hypocrite, he nevertheless came to accumulate tremendous personal power while failing to create a stable polity in seventeeth-century England.

YES

Peter Gaunt

THE FACES OF CROMWELL

Cromwell's death in September 1658 was followed by attempts to place his life and career in context. His state funeral was badly organized and no funeral sermon was delivered or subsequently published. There were, however, a number of memorial services for the late Protector, and at least two of the sermons preached on those occasions found their way into print, together with memorial verses by Marvell, Dryden and others. No official or state-sponsored biography appeared, but at least three full-length biographical studies were published between Cromwell's death and the Restoration, written by Richard Flecknoe, Samuel Carrington and 'L. S.', the otherwise anonymous author of *The Perfect Politician*.

These three biographies have much in common. They all skate very briefly over Cromwell's life before 1642, tend to focus on the interregnum and, to a greater or lesser degree, become narratives of key events and policies post-1649 rather than tightly focusing on Cromwell's own role and personal contribution. In their approach to the man, however, the three diverge quite sharply. Flecknoe and Carrington are overwhelmingly favourable towards Cromwell, Flecknoe dismissing the 'envy and malice' of others to produce a highly flattering conclusion... while Carrington makes Cromwell's continuing humility and compassion the dominant feature of his career post-1649....

In contrast, *The Perfect Politician* takes a generally more critical line, underscoring even apparently complimentary or neutral passages with barbed comments, as in the account of Cromwell's attempts to readmit the Jews— 'our Protector having a large (I say not conscience, but) heart, and being of tender bowels, his charity extended so far, as to plead for the re-entertainment of these guests'—and alleging that ambition and cunning could be seen even in Cromwell's different speaking styles:

> His Speeches were for the most part ambiguous, especially in publicke meetings; wherein he rather left others to pick out the meanings, then did it himself. But when Offenders came under his own examination, then would he speak plain English, and declare his power unto them in a ranting stile.

The author claims that all the developments in Cromwell's life and career, including his championing of religious liberty and his rejection of the crown, were aimed at personal advancement and the acquisition of power:

> We finde him in the beginning of England's Distractions, a most active Instrument to carry on the Cause for King and Parliament; this pretence holding water, and proving prosperous, he then became the main stickler for Liberty of Conscience without any limitation. This toleration became his Masterpiece in Politicks; for it procured him a party that stuck close in all cases of necessity. These Libertines in general, being divided into several particular Fractions... did all of them serve as steps to mount our Protector to the highest pitch of Preferment. After he had made use of all that could augment his Interest, then Humility condescended to look thorow his fingers at a crown; but still waving the ayrie title of King, he rather chose to accept the substantial Power of Protector.

However, the author clearly retained much admiration for Cromwell's achievements and *The Perfect Politician* is by no means unremittingly condemnatory. The closing words of the biography, written from the vantage point of 1659–60, with the Protectorate long gone and the army-backed regime which replaced it tottering, capture this ambivalence perfectly:

> To take him in the whole, he was a Man better fitted to make a Prince of, then the People was to receive him: this we see sufficiently in the management of the Government to his Death. But afterwards, the sudden disaster which befel his Posterity was so admirable, that it cannot be imputed to any thing else but Digitus Dei.

If contemporaries such as these were puzzled by many aspects of Cromwell's character and career and produced such starkly differing assessments, it is all the more impossible for historians writing centuries later to produce a comprehensive, all-encompassing or definitive portrait. No interpretation will ever command the total support and approval of historians and biographers and no conclusions are likely to rise above doubt and criticism in their own day and the need for future revision in the light of further work. None the less, it may prove useful to pull together some of the themes of Cromwell's life and career and to summarize of some of the key facets of the man.

APPEARANCE, HEALTH AND CHARACTER

His body was wel compact and strong, his stature under 6 foote (1 beleeve about two inches) his head so shaped, as you might see it a storehouse and shop both of a vast treasury of natural parts. His temper exceeding fyery, as I have known, but the flame of it kept downe, for the most part, or soon allayed with thos moral endowments he had. He was naturally compassionate towards objects in distresse, even to an effeminate measure; though God had made him a heart, wherein was left little roume for any fear, but what was due to himselfe, of which there was a large proportion, yet did he exceed in tendernesse towards sufferers. A larger soul, I think, hath seldome dwelt in a house of clay than his was. I do believe, if his story were impartialy transmitted, and the unprejudiced world wel possest with it, she would adde him to her nine worthies, and make up that number a decemviri. He lived and dyed in comfortable communion with God, as judicious persons neer him wel observed. He was that Mordecai that sought the welfare of his people, and spake peace to his seed, yet were his temptations such, as it appeared frequently, that he, that hath grace enough for many men, may have too little for himself; the treasure he had being but in an earthen vessel, and that equally defiled with original sin, as any other man's nature is.

This justifiably famous and much quoted pen-portrait of Cromwell was written in 1659 by John Maidstone, formerly steward and cofferer to the late Protector. As a close personal servant and colleague, Maidstone was very well placed to observe both his master's physical appearance and his personality traits, and there is good reason, therefore, to accept the veracity of this account. Around the same time, Flecknoe and Carrington published briefer sketches within their biographies. Flecknoe claimed that Cromwell 'was of stature rather well set then tall; strong and robustious of constitution; of visage Leonin, the true phisiognomy [of] all great and martial men, yet as much Lamb in the Chamber as Lion in the field, courteous, affable and obliging to all', Carrington that 'he somewhat exceeded the usual middle stature, but was well proportioned accordingly, being of a becoming fatness, well shaped, having a masculine face, a sparkling eye, both courteous and harsh at once according as there was occasion'.

Maidstone, Flecknoe and Carrington were writing in 1659, after Cromwell's death, and their sketches were probably based on impressions drawn from the final stages of Cromwell's career, most notably the Protectorate. Other accounts present images of a younger Cromwell, the Cromwell of the early 1640s at the beginning of his political career. However,

they were written or published many years later, and they must be approached with some caution, for they may well have been embellished by hindsight and the knowledge of Cromwell's subsequent career. For example, in his *Memoirs*, Sir Philip Warwick claimed to recall how, coming to the House one morning in November 1640, during the opening weeks of the Long Parliament, he

perceived a gentleman speaking, (whom I knew not,) very ordinarily apparelled, for it was a plain cloth-suit, which seemed to have been made by an ill country tailor; his linen was plain, and not very clean, and I remember a speck or two of blood upon his little band, which was not much larger than his collar; his hat was without a hat-band, his stature was of a good size, his sword stuck close to his side, his countenance swolen and reddish, his voice sharp and untuneable, and his eloquence full of fervour, for the subject matter would not bear much of reason... And yet I lived to see this very gentleman, whom out of no ill will to him I thus describe, by multiplied good successes, and by real, but usurped power, (having had a better tailor, and more converse among good company)... appear of a great and majestic deportment and comely presence. Of him therefore I will say no more, but that verily I believe he was extraordinarily designed for those extraordinary things, which one while most wickedly and facinorously he acted, and at another as successfully and greatly performed.

Again, in his published *Memoirs*, Sir Richard Bulstrode claimed to have recalled another exchange early in the Long Parliament, when Lord Digby asked John Hampden to identify an MP who had spoken in the House that day. Hampden identified the 'slovenly fellow...

who hath no ornament in his speech' as Cromwell, supposedly adding a prediction that, if it came to war, Cromwell would become 'one of the greatest men of England'.

As well as pen-portraits of this sort, we also possess a number of illustrative likenesses of Cromwell. Most famous are the portraits. The earliest, probably dating from the late 1640s, was painted by Robert Walker, and shows Cromwell three-quarter length in dark armour. In the early 1650s Samuel Cooper produced a string of miniatures of Cromwell, usually of the head and shoulders alone, sometimes showing Cromwell in shirt and coat, sometimes in armour. The best in this series appears incomplete and may have served as a master study from which replicas could be produced. Slightly later, perhaps in 1653–4 around the beginning of the Protectorate, Cromwell was painted by Sir Peter Lely, who again produced a head and shoulders likeness, usually in armour and within an oval frame. In each case, a number of different versions survive, some by the principal artist, some by other hands. As well as these and other contemporary portraits, there are a number of engravings which were published during Cromwell's lifetime, the busts and profiles of Cromwell which Thomas Simon produced for the coins and medals of the Protectorate, copies of a death mask taken in 1658 and photographs of the semi-mummified head, reputed to be Cromwell's, finally buried in 1960....

There is no doubt that Cromwell was an emotional man and that, from time to time during the decades of military and political conflict, those emotions swung from high to low. In 1628 [Sir Theodore] Mayerne had diagnosed acute depression as the underlying cause of many of Cromwell's more physical afflictions, and his letters and speeches of the 1640s and 1650s point to periods of despondency and gloom, at times verging on an utter despair from which he was saved only by his faith in God. Equally, there is no doubting his elation in the wake of military and political success, the euphoria breaking through in the letters which he wrote after the battles of Marston Moor, Dunbar and Worcester and after the vote of no addresses of January 1648, and in the speeches with which he opened both the Nominated Assembly and his first Protectorate Parliament. It would have been strange, indeed, if the letters which he wrote within hours of his major military victories had been anything other than imbued with a sense of great joy and elation. Sometimes, too, high emotion ran away with him. His angry arguments in 1630 over the new Huntingdon charter carried him before the Privy Council and, briefly, into custody, and during the opening years of the Long Parliament his passion, perhaps exacerbated by an inexperience of parliamentary procedures, was often counterproductive and occasionally earned him stiff rebuke. In the first two years of the war, his criticisms of his military and social superiors, culminating in his detailed testimony against the Earl of Manchester, were sometimes ill-judged or unwise. At the army's Reading debates in 1647, Cromwell acknowledged that he was often accused of going 'too fast', of underestimating 'dangers' and of 'always making hast, and more some times perhaps then good speede'. In a letter of October 1651 he wrote of his 'weaknesses' and 'inordinate passions'. But even in the closing years of his life and career, as an experienced politician and head of state, he could still be headstrong. He angrily turned on the senior army officers in February 1657 and put them in their place with a stinging recital of home truths, bolstered—if surviving accounts of the tirade are accurate—with a measure of distortion and invention.

However, there is also evidence that, when faced with a major decision, a complex situation or some other personal or political crisis, Cromwell could withdraw into himself, to become introspective and hesitant. Cromwell explained this as a need to seek the Lord, to spend time searching for a better understanding of where God and divine providence were leading. His critics, both contemporaries and many later historians, interpret this as evidence of uncertainty, over-caution, chronic inaction and an unwillingness to commit himself. Examples might be found in spring 1647, when he was torn between loyalty to Parliament and to the army, the latter half of 1647 and the period 1652–3, when he wrestled with suggestions that the army be used to intervene in central government, the latter half of 1648, when he agonized over military intervention and regicide, and spring 1657, when he gave the impression of being uncertain whether or not to accept the crown. In some cases, the agonizing was ended by the decisive action of others—Joyce's seizure of the King in 1647, the decision of London-based officers to purge Parliament in December 1648, the intervention of moderates within the Nominated Assembly to terminate its power. On other occasions, Cromwell himself eventually reached a clear decision and then acted decisively to implement it and thus change events—his tardy but then very active support for regicide, his ejection of the Rump, his firm rejection of the crown. This pattern, with phases of inaction and introspection, and of high activity and decisive interventions, is

sometimes described as symptomatic of a manic depressive, but the comparison seems strained. For long periods during the 1640s and 1650s, Cromwell seems to have been neither manic nor depressive, neither excessively euphoric nor engulfed in a slough of despair. Instead, he appears to have been working steadily and in an emotionally balanced way to tackle his military and political workload. Although there is no denying the periods of depression and inaction, and of euphoric activity, overall Cromwell does not come across as someone who could be described in medical terms as emotionally disturbed or mentally ill....

SOLDIER AND POLITICIAN

'It is obvious to all, he studied Men more than Books', commented the anonymous author of *The Perfect Politician*. Cromwell was far from stupid and had received the solid education of a gentleman's son, including a spell at Cambridge University, though he left well before completing his studies or obtaining a degree. He may have obtained a smattering of legal knowledge by attending one of the London Inns for a time—Carrington commented that 'his parents designed him for the Study of the Civill Law, which is the foundation of the Politicks'—though the evidence is inconclusive. He could read and write English well enough and had adequate Latin. In 1650 he recommended that his son study business, mathematics, cosmography and 'a little' history, particularly Raleigh's *History of the World*. But Cromwell does not come across as a great intellectual or a highly original thinker, and there is little sign that he had an unusually wide or deep academic knowledge. In presenting a set of financial accounts to Parliament in April 1657, he claimed that the business was 'exceed ingly past my understanding, for I have as little skill in Arithmetic as I have in the Law'; earlier in the same speech he had pleaded ignorance of legal terms and claimed that, although he had heard talk of 'demurrers', such matters were beyond his understanding. His surviving letters and speeches reveal no more than a passing acquaintance with classical and recent British history, and certainly do not point to a man of wide academic, literary and historical tastes. Instead, Cromwell usually drew on a single book for his intellectual and literary references, and all his speeches and many of his letters were weighed down with repeated references to the Bible, far more often to the Old than to the New Testament.

This apparently somewhat narrow academic and intellectual background was reinforced by a comparative lack of practical experience. During the 1620s and 1630s Cromwell had been a small-scale East Anglian farmer, at or near the bottom of the gentry class. He may well have strayed no further than East Anglia, the east Midlands and London. In 1640 Cromwell probably had no military experience at all, had never been a county JP, had played no more than quite minor roles in town and county administration and had served inconspicuously in a single Parliament. When the political and military conflict of the years after 1640 catapulted Cromwell ever higher, he had only a very limited intellectual and practical grounding upon which to draw. The military and political skills which he displayed in the 1640s and 1650s were built upon slender foundations.

Cromwell has often been described as a natural military genius and compared with several of the outstanding military figures which Britain has produced,

most notably Marlborough, Wellington and Montgomery. There is no doubting that during the 1640s Cromwell swiftly acquired and exercised a range of military skills and that he emerged as one of the most successful commanders of the entire civil war, a path which carried him from an inexperienced captain to all-conquering commander-in-chief in less than eight years. Cromwell explained this in terms of God's providence, arguing that he was unworthy and unskilled and that the Lord's intervention alone had enabled him to gain victories and to recover from occasional reverses. Consistent with this is Cromwell's oft-repeated claim that, in raising his own regiment, he recruited 'godly' and 'honest' men, and his oft-repeated advice to others that they should do likewise. Such men would be more likely to win God's favour and to be the instruments of His providences and, more prosaically, they would also tend to be strongly motivated by a belief that they were doing God's work and to accept more readily both self-discipline and the sort of tight discipline which Cromwell and his subordinate officers imposed. It was this discipline which enabled Cromwell—unlike many cavalry commanders—to keep tight control of his cavalry on the battlefield, to prevent the horse charging off the battlefield in pursuit of their broken enemy and instead then to regroup and to tear into the vulnerable enemy foot. He also learnt very early the value of keeping one or two waves of cavalry in reserve, to be deployed at the vital moment to support the first attack and to relieve units which had met with unexpected pressure or a reverse. These skills were bolstered both by attention to details of pay and supply—seen most clearly in the long, painstaking preparations for the Irish campaign—and by a conviction that the war was necessary and just and that, whatever may then follow in political and constitutional affairs, it was vital to score a complete military victory. In many ways, Cromwell was the most successful military commander of the civil war, and his reputation was built upon solid and often outstanding achievements....

Two traits underpinned Cromwell's political approach and outlook from the mid-1640s, when he began to play a significant role in central government and national politics, until his death twelve years later. The first... was his lack of profound or original ideas. Cromwell was not a great political theorist and he tended to be led by, or to react to, initiatives and ideas formulated by others. When the debates held at Reading and Putney during 1647 turned from the role of the army, upon which Cromwell had plenty to say, to deeper political and constitutional matters, his recorded contributions quickly dwindled. Other officers, particularly Ireton, took the lead, displaying a sharpness of mind which was perhaps beyond Cromwell. The constitutional theorizing which produced the Nominated Assembly in 1653 emanated from debates in the Council of Officers reportedly dominated by John Lambert and Thomas Harrison, not from Cromwell either acting alone or imposing his distinctive will. Although he requested and obtained revisions to the Instrument of Government and the Humble Petition and Advice, both Protectoral constitutions were initiated and drafted by others. In 1657–8 he repeatedly claimed that most of the key domestic policy developments from 1653 onwards had been initiated by the army or the Council, though

here Cromwell was probably being disingenuous.

The second trait was Cromwell's flexibility, most clearly enunciated at Reading in July 1647, when he asserted that he was not 'wedded and glewed to formes of Governement'. For Cromwell, the importance lay in the ends not the means, and if the government appeared to be doing God's work and bringing closer God's eternal salvation, he was not too concerned about the precise form which that mortal and transitory government took. Thus Cromwell was willing to support different forms, to experiment, and to abandon a government which no longer appeared to have divine support or to be working towards God's chosen ends. According to his interpretation of God's will, he shifted between supporting monarchical and republican forms of government. At times, he laid great stress upon the sovereignty of the people and the sanctity of parliament, yet at other times he could dismiss popular opinion, snarling that the important thing was the people's 'good, not what pleases them', and he was involved in the purging and ejection of elected parliaments and in the establishment of a non-elected assembly. At that point, in spring 1653, he seemed to share many of the millenarian assumptions of the Fifth Monarchists and others, but he clearly shied away from them later in the 1650s, in several speeches bitterly condemning claims by Fifth Monarchists 'to entitle themselves on this principle, that they are the only men to rule kingdoms, govern nations, and give laws to people' He came to view the Protectoral system of government as an effective means to pursuing God-given ends, though even then he was willing to change the forms, perhaps seriously contemplating taking the crown in spring 1657 and around the same time hinting that the entire Protectorate was a temporary experiment.

In several of his speeches during the Protectorate, Cromwell asserted that the chief ends of government were 'maintaining of the liberty of these nations; our civil liberties, as men; our spiritual liberties, as Christians'. Of the two, he claimed that the religious goal, 'the preservation of the professors thereof, to give them all due and just liberty, and to assert the truths of God', was foremost, but he argued that care for 'civil liberties and interests of the nations' was 'the next best God hath given men in the world... to fence the people of God in their interest' Cromwell wanted everyone to share in the peace and well-being of the commonwealth, to enjoy their liberty and their own property free from illegal interference, protected by the law and the magistrate. He was aware that injustices and imperfections continued, and he sought, both via his own reformist initiatives as Protector and by urging various parliaments to undertake reform, to reduce or remove some of these imperfections. Cromwell concentrated upon the unduly harsh nature of some laws and the inefficiency and unwarrantable expense of the legal system. On several occasions, most notably in the letter which he wrote after the battle of Dunbar in 1650, he also called for a measure of social justice, asserting that 'if there be any one that makes many poor to make a few rich, that suits not a Commonwealth'. On the other hand, he strongly defended the established, hierarchical social order, referred to both liberty and property as 'badges of the kingdom of Christ' and fiercely condemned any institution or group—the Nominated Assembly, the Levellers and other radical sects—which appeared to be threatening

the existing social order or to be advocating enforced redistribution of property. Similarly, he supported only modest extensions to the franchise and strongly condemned any proposal to extend the vote to those with little or no property. Cromwell was no social revolutionary.

CROMWELL AND RELIGION

From his conversion experience at some point in the 1630s until his death, Cromwell possessed a deep and overriding belief in an active and all-powerful God, who was guiding the nation and its people along His chosen path and who had summoned Cromwell to be one of His servants and instruments in that work. Here, most historians now agree, was the driving force which pushed Cromwell forward and which shaped most of his subsequent thoughts and actions. From the mid-1630s until his death, almost all Cromwell's surviving letters and recorded speeches are loaded with references to the Bible and allusions to God and God's will. Repeatedly during the 1640s and 1650s, he justified the key developments which he initiated or in which he was involved—the civil war itself, Pride's Purge, regicide, the Irish and Scottish campaigns, the ejection of the Rump, the rejection of the crown and so on—in terms of God's will. The Lord had brought them about, and Cromwell was participating merely as God's servant. In our more secular age, this can all too easily be dismissed as cant, as a false veneer to cover his very mortal actions and ambitions and to apply pressure on political opponents. Some contemporaries thought the same, most notably the authors of *The Hunting of Foxes*, who in 1649 famously alleged that 'You shall scarce speak to Cromwell about anything, but he will lay his hand on his breast, elevate his eyes, and call God to record; he will weep, howl and repent, even while he doth smite you under the first rib.' But a belief in God's controlling hand emerges so fervently and so consistently in Cromwell's letters, even those addressed to close personal friends and family, that it is impossible to dismiss such expressions as conscious and deliberate falsehoods.

Cromwell believed sincerely that God was active in the world and that the Lord guided and directed all the key military and political developments of the 1640s and 1650s. At the end of August 1650, as he and his army were trudging back towards Dunbar on an overnight march, an attempt by the Scots to engage the rear of the army was thwarted when 'the Lord by His good Providence put a cloud over the moon'; even the movement of a cloud was directed by God. Time and again, Cromwell stressed that he was utterly worthless and unfit; his military and political colleagues were equally unworthy. It was the Lord alone who had employed and empowered such pitiful creatures to secure victory and to advance the godly cause. Thus Cromwell repeatedly begged that all glory and credit for victory should lie with the Lord, not with His mortal servants, though such mortals might draw comfort and strength from the knowledge that they were doing the Lord's work and were pleasing to Him. Conversely, defeats and setbacks were seen as warnings from God, indicating that in some way the Lord was displeased and was testing or admonishing His servants. Several times during the 1640s and 1650s, and over key issues, Cromwell came to believe that divisions among, and defeats suffered by, the parliamentary cause were divine rebukes, signs that somehow he and his colleagues had parted from the chosen path, sinned themselves or condoned sins in others, and so earned God's disfavour. Thus God was delivering a warning, to which the recipients should respond by searching out and extirpating sins and errors. For example, Cromwell came to interpret the divisions of 1647 both among the parliamentary army and between that army and Parliament, culminating in the slide into renewed civil war in 1648, as a sign of God's disfavour, caused by their attempts to negotiate with Charles I. Again, the failure of the first Protectorate Parliament and the defeat in Hispaniola in 1655 apparently triggered in Cromwell another, more personal bout of self-doubt and inquiry, born of a suspicion that the Lord's favour had been lost, perhaps in part because of his own failings. Cromwell's providentialism might strengthen and reassure in times of success, but at the price of intensifying the uncertainties and terrors of failure.

In several speeches delivered during the Protectorate, Cromwell made clear his belief that the Lord had chosen the nation for special treatment and favour. Repeatedly referring to the biblical story of Moses leading his people out of Egypt, he claimed that the nation and its people had come through a period of bondage and trial, were currently in the wilderness purging their sins, but were approaching the Promised Land. Hence his attempts, first seen in letters written during the later 1640s but broadcast with greater assurance through words and action during the 1650s, to institute reforms which would reduce the level of sin and immorality and produce a more godly nation, as well as to encourage other institutions and officials to pass further legislation against mortal sins and to enforce more effectively existing measures. Thus the cause of godly reformation would be advanced. Although the high tide of Cromwell's millenarianism apparently turned in 1653 and thereafter his letters and speeches made fewer explicit references to the second coming, he continued to see a necessity for preparing the nation and its people for the day when 'Jesus Christ will have a time to set up his reign in our hearts', as he put it in 1654. To Cromwell, these divine ends alone mattered; the worldly means by which they might be achieved were immaterial. In autumn 1647 Cromwell approvingly quoted St Paul's reference to mortal government as but 'drosse and dunge in comparison of Christ'.

Just as Cromwell did not care much about worldly forms of government, as long as they facilitated progress towards divine ends, so he was not too concerned about the outward forms of religion and religious organization. Repeatedly during the 1640s and 1650s he stressed that a variety of Protestant churches all contained an element of God's truth and should flourish. What mattered to Cromwell was that people should understand God's fundamental truths and should earn salvation. He disliked dividing people up into distinct churches and labelling them as a particular variety of Protestant. Equally, it is impossible to categorize Cromwell as belonging to a particular denomination or confessional group, independent, presbyterian or whatever. Instead, he wanted broad religious liberty, in the belief that all the Protestant faiths contained some element of God's truth, and in the hope that, in due course, they would all coalesce to reveal a complete and united picture. This desire for ultimate religious unity appears opaquely or clearly in a number of Cromwell's letters and speeches, most notably in a letter to Robert Ham-

mond of late 1648: 'I profess to thee I desire from my heart, I have prayed for it, I have waited for the day to see union and right understanding between the godly people (Scots, English, Jews, Gentiles, Presbyterians, Independents, Anabaptists, and all).'

Religious freedom or 'liberty of conscience' became a cornerstone of Cromwell's religious aspirations and policies. He condemned the pre-war church for denying such liberty, for oppressing and persecuting good Protestants and for forcing thousands of them to emigrate to the New World. Several times, he claimed that the desire to secure liberty of conscience was the main factor which had motivated him and others to take up arms and to continue the bloody and terrible war—'all the money of this nation would not have tempted men to fight, upon such an account as they have engaged, if they had not had hopes of liberty, better than they had from Episcopacy'—and had become the central principle and objective of the entire parliamentary cause: 'undoubtedly this is the peculiar interest all this while contended for'. This liberty was not total and, both because it operated within certain limits and because its ultimate goal was religious unity not permanent plurality, it is misleading and anachronistic to equate it with the modern concept of religious toleration. It is noticeable that in his letters and speeches Cromwell usually cited just three denominations—presbyterians, independents and baptists—as examples of Protestant groups which contain elements of God's truth, though in practice during the 1650s as a whole and Cromwell's Protectorate in particular, liberty was extended to other individuals and groups. However, Cromwell was adamant that those whose religious practices disrupted the peace or challenged magistracy—itself divinely appointed—or contained elements which went beyond fundamental truths and strayed into blasphemy and heresy, were not to enjoy liberty. The very opposite—the existing laws against blasphemy, heresy and civil disturbance should be swiftly and rigorously imposed by the magistracy. Time and again, he stressed that liberty of conscience would not be used as a cover for heresy or as a shield to protect heretics from the law.

More often, however, Cromwell laid stress on the need to prevent the persecution of those who possessed an element of God's truth and to stop one religious group attacking another. Time and again, he condemned the attitude of men who now enjoyed liberty but who were attempting to prevent others sharing that liberty. Late in 1654 Cromwell reportedly bewailed, 'Where shall wee have men of a Universall Spirit? Every one desires to have liberty, but none will give it.' In a speech to Parliament in January 1658, he condemned the way in which the sects attacked one another as 'an appetite to variety, to be not only making wounds, but as if we should see one making wounds in a man's side and would desire nothing more than to be groping and grovelling with his fingers in those wounds'. But Cromwell's fullest and most eloquent exposition of the point is to be found in his speech of January 1655, dissolving the first Protectorate Parliament:

I say, you might have had opportunity to have settled peace and quietness amongst all professing Godliness, and might have been instrumental, if not to have healed the breaches, yet to have kept the Godly of all judgments from running one upon another... Are these things done? Or anything towards them? Is there not yet upon the spirits of men a strange itch? Nothing will satisfy them, unless they can put their finger upon their brethren's consciences, to pinch him there. To do this was no part of the contest we had with the common adversary; for religion was not the thing at the first contested for, but God brought it to that issue at last, and give it to us by way of redundancy, and at last it proved that which was most dear to us. And wherein consisted this, more than in obtaining that liberty from the tyranny of the bishops to all species of Protestants, to worship God according to their own light and consciences?... Those that were sound in the faith, how proper was it for them to labour for liberty, for a just liberty, that men should not be trampled upon for their consciences? Had not they laboured but lately under the weight of persecutions, and was it fit for them to sit heavy upon others? Is it ingenuous to ask liberty, and not to give it? What greater hypocrisy than for those who were oppressed by the bishops, to become the greatest oppressors themselves so soon as their yoke was removed? I could wish that they who call for liberty now also, had not too much of that spirit, if the power were in their hands.

In his burning desire to extend and defend liberty, we see Cromwell at his most attractive; in his expectation that the nation would share this vision and link arms with him, we see him at his most futile. Herein rest the triumph and the tragedy of Oliver Cromwell.

NO

John Morrill

OLIVER CROMWELL AND
THE ENGLISH REVOLUTION

Any man who moves on at the age of forty from a life as a provincial farmer and businessman to become by the age of fifty-three Head of State and who is prevented only by his own scruples from accepting an offer from a parliament to have him crowned as king of England, Scotland and Ireland is clearly one of the great men of history. Oliver Cromwell dominates our knowledge and our mental picture of the civil wars and interregnum, of the Puritan Revolution, as surely as Napoleon dominates our view of the French Revolution and Lenin our view of the Russian Revolution. Yet his precise achievement, and the extent of his responsibility for the shaping of events and for the failure of the Revolution, remain matters of great dispute. On 3 September every year, members of the Cromwell Association (and how many other Englishmen have societies founded essentially to commemorate their lives and achievements?) meet by the nineteenth-century statue of Oliver next to the Houses of Parliament to recall his championship of religious liberty and civil liberties and his role in the defeat of Stuart tyranny. Yet there also exists a powerful folk memory of him as a bigot and tyrant, the man who presided over one of the great iconoclasms of English history, a sleighting of castles and sacking of churches, with a destruction of stained glass, wood and statuary equal to if not greater than that of the early Reformation, and the man who butchered the Irish and launched an unequalled assault on the rights of the native inhabitants of Ireland. Yet another image of him is as the man who led the Parliamentarians to victory over the king only to betray the cause from the time of his suppression of popular democratic rights in and around Burford church in May 1649.

In a sense, of course, he was all these things; each is a caricature that exaggerates an important truth about him. Nonetheless it is obviously easier to catalogue his failings and failures than his achievements. His failure to leave as an enduring and irreversible legacy any of the things he held dearest —above all liberty of conscience and 'a reformation of manners' that would turn the people from the things of the flesh to those of the spirit—and the return of political and religious values he associated with a broken past rather

From John Morrill, "Introduction," in John Morrill, ed., *Oliver Cromwell and the English Revolution* (Longman, 1990). Copyright © 1990 by Addison Wesley Longman, Ltd. Reprinted by permission. Notes omitted.

than with a glorious future, are very palpable. At best, some toughened seeds were left below the topsoil waiting for a long, long drought to end before blossoming forth again as the liberal values of the nineteenth century; at worst, Cromwell's vision of a particular kind of godly society, in which men and women learnt the self-discipline of obedience to a stern Calvinist God and were rewarded by that stern God with peace and plenty, was a futile vision that died with him. His greatness in that case lay in the integrity with which he clung to a noble but unrealizable vision, not in anything lasting. At the end of an essay on another man—Thomas, Cardinal Wolsey, who rose from humble East Anglian roots to dominate his world—Sir Geoffrey Elton wrote that:

> to recognize that [he] contributed virtually nothing to the future is not to discard his present. For fifteen years he impressed England and Europe with ... his very positive action in the affairs of the world. He often achieved what he set out to do, even if subsequent events showed his aims to have been mistaken and his solutions to have been patchwork. He made a great and deserved name, and his age would have been very different without him. And surely, this is something; surely it is enough.

And surely this goes for Cromwell too. Only (we might add) unlike Wolsey, that achievement was not vitiated by any of the greed or the agglomeration of wealth and pomp that Wolsey insatiably craved. What other self-made ruler with the world at his feet has ever taken less for himself and for his family of what the world has to offer in goods and services? ...

* * *

Oliver Cromwell's life falls naturally into three sections: his forty years of obscurity in East Anglia, his twelve years as an MP and as a senior officer in the parliamentarian and republican armies, and his five years as Lord Protector of England, Scotland and Ireland.

... Here we should simply note how, in all respects but one, [those first forty years] were a poor preparation for a public career. Cromwell was a man of humble circumstances. His income fluctuated between £100 and £300 per annum: he held little freehold land and no offices that gave him experience of governing; he had no military training—not even, it seems, in the militia. Huntingdon, where he lived until 1631, and, even more, St Ives, where he lived from 1631 to 1636, were backwaters, although Huntingdon did lie on the Great North Road and one of Cromwell's friends, William Kilborne, was the postmaster of the town; so he may have been better able than many minor country figures to keep up with the latest news and gossip from the capital. He spent one year in Cambridge in his teens and seems to have spent three years in London from the ages of nineteen to twenty-two. He was present at the parliament of 1628–29. Otherwise he is not known to have moved more than a few miles from his home until after 1640. The evidence of close links with certain London merchants and with prominent gentry families in Essex, to whom he was related through his mother and through his wife, hint, however, he may have had a more active and mobile life than we have hitherto realized. However, this achievement in the 1640s and 1650s cannot be predicated upon his training as a man of action and administration in his prime years.... [T]he nature and scale of the spiritual crisis he went through in the period 1629–31 helps greatly to explain his later dynamism. He knew ... what it was to be stripped of all those things we take for granted—wealth, reputation, health—so that he could be new modelled by God. In the 1640s he witnessed that which had happened to him happening to England. Just as God had destroyed the illusory values of this world in order to make Cromwell an obedient and justified servant, so now He overthrew monarchy, the House of Lords and the established Church in order that a process of national salvation could take place. Cromwell's long apprenticeship taught him only one thing, but it was to govern the rest of his life: Trust God in all things.

Cromwell was more prominent than most MPs, certainly than most MPs of his humble circumstances, in the early years of the Long Parliament; and he quickly identified himself with those committed first and foremost to reforming the Reformation, to a liberation of the pulpits from the Laudian gag and the cleansing of the churches of surviving and recently reinforced remnants of popery and superstition. More remarkable was his unhesitating willingness to resort to arms to impose a settlement in the summer of 1642. Sent down by the House of Commons to organize the local defence forces in the Cambridge/Ely area, in the face of footdragging by the local gentry, he showed resolve and initiative. With a general commendation from the Houses to mobilize the militias, but without a specific military commission, he gathered together a band of vigilantes whom he used both to seize the Castle at Cambridge with its munitions and, more dramatically, to prevent the plate of the Cambridge colleges from being sent to the king at York and to put it to the use of the parliament. C. H. Firth's judgement that 'the promptitude with which he assumed responsibility and anticipated the (Parliament's) orders by his acts was extremely characteristic' seems an understatement. War was not yet declared; he was committing highway robbery; he had no warrant for what he opted to do. He might have been sacrificed by the more pragmatic members of both Houses if peace had broken out.

The king did, however, raise his standard a few weeks later, and Cromwell was commissioned by the earl of Essex as a captain, quickly raising a company of sixty horse in and around Huntingdon. He was present at Edgehill and then returned to Ely and Cambridge to see to their defence and fortification. In the course of 1643 he was promoted to colonel, and took part in at least eight sieges, skirmishes and battles and campaigned in at least nine counties. Similarly in 1644, he was at the major battles of Marston Moor in Yorkshire and Newbury in Berkshire, at a series of successful sieges, and campaigned in eight counties in a rather wider arc in the north and south midlands. In 1645 he was commissioned into the New Model on a series of forty-day to six-month commissions that took him through the south midlands and deep into the south west. His war ended only in June 1646 when he was party to the surrender of Oxford. In the period from June 1642 to June 1646 he was far more of a soldier than an MP: he returned to Westminster for two weeks in September 1642, a week in January 1643, a month in early 1644 and three months in the winter of 1644/45, a total of 20 out of 200 weeks. Military life had had its frustrations—as the succession of charges of incompetence and dilatoriness he brought against colleagues and superior officers shows—but it had its rewards too, especially for a soldier who never experienced defeat and who saw God make their common enemies stumble to the swords of Cromwell's troopers. His brief returns to Westminster and, much more, the nine months he spent there after the end of the fighting were an altogether more dispiriting experience.... Life in the Palace of Westminster and in St Stephen's Chapel had all the bickering and none of exhilaration of life in the army camp. It brought oil the next great crisis of his life, the agonizing choice of loyalties which spanned the period April to December 1647. It is clear that he tried desperately hard to unite army and parliament, even if it meant purging both; and the aim of maintaining that unity was to reach a settlement with the king. But when choices had to be made and loyalties betrayed, he saw that loyalty to a particular parliament was no more unconditional than loyalty to a particular king. God's will was manifest in his saints, who were concentrated in the army.

Cromwell seems not to have doubted that a settlement had to be made with the king until after the outbreak of the Second Civil War in early 1648. He threw his weight behind the *Heads of the Proposals*, drawn up by his army colleague and son-in-law Henry Ireton, in the summer of 1647; and at the time of the Putney debates in November he would not contemplate any thought of a settlement without Charles. As C. H. Firth wrote of Cromwell, it was the king's flight from the army to Carisbrooke and the revelations of his intrigues with the Scots that 'showed him on what a rotten foundation he had based his policy'. On 3 January 1648, it is reported that he announced that 'parliament should

govern and defend the kingdom by their own power and resolution and not teach the people any longer to expect safety and government from an obstinate man whose heart God had hardened'. By the time of the Scots invasion, Cromwell was clear that God was willing His servants to administer justice to the king. As one army statement arising from a prayer meeting had declared:

> it is their duty, if ever the Lord brought them back to peace, to call Charles Stuart, that man of blood, to account for all he had shed and mischief he had done.

Cromwell's view of the Second Civil War and of the Scottish invasion was unambiguous:

> This [is] a more prodigious treason than any that had been perpetrated before: because the former quarrel on their part was that Englishmen might rule over one another; this to vassalize us to a foreign nation. And their fault who hath appeared in this summer's business is certainly double theirs who were in the first, because it is the repetition of the same offence against all the witnesses that God has borne.

'Take courage,' he wrote to the Houses from the battlefield of Preston, 'they that are implacable and will not leave troubling the land may speedily be destroyed out of the land.'

In 1648 he led one half of the New Model against insurgents in South Wales and Yorkshire before joining Fairfax to defeat the invading Scots at Preston. By this stage, Fairfax ran the army as a military force, and Cromwell led it as a political force, informing Fairfax of what was being done or had been done rather than consulting him. But it was on Fairfax's instruction that he led the pursuit of the remnants of the Scots army back into Scotland and occupied Edinburgh. Within months of the king's execution, he was engaged in the conquest of Ireland —a task undertaken with a ruthless efficiency. He returned, the back of the problem broken, ten months later. But within a month he was off again, this time to conquer Scotland. He crossed the Border on 24 July 1650 and remained north of it for just over the year, once more, as in Ireland, achieving what for centuries no English commander had achieved, a clinical military conquest and occupation as a prelude to an incorporative union of the three kingdoms. He returned to England hot on the heels of the last of the Scottish armies. He crushed that army at Worcester on 3 September 1651. After twelve years of almost constant movement and action, he returned to London on 12 September and was accorded a military triumph in the classical mould. He was never to leave London again until his death in 1658. Although the New Model was to export its triumphs to the Continent in the ears to come—to give English arms a reputation they had not had since the days of the Black Prince and Henry V, 250 years before—his own fighting days were over.

But there was to be no retirement. Ahead of him lay the restless search for a way to make the freedoms released by the revolution into a reality: how to make the people able to take up the responsibilities of freedom. Until they were demystified and able to see for themselves what God willed for them, he must govern on their behalf. Government would have to be 'for the people's good, not what pleases them'. His would be a vanguard State, a State controlled by the godly on behalf of the still unregenerate masses. But the aim must be to spread enlightenment, to make 'all men fit to be called'. To that end,

he used the army to drive out the Rump, a body lacking the vision and the vim necessary to institute a programme of political education and spiritual renewal; he called together representatives of the godly to be a constituent assembly, the born-again leaven in the national lump; he reluctantly took office as Lord Proctector to wheedle the people towards acknowledging their call to be a nation elect by God through a policy of 'healing and settling', and when that proceeded too slowly he sent his senior army officers out into the provinces as major-generals to revitalize the call to personal and collective reformation. Although, as early as 1651, his name was linked to the kingship, he refused the offer when it was formally preferred. . . . Derek Hirst and Anthony Fletcher [have] examine[d] the policies of the Protectorate and Cromwell's personal responsibility for them. Not everything done in his name was done at his instigation or even with his knowledge and consent. He died in office and in harness on 3 September 1658, the anniversary of his two final victories—Dunbar in 1650 and Worcester in 1651. He had come a long way from the modest town house in Huntingdon in which he had grown up and spent his early manhood.

Cromwell was a man of action, not of reflection. He was no intellectual in politics. His personal letters and speeches are suffused with quotations, paraphrases and resonances from scripture. However, although Cromwell had a conventional classical education, one looks in vain for evidence of classical allusions or of patristic and modern theologians in what he wrote or said. Almost the only book, other than the Bible, that he ever mentioned by name was Sir Walter Raleigh's *History of the World*, which he commended in 1650 to his son Richard. If we take a speech to parliament in January 1655 seriously, when he said that 'what are all our Histories, and other traditions of actions in former times, but God manifesting Himself' then perhaps he did study more than Raleigh. He seems to have been proficient enough in Latin to converse in it with ambassadors. But he was not bookish.

There is overwhelming evidence that he had an impulsive, forthright nature. Once his mind was made up, he acted without flinching. He did not mince words. In 1630 he got himself into serious trouble for an intemperate attack on the mayor and recorder of his home town which caused him to be hauled before the Privy Council and to face humiliation before his neighbours and friends. In the early days of the Long Parliament, his ill-considered outbursts were an embarrassment to those who were attempting an orderly reformation of Church and State. No less than four times in the first three years of the civil war he caused bitter division within the parliamentarian cause by denouncing his peers (the Hothams, the heroes of 1642, when they had barred the gates of Hull— and the armaments stored there—to the king, but who got cold feet about the war in 1643; and Major-General Crawford, an influential Scots professional) and his superiors (Lord Willoughby in 1643, dilatory commander of the Lincolnshire forces, and the second earl of Manchester, Cromwell's immediate superior and officer commanding the forces of the Eastern Association in 1643–44). They in turn countercharged that he promoted not so much godly reformation as religious licence; his troopers, for example, had allowed Ely (of which he was now governor) 'to become a mere Ams-

terdam'. Later in his life, he showed the same bull-headedness when he used the army physically and precipitously to get rid of the Rump in April 1653, or when he purged the army of dissident elements without stopping to calculate the consequences on several occasions during the Protectorate. He was a man who found it hard to disguise his emotions. Those who give us physical accounts of him speak of a florid intensity: rubicund, demotic, a manic depressive who was usually manic. One of the best descriptions comes from the steward and cofferer of the protectoral Household, John Maidstone:

> His body was well compact and strong, his stature under six feet, I believe about two inches, his head so shaped as you might see it a storehouse and shop, both of a vast treasury of natural parts... His temper was exceedingly fiery, as I have known; but the flame... was soon allayed with those moral endowments he had. He was naturally compassionate towards objects in distress, even to an effeminate measure... a larger soul hath seldom dwelt in a house of clay.

He thus not only had a fiery temper. After his victory at Dunbar, he laughed uncontrollably, exulting in his sense of God's presence which had given him victory against the odds. At the end of a long, tense meeting, he could pick up a cushion, throw it at a colleague and flee the room; but it is his dyspeptic loss of self-control and descent into a ranting, uncontrolled fury that is most often remembered. Clarendon recalled that at a committee of the Long Parliament in the summer of 1641, examining riots in the Cambridgeshire Fen, Cromwell bullied the witnesses, interrupted other members of the committee, and rounded on the chairman when the latter reproved him for his conduct:

> ... his whole carriage was so tempestuous, and his behaviour so insolent, that the Chairman found himself obliged to reprehend him; and tell him that if he proceeded in the same manner, he would presently adjourn the Committee, and the next morning complain to the House of him.

Along with this impulsiveness and uncontrolledness went occasional lassitude and hesitation. He was a man who clearly often did not know his own mind, or, as he would have put it, who could not discern the will of God in a particular situation. Often he needed to get his ideas from others. This is most obviously the case in November/December 1648 when he hung back from returning to London as the crisis between the parliamentary majority and the army mounted, in the spring of 1653 after his impetuous dissolution of the Rump, in December 1653 when the Nominated Assembly collapsed, and again in 1657 when the offer of the Crown was made. Once he had been given a solution, and more specifically when some external event persuaded him that God had given him a nudge and a wink, he acted decisively, forcefully, unhesitatingly. But it sometimes took time.

More controversial was his persistent claim that he was a reluctant Head of State. In his very last speech, for example, at the bitter dissolution of his second Protectorate Parliament in 1658, he said that

> I cannot [but] say it in the presence of God, in comparison of which we that that are here [like] poor creeping ants upon the earth, that I would have been glad, as to my own conscience and spirit to

have lived under a woodside, to have kept a flock of sheep, rather than to have undertaken such a government as this was.

Or, as he put it four years earlier, discussing in his first Protectorate Parliament his reasons for setting up the Nominated Assembly in 1653:

> As a principal end in calling that assembly was the settlement of the nation, so a chief end to myself was that I might have opportunity to lay down the power that was in my hands. I say to you again, in the presence of that God who bath blessed and been with me in all my adversities and successes, that was, as to myself my greatest end. A desire perhaps (and I am afraid) sinful enough to be quit of the power God had most providentially put into hand, before he called for it, and before those honest ends of our fighting were attained and settled.

This is not how he struck many of his contemporaries, especially those writing from beyond the Restoration gauze. Richard Baxter is typical of those who saw him as a good man corrupted by power:

> Cromwell meant honestly in the main, and was pious and conscionable in the main part of his life till prosperity and success corrupted him. Then his general religious zeal gave way to ambition which increased as successes increased. When his successes had broken down all considerable opposition, then he was in face of his strongest temptations, which conquered him when be had conquered others.

A comparable picture of progressive corruption by the exercise of power comes in a tract published by the veteran republican Slingsby Bethel in 1668.

His want of honour, as well as honesty, appeareth yet further, in that, having, by a long series of pious deportment gained by his dissimulation, good thoughts in his masters, the long-parliament; and, by his spiritual gifts, wound himself into so good an opinion with his soldiers (men generally of plain breeding, that knew little besides their military trades, and religious exercises) that he could impose, in matters of business, what belief he pleased upon them; he made use of his credit he had with each, to abuse both, by many vile practices, for making himself popular, and the parliament and army very odious to one another... [all this] being for his own single advancement... and leaves him a person to be truly admired for nothing but apostasy and ambition...

These charges are all too common in the memoirs of his contemporaries. And yet they never seem sustainable. Those like Edmund Ludlow, Richard Baxter and Lucy Hutchinson who see him as aspiring to the Crown and as betraying the Revolution were never able to explain why he set up the Nominated Assembly in 1653. He had absolute power in his hands and he chose to surrender it; he refused to sit in the Assembly or to serve on its Council of State. He sat back and prayed that it—an assembly of men drawn from 'the several sorts of godliness in this nation'—might find a way to enlighten the whole nation, to make them turn from the things of the flesh to the things of the spirit. He yearned that the people might learn the responsibilities of freedom, might recognise the will of God, be willing to act on it, and thus fitted to govern themselves. When, instead, the godly created not a new Temple of Jerusalem but a new Tower of Babel, he accepted power as Lord Protector, but he rejected the title of king. Similarly in

1657 it was inner conviction that God had overturned the title and office of king ('I would not seek to set up that Providence hath destroyed and laid in the dust, and I would not build Jericho again') rather than calculation of what he could get away with that almost certainly persuaded him to decline the title again.

What gives the charge against Cromwell—that he was the great dissembler—residual credibility is the quite remarkable number of instances in which he got what he wanted in controversial circumstances and in which his denials of foreknowledge and responsibility strain credulity: his exemption from the terms of the Self-Denying Ordinance; his denial of involvement of the seizure of the king from Holdenby House in June 1647; the significance of his contacts with Robert Hammond, Governor of the Isle of Wight, days before the king escaped and took refuge on the isle in the dangerous days after the Putney debates; Cromwell's deliberate(?) delay in coming south at the end of the Second Civil War so as to arrive in London hours after Pride's Purge, late enough to deny complicity in it but not too late to take advantage of it; the almost certainly false accounts he gave of what the Rump was up to on the morning he dissolved it[44]; the convenient way the major-generals were quietly abandoned just before the presentation of the Humble Petition and Advice, which has led some to argue that he wished to clear the decks for an initiative he would maintain had taken him by surprise.

In each of these cases—and more—Cromwell was the beneficiary of initiatives of which he pleads ignorance. The frustrating thing is that his guilt cannot be conclusively established in any of them. Can there be so much smoke without fire? My personal view is that in this case there can. The balance of the evidence points towards Cromwell's insouciance and impulsiveness and against a calculated cunning and deliberate, brazen hypocrisy. He was hardly guileless. It is unthinkable he could have risen from his humble station in 1640 to be Head of State if he had had Fairfax's naïveté (once overpromoted, the latter became an increasingly irrelevant figure politically even while he retained the leadership of the army). But what drove Oliver was a fierce commitment to a cause he believed in, a trust in God that made him openly ruthless and uncompromising, not furtive and conspiratorial. The sense of betrayal experienced by so many of his contemporaries and erstwhile friends lay in this: that in each case he briefly identified their cause as his cause. But as he moved on, he cast each of his friends aside in turn. He was loyal to no-one but God.

Cromwell repeatedly called himself a seeker. He did not know exactly what God's will was for him or for England. He simply believed that God had *a* purpose for England. Just as Cromwell's personal sufferings in the 1620s and 1630s had had a purpose which had only become clear in the 1640s, so England's sufferings in the 1640s had a deeper purpose as yet unrevealed. Cromwell had been called to lead God's new chosen people from under the yoke of popery and tyranny to a new freedom. When the Israelites escaped from slavery in Egypt, it took them forty years in the desert to discover enough self-discipline and obedience to God's call to be allowed to enter the Promised Land, the land of milk and honey. So it was to be for England. The benefits that regicide and the destruction of the old structures and tyrannies of Church and State made possible had to be earned. It had taken the Israelites forty years; it might take the English four, or fourteen or forty or four hundred years. Cromwell could only seek to create transitional structures that would help the people to learn their duty of obedience to the will of God.

Cromwell cared about ends not means; giving substance to a shadow from the future, not sheltering in structures inherited from the past. He was, he said in 1647, 'not wedded or glued to forms of government', or, as he put it in ten years later as he pondered the offer of the Crown, 'not scrupulous about words or names or such things', and he scorned 'men under the bondage of scruples' who could not 'rise to the spiritual heat'. This disregard for propping up the sagging forms of ancient constitutionalism went along with a maverick attitude to existing civil rights. His opening speech to the second Protectorate Parliament was a paean to the triumph of necessity (defined by him as conformity to the will of God) over legalism. On the general proposition that the government was constrained by the rule of law, he argued that:

> If nothing should be done but what is according to law, the throat of the nation may be cut while we send for some to make a law.

The major-generals and the Decimation Tax, both created on Protectoral authority alone, were 'justifiable as to necessity [and] so honest in every respect'. Arbitrary imprisonment without cause shown or trial by jury was justified as follows:

> I know there are some imprisoned in the Isle of Wight, Cornwall and elsewhere, and the cause of their imprisonment was, they were all found acting things that tended to the disturbance of the

peace of the nation. Now these principles made us say to them, pray live quietly in your own counties, you shall not be urged with bonds or engagements, or to subscribe to the government. Yet they would not so much as say, we will promise to live peaceably...

This restlessness, this refusal to settle for the piecemeal conformity of the nation under his government was at the heart of his inability to generate stability. In 1648, he told Oliver St John:

Let us all not be careful what use men will make of these actings. They shall, will they, nill they, fulfil the good pleasure of God, and so shall serve our generations. Our rest we expect elsewhere: that will be durable.

Cromwell's restlessness did not win him the battle for hearts and minds. It led him to alienate his friends as well as to alarm those who hated the regicide but sought to come to terms with its consequences. A majority of the nation never reconciled themselves to regicide and to the government that was set up in its wake. That majority acquiesced in the face of Cromwell's monopoly of military force, but they never *committed* themselves to this rule. The orthodox puritan minister Adam Martindale took the Engagement oath in 1651 to obey a government without a king or House of Lords, but his tart self-justification for taking it showed the limits of that obedience:

... they deserve to be tried for fools if they believed that the royalists or the presbyterians which generally were more averse to it, would ever be cordial friends, so as to suffer with or for them, or to help them up if once thrown down.

Such an attitude is emblematic of the feelings of those Cromwell had to win over as his instruments if his godly reformation was to succeed. Their support proved unattainable. Many—perhaps most—of those who exercised authority in the 1650s saw the Revolution of 1649 not as a beginning but as an end, not as a dawn of liberty but as desperate expedient to prevent the loss of traditional liberties either to a vengeful king or to social visionaries like the Levellers. The regimes of the 1650s were progressively less radical than the circumstances that brought them into being. In most respects there was a rush to restoration: of the old familiar forms of central and local government (exchequer, quarter sessions, etc.) and of gentry power in the localities. And there was a silencing of radical demands for land reform or for greater commercial freedom or questionings of social patenialism.

Cromwell was not intellectually rigorous and consistent enough, or not courageous enough, to believe that God might want to overturn social forms as well as political and religious ones. He believed the new godly order would be erected within the context of the existing social order. What needed reformation was the beliefs and actions of individuals. If the gentry governed compassionately in the general interest, if the yeomen work to produce a surplus to be sold at fair prices, if the labourer did an honest day's work for an honest day's pay, and if the destitute took their charity with due humility, then the divine plan would be being fulfilled. There was just enough about Cromwell's concern for the existing social order, for the reform of procedures, rather than anything more fundamental in the administration of justice —'not that the laws are a grievance, but there are laws that are grievance, and the great grievance lies in the execution and administration'—to permit some of those to whom the 1650s were based upon a politics of regret to work alongside him. But they constantly sought to tranquilize him, to restrain him from excesses of religious enthusiasm, to constrain him with the language of prudence. They tried to do this above all by the offer of the Crown in 1657. This would have placed the shackles of custom and ancient constitutionalism upon him. They found that the fire in his belly was not to be extinguished with their sweet talk of settlement.

Yet as he toiled in vain to reconcile faint hearts to him and to persuade them to join him in his trek from Egypt to the Promised Land, he was steadily losing those who, like him, saw the Revolution as a dawn of liberty, an opening up of a new-modelled commonwealth. He turned to different groups of the godly in turn, trying out their scheme for government. But as each form failed to bring *his* vision any closer to realization, he jettisoned and cast out its proponents. His career from 1649 is therefore littered with his betrayals of those he had previously embraced and called his friends—the Levellers, above all his old friend John Lilburne in 1647–49, the civil republicans in 1651–53, Harrison and the Fifth Monarchists in 1653, veteran army colleagues in 1654, Lambert and the paper constitutionalists in 1657. That very energizing power and that very enthusiasm (in both its senses) with which he took them up, led him to drop them without compunction and without regret when God's will was not being effected by the forms they had proposed to him.

It is this which explains above all his apparent incoherence and his erratic political behaviour—that which led Hugh Trevor-Roper to say that 'no career is as full of undefended inconsistencies' as that of Oliver Cromwell. I would rather say: 'incoherently defended consistencies'. Cromwell struggled in his letters and speeches to make clear that means are always subordinate to ends; forms of government ('dross and dung in comparison with Christ') had to be cast aside if they did not build the Kingdom of Christ. Here is Cromwell at his passionate, his most yearning, his most opaque:

> When you were entered upon this Government... (I hope for] such good and wholesome provisions for the good of the people of these nations, for the settling of such matters in things of religion as would have given countenance to a godly ministry and yet would have given a just liberty to godly men of different judgments, men of the same faith with them as that you call the orthodox ministry in England, as it is well known the Independents are, and many under the form of Baptism, who are sound in the Faith... looking at salvation only in the blood of Christ, men professing the fear of God, having recourse to the name of God as to a strong tower... Are these things done? Or anything towards them? Is there not yet upon the spirits of men a strange itch? Nothing will satisfy them, unless they can put their finger upon their brethren's conscience, to pinch them there. To do this was no part of the contest we had with the common adversary; for religion was not the thing first contested for, but God brought it to that issue at last, and gave it unto us by way of redundancy, and at last it proved to be that which was most dear to us. And wherein consisted this, more than obtaining that liberty from the tyranny if the bishops to all species of Protestants, to worship God according to their own light and conscience?... Is it not ingenuous to ask liberty and not to give it? What

greater hypocrisy than those who were oppressed by the Bishops to become the greatest oppressors themselves, so soon as their yoke was removed? . . . As for profane persons, blasphemers, such as preach sedition, the contentious railers, evil speakers who seek by evil words to corrupt good manners, persons of loose conversation, punishment from the civil magistrate ought to meet with them, because if they plead conscience, yet walking disorderly, and not according but contrary to the Gospel and even natural light, they are judges of all, and their Sins being open, makes them subjects of the magistrate's sword, who ought not to bear it in vain.

Here is the essence of his authoritarian libertarianism.

The people must be free to exercise liberty of conscience without the luxury of being allowed to run to licence. Christian liberty consists of the ability to perceive and to obey the will of God. Government is indeed for the people's good, not what pleases them. For Cromwell, freedom was rooted in a belief that human institutions could be designed to bring men and women nearer to an internalized discipline that made them willingly obedient to a protestant God. He saw himself as accountable not to those he strove to liberate, but to that same God.

In the regicide and its aftermath, therefore, we must recognize the greatest paradox of all. In confronting and destroying Charles I, Oliver Cromwell was concerned not to establish constitutional government, a balanced polity in which those who exercised authority were accountable to those they governed. The destruction of divine right kings was to make room for a divine right revolutionary.

POSTSCRIPT

Did Oliver Cromwell Advance Political Freedom in Seventeenth-Century England?

As Gaunt points out, opinion about Cromwell diverged among his biographers immediately after his death. The diversity of opinion continues as year after year historians attempt to assimilate the information of Cromwell's life into a coherent and convincing portrait. However, Gaunt hits the nail on the head when he writes, "If contemporaries... were puzzled by many aspects of Cromwell's character and career and produced such starkly differing assessments, it is all the more impossible for historians writing centuries later to produce a comprehensive, all-encompassing or definitive portrait." Gaunt focuses repeatedly on Cromwell's conviction that he was an instrument of God's will. He points out that Cromwell himself attributed his military success to his own devotion and to that of the men he recruited to the parliamentary cause. He argues that Cromwell's sometimes manic emotionalism, which Morrill also observes, was always tempered by his religious faith. Ultimately, Cromwell's greatest strengths came from his religious attitudes, which produced in him a flexibility toward governmental forms that kept him from assuming the role of autocratic tyrant and allowed him to promote a religious tolerance that was remarkable for its day, if not for ours. It is in this flexibility and tolerance that Gaunt finds the greatness of the country gentleman turned Lord Protector.

Morrill, on the other hand, sees Cromwell's religious self-vision as noble in a quixotic sense, but he writes, "His greatness in that case lay in the integrity with which he clung to a noble but unrealizable vision, not in anything lasting." In fact, Morrill argues, Cromwell's inability to clarify his own thinking, his unwillingness to overthrow traditional social forms, and his adherence in the long run to divine right—if not that of the king, at least of himself—kept him from achieving anything permanent and significant outside of his own time. Morrill concludes that Cromwell was only libertarian in matters of religious freedom for Protestants, but in politics he remained authoritarian, while believing himself to be "not wedded or glued to forms of government."

A few good biographies of "our chief of men" are Christopher Hill's *God's Englishman: Oliver Cromwell and the English Revolution* (Weidenfeld & Nicholson, 1970), which concludes with a marvelous historiographical analysis; *Oliver Cromwell* by John Buchan (Hodder & Stoughton, 1934), which is a classic; and Barry Coward's *Oliver Cromwell* (Longman, 1991), which contains some of the latest material and interpretations.

ISSUE 16

Did Indian Emperor Aurangzeb's Rule Mark the Beginning of Mughal Decline?

YES: Jadunath Sarkar, from *A Short History of Aurangzib, 1618–1707,* 3rd ed. (M. C. Sarkar & Sons, 1962)

NO: S. M. Ikram, from *Muslim Civilization in India* (Columbia University Press, 1964)

ISSUE SUMMARY

YES: Historian Jadunath Sarkar argues that the Indian emperor Aurangzeb's reign aggravated already-contentious divisions between Muslims and Hindus.

NO: Historian S. M. Ikram defends the reign of Aurangzeb as the last effective defense of Muslim rule on the subcontinent.

In 1526, having plunged his 12,000 well-seasoned troops through the Khyber Pass, Babur, a descendant of the Mongol khans (rulers) and Tamerlane the Terrible, marched into northern India intent on conquering the Delhi Sultanate. In two years of campaigns Babur united the land from the Indus to the Ganges Rivers and founded the last of the great Indian empires, the Mughals. This dynasty ruled over a combined population of Hindus and Muslims. Muslim themselves, the Mughals were a minority in the vast subcontinent, even though the Muslims had consolidated their hold on northern India some 500 years before. Although Babur held on to his conquests with an iron hand, his son Humayan was successfully challenged by Hindu armies invading from the Rajputs (Hindu kingdoms) in the west. Retreating into Afghanistan, Humayan was able to reinvade India in 1556 and restore his lost empire. Dying immediately after, he left his throne to his son Jal-al-ul-din Muhammed, better known as Akbar, meaning "the great." Akbar ushered in a golden age of Indo-Islamic culture. Expanding the Mughal holdings farther south and establishing an efficient administration over the whole, Akbar attempted through patronage of the arts and social reform to synthesize the diverse cultures of Hinduism and Islam. His court at Fatehpur Sikri welcomed scholars, artists, philosophers, and theologians from all religious faiths, inviting them to discuss their philosophies with each other and the emperor.

Akbar's social policies were tolerant and inclusive of the Hindu princes and populace; Akbar encouraged intermarriage and included Hindus in the running of the imperial bureaucracy. At his most extreme, Akbar attempted to create a new religion, a combination of faiths called Din-i-Ilahi. By doing so he hoped to end the religious divisions that hindered the further unification and expansion of the Mughal Empire. In this he failed, but there is no question that Akbar's social and political reforms provided the basis for long-term Mughal rule. Akbar's successors, Jahangir and Shah Jehan (the builder of the Taj Mahal, which is considered the most outstanding example of Indo-Islamic architecture), continued to adhere to a policy of toleration toward their Hindu subjects, and, as a result, their governments flourished, as did Indian cultural development. However, both these rulers avoided instituting any further social, administrative, or military reforms that might have kept the empire from descending into moral decay and external weakness.

When Aurangzeb, the son of Shah Jehan, ascended the throne in 1657, the empire was in sore need of rejuvenation socially, militarily, politically, and economically. Unfortunately, although he was personally brave, incorruptible, and austere, Aurangzeb refused to continue the expansive tolerance practiced by his predecessors. He blamed Hindu influence in the court and administration for the decadence and corruption he found there and vowed to purge it from the empire. At the same time, he desired to subjugate the entire subcontinent, diverting his attention from needed domestic reforms and focusing his resources on the application of large-scale warfare with his powerful competitors in the south. As Aurangzeb's attention became more and more distracted from internal affairs, local rulers in northern India were able to consolidate their positions and act with increasing autonomy, including active revolt.

Although it is true that by the end of Aurangzeb's reign the Mughal Empire was larger territorially than it had ever been, the question of whether or not his policies ultimately destroyed the ability of the dynasty to continue to be the dominant power in India remains. The popular view is that Aurangzeb's tyrannical bigotry and aggressive purging of Hindus from the administration, as well as the reimposition of a head tax on non-Muslims, effectively demolished the carefully established atmosphere of cooperation on which the Indo-Islamic synthesis had been built. Seen as an open attack on Hindu tradition, his policies instigated a Hindu revival, in particular that of the Mahrattas, ensuring that the two cultures would continue to see each others as rivals.

It is this rivalry that weakened the Mughal empire irreparably and opened the way for the European exploitation of India in the following two centuries. The role of Aurangzeb in the empire's demise is debated by Jadunath Sarkar and S. M. Ikram in the following selections.

YES
Jadunath Sarkar

AURANGZIB'S CHARACTER AND THE EFFECT OF HIS REIGN

PEACE THE ROOT-CAUSE OF INDIA'S PROSPERITY

To all outer observers the Mughal empire seemed to have attained to its highest splendour and power when Aurangzib ascended the throne of Delhi. "The wealth of Ind" had become poverbial in far off countries, and the magnificence of the Court of the Great Mughal had "dazzled even eyes which were accustomed to the pomp of Versailles." And when a trained administrator and experienced general like him, who was also a puritan in the simplicity and purity of his private life, succeeded to the guidance of this rich heritage in the fulness of his physical and mental powers, all people hoped that he would carry the empire to unimaginable heights of glory. And yet the result of Aurangzib's long and strenuous reign was utter dissolution and misery. The causes of this strange phenomenon—it is the duty of the historian to investigate.

In a warm, moist and fertile country like India,—where the lavish bounty of Nature speedily repairs the ravages of hostile man and beast, of inclement sun and rain,—order is the root of national life, in an even greater degree than in other lands. Given peace without and the spirit of progress within, the Indian people can advance in wealth, strength and civilization with a rapidity rivalled only by the marvellous growth of their vegetation after the first monsoon showers. A century of strong and wise government under Akbar and his son and grandson had given to the richer and more populous half of India such peace and impulse to improvement. A hundred victories since the second Panipat had taught the Indian world to believe that Mughal arms were invincible and Mughal territory inviolable, Shivaji broke this spell. Mughal peace—the sole justification of the Mughal empire—no longer existed in India at Aurangzib's death.

In a predominantly agricultural country like India, the tillers of the soil are the only source of national wealth. Directly or indirectly, the land alone adds to the "annual national stock." Even the craftsmen depend on the peasants and on the men enriched with the land revenue, for the sale of their goods,

From Jadunath Sarkar, *A Short History of Aurangzib, 1618–1707*, 3rd ed. (M. C. Sarkar & Sons, 1962). Copyright © 1962 by Orient Longman, Ltd. Reprinted by permission. Notes omitted.

and if the latter have not enough food-stuff to spare, they cannot buy any handicraft. Hence, the ruin of the peasants means in India the ruin of the non-agricultural classes too. *Pauvres paysans pauvre royaume,* is even truer of India than of France. Public peace and security of property are necessary not only for the peasant and the artisan, but also for the trader, who has to carry his goods over wide distances and give long credits before he can find a profitable market. Wealth, in the last resort, can accumulate only from savings out of the peasant's production. Whatever lowers the peasant's productive power or destroys his spirit of thrift by creating insecurity about his property, thereby prevents the growth of national capital and impairs the economic staying power of the country. Such are the universal and lasting effects of disorder and public insecurity in India. And the reign of Aurangzib affords the most striking illustration of this truth.

ECONOMIC DRAIN OF AURANGZIB'S CEASELESS WARFARE

The economic drain caused by Aurangzib's quarter century of warfare in the Deccan was appalling in its character and most far-reaching and durable in its effect. The operations of the imperial armies, especially their numerous sieges, led to a total destruction of forests and grass. The huge Mughal forces, totalling 1,700,000 troops according to the official records with perhaps ten times that number of non-combatants, soon ate up everything green wherever they moved. In addition, the Maratha raiders destroyed whatever they could not carry off,—feeding their horses on the standing crops, and burning the houses and prop-erty too heavy to be removed. Hence, it is no wonder that when at last in 1705 Aurangzib retired after his last campaign, the country presented a scene of utter desolation. "He left behind him the fields of these provinces devoid of trees and bare of corps, their places being taken by the bones of men and beasts." (Manucci). This total and extensive deforestation had a most injurious effect on agriculture. The financial exhaustion of the empire in these endless wars left Government and private owners alike too poor to repair the buildings and roads worn out by the lapse of time.

The labouring population suffered not only from violent capture, forced labour, and starvation, but also from epidemics which were very frequent during these campaigns. Even in the imperial camp, where greater comfort, security and civilization might have been expected, the annual wastage of the Deccan wars was one lakh of men, and three lakhs of horses, oxen, camels and elephants. At the siege of Golkonda (1687) a famine broke out. "In Haidarabad city the houses, river and plain were filled with the dead. The same was the condition of the imperial camp.... Kos after kos the eye fell only on mounds of corpses. The incessant rain melted away the flesh and skin.... After some months when the rains ceased, the white ridges of bones looked from a distance like hills of snow." The same desolation overtook tracts which had hitherto enjoyed peace and prosperity. The acute observer Bhimsen writes about the Eastern Karnatak, "During the rule of the Bijapur Golkonda and Telinga [dynasties] this country was extensively cultivated. But now many places have been turned into wilderness on account of the passage of the imperial armies, which have inflicted hardship and oppression on the people." And he noticed the same thing in Berar also.

In 1688, Bijapur was visited by a desolating epidemic of bubonic plague, which is estimated to have carried off a hundred thousand lives in three months. So, too, we read of a plague in Prince Azam's camp in Aug. 1694. The English factors at Surat report similar devastating epidemics throughout Western India in 1694 and 1696 (when 95,000 men perished). To take one example only, the drought and plague of 1702–04 killed two millions of men. In addition to disease, great natural calamities like flood, drought and excessive and unseasonable rainfall were frequent in the Deccan at the beginning of the 18th century, which aggravated the sufferings of invaders and natives alike and still further reduced the population. The state of war, spread over nearly a generation of time, had left no savings, no power of resistance in the common people; everything they produced or had stored up was swept away by the hordes on both sides, so that when famine or drought came, the peasants and landless labourers perished helplessly like flies. Scarcity was chronic in the imperial camp and often deepened into famine. The former remarkable cheapness of grain now became a forgotten myth in many parts of India.

INJURY TO TRADE AND INDUSTRY BY WAR, DISORDER, AND OFFICIAL EXACTIONS

There being in many places no peace or safety for tillage, the starving and exasperated peasantry took to highway robbery as the only means of living. In the Deccan they gathered arms and horses and used to join the Marathas in their raids. Raiding bands were, also, locally formed, which gave employment to many and chances of glory and wealth to the more spirited among the villagers. Trade almost ceased in the Deccan during this unhappy quarter century. Caravans could travel south of the Narmada only under strong escort; hence, they had to wait in the fortified towns for months before they could get an opportunity of advancing further towards their destination in safety. We even read of the royal mail and baskets of fruits for the Emperor's table being held up for five months at the Narmada by Maratha disturbances in the roads beyond it.

Even where war was not raging (as in Bengal), the weakening of the central Government emboldened provincial governors to disregard imperial prohibitions, and to make money by forcing goods from traders at absurdly low prices and then selling them in the public marts, and also by exacting forbidden *abwabs* from craftsmen and merchants. In the absence of security at home and the impossibility of making purchases at distances, arts and crafts ceased to be practised except in the walled cities. Village industries and industrial classes almost died out. The Madras coast, for instance, with its teeming weaving population, was so unsettled by the Mughal-Maratha struggle for the Karnatak (1690–1698) that the English and the French factors found it difficult to get enough clothes for loading their Europe-going ships. Thus ensued a great economic impoverishment of India—not only a decrease of the "national stock", but also a rapid lowering of mechanical skill and standard of civilization, a disappearance of art and culture over wide tracts of the country.

The Mughal soldiers on their march often trod down the crops, and though the Emperor had a special body of officers for compensating the peasants for this loss *(paimali-i-zarait)*, his financial difficulties led to the neglect of this humane rule. The worst oppressors of the peasants, however, were the tail of the army the vast nondescript horde of servants, day labourers, *darvishes* and other vagrants who followed Aurangzib's "moving city of tents" in the hope of picking up crumbs where such a crowd had gathered together. Particularly the Beluchi camel-owners who hired out their animals to the army, and the unattached Afghans searching for employment, plundered and beat the country people most mercilessly. The *banjaras* or wandering grain-dealer tribe, who moved in bodies, sometimes of 5,000 men, each with his couple of bullocks loaded with grain, were so strong in their strength of numbers and contempt for the petty officers of Government, that they sometimes looted the people on the wayside and fed their cattle on the crops in the fields, with impunity. Even the royal messengers (called *mewrahs* in Gujrat) who carried Government letters, reports of spies, and baskets of fruits for presentation to the Emperor, used to rob the people of the villages they passed by. In the trail of the Maratha soldiers appeared the Berads and even the Pindaris—who were brigands pure and simple.

Then, there were the land-stewards of rival jagirdars,—the incoming and the outgoing—of the same village. Under the plea of the never-to-be satisfied arrears of revenue, the late jagirdar's collector tried to squeeze everything out of the peasantry before he left, and even continued to stay in the village for some months after the arrival of his successor.

And the new-comer, in order not to starve himself, passed the half-dead peasants through his fiscal grinding-mill. . . .

Thus, the last reserve of the empire was exhausted, and public bankruptcy became inevitable. The salaries of the soldiers and civil officers alike fell into arrears for three years. The men, starving from lack of pay and the exhaustion of their credit with the local grocers, sometimes created scenes in the Emperor's Court, sometimes abused and beat their general's business manager. The imperial Government made reckless promises of money grant and high command to every enemy captain who was induced to desert and every enemy *qiladar* who was persuaded to surrender his fort. It was not humanly possible to keep all of these promises. The result was that the entire land in the empire proved insufficient for the total amount of *jagir* needed to satisfy the dues of all the officers included in the swollen army-list. Even when the grants of land in lieu of salary were drawn up by the Pay Office, they remained for years as mere orders on paper, the actual delivery of the villages to the grantees being impossible. The interval between the order and the actual possession of the jagir, it was sarcastically said, was long enough to turn a boy into a grey-beard. Even a minor Maratha hill-fort cost on an average. Rs. [rupees] 45,000 in cash to take it by bribing its qiladar, and the Emperor might well despair of taking all of them at this rate. And yet he obstinately went on capturing fort after fort by heavy bribery or by regular sieges which were ten times more costly.

The spirit of the Mughal army in the Deccan was at last utterly broken. The soldiers grew sick of the endless and futile war, but Aurangzib would listen to no protest or friendly advice. Even his grand wazir Asad Khan, who had ventured to suggest that now that Bijapur and Golkonda had been conquered he had no more work to do and might as well return to Delhi, received a sharp reprimand, "I wonder that a wise old servant like you has made such a request. . . . So long as a single breath remains in this mortal body, there is no release from labour." A generation of imperial followers grew up in the Deccan who had never entered a city or house of brick or stone, but passed all their lives in tents, marching from one encampment to another. The Rajput soldiers complained that their race would not be able to serve the empire in the next generation, as they had to pass their life-time in the Deccan campaigns, without getting any respite for going home and rearing up children. One home-sick noble in the Deccan camp offered the Emperor a bribe of one lakh of Rupees for transferring him to Delhi! . . .

DECAY OF INDIAN CIVILIZATION UNDER AURANGZIB, ITS CAUSES AND SIGNS

The retrogression of mediæval Indian civilization under Aurangzib is noticeable not only in the decline of the fine arts, but still more in the low intellectual type of the new generation. As the 17th century wore on, the older nobility nourished on the manly traditions of Akbar and Shah Jahan, gifted with greater independence of spirit, and trained with greater resources and responsibility,—gradually died out, and their places in camp and Court were taken by smaller men, supplied with poorer resources by the suspicious Aurangzib, afraid to exercise responsibility

and initiative, and seeking to advance themselves by sycophancy. The exceptionally prolonged life of Aurangzib with its ever increasing store of experience and information, made him intellectually dwarf the younger generation. His self-sufficiency and obstinacy increased with age; till at last none dared contradict him, none could give him honest advice or impart unpleasant truth. With the lack of leisure amidst the incessant warfare and rough camp-life in the far off South, the culture of the aristocracy decayed, and, as the nobles set the tone to society, the whole of the intellectual classes of India steadily fell back to a lower level. A coarse Jafar Jatali took the place of a chaste Faizi for their delectation.

The growing pessimism of the older men, which we find reflected in the letters and ancedotes of the time and even in the works of thoughtful historians, bears witness to the moral decay of the governing classes. It was too deep and too sincere to be set aside as an example of the familiar oriental habit of imagining a golden age in the past and looking down upon the present generation as the degenerate successors of their glorious ancestors. The historians Bhimsen and Khafi Khan were struck by the hopeless change for the worse that had seized the Indian world and looked wistfully back at the virtues and glories of the men of the times of Akbar and Shah Jahan. We find the aged Aurangzib himself dolefully shaking his head over the prospect of the future and predicting a deluge after his death. It is true, as Sadullah remarked in reply to a pessimist, "No age is without men of ability. What is needed is a wise master to find them out, cherish them, get his work done by them, and never lend his ears to the whispers of selfish men against such officers." But this wise principle was not followed in Aurangzib's latter years, and it was altogether discarded by his successors. Career was not freely opened to talent. The public service was not looked upon as a sacred trust, but as a means of gratifying the apostate, the sycophant, the well-groomed dandy, the great man's kinsmen, and sons of old official families. Bigotry and narrowness of outlook under Aurangzib and vice and sloth under the later Mughals, ruined the administration of the empire and dragged down the Indian people along with the falling empire.

MORAL DEGENERATION OF THE MUGHAL ARISTOCRACY

This moral decay was most noticeable among the nobility and it produced the greatest mischief. The character of the older nobility in the late 17th century was deplorable. In a mean spirit of jealousy they insulted and thwarted "new men" drawn from the ranks and ennobled for the most brilliant public services, and yet they themselves had grown utterly worthless. We have a significant example of the moral degeneration of the Mughal peerage. The prime minister's grandson, Mirza Tafakhkhur used to sally forth from his mansion in Delhi with his ruffians, plunder the shops in the bazar, kidnap Hindu women passing through the public streets in litters or going to the river, and dishonour them; and yet there was no judge strong enough to punish him, no police to prevent such crimes. "Every time such an occurrence was brought to the Emperor's notice by the new-settlers or official reports, he referred it to the prime minister and did nothing more."

All the surplus produce of a fertile land under a most bounteous Providence was swept into the coffers of the Mughal nobility and pampered them in a degree of luxury not dreamt of even by kings in Persia or Central Asia. Hence, in the houses of the Delhi nobility luxury was carried to an excess. The harems of many of them were filled with immense numbers of women, of an infinite variety of races, intellect and character. Under Muslim law the sons of concubines are entitled to their patrimony equally with sons born in wedlock, and they occupy no inferior position in society. Even the sons of lawfully married wives became, at a precocious age, familiar with vice from what they saw and heard in the harem, while their mothers were insulted by the higher splendour and influence enjoyed in the same household by younger and fairer rivals of servile origin or easier virtue. The proud spirit and majestic dignity of a Cornelia are impossible in the crowded harem of a polygamist; and without Cornelias among the mothers there cannot be Gracchi among the sons.

There was no good education, no practical training, of the sons of the Mughal nobility. They were too much petted by eunuchs and maid-servants and passed through a sheltered life from birth to manhood, every thorn being removed from their path by attendants. Early familiarized with vice, softened in their fibres by pleasure, they were yet taught to have an inordinately high opinion of their own wealth and importance in the scale of creation. Their domestic tutors were an unhappy class, powerless to do any good except by leave of their pupils, brow-beaten by the eunuchs (with the support of the ladies of the harem), disobeyed by the lads themselves, and forced to cultivate the arts of the courtier and the sneak, or to throw up their thankless office. The free give and take life in a public school (which hardens character and at the same time removes its angularities), the salutary discipline of training as subalterns in an orderly army, were unknown to the sons of the Mughal aristocracy. Hence, their moral decline was startingly rapid and unchecked. Most of them, and even sons of Aurangzib like Shah Alam and Kam Bakhs, were beyond correction. As Aurangzib, worn out with giving them unheeded counsels, cries out in despair, "I have become a babbler by talking and talking; but none of you have taken heed from my words."

In addition to unbridled sexual licence and secret drinking and gambling, many members of the nobility and the middle class were tainted by pederasty, a vice from which many of the so-called saints were not free. All Aurangzib's prohibitions and all the activity of his Censors of Public Morals failed to hold the Mughal aristocracy back from drink. The freak pleasures and queer fancies of some of the nobles are noticed in the contemporary accounts....

CHARACTER OF AURANGZIB

In the mediæval world, and nowhere more so than in India, the king was held responsible for the happiness of his people, and with good reason. He was God's representative on earth, invested with unlimited, unquestioned authority and the entire property in the land. Therefore, when towards the close of Aurangzib's reign all things began to go wrong, the contemporary historians turned to examine the Emperor's character, in order to account for the destruction of the empire and of public peace.

Aurangzib was brave in an unusual degree. All the Timurids, till the days of his unworthy great-grandsons, had personal courage; but in him this virtue was combined with a coldness of temperament and a calculating spirit which we have been taught to believe as the special heritage of the races of Northern Europe. Of his personal fearlessness he had given ample evidence from the age of fifteen, when he faced a furious elephant unattended, to his 87th year, when he stood in the siege trenches before Wagingera. His calm self-possession, his cheering words amidst the thickest danger, and his open defiance of death at Dharmat and Khajwa have passed into the famous things of Indian history.

In addition to possessing constitutional courage and coolness, he had early in life chosen the perils and labour of kingship as his vocation and prepared himself for this sovereign office by self-reverence, self-knowledge, and self-control. Unlike other sons of monarchs, Aurangzib was a widely read and accurate scholar, and he kept up his love of books to his dying day. Even if we pass over the many copies of the *Quran* which he wrote with his own hand, as the mechanical industry of a zealot, we cannot forget that he loved to devote the scanty leisure of a very busy ruler to reading Arabic works on jurisprudence and theology, and hunted for rare old MSS. of books like the *Nehayya*, the *Ahiya-ul-ulum*, and the *Diwan-i-Saib* with the passion of an idle bibliophile. His extensive correspondence proves his mastery of Persian poetry and Arabic sacred literature, as he was ever ready with apt quotations for embellishing almost every one of his letters. In addition to Arabic and Persian, he could speak Turki and Hindi freely. To his initiative and patronage we owe the greatest digest of Muslim law made in India, which rightly bears his name,—the *Fatawa-i-Alamgiri* and which simplified and defined Islamic justice in India ever after.

Besides book-learning, Aurangzib had from his boyhood cultivated control of speech and action, and tact in dealing with others. As a prince, his tact, sagacity and humility made the highest nobles of his father's Court his friends; and as Emperor he displayed the same qualities in a degree which would have been remarkable even in a subject. No wonder that his contemporaries called him "a *darvish* clad in the imperial purple."

His private life,—dress, food and recreations,—were all extremely simple, but well-ordered. He was absolutely free from vice and even from the more innocent pleasures of the idle rich. The number of his wives fell short even of the Quaranic allowance of four, and he was scrupulously faithful to wedded love. The only delicacies he relished, —the reader will smile to learn,—were the acid fruit *corinda (Carissa carandas)* and a sort of chewing gum called *khardali.* His industry in administration was marvellous. In addition to regularly holding daily Courts (sometimes twice a day) and Wednesday trials, he wrote orders on letters and petitions with his own hand and dictated the very language of official replies. The Italian physician Gemeli Careri thus describes the Emperor giving public audience (21 March 1695): "He was of a low stature, with a large nose, slender and stooping with age. The whiteness of his round beard was more visible on his olive-coloured skin.... I admired to see him endorse the petitions [of those who had

business] with his own hand, without spectacles, and by his cheerful smiling countenance seem to be pleased with the employment."

Muslim historians have observed that though he died in his 90th year, he retained to the last almost all his faculties unimpaired. His memory was wonderful: "he never forgot a face he had once seen or a word that he had once heard." All his physical powers retained their vigour to the end, if we except a slight deafness of the ear, which afflicted him in old age, and a lameness of the right leg, which was due to his doctor's unskilful treatment of an accidental dislocation.

HIS BESETTING SIN OF OVER-CENTRALIZATION: ITS DISASTROUS EFFECT ON THE ADMINISTRATION

But all this long self-preparation and splendid vitality, in one sense proved his undoing, as they naturally begot in him a self-confidence and distrust of others, a passion for seeing everything carried to the highest perfection according to his own idea of it,—which urged him to order and supervise every minute detail of administration and warfare personally. This excessive interference of the head of the State kept his viceroys and commanders and even "the men on the spot" in far off districts in perpetual tutelage; their sense of responsibility was destroyed, initiative and rapid adaptability to a changing environment could not be developed in them, and they tended to sink into lifeless puppets moved to action by the master pulling their strings from the capital. No surer means than this could have been devised for causing administrative degeneration in an extensive and diversified empire like India. High-spirited, talented and energetic officers found themselves checked, discouraged and driven to sullen inactivity. With the death of the older nobility, outspoken responsible advisers disappeared from his council, and Aurangzib in his latter years, like Napoleon I after the climax of Tilsit, could bear no contradiction, could hear no unpalatable truth, but surrounded himself with smooth-tongued sycophants and pompous echoes of his own voice. His ministers became no better than clerks passively registering his edicts.

Such a king cannot be called a political or even an administrative genius. He had merely honesty and plodding industry. He was fit to be an excellent departmental head, not a statesman initiating a new policy and legislating with prophetic foresight for moulding the life and thought of unborn generations in advance. That genius, though unlettered and often hot blooded, was Akbar alone among the Mughals of India.

Obsessed by his narrow ideal of duty and supremely ignorant of the real limitations of his characters,—and not out of political cunning, as Manucci suggests, —Aurangzib practised saintly austerities and self-abasement and went regularly and even ostentatiously through all the observances of his religion. He thus became an ideal character to the Muslim portion of his subjects. They believed him to be a saint who wrought miracles (*Alamgir, zinda pir!*) and he himself favoured this idea by his acts. Politically, therefore, Aurangzib with all his virtues was a complete failure. But the cause of the failure of his reign lay deeper than his personal character. Though it is not true that he alone caused the fall of the Mughal empire, yet he did nothing to avert it, but deliberately quickened the destructive forces always present in a rigid theocratic form of government, because he was a reactionary by instinct and no reforming statesman. And these forces I shall examine now.

TRUE CHARACTER AND AIM OF THE MUGHAL GOVERNMENT

The Mughal empire did much for India in many ways. But it failed to weld the people into a nation, or to create a strong and enduring State.

The glitter of gems and gold in the Taj Mahal or the Peacock Throne, ought not to blind us to the fact that in Mughal India man was considered vile;—the mass of the people had no economic liberty, no indefeasible right to justice or personal freedom when their oppressor was a noble or high official or landowner; political rights were not dreamt of. While the nation at large was no better than human sheep, the status of the nobles was hardly any higher under a strong and clever king; they had no assured constitutional position, because a constitution did not exist in the scheme of government, nor even had they full right to their material acquisitions. All depended upon the will of the autocrat on the throne. The Government was in effect despotism tempered by revolution or the fear of revolution. The whole power and all the resources of a country produce a Court,—the centre of the Court is the prince; finally, then, the ultimate product of all this gathered life is the self-sufficiency of the sovereign.

In Mughal India, as in all other absolute monarchies, popular happiness even under the best of sovereigns was unstable, because it depended upon the character of one man. "The Mughal system of education and training entirely failed to maintain a line of promising heirs-apparent.... As the princes grew up, the jealousy of rival queens forbade their taking a leading part in the politics of the capital.... A prince who took his proper part in the council of the State was suspected of intriguing against the monarch.... Hereditary succession is only tolerable under a system where the responsibility falls on a ministry, which screens the viciousness or incompetence of the occupant of the throne." "Such a ministry the Mughals were never able to organize." The monarch was obliged to fall back on the mob of adventurers who crowded round his *darbar*, ... whose function was more to amuse their master than to act as a modern Cabinet.... It was never the Mughal policy to foster the growth of a hereditary aristocracy." [Crooke].

By its theory, Islamic Government is military rule—the people are the faithful soldiers of Islam, the Emperor (*Khalifa*) is their commander. In an army it is not for the officers, any more than for the privates, to reason why or to seek reply from the supreme leader. The Khalifa-Emperor is the silhouette of God (*zill-subhani*), and in God's court there is no "why or how." No more could there be in the Padishah's administration, which was a sample of God's Court (*namuna-i-darbar-i-ilahi*). By the basic principle of Islamic Government, the Hindus and other unbelievers were admittedly outside the pale of the nation. But even the dominant sect, the Muslims, did not form a nation; they constituted a military brotherhood, a perceptual camp of soldiers.

DIFFERENCE IN LIFE AND IDEAL MAKES FUSION OF HINDUS AND MUHAMMADANS IMPOSSIBLE

According to the root principles of Muslim polity, there can be no political rights for minorities, the nation must be merged in the dominant sect, and a community homogeneous in creed and social life must be created by crushing out all divergent forms of faith, opinion and life. The nation as a purely political creation was inconceivable and impossible in such a state of things. The evil was aggravated by the fact that in India the politically depressed class or "official minority" was a numerical majority, outnumbering the dominant sect as three to one, and at the same time economically better qualified, stronger in capital and wealth-producing power, and not inferior in intellect or physical vigour.

No fusion between the two classes was possible even with the passage of centuries, as they differed like opposite poles in ideal and life. The Hindu is solitary, passive, other-worldly; his highest aim is self-realization, the attainment of personal salvation by individual effort, private devotions, and lonely austerities. To him birth is a misfortune and his fellow-beings so many sources of distraction from his one true goal. Not by enjoyment of God's gifts but by renunciation, not by joyous expansion but by repression of emotion, is he to attain to true bliss. The Muslim, on the other hand, is taught to feel that he is nothing if not a soldier of the militant force of Islam; he must pray in congregation; he must give proof of the sincerity of his faith by undertaking *jihad* or active exertion for the spread of his religion and the destruction of unbelief among other men. He is a missionary, and cannot be indifferent to the welfare of his neighbours' souls; nay, he must be ever alive to his duty of promoting the salvation of others by all means at his command, physical as much as spiritual. Then, again, Islam boldly avows that it is good for us to be here, that God has given the world to the faithful as an inheritance for their enjoyment.

The practical outlook and social solidarity of the Muslims have made them develop the arts and civilization (excepting literature) in a much higher degree than the Hindus; their pleasures are of a more varied and elegant kind, and the Hindu aristocracy in Mughal times were only clumsy imitators of the Muslim peers. The general type of Muhammadans (excepting beggars and menial labourers) are more refined and accustomed to a costlier mode of life, while Hindus of the corresponding classes, even when rich, are grosser and less cultured. The lower classes of the Hindus, however, are distinctly cleaner and more intellectual than Muslims of the same grades of life.

HINDUS POLITICALLY DEPRESSED AND DEGRADED UNDER AURANGZIB

Apart from the restrictions about food, difference of religious doctrine and ritual, rules forbidding intermarriage, &c., this polar difference in their outlook upon life made a fusion between Hindus and Muslims impossible. In addition to these, the Quranic polity made life intolerable for the Hindus under orthodox Muhammadan rule. Aurangzib furnishes the best example of the effects of that polity when carried to its logical conclusions by a king of exemplary morality and religious zeal, without fear or favour in discharging what he held to be his duty as the first servant of God. Schools of Hindu learning were broken up by him, Hindu places of worship were demolished, Hindu fairs were forbidden, the Hindu population was subjected to special fiscal burdens in addition to being made to bear a public badge of inferiority; and the service of the State was closed to them.

Thus, the only life that the Hindu could lead under Aurangzib was a life deprived of the light of knowledge, deprived of the consolations of religion, deprived of social union and public rejoicing, of wealth and the self-confidence that is begotten by the free exercise of natural activities and use of opportunities,—in short, a life exposed to constant public humiliation and political disabilities. Heaven and earth alike were closed to him as long as he remained a Hindu. Hence, the effect of Aurangzib's reign was not only to goad the Hindus into constant revolt and disturbances but also to make them deteriorate in intellect, organization, and economic resources, and thereby weaken the State of which they formed more than two-thirds of the man-power.

NO

S. M. Ikram

AURANGZEB

Aurangzeb, the third son of Shah Jahan, was born on October 24, 1618, at Dohad, on the frontier of Gujarat and Rajputana. Industrious and thorough, he had distinguished himself as an able administrator during the years that he spent in the Deccan and other provinces of the empire. He was also a fearless soldier and a skillful general, and because of the hostile influence at court of his brother Dara, he had had to learn all the tactics of diplomacy. As emperor, he ruled more of India than any previous monarch, but in a court that had become a byword for luxury, he lived a life of austere piety. Yet of all India's rulers, few pursued policies that have excited more controversy among successive generations. In large measure, this is the result of his religious policies, for it was these that have colored men's evaluation of his reign.

Even as a young man, Aurangzeb was known for his devotion to the Muslim religion and observance of Islamic injunctions, and in some of his letters written during the struggle for the succession he claimed that he was acting "for the sake of the true faith and the peace of the realm." As soon as he was securely on the throne, he introduced reforms which could make his dominion a genuine Muslim state. After his second (and formal) coronation on June 5, 1659, he issued orders which were calculated to satisfy orthodoxy. He appointed censors of public morals in all important cities to enforce Islamic law and he tried to put down such practices as drinking, gambling, and prostitution. He forbade the cultivation of narcotics throughout the empire, and in 1664 he issued his first edict forbidding *sati* or the self-immolation of women on funeral pyres. He also repeatedly denounced the castration of children so they could be sold as eunuchs. In the economic sphere he showed a determined opposition to all illegal exactions and to all taxes which were not authorized by Islamic law. Immediately after his second coronation he abolished the inland transport duty, which amounted to ten percent of the value of goods, and the *octroi* on all articles of food and drink brought into the cities for sale.

From S. M. Ikram, *Muslim Civilization in India* (Columbia University Press, 1964). Copyright © 1964 by Columbia University Press. Reprinted by permission of the publisher. Notes omitted.

Although these measures were partly responsible for Aurangzeb's later financial difficulties, they were popular with the people. But gradually the emperor's puritanism began to manifest itself, and steps were taken which were not so universally approved. In 1668 he forbade music at his court and, with the exception of the royal band, he pensioned off the large number of state musicians and singers. The festivities held on the emperor's birthday, including the custom of weighing him against gold and silver, were discontinued, and the mansabdars were forbidden to offer him the usual presents. The ceremony of *darshan*, or the public appearance of the emperor to the people, was abandoned in 1679.

During the long struggle for the throne the central authority had tended to lose administrative control over the distant parts of the empire, and after he had defeated his rivals, Aurangzeb started to reorganize the civil government. He had used the need of revitalizing the instruments of imperial power as a justification for his seizure of the throne, and his intention of making good his promise was soon felt throughout the empire. The provincial governors began to expand the borders of the empire, and local authorities, who had grown accustomed to ignoring orders for Agra, the imperial capital, discovered that new regime could act swiftly against them. . . .

RELIGIOUS POLICY

While Aurangzeb was extending the empire in the east and south, and consolidating his position on the northwest marches, he was also concerned with the strengthening of Islam throughout the kingdom. His attempt to conduct the affairs of state according to traditional Islamic policy brought to the fore the problem that had confronted every ruler who had attempted to make Islam the guiding force: the position of the Hindu majority in relation to the government. In 1688, when he forbade music at the royal court and took other puritanical steps in conformity with strict injunctions of Muslim law, he affected both Hindus and Muslims. When *jizya*, [taxation of Jews and Christians by Muslim rulers] abolished for nearly a century, was reimposed in 1679 it was the Hindus alone who suffered.

By now Aurangzeb had accepted the policy of regulating his government in accordance with strict Islamic law and many orders implementing this policy were issued. A large number of taxes were abolished which had been levied in India for centuries but which were not authorized by Islamic law. Possibly it was the unfavorable effect of these remissions on the state exchequer which led to the exploration of other lawful sources of revenue. The fact that, according to the most responsible account, the reimposition of *jizya* was suggested by an officer of the finance department would seem to show that it was primarily a fiscal measure. The theologians, who were becoming dominant at the court, naturally endorsed the proposal and Aurangzeb carried it out with his customary thoroughness.

Another measure which has caused adverse comment is the issue of orders at various stages regarding the destruction of Hindu temples. Originally these orders applied to a few specific cases—such as the temple at Mathura built by Abul Fazl's murderer, to which a railing had been added by Aurangzeb's rival, Dara Shukoh. More far-reaching is the claim that when it was reported to him that Hindus were teaching Muslims their "wicked science," Aurangzeb issued orders to all governors "ordering the destruction of temples and schools and totally prohibiting the teaching and infidel practices of the unbelievers." That such an order was actually given is doubtful; certainly it was never carried out with any thoroughness. However, it is incontestable that at a certain stage Aurangzeb tried to enforce strict Islamic law by ordering the destruction of newly built Hindu temples. Later, the procedure was adopted of closing down rather than destroying the newly built temples in Hindu localities. It is also true that very often the orders of destruction remained a dead letter, but Aurangzeb was too deeply committed to ordering of his government according to Islamic law to omit its implementation in so significant a matter. The fact that a total ban on the construction of new temples was adopted only by later jurists, and was a departure from the earlier Muslim practice as laid down by Muhammad ibn Qasim in Sind, was no concern of the correct, conscientious, and legal-minded Aurangzeb.

As a part of general policy of ordering the affairs of the state in accordance with the views of the ulama certain discriminatory orders against the Hindus were issued, for example imposition of higher customs duties, 5 percent on the goods of the Hindus as against 2 percent on those of Muslims. These were generally in accordance with the practice of the times but they marked a departure not only from the political philosophy governing Mughal government, but also from the policy followed hitherto by most Muslim rulers in India.

Aurangzeb has often been accused of closing the doors of official employment on the Hindus, but a study of the list of his officers shows this is not so. Actually there were more Hindu officers under him than under any other Mughal emperor. Though this was primarily due to a general increase in the number of officers, it shows that there was no ban on the employment of the Hindus.

The Aurangzeb's religious policy was unpopular at the time is true, but that it was an important factor, as usually charged, in the downfall of the empire is doubtful. The Hindu uprisings of his reign seem to have had no wide religious appeal, and they were supressed with the help of Hindu leaders. Their significance comes in the following reigns, when the rulers were no longer able to meet opposition as effectively—and as ruthlessly —as had Aurangzeb. His religious policy aimed at strengthening an empire already overextended in Shah Jahan's time; that it failed in its objective is probably true, but the mistake should not be made of assuming that the attempt was a major element in the later political decay. It should be seen, rather, as part of an unsuccessful attempt to stave off disaster. Seen in this light, his religious policy is one element, but not a casual one, save in its failure to achieve its intended goal, among the many that have to be considered in seeking an understanding of Aurangzeb's difficulties....

THE ENIGMA OF
AURANGZEB'S PURPOSES

In the background of all these events— the struggle for the throne, the annexations of great territories in the South, the wasting struggle with the Marathas, the pacification of the northwest frontier, the consolidation of Mughal power in Bengal, the contemptuous treatment of the East India Company—stands the enigmatic figure of Aurangzeb, surely the most controversial personality in the history of Islamic rule in India. Held responsible by some for the downfall of the Mughal empire, by others he is praised for maintaining as long as he did the unity of his vast realm.

So far as Aurangzeb's personal qualities are concerned, however, there is general admiration. R. C. Majumdar writes: "Undaunted bravery, grim tenacity of purpose, and ceaseless activity were some of his prominent qualities. His military campaigns gave sufficient proof of his unusual courage, and the manner in which he baffled the intrigues of his enemies shows him to have been a past master of diplomacy and statecraft. His memory was wonderful, and his industry indefatigable." "He never forgot a face he had once seen or a word that he had once heard." Apart from his devotion to duty, his life was remarkable for its simplicity and purity. His dress, food, and recreations were all extremely simple. He died at the age of ninety, but all his faculties (except his hearing) remained unimpaired.

A well-read man, he kept up his love of books till the end. He wrote beautiful Persian prose. A selection of his letters (*Ruq'at-i-Alamgiri*) has long been a standard model of simple but elegant prose. According to Bakhtawar Khan, he had acquired proficiency in versification, but agreeable to the word of God that "Poets deal in falsehoods," he abstained from practicing the art. He understood music well but he gave up this amusement in accordance with Islamic injunctions.

It is the general attitude to culture that explains why the Mughal court, which under Shah Jahan had been the great center of patronage for the arts, ceased to be so in Aurangzeb's reign. He disbanded the court musicians, abolished the office of the poet-laureate, discontinued the work of the court chronicler, and offered little encouragement to painters. On grounds of both economy and fidelity to the Islamic law he criticized the Taj Mahal, the tomb of his mother, remarking: "The lawfulness of a solid construction over a grave is doubtful, and there can be no doubt about the extravagance involved."

Although Aurangzeb's attitude toward the arts was one of disapproval, his reign was not culturally barren. Large-scale building activity ceased, but this was as much a reflection of a treasury depleted by war as deliberate policy. Other forms of artistic life flourished, partly because they had taken firm foot in Indian soil, and partly because the great nobles made up to some extent for the lack of royal patronage. In the case of poetry, where self-expression yields better results without compliance with a patron's wishes or moods, the abolition of the court patronage and the weakening of the court tradition led to some welcome new developments. The greatest Persian poet of the period, Bedil, turned away from the polished love lyrics of the old court poets and concentrated on metaphysical poetry. Often his fancy ran riot. Many of his metaphors are quaint and far-fetched, and his meaning is frequently obscure, but he is unmatched for profundity of thought and originality of ideas and similes. He is highly popular in Afghanistan and Tajikistan, where his poetry appeals to the serious readers in the same way as does the great *Masnavi* of Rumi. He paved the way for Ghalib, who followed him in aiming at originality and depth of thought, but adopted the polished diction of Mughal court poets.

Perhaps even more important was Wali (d.1707), originally a writer of Deccani, who became the first major poet of modern Urdu. This replacement of Deccani by Urdu was a direct result of Aurangzeb's conquest of the Muslim kingdoms of the south. So long as the kingdoms of Golkunda and Bijapur existed and patronized the poets and writers of Deccani, "it was fully in vogue and its peculiarities immune from criticism and sneers." When this source of patronage dried up and the Hindustani-speaking officers became dominant in the south, the writers of Deccani had to adjust to a new situation. They were forced to shed their peculiarities of dialect, themes, and treatment while the speakers from the north saw the literary possibilities of the spoken language. The two streams of literary tradition mingled, and gave birth to modern Urdu.

These developments owed little to Aurangzeb's deliberate efforts. The cultural activities for which he was directly responsible were the spread of Islamic learning and general diffusion of education. His reign was marked by the extensive grant of patronage and stipends to scholars and students. There were no religious leaders of the caliber of Shah Waliullah or Shaikh Ahmad Sirhindi, but there is no doubt that the foundation of the Islamic religious revival in the eighteenth and nineteenth centuries were laid at this time. The Islamic academic curriculum, known as *Dars-i-Nizamiya*, was begun in his reign, and the emperor was personally responsible for the grant of extensive buildings, known as Farangi Mahal of Lucknow, to the family of Mulla Nizam-ud-din, after whom *Dars-i-Nizamiya* is named. Most of the books included in the *Dars-i-Nizamiya*, other than those of foreign origin, were

written during Aurangzeb's reign. They were mainly the work of two scholars patronized by the emperor—Mir Zahid, the qazi of Kabul, and Muhibullah Bihari, the qazi of Allahabad. Compilation of the comprehensive legal digest, known as *Fatawa-i-Alamgiri*, was also initiated by the emperor.

In turning from Aurangzeb's influence on culture to his work as a statesman, we find that his achievements are obvious but his final years were clouded by difficulties. The strong kingdoms of Golkunda and Bijapur, for long centers of Muslim power in the south, were conquered in less than a year, but the entire might of the Mughul empire was pitted against the Marathas for twenty years, without resulting in decisive gains. And in the struggle the Marathas gained a new confidence and soon moved from the defensive in the Deccan to an offensive in the north.

In the financial field, Aurangzeb's achievements were even less distinguished. When he died, the imperial treasury was almost empty. He left barely 12 crores of rupees—not very much more than the inheritance of a great Mughal noble like Asaf Khan. Towards the end of his reign, the imperial finances were in such straits that the diwan anxiously waited for the receipt of the Bengal revenue, so that the expenses of the Deccan campaign could be met.

It is a tribute to Aurangzeb's control over the affairs of the empire that no major upheaval occurred in the north during his prolonged absence in the Deccan, but there are clear indications of many minor disturbances and a general slackening of administration. In Bengal, for example, Sobha Singh, a petty chief of Midnapur district, joined an Afghan chief to defeat the Hindu zamindar

314 / 16. DID AURANGZEB'S RULE MARK THE BEGINNING OF DECLINE?

of Burdwan. They also seized the fort and city of Hugli and plundered the cites of Nadia, Murshidabad, Malda, and Rajmahal. The emperor removed Ibrahim Khan, the governor (though, it appears, soon to appoint him to Allahabad), and the rebellion was effectively put down, but it exposed the insecure state of the administration. As this disturbance enabled the English and other foreigners to fortify their settlements at Calcutta and elsewhere, its effects were far-reaching.

The basic cause of Aurangzeb's failures did not lie in his own weakness, but in the quality of men at his disposal. Aurangzeb's misfortune was that he began to rule when two generations of unparalleled prosperity had sapped the moral fiber of the Mughal aristocracy. The Mughals were no longer the hardy soldiers and resourceful improvisers of the days of Babur and Akbar. Aurangzeb constantly bemoaned the scarcity of good officers. In one of his letters he says, "My great grandfather [Akbar] had many faithful servants. He entrusted them with the work of gaining successful victories and of performing many affairs, and in the time of my father [Shah Jahan] there came forward many brave and faithful servants, well-behaved officers and able secretaries. Now I want one competent person, adorned with the ornament of honesty, for the Diwani of Bengal; but I find none. Alas! alas! for the rarity of useful men."

A growing weakness of the Mughal officials was that they shirked arduous and difficult assignments. For them the continuous stay in the Deccan, away from the attractions of the capital, was such a calamity that they would probably have preferred the Maratha victory to such an exile. One of Aurangzeb's leading nobles used to say that he would distribute a lakh of rupees in charity if he could see the capital once again. Such ease-loving generals fared badly against the hardy Marathas. They took years to conquer small hill-forts, and many of these forts conquered after long sieges would be quickly lost owing to the sloth and negligence of the officers in charge.

Treachery was rampant in the Mughal army, and the royal princes were sometimes the cause. During the seven-year siege of Ginji, Prince Kam Bakhsh, who was in charge of the operations along with Zulfiqar Khan, was placed under arrest as he was about to join the Marathas with his troops. During the siege of Satara the Marathas bribed Prince Azam to ensure that the provisioning of their garrison wold not be interfered with, and the fort which at the commencement of the siege had provisions to last only for two months was not conquered for six months. With such instruments at his disposal, it is little wonder that Aurangzeb's policies were not successful.

The causes of some of Aurangzeb's difficulties were beyond his control. Others, especially the financial and the administrative ones, arose out of his personal character and its reflection in his basic policies. In making his decision to run his government according to Islamic law, he did more than reverse Akbar's religious policy: he gave up the age-old policy, followed since the inception of the Muslim rule in India, and which had been openly proclaimed by Balban, Ala-ud-din Khalji, and Sher Shah, of subordinating legal and ecclesiastical considerations to practical requirements of administration. Aurangzeb was inspired by high motives, but the policy created many problems.

His financial difficulties were partly due to the wholesome remission of some eighty taxes, and partly to his refusal to levy any tax, not specifically authorized by *shariat*. He failed to see ... that such a policy was inconsistent with military expansion and large-scale warfare. In the administrative field, also, he was opposed to taking any action or imposing any penalty, except in strict accordance with the Islamic law. This resulted in precedence being given to the qazis, which was not liked by many of Aurangzeb's officers. Some of Aurangzeb's ablest generals found the attention given by the emperor to rigid legal procedure irksome. Firuz Jang, the conqueror of Golkunda (whom the emperor held so dear that once when he fell ill and was forbidden melons, Aurangzeb himself gave up this fruit), put to death one Muhammad Aqil on a charge of highway robbery, without formal trial by a qazi. Aurangzeb sternly rebuked him, and asked his wazir to write to the noble that if the heirs of the slain refused to accept the blood-money permitted by law he would have to pass an order of retaliation against him.

There is something truly noble in a ruler reminding his ablest general that he would have to face the full rigors of the law for an unlawful action, and there can be nothing but admiration for Aurangzeb's endeavors to uphold the law and proper judicial procedure. But in the seventeenth century the administrators found this meticulous emphasis on legal procedure and the prominent position of the qazis a hindrance. The contemporary historian Khafi Khan has attributed the imperfect success of Aurangzeb, in spite of his great ability and immense industry, to his reluctance to go beyond

Islamic law. "From reverence for the injunctions of the Law, he did not make use of punishment and without punishment the administration of a country cannot be maintained. Dissensions rose among his nobles through rivalry. So every plan and project that he formed came to little good; and every enterprise which he undertook was long in execution and failed in its objective."

Perhaps the time to make a final assessment of Aurangzeb has not yet arrived. More than five thousand of his letters are extant, but only a handful have been published, and until this rich material is studied, a proper appraisal of his personality is not possible. At present, evidence about him is fragmentary and contradictory, and his personality was more complex than either his admirers or critics are willing to acknowledge. In the context of conflicting evidence the tendency for each group is to emphasize the elements supporting its point of view. These verdicts are liable to be modified in the light of the vast material which remains to be utilized and all judgment of Aurangzeb, at this stage, can only be provisional.

Whatever view it taken should not obscure, however, Aurangzeb's solid and abiding achievements. He greatly enlarged the Mughal empire and much of what he accomplished has endured. A large part of what is East Pakistan today was either conquered or consolidated during his reign. In the Deccan he annexed vast areas which were to remain centers of Mughal culture and administration for more than two centuries. He selected and promoted administrators whose work constitutes a landmark in the history of the regions entrusted to them—Shayista Khan and Murshid Quli Khan in Bengal, and Nizam-ul-Mulk in the Deccan. He tried to reduce the Irani preponderance in administration and attracted some gifted Turani families to the service of the Mughals. He also trained a body of men who were to sustain the empire through a period of foreign invasions and repeated internal struggles for the succession. Viewed in this light, Aurangzeb can be seen not as the instigator of policies that led to ruin but as the guardian of the Islamic state in India.

POSTSCRIPT

Did Indian Emperor Aurangzeb's Rule Mark the Beginning of Mughal Decline?

Sarkar believes that Aurangzeb was a courageous, devout, and hardworking leader. Nevertheless, Sarkar has no doubt that this Mughal ruler instituted policies that encouraged decadence among his court, despite attempts to curb it; diminished the accomplishments of Indian culture; sapped the empire's economic strength; and destroyed the agricultural productivity of the peasantry. It is in this last point that Sarkar finds the greatest fault. Through the waging of incessant and resource-depleting warfare, Aurangzeb bankrupted his empire. He imposed oppressive taxes on the Hindu peasantry and was unable to compensate them for their wartime losses, which led to lowered agricultural output. At the same time, his inattention to local control allowed for further depredations, including the gouging of the populace by village officials. Even the army tired of the endless campaigning of their relentless general. Sarkar finds that Aurangzeb's persecution of Hindus forced them into a revolt that aggravated an already-disturbed situation, ensuring that the empire would not remain as a successful entity for long.

However, even while condemning Aurangzeb as the destroyer of Mughal power, Sarkar asserts that there was an inevitability to its collapse. For him, the differences between Hindu and Muslim were insurmountable. In this Ikram would most likely agree. For him, Aurangzeb did not bring about the downfall of the Mughal empire but implemented policies that allowed it to survive as long as it did. In particular, Ikram rejects the accusation that Aurangzeb's religious policy was oppressive to the point of being debilitating. He points out that more Hindu officers served under Aurangzeb's command than ever before and that there was no general discrimination against Hindu bureaucrats. He states that the reintroduction of the head tax, or jizya, was not an instrument of religious persecution but an economic necessity. As concerns his supposed unfriendliness to the arts, Ikram argues that the emperor played a key role in the development of Islamic scholarship and the spread of education and that in no way did he repress artistic expression. Aurangzeb's removal of the court musicians and poets indicated necessary and sound financial frugality rather than a bigoted religious fanaticism. In essence, says Ikram, Aurangzeb is at worst a mysterious but personally admirable figure and at best "the guardian of the Islamic state in India."

For more information, see Muni Lal's biography *Aurangzeb* (Vikas, 1988), Stanley L. Poole, *Aurangzib and the Decay of the Mughal Empire* (S. Asia, 1990); and M. Athar Ali, *The Mughal Nobility Under Aurangzeb* (Oxford University Press, 1997).

ISSUE 17

Did Peter the Great Exert a Positive Influence on the Development of Russia?

YES: Vasili Klyuchevsky, from *Peter the Great,* trans. Liliana Archibald (Macmillan & Co., Ltd., 1958)

NO: Peter Brock Putnam, from *Peter: The Revolutionary Tsar* (Harper & Row, 1973)

ISSUE SUMMARY

YES: Historian Vasili Klyuchevsky, dismissing the cruelty of Peter the Great's methods, argues that the myriad Petrine reforms helped Russia compete with western European nations.

NO: Historian Peter Brock Putnam argues that the human and financial costs of Peter's reforms outweighed their benefits, particularly for the Russian peasantry.

Peter the Great has long been one of the most dominant figures in Russian history. His reign forms a watershed between the old, backward Russia and the new Russia that attempted to compete with western European nations during the eighteenth and nineteenth centuries.

Peter himself was an extraordinary man. Physically, he towered over other men, standing nearly seven feet tall. With his powerful physique and his restless energy, he seemed a dynamo to his contemporaries. Peter was always in motion, walking with rapid, giant strides even while talking, and Peter's advisers had to struggle to keep pace with him. Vastly ambitious and prone to fierce rages, Peter's personality enhanced the impression of irrepressible power. He possessed an insatiable desire for knowledge, and he often handled the details of government himself, for which he taught himself the intricacies of diplomacy, military arts, justice, administration, education, finance, and industry.

Although Peter did not begin his reign as a reformer, the foreign and domestic circumstances that greeted him soon convinced him that Russia needed to undergo significant changes if he were to achieve his goals. Consequently, Peter pushed, drove, and bullied the Russian people into the eighteenth century. During the course of his reign, Peter virtually re-created the Russian army and conquered new territories in the Baltic; substantially increased Russia's industrial production, particularly in the key iron industry; founded myriad new schools, including the Academy of Sciences; established the first Russian newspaper; expanded the imperial revenue; and liberated upper-class Russian women from the severe restraints that had bound them under the old regime.

According to Vasili Klyuchevsky in the following selection, Peter was an exceptionally complex man whose effects on Russia were equally complex and who is therefore not subject to black-and-white judgments. Although Klyuchevsky concedes that many of Peter's actions were brutal, he excuses Peter's methods by arguing that the czar needed to be ruthless to overcome the entrenched prejudices and opposition of the *boyars* (conservative Russian aristocrats) and the *streltsy* (the imperial militia). Moreover, Peter had to work quickly and under difficult circumstances, including the bitter war with Sweden. The end result, Klyuchevsky maintains, was akin to a powerful spring storm, which strips old growth from the trees but clears the air and hastens the development of new seeds.

In the second selection, Peter Brock Putnam also portrays Peter as a complex figure, but he emphasizes the negative effects of the czar's rule on the Russian people. During his reign, Peter launched numerous despotic practices that have endured to the present, including Russia's first regularly organized secret police. Peter treated the peasantry like slaves, forcing them to perform labor in mines and factories, which is clearly a precedent for the harsh labor policies adopted by Stalin in the 1930s. Peter's wars led to the deaths of thousands of Russian peasants and to taxes that impoverished the Russian people. In the end, Putnam states, Peter's reforms led to slavery and oppression rather than progress and freedom.

YES
Vasili Klyuchevsky

PETER THE GREAT

Our survey of Peter's reforming activities is not yet complete, for we have discussed neither their effects on education and welfare nor the changes they caused in the ideas and customs of the people. Some of his measures were not directly connected with his more urgent reforms; some had effects which were not obvious in his lifetime; and some affected only certain classes. We [believe] that the purpose of all Peter's reforms was originally either financial or military, and . . . we have concentrated on the way in which the reforms, aimed at these particular objects, affected society as a whole. It should now be possible to form an appreciation of the significance and character of Peter's reforming activities, or at any rate of some of their aspects.

The question of the significance of Peter's reforms is largely a question of the development of Russian historical understanding. For over two hundred years Russians have written a great deal, and talked even more, about Peter's activities. Whenever a discussion of isolated facts in Russian history has turned to consideration of their general significance, it has been found necessary to refer to Peter's activities; and anyone discussing Russia's past philosophically has found it necessary to establish his academic respectability by commenting on Peter's activities. Very often, indeed, Russian philosophies of history have been in the form of judgements of the Petrine reforms; and, by a remarkable feat of condensation, the meaning of all Russian history was looked for in the significance of those reforms, and in the relationship between the old and the new Russia. The Petrine reforms became the focus of all Russian history: they were taken as a starting point for the study of the past, and used by historians in an attempt to elucidate the future. . . .

First of all, how did Peter become a reformer? The name of Peter makes us think of his reforms, and indeed 'Peter the Great and his reforms' has become a cliché. 'Reformer' has become his sobriquet, and the name by which he is known to history. We tend to believe that Peter I was born with the intention of reforming his country, and that he believed that this was his predestined historical mission. Nevertheless it was a long time before Peter took this view of himself. He was certainly not brought up to believe that he would reign over a state which was good for nothing, and which he would have to rebuild

From Vasili Klyuchevsky, *Peter the Great*, trans. Liliana Archibald (Macmillan & Co., Ltd., 1958). Copyright © 1958 by Liliana Archibald. Reprinted by permission of Macmillan, Ltd.

from top to bottom. On the contrary, he grew up knowing that he was Tsar, though a persecuted one, and that, as long as his sister and the Miloslavskys were in power, he was in danger of losing his life, and was unlikely to occupy the throne. His games of soldiers and with boats were the sports of his childhood, suggested to him by the conversations of his entourage. He realised very early that when he grew up and began to rule, he would need an army and navy, but he was, it seems, in no hurry to ask why he would need them. He only gradually realised, when he had discovered Sophia's intrigues, that he would need soldiers to control the Streltsy who supported his sister. Peter acted on the spur of the moment, and was not concerned with making plans for the future; he regarded everything he did as an immediate necessity rather than a reform, and did not notice how his actions changed both people and established systems. Even from his first foreign tour he brought back, not plans for reform, but impressions of a civilisation which he imagined he would like to introduce into Russia; and he brought back, too, a taste for the sea, that is to say, a desire to wage war against the country which had won access to the sea away from his grandfather. Indeed it was only during the last decade of his life, when the effect of his reforms was already fairly obvious, that he realised that he had done something new and spectacular. His better understanding of what he had done, however, did not help him to understand how he might act in the future. Peter thus became a reformer by accident, as it were, and even unwillingly. The war led him on and, to the end of his life, pushed him into reforming.

In the history of a country, war generally impedes reform, since foreign war and domestic reform are mutually exclusive and reform prospers best in times of peace. But in the history of Russia the correlation is different. Since a successful war has always served to secure the *status quo*, and an unsuccessful war, by provoking internal discontent, has always forced the government to review its domestic policy and introduce reforms, the government has always tried to avoid war, often to the detriment of its international position. Reforms at home were commonly achieved at the price of disaster abroad. In Peter's time the relationship between war and domestic change was different. Reforms were stimulated by the requirements of war, which indeed dictated the nature of the reforms that were undertaken. In other times the effect of war has been to force change on an unwilling government, but Peter, as he said himself, was able to learn from war what changes were needed. Unfortunately the attempt to carry on both war and reform simultaneously was unsuccessful: war slowed up reform, and reform prolonged the war because there was opposition and frequent revolt, and the forces of the nation could not be united to finish the war.

There were also interminable controversies about whether the reforms had been sufficiently elaborated, and whether they were introduced to meet the needs of the people, or had been forced on them as an unexpected act of Peter's autocratic will. In these discussions the preparations for reform were examined. It was asked whether they were deliberately calculated to bring about improvement, or were simply forced upon Peter by urgent difficulties, and were therefore only by accident measures which led to new possibilities and a new way of life....

It is even more difficult to estimate the influence and effect of the reforms, and this, after all, is the main problem. In order to attempt a solution it will be necessary to dissect minutely its complex component parts. So many clashes of interest, influence, and motive were involved in the Petrine reforms that we must try to distinguish between indigenous and imported ideas, between that which was foreseen and that which was arrived at haphazardly. Indeed we shall not arrive at much understanding of these reforms by looking at some simple point in isolation. We should look at three parts of this problem, first, Peter's relations with the West, second, his attitude to medieval Russia, and third, his influence on the future. In fact this last point should not be surprising, since the work of a great man commonly survives him and is even carried on by others. We must therefore include in our judgement of Peter's reforms effects which only appeared after his death. The three parts of the problem we must look into are, then, how much Peter inherited from unreformed Russia, how much he borrowed from Western Europe, and what he left Russia, or more accurately, what happened to his work after his death.

Peter inherited from medieval Russia sovereign power of a peculiar sort, and an even stranger organisation of society. At the time of the accession of the new dynasty, the sovereign power was recognised as hereditary because of its proprietorial character. As soon as it lost this proprietorial character, it was left with neither definite juridical definition nor defined scope, and began to expand or contract according to the situation and character of the monarch. Peter inherited almost complete authority, and managed to extend it even further. He created the Senate, and by so doing rid himself of the pretensions which were associated with the Boyar Duma; by abolishing the Patriarchate he also eliminated both the risk of further Nikonian scandals and of the cramping effect of the exaggerated and unctuous respect which was accorded to the Patriarch of All the Russias.

At the same time, however, it is important to remember that Peter was the first monarch to give his unlimited power a moral and political definition. Before his reign the notion of the state was identified with the person of the Tsar, in the same way as in law the owner of a house is identified with the house. Peter made a distinction between the two ideas by insisting on two oaths, one to the State, and one to the Monarch. In his ukazes [proclamations of law] he repeatedly insisted that the interests of the state were supreme, and, by so doing, made the Monarch subordinate to the state. Thus the Emperor became the chief representative of the law and the guardian of general prosperity. Peter considered himself a servant of state and country, and wrote as an official would about his victory over the Swedes at Doberau: 'From the time I *began to serve*, I have never seen such firing and such discipline among our soldiers.' Indeed the expressions *interest of the state, public good*, and *useful to the whole nation*, appear in Russian legislation for the first time I think, in Peter's time.

None the less Peter was influenced unconsciously by historical traditions in the same way that he had been unconsciously influenced by instincts. Because he thought that his reforms were in the interest of state, and for the public good, he sacrificed his son to this supreme law. The tragic death of the Tsarevitch led to the Statute of February 5th, 1722, on the law of succession. This was the first law in the history of Russian legislation to have a constitutional character. It stated: 'We issue this Statute in order to empower the ruling sovereign to specify the person to whom he wishes the heritage to pass, and to charge that person according to his judgment.' The Statute, by way of justification recalls the example of the Grand Prince Ivan III who arbitrarily disposed of the succession, appointing first his grandson and then his son to succeed him. Before Peter there had been no law of succession, and its order had been decided by custom and circumstance alone. Under the old dynasty, which looked on the state as its patrimony (*votchina*) it was customary for the father to pass on the throne to his son 'by testament.' A new system of succession, election by the Sobor (the National Assembly) was introduced in 1598. By the seventeenth century the new dynasty did not look on the state as its patrimony, but, while the hereditary system fell into disuse, the elective system was not yet established; the new dynasty was recognised as hereditary for one generation only, and in 1613 the oath was taken to Michael Romanov and his children, but no farther. In the absence of an established system, the throne was occupied sometimes after an election by the Sobor, and sometimes by presenting the heir to the people in the Square at Moscow, as was done by Tsar Alexis with the Tsarevitch Theodore, or as happened when the rebellious Streltsy and an irregular Sobor established the Dual Monarchy of Tsars Peter and Ivan.

Peter replaced the hereditary and elective systems of succession with a system of 'personal nomination' coupled with the right to revoke; that is to say, he re-established succession by testament, legalised a situation for which no law existed, and retarded constitutional law by returning to the *votchina* system of succession. The Statute of February 5th, 1722, merely reiterated the words of Ivan III who said 'To whom I wish to him shall I give the rule.' Not only did Peter irresponsibly reproduce the past in his innovations, but he also let it influence his social legislation.

Peter did nothing to change the organisation of society which had been set up by the *Ulozhenie,* nor did he alter a division of classes which was based on obligations to the state, nor did he attack serfdom. On the contrary, the old system of class obligation was complicated by the imposition of further burdens. Peter made education compulsory for the nobility; he divided the civil service from the military; he organised the urban taxpayers into a compact group first under the administration of the *zemskie izby,* and then under the town councils; and he made the merchants of the guilds, the upper urban class not only pay their ordinary taxes but form companies to lease and run factories and workshops belonging to the state. In Petrine Russia factories and workshops were not privately owned, but were state enterprises administered by a merchant of the guild who was compelled to do so. Nevertheless there were compensations, for the merchants, manufacturers, and workshop superintendents were granted one of the privileges of the nobility, that of buying villages with serfs to work in the factory or workshop. Peter did not alter the nature of serfdom but did modify its structure: the many types of serfdom, each with a different legal and economic position, were combined, and one class of taxable serfs was the result. Some of the 'free idlers' were registered as inferior urban citizens, so that 'idlers shall take themselves to trade in order that nobody shall be without an occupation'; others were conscripted, or forced into bondage. Thus Peter, by abolishing the intermediate classes, continued the work of simplification started by the *Ulozhenie;* and his legislation forced the members of the intermediate classes into one or other of the main classes. It was in Peter's time that Russian society was organised in the fashion planned in seventeenth-century legislation; after Peter's reforms Russian society was divided into clearly defined classes, and every class was burdened with complicated and weighty duties. Peter's attitude to the political and social régime of old Russia... has now been made clear. He neither disturbed old foundations, nor built new ones, but altered existing arrangements by separating classes previously combined, or combining classes hitherto divided. Both society and the institutions of government were made more vigorous by these changes, and the state benefited from their greater activity.

What was Peter's attitude to Western Europe? He had inherited the precept 'Do everything after the example of foreign countries', that is to say Western European countries. This precept combines large doses of despondency, a lack of confidence in Russia's strength, and self-denial. How did Peter interpret this precept? What did he think of Russian relations with Western Europe? Did he see in Western Europe a model to imitate or a master who could be dismissed at the end of the lesson? Peter thought that the

biggest loss suffered by Muscovy in the seventeenth century had been the Baltic littoral, by which Russia was deprived of contact with the civilised nations of the West. Yet why did he want this contact? Peter has often been accused of being a blind and inveterate Westerner who admired everything foreign, not because it was better than the Russian, but because it was unlike anything Russian; and it was believed that he wanted rather to assimilate Russia to Western Europe than to make Russia resemble Western Europe. It is difficult to believe that as sensible a man as Peter was troubled by such fantasies....

What did Peter hope to gain from a rapprochement? Before answering this question, we must [consider] why Peter sent scores of young Russians to study abroad, and ask what type of foreigner he attracted to Russia. The young Russian was sent to study mathematics, the natural sciences, naval architecture, and navigation; the foreigners who came to Russia were officers, naval architects, sailors, artisans, mining engineers, and later on jurists and specialists in administration and finance. With their help Peter introduced into Russia useful technical knowledge and skills lacked by the Russians. Russia had no regular army: he created one. It had no fleet: he built one. It had no convenient maritime commercial outlet: with his army and navy he took the eastern littoral of the Baltic. Mining was barely developed, and manufacturing hardly existed, yet by Peter's death there were more than two hundred factories and workshops in the country. The establishment of industry depended on technical knowledge, so Peter founded a naval academy, and many schools of navigation, medicine, artillery and engineering, including some where Latin and mathematics were taught, as well as nearly fifty elementary schools in provincial and sub-provincial main towns. He even provided nearly fifty garrison schools for soldiers' children. There was insufficient revenue, so Peter more than trebled it. There was no rationally organised administration capable of managing this new and complicated business, so foreign experts were called on to help to create a new central administration.

The above is, of course, an incomplete account of Peter's achievements, but it does show what he hoped to do with the help of Western Europe. Peter called on Western Europe to work and train Russians in financial and administrative affairs, and in the technical sciences. He did not want to borrow the results of Western technique, but wanted to appropriate the skill and knowledge, and build industries on the Western European model. The intelligent Russian of the seventeenth century realised that it was essential to increase Russia's productive capacity, by exploiting the country's natural and virgin riches, in order that the increased requirements of the state might be more easily met. Peter shared this point of view, and gave effect to it as did nobody before or after him, and he is therefore unique in the history of Russia. In foreign policy he concentrated on solving the Baltic problem.

It would be difficult to assess the value of the many industries he introduced. The evidence of the increased wealth was not a higher standard of living, but increased revenue. All increased earnings were, in fact, used to pay for the war. Peter's intention had been general economic reform, but the only evidence of success was the improved financial position. When Pososhkov wrote to Peter in 1724 that 'it was a great and difficult business to enrich all the people', he was not explaining a theory but sadly stating what he, and many others, had observed to be fact. In Peter's time men worked not for themselves but for the state, and after working better and harder than their fathers, probably died a great deal poorer. Peter did not leave the state in debt for one kopeck, nor did he waste a working day at the expense of future generations. On the contrary, he left his descendants rich reserves to draw on. His superiority lies in the fact that he was a creditor of the future, not a debtor. We will pursue this point later when we discuss the results of his reform. Were we to draw up a balance sheet of Peter's activities, excluding those affecting Russia's security and international position, but including those affecting the people's welfare, we would find that his great economic ambitions (which were the basis for his reforms) failed in their purpose, and, in fact, their only success was financial.

Thus Peter took from the old Russia the absolute power, the law, and the class structure; from the West he borrowed the technical knowledge required to organise the army, the navy, the economy, and the government. Where then was the revolution which renewed or transformed the Russian way of life, which introduced not only new institutions, but new principles (whether they were good or bad, is for the moment, immaterial). Peter's contemporaries, however, thought that the reforms were revolutionary, and they communicated their opinion to their descendants. But the reforms did not stop the Russians from doing things in their own way, and it was not the innovations that agitated them so much as the methods Peter used. Some of the results of the reforms were only felt in the future, and their significance was certainly not understood by everyone, and contemporaries anyhow only knew the effect the reforms had on them. Some reactions, however, were immediate, and these Peter had to account for.

The reforms were influenced not only by Peter's personality, but by wars and internecine struggles. Although the war had caused Peter to introduce reforms, it had an adverse influence on their development and success, because they were effected in an atmosphere of confusion usually consequent on war. The difficulties and demands of war forced Peter do to everything hastily. The requirements of war imposed a nervous and feverish tempo on the reforms, and an unhealthily fast pace. Peter's military preoccupations did not leave him time for critical analysis of a situation or careful consideration of his orders and the conditions in which they would be carried out, He could not wait patiently for natural improvement; he required rapid action and immediate results; at every delay or difficulty he would goad the officials with the threats which he used so often that they lost their power. Indeed for any offence against the law, such as petitioning the Tsar without going through the proper authorities, or felling an oak, or even a spruce, or failing to appear at a nobleman's review, or buying or selling clothes of the old Russian pattern, Peter ordered confiscation of property, loss of civil rights, the knout, forced labour, the gallows, or physical and civil death. This extravaganza of punishments produced an increase in wrongdoing, or a general feeling of oppression and perplexity that resulted in neurasthenia. General-Admiral Apraxin, one of Peter's most eager collaborators, has vividly described this state of mind in a letter written in 1716 to Makarov, the Tsar's personal secretary: 'Verily, in all affairs we wander like blind men, not knowing what to do; everywhere there is great agitation, we do not know to whom to turn, or what to do about it for the future; there is no money anywhere, and everything will come to a stop.'

Moreover the reforms were evolved in the middle of bitter internal struggles, which often burst into violence; four terrible uprisings and three or four conspiracies were directed against Peter's innovations, and all appealed to people's feeling for antiquity, to the old prejudices and ideas. These troubles reinforced Peter's hostility to the old customs and habits which to him symbolised the prejudices and ideas of the past. The political education he had received was primarily responsible for this hostility. From his childhood he had witnessed the struggle which had divided Russian society from the beginning of the seventeenth century. On one side were the advocates of change who turned to the West for help, and on the other were the political and religious Old Believers. The beards and clothes of the Old Believers were symbols adopted expressly to distinguish them from the Western Europeans. In themselves these trivialiries of dress were no obstacle to reform, but the sentiments and convictions of their wearers were certainly an obstacle. Peter took the side of the innovators, and hotly opposed these trifling practices, as well as the ancient traditions that the Russian insisted on observing. The memories of childhood were responsible for the Tsar's excessive attention to these details. He associated these symbols with the risings of the Streltsy and the Old Believers. To him, the beard worn by an Old Believer was not a detail of masculine appearance, but, like the long-skirted coat, the mark of a political attitude, the spirit of opposition. He wanted to have clean-shaven subjects wearing foreign clothes, in the belief that this would help them to behave like Western Europeans.

When he returned to Moscow in 1698, on hearing of the rising of the Streltsy, one of the first things he did was to shave beards, cut the long coats of his entourage, and introduce wigs. It is hard to imagine the difficulties of legislation, and the uproar that was produced by this forcible transformation of costume and fashion. The clergy and the peasants, however, were not affected by these measures; they retained their class privilege of remaining orthodox and conservative. In January 1700, the order that, by next Shrovetide, everyone else was to appear in a Hungarian kaftan, was proclaimed with rolling drums in streets and squares. In 1701 a new ukaze was issued: men were to wear a jacket in the French or Saxon style, a waistcoat, breeches, gaiters, boots, and caps, in the German style; women were to wear bonnets, petticoats, skirts and shoes, in the German style. Censors of dress and beards were posted at the gates of towns, with instructions to fine the wearers of beards and illegal dress, which was to be torn to pieces. Noblemen who appeared at reviews with beards and moustaches were unmercifully beaten. The bearded Old Believers were compelled to wear special clothes, while their wives, though spared by nature from paying a fine on beards, had, because of their husbands' beards, to wear long robes and peaked bonnets. Merchants who sold old-fashioned clothes were knouted, had their property confiscated, and were sent to forced labour.

All this might be amusing if it were not so contemptible! It was the first time that Russian legislation abandoned its serious tone and concerned itself with trifles better left to hairdressers and tailors. These caprices aroused much hostility among the people. These petty annoyances explain the disproportion, which is so striking, between the sacrifices involved in Peter's internal reforms, and their actual achievements. Indeed it is astonishing to find the number of difficulties that had to be overcome to achieve even modest results. Even Peter's fervent admirer, Pososhkov, vigorously and appropriately described the difficulties Peter had to overcome, Peter who alone pulled the chariot of state up the hill, while millions pulled in the opposite direction. Another of Peter's admirers, one Nartov, a turner, wrote in his memoirs of everything 'that has been conceived against this monarch, what he underwent, and the hurt he suffered'. Peter went against the wind, and by his rapid motion increased the resistance he encountered. There were contradictions in his actions which he was unable to resolve, discordances which could not be harmonised.

As he grew older, and left his unruly youth behind him, he became more anxious than any other Tsar had been for the welfare of his people, and he directed the whole of his forceful energy to its improvement. His devotion attracted such intelligent men as Bishop Mitrophan, Nepluev, Pososhkov, and Nartov, who understood what it was that was driving Peter on, and who became his fervent admirers. Nartov, for instance, in calling Peter a god, added 'without fear we call him father; he has taught us truth and a noble fearlessness'.

Unfortunately Peter's methods alienated those indifferent to his reforms, and turned them into stubborn opponents. Peter used force, not example, and relied on mens' instincts, and not on their moral impulses. Governing his country from the post-chaise and stagehouse, he thought always of business, never of people, and, sure of his own power, he neglected to pay sufficient attention to the passive resistance of the masses. A reforming zeal and a faith in autocracy were Peter's two hands; unfortunately one hand paralysed the energy of the other. Peter thought that he could supplement the lack of proper resources by using power to urge people on, and aimed at the impossible. As a result the officials became so intimidated and inefficient that they lost their ability to do what they were normally quite capable of doing. As Peter, for all his zeal, was unable to use people's strength, so the people, in their state of inert and passive resistance, were unable to appreciate Peter's efforts.

Thus without exaggerating or belittling the work of Peter the Great, we can summarise it as follows: the reforms were brought on by the essential requirements of state and people; the need for reform was understood by an authoritative, intelligent, energetic, and talented individual, one of those who, for no apparent reason, appear from time to time. Further, he was gifted, and, animated by a sense of duty, was resolved 'not to spare his life in the service of his country'. When Peter came to the throne, Russia was not in an advantageous position compared with other European countries. Towards the end of the sixteenth century the Russians had created a great state, which was one of the largest in Europe; in the seventeenth century, however, it began to fail in moral and material strength. Peter's reforms did not aim directly at changing the political, social, or moral order, nor did they aim at forcing Russian life into an alien Western European pattern. The reforms only aimed at providing the Russian State and people with Western European intellectual and material resources, so that Russia might take its just position in Europe, and its people increase their productive capacity. But Peter had to do all this in a hurry, in the middle of a dangerous and bitter war, by using constraint at home; he had to struggle with the rapacity of his rascally officials, a gross landed nobility, and the prejudices and fears instilled by an ignorant clergy. The first reforms had been modest and limited, aimed only at reconstructing the army and developing the financial resources of the state; later, however, the reforms were the occasion for an obstinate battle which disturbed the existing pattern of living, and upset society. Started and carried through by the sovereign, the people's usual leader, the reforms were undertaken in conditions of upheaval, almost of revolution, not because of their objects but because of their methods, and by the impressions they made on the nerves and imaginations of the people. Perhaps it was more of a shock than a revolution, but the shock was the unforeseen and unintended consequence of the reforms.

Let us end by giving our opinion of Peter's reforms. The contradiction in his work, his errors, his hesitations, his obstinacy, his lack of judgement in civil affairs, his uncontrollable cruelty, and, on the other hand, his wholehearted love of his country, his stubborn devotion to his work, the broad, enlightened outlook he brought to bear on it, his daring plans conceived with creative genius and concluded with incomparable energy, and finally the success he achieved by the incredible sacrifices of his people and himself; all these different characteristics make it difficult to paint one painting.

Moreover they explain the diverse impression he made on people; he sometimes provoked unqualified admiration, sometimes unqualified hostility. Generally the criticism prevailed because even his good actions were accompanied by disgusting methods.

Peter's reforms were the occasion for a struggle between the despot and the people's inertia. The Tsar hoped to arouse the energies and initiative of a society subdued by serfdom with the menace of his power, and strove, with the help of the noblemen, the oppressors of serfs, to introduce into Russia the European sciences and education which were essential to social progress. He also wanted the serf, while remaining a serf, to act responsibly and freely. The conjunction of despotism and liberty, of civilisation and serfdom, was a paradox which was not resolved in the two centuries after Peter. It is true that Russians of the eighteenth century tried to reconcile the Petrine reforms with humanitarian instincts, and Prince Shcherbatov, who was opposed to autocracy, devoted a treatise to explaining and even justifying Peter's vices and arbitrary conduct. Shcherbatov recognised that the enlightment introduced into Russia by Peter benefited the country, and attacked Peter's critics on the grounds that they themselves had been the recipients of a culture, bestowed on them by the autocracy which permitted them to distinguish the evils inherent in the autocratic system. Peter's faith in the miraculous power of education, and his respect for scientific knowledge, inspired the servile with little understanding of the meaning of civilisation; this understanding grew slowly, and was eventually transformed into a desire for truth and liberty.

Autocracy as a political principle is in itself odious. Yet we can reconcile ourselves to the individual who exercises this unnatural power when he adds self-sacrifice to it, and, although an autocrat, devotes himself unsparingly to the public good, risking destruction even on difficulties caused by his own work. We reconcile ourselves in the same way to the impetuous showers of spring, which strip branches from the trees, but none the less refresh the air, and by their downpour bring on the growth of the new seed.

NO

Peter Brock Putnam

PETER: THE REVOLUTIONARY TSAR

When Peter interrupted his homecoming audience to shear off Generalissimo Shein's beard, he signaled the beginning of a revolution. His attack on beards was based on a radical new concept of the state. The absolute authority of the Tsar had been growing for centuries, and there was no institution or class that could oppose it, yet the power of the autocracy was limited. It was limited not by law, but by custom.

Custom played a major role in the life of the people. Over the years there had been many changes in Muscovy, but they had come about so gradually that it was easy to believe life was still going on in the same old way. There were wars, invasions, uprisings, plagues, and famines, but when they passed, the people went back to the customs of their ancestors. The Tsar could and did sponsor changes in institutions, but he seldom interfered in the private lives of his subjects, or, if he did, it was on the side of custom and against change.

There had been one notable exception to this rule. When Tsar Alexis had supported the reforms of the Patriarch Nikon, he attacked custom and sponsored change in the most sensitive area of Muscovite life—religion. When Peter began to shave his courtiers, he was, in a sense, renewing his father's battle with the Old Believers and affirming the Tsar's right to regulate the private life of the people. Beards were sacred. They had been given to men by God to distinguish them from the lower animals. "Nothing but the absolute authority of the Tsar," wrote John Perry, an English engineer in Peter's service, "could ever have prevailed with the Russes to have parted with their beards." Peter claimed such authority. "His Majesty is absolute monarch who need not answer for his acts to anyone in the world, but has power and authority as a Christian sovereign to govern his states and lands according to his will and his benevolent understanding." It was his benevolent understanding that beards were the sign of a backward Asiatic people, and it was his will to eliminate them.

Perry described the Voronezh workmen's reaction to the shaving. When he jokingly asked one of them what he had done with his beard, "he put his hand in his bosom and pulled it out, and showed it to me: further telling me,

From Peter Brock Putnam, *Peter: The Revolutionary Tsar* (Harper & Row, 1973). Copyright © 1973 by Peter Brock Putnam. Reprinted by permission of HarperCollins Publishers.

that when he came home, he would lay it up to have it put in his coffin and buried along with him, that he might be able to given an account of it to St. Nicholas when he came to the other world."

Peter tried to turn such superstition to his advantage by establishing a beard tax. It ranged from one sixth of a kopeck a year for a peasant to one hundred rubles a year for a rich merchant. As receipts for payment, they were issued bronze tokens to wear around their necks like dog licenses. Courtiers, officials, army officers, and soldiers were forced to shave, but the vast majority of merchants and peasants, and all monks and priests, kept their beards.

Peter used similar methods in ordering his people to give up their Muscovite costumes. Devout believers felt it would be sacrilege to worship in a Russian church dressed like a German heretic. The Tsar ordered all members of the court or persons in government service to wear western dress. He had samples of such clothes hung up on all the gates of the city of Moscow and commanded that all the inhabitants except common peasants should have their clothes made like them. Nobles and merchants entering the capital in their caftans either were fined or had their skirts cut off at the knees.

The Tsar's "revolution" had its limits. He lacked the practical power to force all the millions in his vast country to change their ways. Only courtiers or those in government service came within his effective reach. They obeyed him and in appearance at least, followed him into eighteenth-century Europe. Peasants, merchants, and churchmen remained in the Asiatic past.

Peter could argue that western clothes were more practical than flowing robes,

but convenience was not his sole object. Shaving was a nuisance, not a convenience. Peter disliked beards and caftans as remnants of the Mongol period. To make his people behave like Europeans, he wanted them to look like Europeans. His reasoning was naive, but the effect was valuable as a kind of discipline. The courtiers and officials he forced to shave were daily reminded of the Tsar's authority over them. They could not forget that they were wearing their new foreign clothes by his order. Their razored cheeks and western dress set them apart from the people and proclaimed them as the Tsar's men employed on the Tsar's business.

Peter's revolution was more radical for women than for men. His sister Natalia set the fashion of wearing western costume, but the change in the women's dress style was less important than the change in their life style. The Tsar who confined his own wife to a convent freed the wives of his nobles from the confinement of the terem. He ordered that "at all weddings and all other public entertainments, the women as well as the men should be invited... and that they should be entertained in the same room with the men, like as he had seen in foreign countries, and that the evening should be concluded with music and dancing."

* * *

... Peter had neither the time nor the temperament to thoroughly rebuild the antiquated machinery of the Muscovite state. Instead, he tinkered with it. He forged, welded, patched, and mended. He invented new parts or adapted old ones to new uses. He improvised as he went along, and his reforms often fell short of the mark. For example, he removed the collection of many taxes from his corrupt military governors and gave it to town councils elected by the merchants. This was a temporary improvement, but the merchants soon became nearly as corrupt as the military governors.

In the week before Lent, Peter arranged a perfect orgy of feasting to dedicate a new palace he had given Franz Lefort. On the dawn following the last night, he said good-bye to his favorite and drove away to Voronezh. In March, he had word that Lefort was seriously ill. He died before Peter could reach his side. Grief-stricken, the Tsar sobbed, "Now I am left without one friend I can trust!"

This was near the truth. As supreme autocrat, Peter could have no real friends, because he had no real equals; but Lefort had come close. He had shared Peter's enthusiasms and encouraged his ambitions. He was both honest and unselfish. All Peter's Russian favorites heaped up vast fortunes by corruption. Lefort lived in princely style, but he died nearly as poor as when he had come to Russia....

* * *

Peter was an enlightened despot fifty years before enlightened despotism came into vogue. He was enlightened in that he attacked ignorance, superstition, corruption, and conservatism. He introduced scientific education, rational administration, and modern industry. He emancipated women, subsidized printing, and expanded commerce. A humanitarian desire to improve the life of his people motivated one reform after another.

Yet he was often ruthlessly despotic in the demands he made on these people. He aimed at progress, but the tool that lay ready to his hand for achieving it was the tsarist autocracy he had inherited

from the past. That autocracy rested on serfdom, and the more ambitious his programs became, the heavier were the burdens on the serfs. In this sense, Peter's efforts to modernize Muscovy led not to freedom, but to slavery, not to progress, but to oppression.

The Northern War was a tremendous drain on manpower. From 1700 to 1709, more than 300,000 peasants were drafted into the army. The new mines, foundries, and factories required vast numbers of industrial serfs. Drafts of forced labor to work on Peter's expanding construction projects were even greater. Although the fortification of Azov and Taganrog began in 1696, it was still calling for 30,000 men a year ten years later. The repeated attempts to construct a Don-Volga canal consumed labor on the same scale. Workers in the Voronezh dockyards were regularly in short supply, and after the conquest of the Neva, Peter began building a fleet for the Baltic as well as for the Black Sea. The construction of St. Petersburg and Kronstadt was the most demanding of all.

Living and working conditions were appalling. Disease flourished in the Tsar's boomtowns. Malaria and other fevers lurked in the swamps of St. Petersburg. Its distance from the crop-producing regions made food scarce and expensive. Some historians have estimated that the building of the new capital cost half a million lives. Both soldiers and laborers escaped whenever they could. Nearly half of 15,000 dragoons stationed in Poland deserted. The number of Cossacks in the Ukraine and on the Don was swelled by thousands of fugitives from the army and labor forces.

To plug up this drain on his manpower, Peter tightened controls. Peasants were required to carry official identity cards or passports. Attempts to track down fugitives and deserters were intensified. When he disbanded the Streltsy, Peter turned over their police powers to the Preobrazhensky Guards, and the Office of the Preobrazhensky developed a secret section that was the first regularly organized secret police in Russia. Under Romodanovsky, it became an instrument of savage oppression.

The need for money produced a multitude of new taxes. Kurbatov and his "profit makers" devised taxes on births and marriages, caps and boots, baths and lodging houses, firewood, stovepipes, and even drinking water. In the long run, these produced little income, but they created enormous ill will. To former state monopolies like alcohol and potash were added tobacco, playing cards, chessmen, and oak coffins. Worst of all was the monopoly on salt. In 1705, salt was priced so high that it was put beyond the reach of many poor peasants, who sickened and died without it.

Peter was not the first Tsar to levy burdensome taxes, require forced labor, or wage an unpopular war; but he was the first to do so on such a large scale, and the first to make his role so clearly visible. Earlier rulers had been screened from view by Byzantine tradition. Behind the high walls of the Kremlin, the Tsar was a remote and shadowy figure. The peasants had a saying, "God is high, and the Tsar is far off." Cruelty and injustice were considered the work, not of the Tsar, but of wicked boyars and ministers....

* * *

Peter's detractors argue that every one of his innovations had a precedent in the reign of an earlier Tsar. Ivan the Terrible had established a printing press. Boris Godunov had sent nobles to study abroad. The Slavonic Greek–Latin Academy had been founded under Peter's half brother, Fyodor. Even in the creation of the Russian navy, Peter's father had pioneered the way. Brandt, the Dutch carpenter who taught Peter to sail, had been hired by Tsar Alexis to build a ship for the navigation of the Caspian. On the basis of such evidence, some historians argue that Russia was already on the road to westernization and would have come to it even without Peter.

But she would not have come to it so suddenly. Evolution is not the same as revolution. It was the pace, scope, and violence of Peter's reforms that made them revolutionary. Moreover, the revolution was personal. He not only sent others abroad, but went himself. He not only hired foreign shipwrights, but built ships with his own hands. Instead of merely importing a printing press, he learned to print and selected what was to be printed. He became the personal instrument and the embodiment of change.

He made giant strides in the field of education. He set up the Academy of Sciences. He founded schools of navigation, artillery, and engineering in the capital, and elementary or "cipher" schools in the provinces. He forced his nobles to study abroad. He established the first Russian newspaper. He redesigned the Russian alphabet to adapt it to movable type and saw to the translation and publication of western books. He impelled Russia from a manuscript culture toward a print culture, and after Peter, it could never again return to the intellectual climate of ancient Muscovy.

Except for his father's support of Nikon's reforms, earlier Tsars had interfered in the conduct of private life only on the side of custom. Peter admitted no such limits to his power. He prescribed new forms of behavior that defied hallowed traditions. Liberating upper-class women from the terem, he revolutionized marriage. He substituted a "German" for a Russian calendar. He told people where they must live and how they must construct their houses. He decreed their dress, their hair style, and even the use of their leisure hours. The image of the old Tsarism had been of a bearded and benevolent Byzantine patriarch, dignified and distant. The symbol of the new Russia was a clean-shaven and sharp-eyed "German" policeman, regulating and spying into everything. Under Peter, Russia's first regularly organized secret police stamped political life with a character that endures to this day.

The police state regulated commerce as well as custom. During Peter's reign, foreign trade quadrupled, but this increased owed less to his mercantile policy than to his military conquest of ports like Riga, where a thriving commerce already existed. Peter managed to expand the trade of St. Petersburg only by ruining that of Archangel, and he never secured a significant share of that trade for native merchants. During his life and long afterward, western nations dominated trade with Russia as thoroughly as if she had been an overseas colony, exchanging raw materials for the finished goods she could not manufacture for herself.

The great exception to Russian dependence on the west was military. Peter saw clearly that unless he could modernize his arms production, Russia would remain a second-class nation. Earlier Tsars had opened iron mines, powder mills, and gun foundries, but Peter manufactured armament on a huge scale. In a single generation, his heavy industry outstripped that of far more advanced nations. His methods were despotic. The

thousands of forced laborers drafted into his mines and factories were little better than industrial slaves, but iron production soared to more than three times that of England and helped to raise Russia to the rank of a great power.

To mobilize the resources of a primitive economy, Peter built on the achievements of his predecessors. The abolition of the Patriarchate and substitution of the Holy Synod institutionalized the state control of the church won by his father. The soul tax was an intensification of the serfdom that had been growing and spreading for centuries. The Table of Ranks was the final and logical step in a long evolution of state service. Yet the combination and culmination of these trends created a new kind of state that bound all classes to lifelong service and made all privileges dependent on such service.

Such a state required a powerful leader at its center. In the dynastic confusion that followed Peter's death, no fewer than seven monarchs ascended the throne in thirty-seven years. Four of them were women, whose rule was grudgingly accepted in a patriarchy. Of the three males, two were minors and the third was mentally unbalanced.

Peter's immediate successor was his wife, Catherine, the first Russian Empress. Two years later, her death brought to the throne Peter's grandson, the twelve-year-old son of Alexis, Peter II. In 1730, he was followed by Anna, the daughter of Peter's half brother Ivan V. In 1740, the infant great-grandson of this same Ivan—Anna's grandnephew—was proclaimed Ivan VI. A year later, he was deposed by Peter's daughter, who became Empress Elizabeth. After her death in 1762, another Peter, the unstable son of Peter's daughter Anna, reigned briefly as Peter III, but was soon murdered with the probable connivance of his German wife, who succeeded him as Catherine II, later called Catherine the Great.

During these shifts and seizures, the Guards became like the Streltsy of Peter's youth, the essential power base for the throne. To court their favor, successive monarchs granted special privileges to the nobles, whose class the Guards represented. In 1762, the nobles won total emancipation from the service forced on them by the Table of Ranks, but retained their rights over the serfs in full force.

Peter's program of westernization had deepened the division he found in the Russian people. The emancipation of the nobles from state service split the nation in two. The aristocracy, the army, and the bureaucracy became increasingly European. The peasantry, the clergy, and the merchant class lived in the Muscovite way. The privileged ruling class shaved and dressed in the western style, built German or Italian villas landscaped with English gardens, and spoke French in preference to Russian. The bearded mass of the peasantry, groaning under a serfdom that became progressively harsher through the century, was a separate and oppressed people. Even before the Napoleonic invasion of 1812, they seemed to have been conquered and enslaved by a western army of occupation.

The intelligentsia reflected this division in the Russian people. The pro-western faction was ashamed of Russian backwardness and held that the only remedy was further westernization. They were opposed by the Slavophiles, who argued that westernization had alienated Holy Russia from her spiritual and cultural roots. Salvation lay not in the science and reason of the west, but in the purity and piety of Greek Orthodoxy. The star of the third Rome must rise in the east.

Westernizers glorified Peter, and Slavophiles condemned him; but his vision was broader than either group recognized. He had gone to school in the west to make war on the west, but his goals were not exclusively western. He fought on the Caspian Sea as well as the Baltic. He sent embassies and expeditions into Persia, central Asia, and China as well as to Europe. He ordered two frigates to Madagascar by way of the Cape of Good Hope and dreamed of a maritime commerce with India. He commissioned Vitus Bering on the Alaskan exploration that opened North America to Russian colonization. The global grandeur of his schemes was worthy of the Emperor of a third Rome.

He attempted far more than he could achieve in a lifetime. At his death, the Ladoga Canal was only half built. The new government buildings and the Academy of Sciences were barely begun. The dockyards at Voronezh and the abandoned Don-Volga canal were already crumbling in neglect. Peter had tried to do too much too fast. He was an impetus to the future, rather than its architect. He was forever making new beginnings in the hope that time would bring them to completion.

He expressed the essence of this hope in refuting critics of the Academy of Sciences who argued that such an academy was premature until there was an adequate school system to provide it with students. Peter countered with a homely parable, in which he likened himself to a farmer with a crop of wheat to grind: "But I have no mill, and there is not enough water close by to build a water mill. But there is water enough at a distance, only I shall have no time to make a canal, for the length of my life is uncertain, and, therefore, I am building the mill first and have only given orders for the canal to be begun, which will the better force my successors to bring water to the completed mill."

In this instance, his optimism proved justified. Within a few years, the Academy of Sciences was nurturing the genius of the great mathematician, philosopher, and historian, Mikhail Lomonosov. Yet, in many instances, Peter's attempt to "force my successors to bring water to the completed mill" imposed a terrible burden.

The very magnitude of his ambition may have been Peter's greatest defect. Undertaking the superhuman, he became less than humane. He was so dazzled by his hopes for the future that he was blind to their present cost. The imagined beauty of St. Petersburg was more real to him than the sufferings of tens of thousands who lost their lives in building it. His programs of construction caused nearly as much human misery as the devastation of his wars.

Peter was a living paradox, a builder and a destroyer, a visionary and a pragmatist, a genius and a buffoon. He was both flexible and adamant, frugal and prodigal, patient and passionate, magnanimous and merciless, self-sacrificing and self-centered. He went from one extreme to the other, a giant of a man with appetites, endowments, and ambitions to match. "God has made the rivers to flow in one way," argued a conservative boyar who opposed the Don-Volga canal, "and it is presumption in man to think to turn them another." Peter's greatness was flawed by a thoroughly Promethean presumption. In the Greek myth, Zeus punished Prometheus, but allowed mankind to keep the fire he had stolen from Heaven. The Russian Prometheus went unpunished, while the vengeance of history fell on those he had meant to elevate. It was the Russian people who paid the price for the flaw in Peter's greatness.

POSTSCRIPT

Did Peter the Great Exert a Positive Influence on the Development of Russia?

Before the breakup of the USSR, historians within the Soviet Union displayed an ambivalent attitude toward Peter the Great. Initially, they denounced Peter (along with all the other czars of the Romanov dynasty) particularly because of his harsh treatment of the Russian peasantry. By the time Stalin assumed power in 1929, however, the official view of Peter's regime had softened. Stalin found much to admire in the way Peter had marshaled Russia's resources and in the way the czar had sought to compete with the western European powers. Peter's reforms, Stalin decided, represented "a singular attempt to jump out of our country's framework of backwardness." Stalin added, however, that Peter ultimately did not achieve his goals because he failed to understand that "the centuries-old backwardness of our country can be liquidated only on the basis of a successful building of socialism."

Soviet historians who feared Stalin's wrath often compared Peter to Stalin, but always to the detriment of the czar. On the other hand, critics of the Soviet regime in the post-Stalin era, including Alexander Solzhenitsyn and Alexander Yanov, denounced Peter for providing such an excellent model of autocratic repression for Russia's communist rulers.

Biographies of Peter from Western historians include Robert Massie's lengthy *Peter the Great: His Life and World* (Alfred A. Knopf, 1980) and B. H. Sumner's *Peter the Great and the Emergence of Russia* (Collier Books, 1965). Those who wish to take a broader view of the topic should consult the magisterial study *Russia Under the Old Regime* by Richard Pipes (Scribner's, 1974).

CONTRIBUTORS
TO THIS VOLUME

EDITORS

JOSEPH R. MITCHELL is a history instructor at Howard Community College in Columbia, Maryland, and an educational consultant for *U.S. News and World Report*. He is also an educational consultant for Summer Productions (educational programmers for the Discovery Channel and the Learning Channel). He received an M.A. in history from Loyola University and an M.A. in African American history from Morgan State University.

HELEN BUSS MITCHELL is a professor of philosophy and director of the women's studies program at Howard Community College in Columbia, Maryland. She is the author of *Roots of Wisdom: Speaking the Language of Philosophy* (Wadsworth, 1996) and *Roots of World Wisdom: A Multicultural Reader* (Wadsworth, 1997). She has received numerous degrees, including a Ph.D. in women's history from the University of Maryland.

WILLIAM K. KLINGAMAN is an instructor at the University of Maryland in Baltimore County. He is the author of many publications, including *1929: The Year of the Great Crash* (Harper & Row, 1989); *The First Century: Emperors, Gods, and Everyman* (HarperCollins, 1991); and *Encyclopedia of the McCarthy Era* (Facts on File, 1996). He received an M.S. and a Ph.D. in history from the University of Virginia.

R. K. McCASLIN is a teacher at the Maryland public schools in Howard County. He also teaches Scottish history under the aegis of the St. Andrew's Society of Maryland. He has published many articles on Scottish history, and he has a B.A. and an M.A. in history from the University of Maryland.

STAFF

David Dean   List Manager
David Brackley   Developmental Editor
Ava Suntoke   Developmental Editor
Tammy Ward   Administrative Assistant
Brenda S. Filley   Production Manager
Juliana Arbo   Typesetting Supervisor
Diane Barker   Proofreader
Lara Johnson   Graphics
Richard Tietjen   Publishing Systems Manager

AUTHORS

RICHARD E. W. ADAMS is a professor of anthropology at the University of Texas at San Antonio. He is also director of the Rio Azul Archeological Project.

MONIQUE ALEXANDRE is a professor at the University of Paris IV-Sorbonne, where her research is concentrated on Hellenistic Judaism and Greek patristics. She is the author of *The Beginning of the Book of Genesis 1–5: The Greek Version of the Septuagint and Its Reception* (in French) (Beauchesne, 1988).

KAREN ARMSTRONG teaches at the Leo Baeck College for the Study of Judaism and the Training of Rabbis and Teachers in London, England. An honorary member of the Association of Muslim Social Sciences, her published works include *Through the Narrow Gate* (St. Martin's Press, 1981); *Beginning the World* (St. Martin's Press, 1983); and *Holy War* (Macmillan, 1988).

KATHRYN A. BARD is an assistant professor of archaeology at Boston University. She received her Ph.D. in Egyptian archaeology from the University of Toronto.

MARY R. BEARD (1876–1958), the founder of the World Center for Women Archives, was a leading suffragist and participant in the labor movement. She coauthored with her husband Charles many works in American history, and she is the author of *A Short History of the American Labor Movement* (Greenwood Press, 1924).

MARTIN BERNAL is a professor of government at Cornell University in Ithaca, New York.

MARCUS BULL is a lecturer in medieval history at the University of Bristol in England. He is the author of *Knightly Piety and the Lay Response to the First Crusade* (Oxford University Press, 1993).

REBECCA L. CANN is an associate professor of genetics and molecular biology in the John A. Burns School of Medicine at the University of Hawaii at Manoa. She received her Ph.D. in anthropology from the University of California, Berkeley.

OWEN CHADWICK was Regius Professor of Modern History at Cambridge University from 1968 to 1983 and vice chancellor of Cambridge University from 1969 to 1971, and he has been chancellor of the University of East Anglia since 1985. He has written many books, including *The Victorian Church*, 2 vols. (Oxford University Press, 1966–1971); *The Popes and European Revolution* (Oxford University Press, 1981), for which he was awarded the Wolfson Prize for History; and *Michael Ramsey: A Life* (Oxford University Press, 1990).

JOHN E. COLEMAN is a professor of classics at Cornell University in Ithaca, New York.

ARTHUR COTTERELL is an English historian specializing in Asian civilizations. His works include *The Early Civilization of China* (Putnam, 1975) and *Chinese Civilization from the Ming Revival to Chairman Mao* (Weidenfeld & Nicholson, 1977), both coauthored with Yong Yap.

GEORGE L. COWGILL is a professor of anthropology at the University of Arizona. He is coeditor, with Norman Yoffee, of *The Collapse of Ancient States and Civilizations* (University of Arizona Press, 1988).

CLINTON CRAWFORD is an assistant professor in the Department of Literature, Communication and Philosophy at Medgar Evers College, City University of New York. His field of specialization is African arts and languages as communication systems.

JOSEPH DAHMUS was a professor of medieval history at Pennsylvania State University. He is the author of many books, including *Seven Decisive Battles of the Middle Ages* (Nelson-Hall, 1983).

BASIL DAVIDSON is considered one of the founding fathers of the movement to rediscover African history. Beginning his career as an English journalist in Africa, he has since written many acclaimed histories of the continent as well as the excellent television documentary series *Africa*.

ARTHER FERRILL is a professor of history at the University of Washington. He is the author of *The Origins of War: From the Stone Age to Alexander the Great* (Westview Press, 1997).

PETER GAUNT, a former president of the Cromwell Association, is a senior lecturer in history at the Chester College of Higher Education in England. He is the author of *A Nation Under Siege: The Civil War in Wales* (HMSO, 1991). His principal research interests are early modern British history, especially the military and political history of the 1640s and 1650s, and British landscape history.

CHARLES HOMER HASKINS (1870–1937) was a history professor and dean of the Graduate School of Arts and Sciences at Harvard University. He is the author of *Studies in the History of Mediaeval Science* (Harvard University Press, 1927).

S. M. IKRAM has been a member of the Pakistani Civil Service and a visiting professor of international affairs at Columbia University. He is the author of *Charles Grant and British Rule in India* and coeditor of *Approaches to Asian Civilization*.

MARIUS B. JANSEN received his Ph.D. from Harvard University. After teaching at the University of Washington from 1950 to 1959, he became director of the East Asian studies program at Princeton University, where he subsequently served as chairman of the Department of East Asian Studies. He is the author of numerous works on modern Japanese history and Sino-Japanese relations, and he is coeditor, with John W. Hall, of *Studies in the Institutional History of Early Modern Japan* (Princeton University Press, 1968).

SOLOMON KATZ is a professor at the University of Washington.

JOAN KELLY-GADOL (1928–1982) was a Renaissance scholar and theorist in women's history. Her works include *Leon Battista Alberti: Universal Man of the Early Renaissance* (University of Chicago Press, 1969).

VASILI KLYUCHEVSKY (d. 1911) held the chair of history at the University of Moscow from 1879 until his death. His five-volume *History of Russia* remains a classic work, the best and most penetrating large-scale history of that nation to date.

KENNETH SCOTT LATOURETTE has held the position of Sterling Professor of Missions and Oriental History and has been a fellow of Berkeley College at Yale University. Well known for his work on the history of East Asia, he is the author of the monumental *History of Christianity* (HarperSanFrancisco, 1975).

MILTON W. MEYER is a professor emeritus of history at California State University at Los Angeles. He has written extensively on Asian history, and his works include *Asia: A Concise History* (Bowman & Littlefield, 1997) and *History of the Far East* (Barnes & Noble, 1972).

JOHN MORRILL is vice-master and reader in early modern history for Selwyn College at the University of Cambridge and president of the Cromwell Association.

MEHDI NAKOSTEEN is a contributor to *Encyclopedia Britannica* and a former professor of history and philosophy of education at the University of Colorado. He received his Ph.D. from Cornell University. He has written several books and articles on education, including *The History and Philosophy of Education* (Ronald Press, 1965).

PETER BROCK PUTNAM received his Ph.D. from Princeton University, where he later served as a lecturer in history. He has written a number of studies on Russian history.

KEVIN REILLY is the author of *The West and the World: A Topical History of Civilization* (Harper & Row, 1980), and he has been an associate with Somerset County College.

JADUNATH SARKAR, an honorary member of the Royal Asiatic Society of Great Britain, is the author of many books on Indian history, including *Fall of the Mughal Empire*, 4 vols. (AMS Press, 1972) and *A Short History of Aurangzib*.

T'ANG HSIAO-WEN is a Chinese scholar whose essay in Li Yu-ning, ed., *The First Emperor of China* appeared in 1974 as part of the Communist regime's reevaluation of early Chinese history.

PAOLO EMILIO TAVIANI is Italy's foremost scholar on Christopher Columbus and a member of the Italian Senate. He is well known in Italy for his scholarly biographies.

ALAN G. THORNE is head of the Department of Prehistory for the Institute of Advanced Studies at the Australian National University. He previously taught human anatomy at the University of Sydney.

HUGH TREVOR-ROPER is an esteemed and prolific English historian who has written for a variety of presses and periodicals. He has also served as Regius Professor of Modern History at Oxford University and as director of Times Newspapers, Ltd.

ALLAN C. WILSON (d. 1991) was a professor of biochemistry at the University of California, Berkeley. He also worked at the Weizmann Institute of Science, the University of Nairobi, and Harvard University. He pioneered the use of DNA in establishing the roots of human origins.

MILFORD H. WOLPOFF is a professor of anthropology at the University of Michigan at Ann Arbor. He coauthored with Rachel Caspari *Race and Human Evolution: A Fatal Attraction* (Simon & Schuster, 1997).

INDEX

Adam, as universal male ancestor, 11
Adams, Richard E. W., on collapse of the Mayan civilization, 162–168
Adrianople, Battle of, 103
Aeschylus, 25
Africa: controversy over, as source of ancient Greek civilization, 44–59; controversy over, as origin of Egyptian civilization, 24–40; controversy over, as site of origin for *Homo sapiens*, 4–20
agriculture: as cause of collapse of the Mayan civilization, 162–168; in the Middle Ages, 184
Agrippa, Henry C., 206
Alaric, 113, 114
Alcuin, 123, 126, 134
Alexandre, Monique, on early Christian women, 82–89
Alfred the Great, 129
Anabaptism, 238
Angles, 129, 188
Aquinas, Saint Thomas, 96–97, 215
aristocracy: of India's Mughal Empire, 303–304; in the Mayan civilization, 162, 164, 166
Aristotle, 25, 153
Armstrong, Karen, on early Christian women, 90–97
art, in ancient Egypt, 36–38
Ashikaga period, in Japan, 262
Astour, Michael, 57, 58
Attila the Hun, 115–116
Augustine, Saint, 95–96
Aurangzeb, controversy over rule of Indian emperor, 298–316
autocracy, and controversy over Peter the Great, 320–336
Avar people, 131
Avicenna, 150

barbarians: and controversy over the Dark Ages, 120–137; and the decline of the Roman Empire, 109–116
Bard, Kathryn A., on the origins of Eqyptian civilization, 33–40
Basque people, 131
Baxter, Richard, 289, 290
Beard, Mary R., on women and the Renaissance, 202–208
beard tax, in tsarist Russia, 330–331
ben-Jochannan, Yosef, 25, 26–28, 30, 31–32
Beijing Man, 10
Bernal, Martin, 30–31, 32, 34, 52, 53, 54; on the origins of Greek civilization, 44–51
Bible, women in, 84–86

blacks: and controversy over the origins of Greek civilization, 44–59; controversy over the origins of Egyptian civilization, 24–40
blood prices, 123–124
Boccaccio, 206
Boetius, 153
Broad Aryan Model, Bernal's, 46, 48, 49–50, 55, 57
Brunson, James, 25, 30
Bulstrode, Sir Richard, 274–275
Bull, Marcus, on the Crusades, 192–198
Burgundians, 125
Bury, J. B., 44–45, 110
Byzantine Empire, 102, 109, 113, 125, 127, 128, 130, 135, 181, 195, 197, 198

Calvinism, controversy over influence of, on democracy in Europe, 238–246. *See also* Christianity
Cann, Rebecca L., on Africa as site of origin for *Homo sapiens,* 4–11
Carter, Howard, 38
Castiglione, Baldassare, 212–213, 214
Catherine the Great, 335
Cavalli-Sforza, Luigi, 10, 11
central authority: disintegration of, and the decline of the Roman Empire, 125; in India's Mughal Empire, 303–304
Chadwick, Owen, on Calvinism, 243–246
chansons de geste, 190
Charlemagne, 123, 125, 126, 129–137, 153, 184
Chaucer, 153
China, controversy over Ch'in dynasty of, 64–78, 254
Christianity, 212, 267; Columbus and, 222–223; controversy over women of early, 82–97. *See also* Crusades; Protestantism
Cistercian monks, 187–188, 189
climate change, and the decline of the Roman Empire, 104–105
Coleman, John E., on the origins of Greek civilization, 52–59
Columbus, Christopher, controversy over, as hero, 220–234
common-sense knowledge, in Muslim education, 148
Confucianism: Ch'in dynasty and, 72–78; in Japan, 253–254, 258, 260, 265
Congregationalists, 241
Constantine, Roman emperor, 102
Cotterell, Arthur, on the Ch'in dynasty of China, 64–71
courtly love, 211–215

Cowgill, George L., on collapse of the Mayan civilization, 169–175

craniometry, physical anthropology and, 28–29, 32, 35

Crawford, Clinton, on the origins of Egyptian civilization, 24–32

Cromwell, Oliver, 241; controversy over, 272–294

Crusades, 128; controversy over, 180–198; and controversy over the Dark Ages, 120–137

cultural factors, as cause of collapse of the Mayan civilization, 162–168

cuneiform writing, 54, 56

Dahmus, Joseph, on the Dark Ages, 129–137

daimyo, Japan's, 255, 257, 263–264

Dark Ages, controversy over ninth century as end of, 120–137

Davidson, Basil, 25, 30; on Christopher Columbus, 229–234

de Pisan, Christine, 207–208

deaconesses, in early Christianity, 87–89

democracy, in Europe, controversy over influence of Calvinism on, 238–246

demographic factors, as cause of collapse of the Mayan civilization, 162–168

Denon, Baron, 24–25, 31

Diet of Worms, 238

Diocletian, Roman emperor, 102

Diodorus of Sicily, 25–26, 49

Diop, Chekh Anta, 25, 26, 28–30, 31–32

disease, as cause of collapse of the Mayan civilization, 162–168

DNA, mitochondrial, and controversy over Africa as site of origin for Homo sapiens, 4–20

Dore, Ronald, 258, 259

dress codes, in tsarist Russia, 326–327, 330–331

East India Company, 266, 311

economic issues, Aurangzeb and, 298–299

education: and controversy over Muslim education as source of universities, 144–158; in the Middle Ages, 202–208; and Tokugawa Japan, 252, 257–260;

Egypt, ancient, controversy over Africa as source of civilization of, 24–40

Einhard, 130, 131, 132

Eliezar, Rabbi, 83–84

Enlightenment, 45, 56, 180–181

environmental factors, controversy over, as cause of collapse of the Mayan civilization, 162–175

Erik the Red, 127

Euclid, 153

Europe, democracy in, controversy over influence of Calvinism on, 238–246

Evans, Sir Arthur, 57

Eve, as universal female ancestor, and controversy over Africa as site of origin for Homo sapiens, 4–20

evolution, and controversy over Africa as site of origin for Homo sapiens, 4–20

Extreme Aryan Model, Bernal's, 46, 50, 57

Ferrill, Arther, on the decline of the Roman Empire, 109–116

feudalism, 125, 183, 185, 211, 213, 215; controversy over Tokugawa Japan and, 250–267

Filioque clause, of the Nicene creed, 132

Firth, C. H., 285, 286

Flavius Josephus, 82, 83, 84

fossils, and controversy over Africa as site of origin for Homo sapiens, 4–20

Franks, 120, 121, 129, 196. See also Charlemagne

French, Marilyn, 97

Friedan, Betty, 97

Frobenius, 25

Gauls, 120

Gaunt, Peter, on Oliver Cromwell, 272–282

genes, and controversy over Africa as site of origin for Homo sapiens, 4–20

Gibbon, Edward, 102, 103, 108, 109, 110, 180, 181, 182, 189, 190

Gloger's law, 28

Godunov, Boris, 333

Gonzaga, Gian Francesco, 204

Gordon, Cyrus, 57, 58

Goths, 123

Gracchi, 107

Greece, ancient, controversy over origins of, 44–59

Guibert of Nogent, 192–193

Hadrian, 84

Hammond, Robert, 281

Han dynasty, China's, 254

Haskins, Charles Homer, on the roots of the modern university, 152–158

Hastings, Battle of, 196

hero, controversy over Christopher Columbus as, 220–234

Herodotus, 25, 26, 45, 57, 232

Hesiod, 54, 55

Hinduism, in India, 310–311

Hippolytus of Rome, 87

Homer, 55

Homo sapiens, controversy over Africa as site of origin for, 4–20

Hu Shih, 251, 261

Hundred Regulations of 1742, Japan's, 265

Huns, 112, 115–116, 121

Hyksos people, 48, 49, 52–53, 54, 58

Ikram, S. M., on Indian emperor Aurangzeb, 309–316

Imperial Declaration of 1868, Japan's, 250

imperialism, controversy over Crusades as Western, 180–198

inconsequential mutations, evolution and, 6
India, controversy over influence of Aurangzeb's rule on, 298–316
intellectual aspects, in the decline of the Roman Empire, 107–108
intuitive knowledge, in Muslim education, 148
Islam: Aurangzeb and, 309–311; controversy over Muslim education as source of universities and, 144–158. *See also* Crusades
isolationism, in Tokugawa Japan, 265–266
Ivan the Terrible, 333

Jansen, Marius B., on Tokugawa Japan, 250–261
Japan, controversy over influence of Tokugawa shogunate on, 250–267
Java Man, 10, 15–16
Jerome, Saint, 93–96
Jesus Christ, 84–86, 90
John, Saint, 85, 86
Jones, A. H. M., 110, 111
Judaism: and women in the Christian era, 82–90. *See also* Semitic culture

Katz, Solomon, on the decline of the Roman Empire, 102–108
Kelly-Gadol, Joan, on women and the Renaissance, 209–215
Klyuchevsky, Vasili, on Peter the Great, 320–329
knighthood, 125, 186, 189. *See also* Crusades; feudalism
Kush culture, in ancient Egypt, 39–40

Lancelot, 212
languages, of ancient Egypt, 34–35
Latourette, Kenneth Scott, on Calvinism, 238–242
Leakey, Louis, 28
Leger, Saint, 122–123
leprosy, 190
Lepsius, 29–30
Locke, John, 242
Lombards, 129, 130, 133, 135
love, and the medieval lady, 211–215
Lowe, John, 163, 164
Lucan the Greek, 25
Luke, Saint, 84
Luther, Martin, 238, 239, 240

MacArthur, Douglas, 251
MacIver, Thomson and Randall, 29
madrasahs, Muslim education and, 145
Magyars, 129, 183, 195
Maidstone, John, 274, 288
Malatesta, Paolo, 204–205
Manetho, 52
Marcus Aurelius, 105, 106, 112
marriage, in the Middle Ages, 202
Martel, Charles, 183
Mary Magdalene, 85, 88
Mary, mother of Jesus, 84–85, 86

Massoulard, Emile, 28–29
maternal lineage, and controversy over Africa as site of origin for *Homo sapiens*, 4–20
Matthew, Saint, 84
Mayan civilization, controversy over causes of collapse of, 162–175
Meiji period, Japan's, 251, 260, 261
melanin, use of, in physical anthropology, 29, 32
Mencius, 73, 252
Meng T'ien, 67–68, 69
Meyer, Milton W., on Tokugawa Japan, 262–267
Middle Ages, 111, 152, 222, 230–231, 240; and controversy over Peter the Great, 320–329; universities of, 152–159. *See also* Crusades; Renaissance
military issues: in the decline of the Roman Empire, 109–116; in collapse of the Mayan civilization, 165, 169–175
Minoan civilization, 53, 54, 56–57
mitochondrial DNA, and controversy over Africa as site of origin for *Homo sapiens*, 4–20
molecular clocks, and controversy over Africa as site of origin for *Homo sapiens*, 6
monasticism, in the Middle Ages, 183, 187
morality, of India's Mughal aristocracy, 303–304
Morrill, John, on Oliver Cromwell, 283–294
Moslem Empire, 126, 127, 128, 131
Mughal Empire, controversy over influence of Aurangzeb's rule on, 298–316
multiregional evolution model, for humans, 10–11, 12–20
Mycenaean civilization, 52, 53, 54, 55, 58

Nakosteen, Mehdi, on the roots of the modern university, 144–151
nationalism, and Tokugawa Japan, 252, 253–257
Neanderthal people, 11, 15, 16–17
Nei, Masatoshi, 10
New World, and controversy over Columbus as a hero, 220–234
Nicene Creed, 132
Nizam-al-Mulk, and Muslim education, 145–147
Nizamiyyas, Muslim education and, 145, 146–147
Noah's ark model, of evolution, 13
Nobunaga, Oda, 262, 263
Normans, 185, 187, 189, 190
Northern War, Russia and, 332
Nubia, 36–39

Old Believers, in Russia, 326–327, 330
original sin, 92
osteologic measurements, in physical anthropology, 29–30, 32
Ostrogoths, 112

parsimony principle, 7
Parsons, J. R., 171
paternal lineage, human evolution and, 11
Paul, Saint, 90

Paula, Saint, 93
Perry, John, 330
Perry, Matthew, 254
Peter the Great, controversy over, 320–336
Petrarch, 206, 207
Petrie, Sir Flinders, 33
Phoenicia, 45, 64, 48
Piganiol, Andre, 110
pilgrimage, First Crusade as, 192–198
piracy, Vikings and, 125–128
Pliny, 88
ploughs, in the Middle Ages, 184, 189
Plutarch, 45, 49, 55
poetry, of Indian emperor Aurangzeb, 312–313
political issues: Christianity and, 240–242; and
    controversy over Oliver Cromwell, 272–294; in
    the decline of the Roman Empire, 106–107
polymerase chain reaction, 8–9
Pope, Geoffrey G., 14
Prayer, David W., 17
priesthood of all believers, Protestantism and, 238
prophetesses, in early Christianity, 86
Protestantism. See Calvinism; Christianity
Portsch, Reiner, 17
psychological aspects, in the decline of the Roman
    Empire, 107–108
Ptolemy, 153
Puritan Revolution, and controversy over Oliver
    Cromwell, 272–294
Putnam, Peter Brock, on Peter the Great, 330–336

Quakers, 241

race suicide, and the decline of the Roman
    Empire, 105
racial issues. See blacks; slavery
Radagaisus, 114
Raleigh, Sir Walter, 276, 287–288
Ramapithecus, 5
Reformation, Protestant, 180, 239, 245
Reilly, Kevin, on the Dark Ages, 120–128
Reisner, George, 35, 39
religion: during the Dark Ages, 135–137; Oliver
    Cromwell and, 279–282. See also Christianity;
    Confucianism; Crusades; Islam; Judaism;
    Protestantism
Renaissance, 222, 228; controversy over women's
    role in, 202–215
Revett, Nicholas, 56
Ricci, Matteo, 70
Robertson, Wilham, 182
Robert I of Normandy, Duke, 196–197
Robert the Monk, 192, 193
Romanesque architecture, 136
Romanticism, 45
Rome, ancient, 121–122, 123, 202; controversy
    over causes of the decline of, 102–116
Romulus Augustulus, 111
Rus people, 126–127

Russia, and controversy over Peter the Great,
    320–336
Ryōma, Sakamoto, 259

Sadatake, Tse, 253
Saladin, 181
Salic Code, 122
salvation by faith, Protestantism and, 238, 239
Salvien, 121–122
samurai, Japanese, 256, 258
Saracens, 129, 135, 183
Sarich, Vincent M., 5, 9
Sarkar, Jadunath, on Indian emperor Aurangzeb,
    298–308
Saxons, 121, 129, 131, 188
Schliemann, Heinrich, 56
Schwartz, Benjamin, 254
scientific knowledge, in Muslim education, 148
Semitic culture, controversy over, as source of
    ancient Greek civilization, 44–59
Seneca, 243
serfs, Russian, 323, 332
sexuality, Renaissance women and, 209–215
Shalom Ima, 83–84
Shi'ite Muslims, 146, 148
Shimkin, Demitri, 166
Shintarō, Nakooka, 255
shoguns, controversy over influence of Tokugawa,
    in Japan, 250–267
Simon, Thomas, 275
Sivapithecus, 5–6
slavery: in ancient China, 76–77; Columbus and,
    229–234;
Slavs, 127, 131, 186, 187, 230
Smiles, Samuel, 260
Smith, Fred H., 17
Smith, Ray Winfield, 27
Snowden, Frank, 25
social classes: as cause of collapse of the Mayan
    civilization, 162–168; and the decline of the
    Roman Empire, 105–106; in tsarist Russia,
    323–324
Socrates, 152
Soho, Tokutomi, 252
soil depletion, and the decline of the Roman
    Empire, 104–105
soldier, Oliver Cromwell as, 276–279
Song of Roland, 190
Sorai, Ogyu, 253
St. John, Oliver, 292
Stilicho, 114–115
Stoneking, Mark, 6, 19
Stuart, James, 56
Stubbings, Frank, 53
succession, laws of, Peter the Great and, 323
Sunni Muslims, university education and, 144–151
syphilis, 190

Tacitus, 125

Talmud, 82
T'ang Hsaio-wen, on the Ch'in dynasty of China, 72–78
Tauber, Irene, 251
Taviani, Paolo Emilio, on Christopher Columbus, 220–228
Teotihuacan civilization, and collapse of the Mayan civilization, 169–178
Tertullian, 87, 91–92, 94, 95, 96
Teutonic Knights, 186
Theodosius, 114
Thorne, Alan G., on Africa as site of origin for Homo sapiens, 12–20
Thucydides, 46
Timothy, Saint, 90, 91
Tokugawa shogunate, controversy over influence of, on Japan, 250–267
Toltec people, 167–168, 171
trade, during the reign of Indian emperor Aurangzeb, 298–302
Trajan, 88
Trevor-Roper, Hugh, 311; on the Crusades, 180–191
triangular trade route, New World and, 230
troubadours, 211
Tung Chung-Shu, 70
Tutankhamen Egypt's pharaoh, 35, 36, 38

Unitarianism, 239
universities, controversy over Muslim education as source of, 144–158
Urban II, Pope, 182, 192–193, 194, 198

Van Sertima, Tivan, 25, 31
Vandals, 113

vendettas, 123–124
Vermeule, Emily, 53
Vigilant, Linda, 9
Vikings, 125–128, 129, 183, 188, 195
Visigoths, 112, 114, 120, 129
Volney, Count C. F., 24, 25, 31

Wainscoat, James, 10
Walbank, F. W., 110
Waldensees, 239
Walker, Robert, 275
war, during the rule of Indian emperor Aurangzeb, 298–302
Warwick, Sir Philip, 274
weary Titan syndrome, 112
Webster, David, 169
Westernization, controversy over Peter the Great's policy of, 320–336
widows, in early Christianity, 86–87
William the Conqueror, 185, 196
Williams, Chancellor, 25, 31
Wilson, Allan C., 13, 15, 19; on Africa as site of origin for Homo sapiens, 4–11
Wolpoff, Milford H., on Africa as site of origin for Homo sapiens, 12–20
women: controversy over early Christian, 82–97; controversy over benefits for, of the Renaissance, 202–215;
Wright, Arthur, 253
Wu Rukang, 16
Wu Xinzhi, 13, 16

Xavier, Saint Francis, 233

Yen Fu, 254